Diversity in the Power Elite

Ironies and Unfulfilled Promises

Third Edition

Richard L. Zweigenhaft
Guilford College

G. William Domhoff
University of California, Santa Cruz

ROWMAN & LITTLEFIELD
Lanham • Boulder • New York • London

Executive Editor: Sarah Stanton
Assistant Editor: Carli Hansen
Marketing Manager: Kim Lyons

Published by Rowman & Littlefield
A wholly owned subsidiary of
The Rowman & Littlefield Publishing Group, Inc.
4501 Forbes Boulevard, Suite 200, Lanham, Maryland 20706
https://rowman.com

Unit A, Whitacre Mews, 26-34 Stannary Street, London SE11 4AB,
United Kingdom

British Library Cataloguing in Publication Information Available

Library of Congress Cataloging-in-Publication Data
Names: Zweigenhaft, Richard L., author. | Domhoff, G. William., author.
Title: Diversity in the power elite : ironies and unfulfilled promises / Richard L. Zweigen-
    haft, Guilford College, G. William Domhoff, University of California, Santa Cruz.
Description: Third Edition. | Lanham : Rowman & Littlefield, [2018] | Revised edition of
    the authors' Diversity in the power elite, c2006. | Includes bibliographical references
    and index.
Identifiers: LCCN 2017047122 (print) | LCCN 2017048655 (ebook) | ISBN
    9781538103388 (electronic) | ISBN 9781538103364 (cloth : alk. paper) | ISBN
    9781538103371 (pbk. : alk. paper)
Subjects: LCSH: Elite (Social sciences)—United States. | Power (Social sciences)—Unit-
    ed States. | Cultural pluralism—United States. | Minorities—United States.
Classification: LCC HN90.E4 (ebook) | LCC HN90.E4 Z944 2018 (print) | DDC 305.5/
    20973—dc23
LC record available at https://lccn.loc.gov/2017047122

♾ ™ The paper used in this publication meets the minimum requirements of American
National Standard for Information Sciences Permanence of Paper for Printed Library
Materials, ANSI/NISO Z39.48-1992.

Printed in the United States of America

Contents

Preface and Acknowledgments

This is the third edition of a diversity project that began in 1994. In this new edition, we explore the career pathways of the new arrivals to the power elite. And now that we have decades of data to draw on, we are better able to step back and look at trends over time. Have things changed in similar ways for the various groups we look at in terms of representation in the political, corporate, and military elites? Why or why not? Have things improved for all groups, stayed the same, or gotten worse? How? And why?

Obviously, in the dozen years since the last edition of the book was published, the country has elected, twice, an African American as president. (It looked as if we were going to elect the first woman president, but that did not happen.) Many white women and people of color have served in presidential cabinets, as directors and CEOs of *Fortune* 500 boards, in the military elite, and also in Congress and on the Supreme Court. Perhaps the most dramatic changes in the larger culture have had to do with the treatment and acceptance of people who are gender and sexual minorities. In our eighth chapter, we explore some of the changes that have taken place, and the extent to which these changes have affected who is in, or remains excluded from, the power elite.

There are many people we want to thank for the considerable help they have given us along the way, which made these three editions possible. This includes many friends and colleagues who have read drafts of chapters and given us feedback. Among other things, they have tried their best to help us avoid language that might offend some of the groups about whom we have written (no easy task, given the linguistic changes that take place over time).

For this help, alphabetically, we thank Richard Alba, Edna Bonacich, Dan Clawson, John D'Emilio, Peter Dreier, Joe Feagin, Aida Hurtado, Jeffrey Janowitz, John Kitsuse, Rhonda F. Levine, Catherine Lew, Wendy Mink, Laura O'Toole, Perry Patterson, Vania Penha-Lopes, Tom Pettigrew, Martha Julia Sellers, Steve Sellers, Earl Smith, David Thomas, Deborah Woo, Steve Wright, and Lisa Young.

Many generously have shared their data, their ideas, and suggestions about how to find what we were seeking, for which we are deeply grateful. Thanks to Carol Bowie, Sheryll Cashin, Jan Combopiano, Amelia Costigan, Nancy DiTomaso, Lisette Garcia, Peter Garrett, Christy Glass, Kelly Glew, Roderick Harrison, Jerry Jacobs, Rory Kramer, Robert Livingston, Frederick B. Lynch, Lory Manning, Charles Moskos, Nicholas Pearce, Cliff Staples, Sandra Timmons, Emily Troiano, and Lynda Woodworth. For this most recent edition, we are especially grateful to political scientist Seth McKee at Texas Tech University for helping us understand the ways in which redistricting led to a large increase in African Americans in the House in the 1990s, to Rachel Riskind, a psychologist at Guilford College, who provided invaluable feedback on an earlier draft of the chapter on LGBT individuals in the power elite, and to Myles B. Caggins III, a lieutenant colonel in the US Army who works in public affairs for the Department of Defense, for providing us with data on women and people of color who have achieved officer rank in the US military.

For all three editions of the book, we have drawn on the good work of generations of undergraduates at Guilford College. Among other things, they have assisted with gathering data on the many people we have been interested in because of their presence in the power elite (or in Congress, or on the Supreme Court), and putting it into readable files. We therefore also wish to thank Cari Boram, Katharine Cannon, Rachel Chmelko, Michael Hamilton, Elizabeth Hayton, Damara Luce, Tess McEnery, Taryn McFadden, Patty Perez, Michael Peterson, Kyle Riplinger, Sierra Say Keo, Jennifer Simms, Sonora Stein, Isaac Studebaker, and Sam Williams.

Last, and very far from least, we have had the help of three peerless editors. The first, Gladys Topkis, a senior editor at Yale University Press when we worked with her on a previous book and the first edition of this book, always broke new ground in bringing issues of gender equality and racial fairness to the attention of both the academic community and the general public. We are equally grateful to Dean Birkenkamp, then an editor at Rowman & Littlefield, who a few years later supported our work on diversity. Now, another dozen years later, Sarah Stanton, our wonderful editor for this third edition, agreed that yet another look at diversity in the power elite was needed in light of the many twists and turns of diversity issues in recent years. For us, it is especially gratifying that this edition of *Diversity in the Power Elite* has come full circle because our present editor was in part mentored by our original editor. In any case, the creation of the book and its continuation owe a great deal to Gladys and Sarah. (For this third edition, we also much appreciate the work done by Jo-Ann Parks, the copy editor. She, Janice Braunstein, and Carli Hansen have provided us with invaluable assistance.)

We hope that our academic efforts to examine the origins, the present, and the likely future of diversity in the higher circles have contributed to the understanding that many Americans have about the way power works, and the importance and complexity of diversity. Along these lines, we hope that the systematic data we have gathered, and the analyses we have made, will contribute to the work that people do to encourage genuine diversity throughout the society, including in the halls of power.

Chapter One

The Ironies and Unfulfilled Promises of Diversity

In 2008, 155 years after slaves were freed and forty-three years after the Voting Rights Act of 1965 was passed, the United States elected an African American president, Barack Obama, who won that election with 51.1 percent of the popular vote, and he was reelected in 2012, with 52.9 percent of the popular vote. Between 1997 and 2016, there were fifty-three women who served as CEOs of *Fortune* 500 companies, and twenty-three of them were sitting in that corner office as of July 2017. Between 1998 and 2016, there were nine Latinos and six Asian Americans appointed to one or another presidential cabinet, and in 2009 the first Latina was appointed to the Supreme Court, where she joined a conservative African American who had been appointed by a Republican president in 1991.

These examples of diversity at the highest levels of American society demonstrate that doors have opened and ceilings have been penetrated. Still, as we will argue in this book, a closer look at the numbers of nonwhite males at the top over time, and at the pathways these newcomers have taken, reveals that the promises of a level playing field that often accompany the arguments for diversity have not been fulfilled. The diversity that has taken place has generated many unexpected outcomes, and it may have reached its peak for most previously excluded groups in the years between 2009 and 2014.

In this book, we look at diversity from a distinctive angle: We examine its impact on the small group at the pinnacles of the American power structure that we call the *power elite*, those who own and manage large banks and corporations, finance the political campaigns of many mainstream Democrats and virtually all Republicans at the state and national levels, and serve in government as appointed officials and military leaders. We ask just how much the decades of civil disobedience, protest, and litigation by civil rights groups, feminists, and gay and lesbian rights activists have resulted in a more diverse power elite. To the extent that the power elite is now diverse, or more diverse than it once was, what effects has this new diversity had on its functioning and on its relation to the rest of society? We suggest that there are many ironies to be found in the history of the movement for diversity that began in the second half of the 1960s under the label "affirmative action."

We also compare our findings on the power elite with those from our parallel study of Congress to see whether there are differences in social background, education, and party affiliation for women and other underrepresented groups in these two realms of power. We explore the possibility that elected officials come from a wider range of occupational and income backgrounds than members of the power elite. In addition, we ask whether either of the major political parties has been more active than the other in advancing the careers of women and minorities. We also ask if the members of previously excluded groups become Republicans or Democrats, and why.

According to many popular commentators, the composition of the higher circles in the United States had already changed by the late 1980s and early 1990s. Some went even further, saying that the old power elite had been pushed aside entirely.[1] Enthusiastic articles in mainstream magazines, such as one in the late 1980s in *U.S. News & World Report* titled "The New American Establishment," also appeared, celebrating a new diversity at the top and claiming that "new kinds of men and women" have "taken control of institutions that influence important aspects of American life." School and club ties are no longer important, the article announced, highlighting the new role of women with a picture of some of the "wise women" who had joined the "wise men" who dominated the old establishment.[2] In a slightly new twist on this old theme, in July 1995, *Newsweek* even ran a cover story titled "The Rise of the Overclass," featuring a gallery of one hundred high-tech, media, and Wall Street stars, including women as well as men and previously excluded racial and ethnic groups as well as whites with Western European backgrounds, all of whom supposedly came from all rungs of the social ladder.[3]

Based on the studies that we have done of diversity in the power elite since the late 1970s, we have long been wary of these claims announcing the demise of the old elites and the arrival of new elites, and are even more so after more than thirty years of the same old story. For one thing, these pronouncements are never documented systematically. Moreover, they are suspect because similar claims have been made repeatedly throughout American history and have been proved wrong each time. In popular books and magazines from the 1830s, 1920s, and 1950s, for example, leading commentators of the day asserted that there used to be a tightly knit and cohesive governing group in the United States, but no longer. A closer look several decades later at each of these supposedly new eras invariably showed that the new power group was primarily the old one after all, with a few additions and alterations here and there.[4] If anything, as we already have noted, we now wonder if diversity in the power elite has leveled off.

Since the 1870s, the refrain about the new diversity of the governing circles has been closely intertwined with a staple of American culture created by Horatio Alger Jr., whose name has become synonymous with upward mobility in America. Far from being a Horatio Alger himself, the man who gave his name to upward mobility was born into a patrician family in 1832; his father was a Harvard graduate, a Unitarian minister, and a Massachusetts state senator. Horatio Jr. graduated from Harvard at the age of nineteen, after which he pursued a series of unsuccessful efforts to establish himself in various careers. He found his literary niche and his subsequent claim to fame: writing books in which poor boys make good. His books sold by the hundreds of thousands in the last third of the nineteenth century, and by 1910, they were enjoying annual paperback sales of more than one million.[5]

The deck is not stacked against the poor, according to Alger. When they simply show a bit of gumption, work hard, and thereby catch a break or two, they can become part of the American elite. The persistence of this theme, reinforced by the annual Horatio Alger Award given to such well-known figures as football player John Elway, corporate executives such as Roger Ailes, and evangelist Billy Graham, suggests that we may be dealing once again with a cultural myth.

In its early versions, of course, the story concerned the great opportunities available for poor white boys willing to work their way to the top. More recently, the story has featured black Horatio Algers who started in the ghetto, Latino Horatio Algers who started in the barrio, Asian American Horatio Algers whose parents were immigrants, and female Horatio Algers who seem to have no class backgrounds, all of whom now sit on the boards of the country's largest corporations.[6] And so the award in recent years has gone to highly visible people of color such as baseball player Hank Aaron, television star Oprah Winfrey, and presidential cabinet members such as Condoleezza Rice, Colin Powell, and Ben Carson.

For many decades scholars have shown that when it comes to those in the corporate elite, very few have legitimate Horatio Alger stories to tell. When William Miller of the Harvard University Research Center in Entrepreneurial History studied the backgrounds of 190 men who were business leaders between 1901 and 1910, individuals "at the apex of some of the mightiest organizations the world up to then had seen," he found that very few had come from impoverished backgrounds or even from working-class or foreign origins. In fact, 79 percent had fathers who were businessmen or professionals; only 12 percent had fathers who were farmers, and only 2 percent had fathers who were "workers." Miller concluded that "American historians . . . stress this elite's typically lower-class, foreign, or farm origins and speculate on the forces that impelled men upward from such insalubrious environs. Yet poor immigrant boys and poor farm boys together actually make up no more than 3 percent of the business leaders who are the subject of this essay. . . . Poor immigrant and poor farm boys who become business leaders have always been more conspicuous in American history books than in American history."[7]

In another study of the backgrounds of business leaders, this one looking at the highest-ranking businessmen in 1900, 1925, and 1950, Mabel Newcomer, chair of the economics department at Vassar, also found that they tended to come from the upper levels of the class structure. Fully 55.7 percent of the fathers of the 1950 executives had been business executives (seven times the proportion of business executives in the US population at the time the executives were born), and another 17.8 percent had been professionals (six times the proportion of professional men in the population). When she divided the families of the 1950 executives into three classes and defined the lowest of the three as "poor," by which she meant those families that had not been able to contribute to their children's education beyond high school, she found that only 12.1 percent came from poor families. (The figure was virtually the same for the men who were top executives in 1900.)[8]

When the iconoclastic sociologist C. Wright Mills examined the backgrounds of the "very rich" in 1900, 1925, and 1950 in his classic book, *The Power Elite*, he found no support for the prevailing myth that most were the sons of immigrants who had pulled themselves up by their own bootstraps. Instead, the data led Mills to the following characterization: "American-born, city-bred, eastern-originated, the very rich have been from families of higher class status, and, like other members of the new and old upper classes of local society . . . they have been Protestants. Moreover, about half have been Episcopalians, and a fourth, Presbyterians."[9]

The "very rich" identified by Mills were not exactly the same people who occupied positions in the political, corporate, and military elites, but there was, Mills found, considerable overlap, especially between the very rich and the corporate elite. When he looked separately at the men who made up the political, corporate, and military elites, he found, in each case, that most were Protestant and that they were especially likely to be Episcopalians and Presbyterians. For example, Mills wrote that the members of the corporate elite in 1950 were "predominately Protestant and more likely, in comparison with the proportions at large, to be Episcopalians or Presbyterians than Baptists or Methodists. The Jews and Catholics among them are fewer than among the population at large."[10]

Few people read Horatio Alger today, but some still believe in upward mobility, even in an era when real wages have been stagnant for the bottom 80 percent since the 1970s, and the rate of upward mobility has declined.[11] As we explain in the concluding chapter, it does not take many anecdotal examples to reinforce a strongly held cultural belief when people have a tendency to believe in a just world.

But is any of the talk about Horatio Alger and upward mobility true? Can anecdotes, dime novels, and self-serving autobiographical accounts about diversity, meritocracy, and upward social mobility survive a more systematic analysis based on the past few decades? Just how many women or members of other previously excluded groups made it to the top? And, for those who have made it, is there more evidence of class privilege than first meets the eye, or, as we have found consistently in our earlier research, are those now making it into the power elite still likely to have come from the upper or upper-middle classes?

In this book, we address these and related questions within the framework provided by Mills in *The Power Elite*, published more than sixty years ago in 1956 when the media were in the midst of what Mills called the "Great American Celebration." In spite of the Great Depression of the 1930s, Americans had pulled together to win World War II, and the country was both prosperous at home and influential abroad. Most of all, according to enthusiasts, the United States had become a relatively classless and pluralistic society, where power belonged to the people through their political parties and public opinion. Some groups certainly had more power than others, but no group or class had too much. The New Deal and World War II had forever transformed the corporate-based power structure of earlier decades. The pervasive sexism, racism, and homophobia of the decade were almost entirely ignored in the mass media, and now even more in nostalgic accounts of that bygone era.

It is our purpose, therefore, to take a detailed look at the social, educational, and occupational backgrounds of the leaders of these three institutional hierarchies to see whether they have become more diverse in terms of gender, race, ethnicity, and sexual orientation, and also in terms of socioeconomic origins. Unlike Mills, however, we think the power elite is more than a set of institutional leaders; it is also the leadership group for the small upper class of owners and managers of large, income-producing properties, the 1 percent of American households that own such a disproportionate amount of all privately held stock, financial securities, and business equity. Emmanuel Saez, who tracks income inequality over time, writes, with his colleague Gabriel Zucman, that "the richest 1% of households owned 36% of the wealth in 2013, up from 30% in 1992," and "wealth concentration was high in the beginning of the twentieth century, fell from 1929 to 1978, and has continuously increased since then. The top 0.1% wealth share has risen from 7% in 1978 to 22% in 2012, a level almost as high as in 1929." Not surprisingly, we think the primary concern of the power elite is to support the kind of policies, regulations, and political leaders that maintain this structure of privilege and income inequality for the very rich. [12]

We first study the directors and chief executive officers (CEOs) of the largest banks and corporations, as determined by annual rankings compiled by *Fortune* magazine. The use of *Fortune* rankings is now standard practice in studies of corporate size and power. Over the years, *Fortune* has changed the number of corporations on its annual list and the way it groups them. For example, the separate listings by business sector in the past, such as "life insurance companies," "diversified financial companies," and "service companies," have been combined into one overall list, primarily because many large businesses are now involved in more than one of the traditional sectors. Generally speaking, we use the *Fortune* list or lists available for the period under consideration.

Second, again following Mills, we focus on the appointees to the president's cabinet when we turn to the "political directorate," Mills's general term for top-level officials in the executive branch of the federal government.

We also have included the director of the CIA in one chapter because of the increased importance of that agency since Mills wrote. Third, and rounding out our portrait of the power elite, we examine the same two top positions in the military, generals and admirals, that formed the basis for Mills's look at the military elite.

As we have noted, we also study Congress. We include findings on senators and representatives from underrepresented groups for two reasons. First, this allows us to see whether there is more diversity in the electoral system than in the power elite. Second, we do not think, as Mills did, that Congress should be relegated to the "middle level" of power. To the contrary, we believe that Congress is an integral part of the power structure in America. Similarly, unlike Mills, because we think that the Supreme Court is a key institution within the power elite, we have added information on Supreme Court appointments.

Until the 1980s, most Northern Republicans and most Southern Democrats supported the power elite on the labor, welfare, and business-regulation issues critical to it, whereas a majority of Democrats outside of the South were sympathetic to a coalition of liberals, organized labor, and underrepresented groups. Due to the Voting Rights Act of 1965 and the gradual industrialization of the South since World War II, Southern conservatives moved steadily into the Republican Party until 1994, when the newly won Republican control of Congress was strengthened further when five representatives, all from the South, switched their party affiliations from Democrat to Republican, as did two senators (Richard Shelby of Alabama, and Ben Nighthorse Campbell of Colorado). At the same time, many moderate Republicans outside the South now have been defeated by Democrats, leading to a situation in which each of the two major power coalitions, the corporate-conservative coalition and the liberal-labor coalition, is housed almost exclusively in just one of the two dominant political parties. Starting in 1996, therefore, we can use party preference to gauge whether members of underrepresented groups who join the power elite differ from their counterparts who are elected to Congress. Do they become Republicans, or do some or most remain Democrats, even though the Democratic Party is now primarily the home of the liberal-labor coalition (and does this differ for the different groups we examine)?

In addition to studying the extent to which women and other previously excluded groups have risen in the system, we focus on whether they have followed different avenues to the top than their predecessors did, as well as on any special roles they may play. Are they in the innermost circles of the power elite, or are they more likely to serve as ambassadors, go-betweens, and tokens? Do they go just so far and no farther? What obstacles does each group face?

We also examine whether their presence affects the power elite itself. Do they influence the power elite in a more liberal direction, or do they end up endorsing traditional conservative positions, such as opposition to trade unions, high corporate taxes, government regulation of business, and progressive income taxes? In the final chapter, we argue that the diversity forced on the power elite has had the ironic effect of strengthening it by providing it with a handful of people who can reach out to the previously excluded groups, and thereby seemingly provide evidence for the claim that the American system can deliver on its most important promise, an equal opportunity for every individual. More specifically, we draw on some counterintuitive findings in social psychology that reveal that the mere presence of a few women or a few people of color in prominent positions can decrease the sense of collective exclusion on the part of an out-group, thus making them less likely to mobilize to pressure for change. The presence of this handful of people who previously would have been excluded inadvertently raises questions such as "If they could make it, why didn't I? What is wrong with me? Is it my fault?" These questions, and the self-reproach they may engender, feeds into the subtle ideology of "blaming the victim," one of the downsides of a highly individualistic worldview. [13]

The issues we address are not simple. They involve both the nature of the American power structure and the way in which people's need for self-esteem and a coherent belief system, along with the human tendency to feel guilty for being less than perfect, mesh with the hierarchical social structure they face. Moreover, the answers to some of the questions we ask vary greatly depending on which previously disadvantaged group we are talking about. Nonetheless, in the course of our research, some general patterns have emerged that we examine throughout the text and then tie together in chapter 8. Eight general points may help readers to see the patterns develop as we embark upon a narrative in the next six chapters that focuses on specific issues related to entry into the power elite by Jews, women, blacks, Latinos, Asian Americans, and, finally, lesbian, gay, bisexual, and transgender (LGBT) individuals.

1. The power elite now shows considerable diversity, at least as compared with its state in the 1950s, but its core group continues to consist
   of wealthy, white, Christian males, most of whom are still from the
   upper third of the social ladder. Like the white, Christian males, those
   who are newly arrived to the power elite have been filtered through
   the same small set of elite schools in law, business, public policy, and
   international relations that the original wealthy white Anglo Saxon
   Protestant (WASP) elites used to exclude Catholics and Jews. [14]
2. In spite of the increased diversity of the power elite, for most of the
   groups we look at, high social origins continue to be the most important factor in making it to the top. There are relatively few rags-to-
   riches stories, and those we did find tended to have received scholarships to elite schools or to have been elected to office, usually within
   the Democratic Party.
3. The new diversity within the power elite is transcended by common
   values and a subjective sense of hard-earned and richly deserved class
   privilege. The newcomers to the power elite have found ways to signal
   that they are willing to join the game as it has always been played,
   assuring the old guard that they will call for no more than relatively
   minor adjustments, if that. There are few liberals and fewer crusaders
   in the power elite, despite its newly acquired diversity. Class backgrounds, current roles, and future aspirations are generally more powerful in shaping behavior in the power elite than gender, ethnicity,
   race, or sexual orientation.
4. Not all the groups we studied have been equally successful in contrib-
   uting to the new diversity in the power elite. Women, African
   Americans, Latinos, Asian Americans, and openly gay men and lesbians are all underrepresented, but to varying degrees and with different rates of increasing representation. In fact, we find that white wom-
   en have been the major beneficiaries of the pressure to diversify generated by affirmative action, which helps to explain, for example, why
   the corporate elite is still 87.7 percent white. [15]
5. Moreover, there is a real possibility that Americans are replacing the
   old black-versus-white distinction with a black-versus-nonblack divid-
   ing line. Based on the evidence that the new immigrants since the late
   1960s are assimilating and intermarrying in the same way that the
   white "ethnic" immigrants did, and also intermarrying with white
   Americans of the same education level they have attained, we think

that the category of "white" may be in the process of becoming just another word for the in-group, with many second- and third-generation Latinos and Asian Americans defining themselves in terms of both their ethnicity and light skin color. Although we believe that the black-versus-nonblack distinction will be a crucial one, we are also aware that within nonblack groups, skin color, or what is now generally referred to as "colorism," is likely to be in play. There is now an extensive literature showing that African Americans and Latinos with lighter skin receive better treatment in various settings, and they are more likely to be found in elite positions, than African Americans and Latinos with darker skin color. We will explore the many findings that support these patterns, and the likely complex interactions between the black-versus-nonblack distinction and colorism, at relevant points in subsequent chapters and in our final chapter.

6. There is greater diversity in Congress than in the power elite, especially in terms of class origins, and the majority of these more diverse elected officials are Democrats, whose presence has forced the Republicans to try to play catch-up by including some token candidates from the previously excluded groups.

7. Although the corporate, political, and military elites initially accepted diversity only in response to pressure from social-movement activists and feminists, the power elite has benefited from the presence of new members. Some serve either a buffer or a liaison function with such groups and institutions as consumers, angry neighborhoods, government agencies, and wealthy foreign entrepreneurs. More generally, and ironically, studies by social psychologists suggest that their simple presence at the top turns out to decrease the possibility of collective protest against institutions of power because young women and people of color may wonder if they are being excluded due to some personal inadequacy. So the presence of a few, which is usually called tokenism, even when it is seen by elites as a first step, works in terms of reassuring the general population that the system is fair, as documented in studies discussed in chapter 8.

8. Globalization has clearly come to the power elite, especially the corporate elite. Our look at the Latinos and Asian Americans who have joined the power elite in the last decade, especially the South Asians, reveals an increased presence of corporate directors and CEOs born to privilege and educated at elite schools outside the United States,

though many have supplemented their secondary school and under-graduate education with higher degrees from elite schools in the United States.

To provide a starting point for understanding the diversity we focus on in this book, we begin with the story of how a previously rejected and excluded out-group, the Jews, gradually became fully participating members of the power elite, especially after the 1960s. However, we recognize that the changed situation for Jews does not provide a perfect basis for comparison with the experiences of other underrepresented groups. For one thing, Jews accounted for only 3.3 percent of the population in 1950, at a time when 10 percent of the population was African American, and they make up only about 2 percent now, when African Americans constitute about 13 percent and Latinos about 16 percent. Also, many Jews, more than are generally realized, came to the United States with economic or educational advantages, especially those who became major corporate figures. [16]

Nonetheless, the fact remains that over 40 percent of other white Americans held clearly anti-Semitic views until the years after World War II, when the full extent of the Holocaust became widely known. [17] As late as the 1940s, there were quotas on the number of Jews who were allowed to attend elite private colleges such as Harvard, Yale, and Princeton, and successful Jewish business leaders were not permitted to join Gentile social clubs until the civil rights movement highlighted the extent of all forms of discrimination. For example, it was not until 1977 that the most exclusive downtown club in Los Angeles accepted Jewish members, a change that was accomplished in a hurry when Harold Brown, the Jewish president of the California Institute of Technology, was selected to be the secretary of defense by the newly elected Jimmy Carter. [18] In addition, the assimilation of Jews into the power elite and Congress has been studied in detail, which means that their experiences and pathways can serve as benchmarks.

Despite the apparent assimilation of many Jews into the upper-middle and upper classes after decades of vilification and exclusion (these decades of vilification and exclusion may come as a complete surprise to those who were born after 1975), the potential for a resurgence of the kind of scapegoating that has haunted Jews over the past 2,400 years can be seen in the outbursts of overt anti-Semitism in 2016 among the white nationalists called the "alt-right," and by the meeting of neo-Nazis in the nation's capital shortly after Donald Trump's election in November 2016. [19]

Although anti-Catholicism nearly reached the levels of anti-Semitism in some contexts early in the twentieth century, and especially in the South, we do not use the acceptance of Catholics into the power elite as a baseline for several reasons. Discrimination against Jews, unlike discrimination against Catholics, had cultural and racist overtones that went far beyond religious differences. Moreover, the exclusion of Jews was more complete than was the exclusion of Catholics, and the acceptance of Catholics into the establishment occurred earlier than did the acceptance of Jews. In 1954, when he published his classic work *The Nature of Prejudice*, Gordon Allport was still concerned about anti-Catholicism.[20] By the late 1950s, however, anti-Catholicism had declined dramatically, a condition that was confirmed by the election of the Irish Catholic John F. Kennedy as president in 1960. As sociologist E. Digby Baltzell (himself a member of the upper class) pointed out in *The Protestant Establishment*, Kennedy's election "marked a definite trend toward a representative establishment as far as the Catholic community is concerned."[21] In clear contrast, Jews still faced considerable discrimination at that time, both inside and outside of the establishment.[22]

Following the chapter on Jews (chapter 2), we present empirically based chapters on women (chapter 3), blacks (chapter 4), Latinos (chapter 5), and Asian Americans (chapter 6) in the power elite. We also have included a chapter on LGBT individuals (chapter 7) in which we faced challenging research issues. We know that there are Jews, women, blacks, Latinos, and Asian Americans in the power elite, but, unless they have chosen to be public about their sexual orientation (or, as has sometimes been the case, been outed), we can only assume that some of those in the power elite are lesbian, gay, bisexual, or transgender. From our perspective, the relevant issue is not how many in the power elite are LGBT individuals, or who they are, but whether those who are members of the power elite feel comfortable about acknowledging this publicly. Given the dependence of the researcher upon self-disclosure, sexual and gender orientation is an especially difficult topic to study, so the data we draw upon to address this issue are not as systematic as in other chapters.

Because people have more than one identity and, therefore, are not solely women, black, or heterosexual, overlaps and cross-weavings in our presentation are inevitable. We have organized our findings into chapters that focus on a single identity at a time. When relevant, however, we attempt to address the complexity that can emerge when two or more identities seem to matter to a person's career.

Although our range of groups is a wide one, we have not tried to be completely inclusive. First, we have not analyzed the fortunes of recently arriving groups that have fewer than a million members in the United States. These include immigrants from Thailand, small Pacific islands, and various countries in Africa, as well as refugees from countries such as Cambodia and Vietnam, whose situation is different from that of many other immigrants because they left their countries out of necessity in the face of starvation conditions or threats of imminent harm from more powerful groups in their home countries. Nor have any of these groups, immigrants or refugees, been here long enough to establish a clear pattern, and there is less information available on them than there is on the groups that we have chosen to write about. Further, we see little evidence that any of them are as yet represented in the highest levels of the American power structure.

Second, we have not dealt with the diverse group of tribes variously called American Indians or Native Americans. There are several reasons for this decision. To begin with, based on census data, there are only 6.6 million American Indians or Alaska Natives—about 2 percent of the population—and 59 percent of those who are married are married to non-Indians.[23] Although some Native American groups have become collectively well off from owning casinos or leasing valuable mineral lands to corporations, none, as far as we know, have become part of the power elite. In addition, about one-fifth of those who identified themselves as members of one or another Native American group live on reservations apart from the rest of American society, which means that they are not likely to become part of the power elite or to be elected to Congress.[24]

Finally, we do not discuss in detail why the power elite has accepted some degree of diversification because we take it for granted that it would not have done so had it not been for the long and heroic efforts of the African American civil rights movement, a point all too easily overlooked in a day when corporations and elected officials in Washington, DC, brag about their diversity. We also think that the most internationally oriented elements of the power elite, and especially the leaders of multinational corporations and in the State Department, felt compelled to accept some degree of diversity because the ongoing segregation of African Americans was an embarrassment to them in their high-stakes competition with the Soviet Union for the loyalty of people of color in the many emerging nations around the globe.[25] Moreover, the feminist and gay and lesbian movements that grew out of the civil rights and women's movements of the 1960s also fueled the pressure on corporate America to diversify. Although not many white male corporate directors had blacks, Latinos, or Asians in their families, almost all of them had females (either wives, siblings, daughters, or nieces) in their families, and in the families of their friends, which sensitized at least some of them to sexual discrimination. More recently, they may have had children, or other relatives or friends, who have come out as gay men or lesbians, which forced them to think about homophobia in a more personal way. These more personal reminders and pressures may have helped to legitimate the need for diversity in the corporate elite.

As already noted, in the final chapter we build on these points in the process of exploring a number of ironic effects of diversity in the power elite, including the various ways that those in power have used it to increase their dominance.

Although the power elite is much more diverse than it used to be, the data for the past decade indicates something that we have mentioned, and now wish to make more explicit: the pace of diversification has slowed, and in some cases the presence of women and people of color has either remained static or declined. By early 2014 it seemed that the heyday of diversity may have come and gone, and by 2016 it seemed as if the "twilight of diversity" may have set in. This trend was already in motion during the Obama years, and now, with Republican control of both Congress and the White House, diversity in the power elite may be on the ropes. We think there may again be a time when diversity increases, but if it does happen, it will come in unexpected ways and places, and perhaps in fits and starts, as it did between 1965 and 1980. If the 1960s are any guide, a renewed push for greater diversity will be the result of action on the part of those who continue to be excluded. That effort will most likely be aided by the ongoing work of the foundation-funded nonprofits on the liberal and moderate fringes of the power elite, which have been quietly supporting diversity against great odds for many decades.

Chapter Two

Jews in the Power Elite

For most intents and purposes, the twenty-first-century American Jewish community appears to be a fully assimilated religious and ethnic minority that includes at most 2–3 percent of the country's 325 million people, with the great majority of them residing in New York, California, southern Florida, and a few large urban centers in other states. (There are only 1,525 Jews in Mississippi and 250 in South Dakota.) This 2–3 percent estimate includes enclaves of recent immigrants from Russia and Eastern Europe in and around New York City, who are only now beginning to seek assimilation, as well as a few tens of thousands who belong to ultraorthodox sects (with perhaps 90,000 to 100,000 members) that strive to remain separate from all other Americans, including other Jews, through distinctive lifestyles, clothing, and hairstyles.

However, the vast majority of American Jews are well-educated members of the middle and upper-middle classes, a blending of the 150,000 German Jews who immigrated between 1820 and 1880, and became peddlers and store owners throughout the country, and the much more numerous Eastern European Jews, approximately three million in all, who were part of the major wave of immigration from Eastern and Southern Europe that brought about twenty million new immigrants, many of them Catholics, to the United States between 1880 and 1924. At that point the large American Protestant population that had arrived earlier from ethnic groups in the British Isles and Northern Europe, led by ultraconservative Republicans and Southern Democrats sympathetic to the Ku Klux Klan, closed off the immigration that had been encouraged by a burgeoning corporate community in need of industrial workers.

Although these new immigrants were not welcomed with open arms by most Americans, who saw them as threats to both their jobs and their way of life, assimilation was especially problematic for the Eastern European Jews because of the 2,500 years of anti-Semitism that Jews had endured at the hands of successive conquerors (Assyrians, Babylonians, and Romans).

Henry Ford, one of the most influential and respected Americans of the 1920s (one survey of college students found that he was rated the third "greatest man of all time," right after Napoleon and Jesus Christ), was a virulent anti-Semite. His public statements and his publications earned him the attention of many who hated Jews and presumably helped to persuade others to do so. In fact, Adolf Hitler periodically expressed his admiration for Ford, stating that "we look to Ford as the leader of the growing Fascist party in America," and "I regard Henry Ford as my inspiration."[1]

Nor were the most prestigious colleges and universities free of discrimination against Jews, either in their hiring or in their admissions policies. In 1922, the president of Harvard urged the university to adopt a quota system to solve "the Jewish problem." The president of Columbia University took a similar stance. Many medical schools and other professional schools joined a growing number of undergraduate colleges in restricting admissions for Jewish students. Jewish academicians had a difficult time obtaining positions or attaining tenure at these schools.

The exclusion and hazing of Jews extended to the military as well. From the day Leonard Kaplan arrived at the US Naval Academy as one of 955 members of the class of 1922, his experience consisted of four years of vicious and abominable treatment by his classmates. In the jargon of that day, he was "sent to Coventry"—no one spoke to him or even acknowledged his presence. He lived alone for four years. When the yearbook appeared at the end of his senior year, it included a crude cartoon of him, a derogatory biographical sketch (claiming, for example, that he was "born in the township of Zion, county of Cork, State of Ignorance"), and his name was omitted from the index; moreover, unlike all the other pages in the yearbook, the page about him was perforated so that it could be torn out and discarded with ease.[2]

In the 1930s anti-Semitism was strongly politicized by ultraconservatives in the face of the New Deal and the overwhelming support for it by Jewish voters in 1936 and thereafter. Roosevelt's two or three Jewish advisers were one flashpoint, and Roosevelt himself was called "Rosenfelt," and said to be from a Jewish family that had changed its name. The "New Deal" became the "Jew Deal," with Henry Ford once again in the forefront.[3] The fact that Eleanor Roosevelt, the First Lady, was sympathetic to black causes led to a refrain that expressed a suspicion of a Jewish-black alliance: "You kiss the Negroes, I'll kiss the Jews, We'll stay in the White House, As long as we choose."[4] With the advent of public-opinion polling in the 1930s, various polls in the late 1930s and early 1940s found that over half the general public thought Jews were greedy and dishonest, had too much power, were a greater threat to the country than any other religious or racial group, and should face various restrictions in their activities.

Anti-Semitism declined rapidly after World War II, perhaps in part due to Nazi expressions of Germanic racial superiority and increasing awareness of the full extension of the horrors of the Holocaust, as well as to patriotic participation in the war by American Jews. However, traces of highly negative attitudes toward Jews nonetheless remained on the fringes of the extreme right. More importantly especially for our purposes, Jews were also excluded from elite Gentile social circles, which did not admit Jews to their exclusive social clubs until the 1970s, and even then it was due to social pressure and campaigns by the American Jewish Committee.[5]

In the 1950s, after Henry Ford died, reflecting greater acceptance of Jews in the larger corporate community, Sidney Weinberg, a Jewish investment banker from Goldman Sachs, became the Ford family's primary financial adviser; he sat on the board of Ford Motors, as well as on the boards of a number of other corporations, including B. F. Goodrich, Kraft, and Cluett-Peabody.[6] But vigilance on the part of Jews remained high. Expressing a widespread wariness, billionaire Laurence Tisch, who grew up in the 1940s, told us in an interview in 1980 that he thought it was a mistake for Jews to work for a large corporation, unless it was a company founded by Jews.[7]

Nor did it seem to be a good idea for Jews to seek elected office. When a journalist of German-Jewish heritage, Stephen Isaacs, who grew up in Kentucky, published his book on *Jews and American Politics* in 1974, he reported widespread Jewish involvement in all aspects of politics, motivated in fair measure by the fear that "It could happen here." But his interviews also made clear that it seemed too risky to most Jews to run for office anywhere outside of New York in the face of lingering anti-Semitism.[8]

Still, by the 1970s more than a third of young Jews were intermarrying with non-Jews. In 1986 Laurence Tisch was invited to buy a 24.9 percent stake in CBS. He then became a member of its board of directors, and soon thereafter became the company's CEO. By the 1990s, far more Jews had been elected to the Senate and the House than would have been expected based on their representation in the population at large, in some cases even from districts with very few Jewish voters. In 2016, when Bernie Sanders, a secular and unaffiliated Jew, ran for president, few people seemed to care that he is Jewish (they were much more concerned that he is a democratic socialist, though he still won twenty-two primaries and caucuses, and received more than thirteen million votes).

By the mid-1970s, one-third of the faculty at Harvard and almost half the faculty at the Yale Law School were Jewish. At the same time, approximately one-fourth of the students at Harvard, Yale, Princeton, and Columbia were Jewish. The acceptance of Jews in prestigious Gentile universities extended to the highest administrative levels. In 1993, for example, Jews headed five of the eight Ivy League institutions.[9] More generally, by any of the standard measures, Jews have become more successful than any other white immigrant group. As sociologists Seymour Martin Lipset and Earl Raab wrote as early as 1955, Jews are "the best educated, the most middle-class, and, ultimately, the most affluent ethnoreligious group in the country. No other immigrant group has evinced such rapid and dramatic success."[10]

But anti-Semitism is certainly not dead in America. During Donald Trump's 2016 presidential election campaign, the Republican nominee used advertisements that included anti-Semitic imagery, and earlier in his life he kept a copy of a book by Adolf Hitler in a cabinet beside his bed.[11] And even now, previously all-Gentile male social clubs are not fully integrated (for either Jews, people of color, or women). As a result, there remains a parallel set of downtown clubs and country clubs for Jews, which sometimes include members of other excluded groups as well. (In 2017, former President Obama joined one of these country clubs.)[12]

Perhaps due to these continuing exclusions and insults, along with some concern with the fact that the Christian right in the Republican Party now claims to love Jews (though they also hope to convert them) and definitely loves Israel, most Jews in the United States have tended to vote Democratic (69 percent and 71 percent in the 2012 and 2016 presidential elections), despite their high socioeconomic standing. Jews in the corporate community tend to agree with the rest of the Jewish community in terms of the party preferences. In a comparison of campaign donations to the presidential elections in 2008 by thirty-one present and past male Jewish CEOs and seventy-eight non-Jewish white male CEOs, we found that 45 percent of Jewish CEOs gave exclusively to the Democrats and they were 4.5 times more likely to give to the Democrats than were the Gentile CEOs.[13]

Nor was this a new pattern, as a wide range of studies show. As early as 1940 and 1944, a majority of Jews who gave $1,000 or more to a presidential campaign supported Democrats, and that figure increased after President Harry S. Truman recognized the state of Israel in 1947. In 1968, when the Democrats raised money for a last-minute flurry of ads to tip the presidential election to Senator Hubert Humphrey of Minnesota, fourteen of the twenty-two donors who gave $95,000 or more for these ads were Jewish.[14]

In our view, the fact that Jews continue to vote Democratic, and donate to Democrats, the political party that is clearly identified with the liberal-labor coalition, is a sign that most Jews, even wealthy Jews, still feel a certain amount of wariness about the strong conservatism of the Republican Party and its clear identification with white Christians and their desire to eliminate some if not all of the barriers that have separated church and state since the founding of the country. Clearly there are some highly visible exceptions, most of whom are devoutly religious or are strong supporters of those Israeli leaders who want to continue to limit Palestinian rights. But are Jews more than the most affluent white immigrant group? Despite their tendency to support Democrats, how central a role have they come to play in the power elite? It is useful to look at the dramatic change Jews have experienced, moving from an ostracized minority to full-fledged members of the power elite, for clues to understanding the prejudice and obstacles that face women and people of color as they demand entry into the higher levels of society. First, however, a tricky preliminary question must be addressed.

SO, WHO'S JEWISH ANYHOW?

It is not easy to determine who is Jewish. A noted anthropologist, Melville Herskovits, claimed that "of all human groupings, there is none wherein the problem of definition has proved to be more difficult than for the Jews."[15] Defining who is Jewish may not be the most difficult of "all human group-ings"—as we will see in subsequent chapters, defining who is black, Hispan-ic, or Asian American is no easy task either—but it is certainly a matter of considerable complexity.

In general, four different criteria have been used in different times and places to determine whether someone is Jewish. The first and most traditional comes from Jewish religious law, which states that a person is Jewish if he or she was born to a Jewish mother or has followed a prescribed set of procedures to convert to Judaism. A second way to define Jewishness is based not on birth or conversion, but on conviction. According to this definition, people are Jewish if they consider themselves Jewish. This includes those whose mothers were Jewish and who see themselves as Jewish, those whose fathers were Jewish and who see themselves as Jewish, and those who have converted. A third way to define Jewishness is based on an ancestral tabulation, according to which a person who has one Jewish parent is half-Jewish, a person who has one Jewish grandparent is one-fourth Jewish, and so on. A fourth definition of Jewishness, somewhat similar to the second, is based on membership in Jewish institutions such as synagogues or Jewish clubs. These memberships not only imply that people's identity includes being Jewish, but they also suggest some willingness to make Jewish affiliations a part of their public identity.

In this chapter, we generally draw on self-definitions as our starting point. We will also pay attention to whether a person's parents or grandparents were Jewish. If, for example, a member of the political, corporate, or military elite had a parent or grandparent who was Jewish but was not told about this, or knew it and denied it, this may be sociologically revealing, because it demonstrates just how powerful the pressures were to assimilate. For example, it is one thing to say that Walter Lippmann, one of the country's most prominent journalists from the 1930s through the 1960s, did not consider himself Jewish; it is quite another thing to say that he was born to wealthy and well-assimilated Jewish parents, but he would not join any Jewish organizations or even speak before any Jewish groups, and even refused to accept an award from the Jewish Academy of Arts and Sciences.[16]

We will also make use of listed membership in a Jewish organization in published sources, which can serve as a proxy for personally stating self-identification as Jewish. Finally, we will pay attention to the definition based on the religion of one's parents and grandparents because it has often been used by others to decide if a person is Jewish, and in some situations, other people's definitions of who we are take precedence over our own. As Laurence Tisch put it in our interview with him, "When Hitler came around he didn't ask questions whether you were or you weren't—it wasn't what you said, it was what he said."[17] Similarly, if the senior executives at a corporation did not want Jews in their midst, it was likely to be their definition of who was or was not Jewish that mattered. So, in order to understand why the power elite has been willing to accept more Jews into its ranks, we have to understand whom they have perceived as Jewish and why this is apparently no longer of such concern to them.

By our flexible criteria, the senator from California since 1992, Dianne Feinstein, is Jewish because she says she is—and she has been married to three different Jewish men. As a girl named Dianne Goldman, she had a double exposure to religion because her mother was Catholic and her father was Jewish. As she recalls her childhood, "I was brought up supposedly with some Catholic religion and some Jewish, and I was to choose. I went to a convent and I went to a temple at the same time, but I don't think that works very well."[18] But Larry Page, a cofounder of Google, and the CEO of Alphabet, the parent company of Google, is not Jewish. His mother, Gloria, was raised Jewish, but he was not raised in a religious household, and he does not consider himself to be Jewish.

JEWS IN THE CORPORATE ELITE

On December 14, 1973, readers of the *Wall Street Journal* awoke to the following headline: "Boss-to-Be at DuPont Is an Immigrant's Son Who Climbed Hard Way." This was news, indeed, for the boss-to-be was not merely an immigrant, nor had he merely climbed the hard way. He was Irving Shapiro, a Jew who had been named chairman of the board and chief executive officer of one of the oldest and largest corporations in America. Never before had a Jew achieved such a prominent position in a corporation that had not been founded or purchased by Jews. Shapiro assumed that his appointment was a harbinger of things to come and that the barriers that had prevented Jews from rising to the top in the corporate world were finally coming down. As he explained in an interview with us shortly before his retirement in 1981: "That's really been the great dividend from my position. All kinds of people have moved up in banks and other corporations simply on the premise that there is no longer a barrier."[19]

In order to show just how many doors to the corporate elite have opened for Jews, we will look at the presence of Jews in the higher circles of the corporate world throughout the twentieth century, and now into the twenty-first, paying special attention to their career pathways and to how their presence affected their identities as Jews. In later chapters, we will compare these pathways with those taken by women, African Americans, and other previously excluded groups.

The Overrepresentation of Jews in the Corporate Elite

For the most part, the religious makeup of the corporate elite changed very little throughout the first half of the twentieth century, though there is evidence of a slight increase in the percentage of Jews during that time. In his study of the backgrounds of business leaders between 1901 and 1910, discussed in the first chapter, Miller found that 90 percent were Protestant, 7 percent were Catholic, and 3 percent were Jewish.[20] In her study of the backgrounds of presidents and chairmen of the largest companies in 1900, 1925, and 1950, Newcomer found that the percentage of Jews in the corporate elite was 3.4 percent at the turn of the century, had risen to 4.3 percent by 1925, and to 4.6 percent by 1950. Jews were "heavily concentrated in the merchandising, entertainment, and mass communications fields," but very few were to be found in "heavy industry or public utilities, and none at all among the railroad executives." Moreover, she estimated that 40 percent of the Jews in her 1950 sample had "organized their own enterprises."[21]

A number of studies of the postwar era reveal that the percentage of Jews in the corporate elite continued to climb. Although these studies used different samples and methods, all looked at the ethnic backgrounds of *Fortune*-level corporate directors. The results are compelling in their consistent finding that Jews have been increasingly overrepresented.

In 1972, as part of the American Leadership Study by the Bureau of Applied Social Research at Columbia University, a sample of directors of *Fortune*-level companies and "holders of large fortunes" were interviewed. Although Jews constituted only about 3 percent of the national population at that time, 6.9 percent of these business leaders and affluent men were Jewish.[22] These findings mirrored those of a 1976 survey conducted by *Fortune*, which showed that 7 percent of the chief executive officers of eight hundred American corporations were Jewish.[23] At about the same time, Frederick Sturdivant and Roy Adler examined the backgrounds of 444 executives from 247 major American corporations. They found that 6 percent of their sample was Jewish.[24]

In a series of systematic studies performed in the late 1970s and in interviews with thirty Jewish corporate directors conducted in 1980 and 1981, we found that Jews were well represented in the corporate elite but were more likely to be in small *Fortune*-level companies than large ones. We also found that they had traveled different pathways in getting to the corporate elite than had their Gentile counterparts. Whereas Gentile executives were most likely to have advanced through the managerial ranks of the corporation, the Jewish directors were most likely to have joined the boards as outsiders with expertise in such areas as investment banking, corporate law, or public relations, unless they had risen through the ranks of companies owned or founded by Jews.[25]

It is both noteworthy and informative that many of these Jewish directors had attained skills in areas that subsequently became necessary to the corporations. Rather than merely figuring out ways to gain entry into the corridors of corporate power or waiting until the doors opened enough to let them in, many pursued less traditional areas, areas open to Jews, and the skills they developed later served as their entrée. In *A Certain People,* Charles Silberman describes the same pattern in prominent law firms and in the legal departments of large corporations in the postwar years. Both the corporations and law firms discovered that they needed lawyers who knew how to negotiate with trade unions and interpret the increasingly arcane tax laws.[26]

By the mid-1980s, studies indicated that the percentage of Jews in senior executive positions had climbed a bit higher. In a 1986 survey of the CEOs of *Fortune* 500 and Service 500 companies, modeled after Newcomer's 1955 study, *Fortune* found that 7.6 percent identified themselves as Jewish.[27] That same year, in a survey of 4,350 senior executives just below the chief executive level, Korn/Ferry International, an executive search firm, found that 7.4 percent were Jewish. More dramatic was the finding that 13 percent of those under the age of forty were Jewish.[28]

In order to determine whether Jews are more or less likely to be on the largest *Fortune*-level boards, we used an atypical technique, but one that has been useful in various studies of Jews and other ethnic groups. We also employ it in the chapters on Latinos and Asian Americans. For years, demographers have used the distinctive names within racial and ethnic groups to estimate the size of various populations. It is a strategy that eventually will lose its usefulness as distinctive groups intermarry and their children take on multiple social identities, but, for now, it is still accurate for Jews, Latinos, and Asian Americans over the age of forty-five or so. As early as 1942, Samuel Kohs compiled a list of those names that appeared most frequently in the files of the Los Angeles Federation, an umbrella group for Jewish congregations and organizations in the Los Angeles area. Kohs found that the 106 most-common surnames accounted for about 16 percent of the names on various other Jewish Federation lists and that thirty-five names accounted for about 12 percent of the names on most lists. Various other researchers have since used his list of thirty-five names, or variations of it, and have found that the proportion of Jews with these distinctively Jewish names has remained relatively constant over time. Moreover, no meaningful differences in attitudes or behaviors have been found between Jews with distinctive and nondistinctive names.[29]

In order to estimate the number of Jews on *Fortune* 500 boards, we used a list of the 4,323 men and women who sat on the boards of directors of the *Fortune* 500 companies in 2011 (we have used this list in a number of studies over the past few years,[30] and we will also draw on it in subsequent chapters on women, African Americans, Latinos, and Asian Americans). We simply counted the number of times the thirty-five distinctive Jewish names appeared. Since these thirty-five distinctive Jewish names account for about 12 percent of the overall Jewish population, this gives us a factor of 8.33 for estimating the total number of Jews on these boards. That is, because 8.33 × 12 percent equals 100 percent, multiplying the number of times these thirty-five names appear by 8.33 provides an estimate for the total number of Jews on the boards. The results indicated that 8.7 percent of the 2011 *Fortune* 500 directors were Jewish.

We had previously used this same technique to assess the percentage of Jews on of the boards of the top one hundred companies and each of the companies ranked between #401 and #500 for 1975, 1985, 1995, and 2004 editions of the *Standard & Poor's Directory*, which includes all the names of the men and women who sit on boards of directors. Table 2.1 includes the estimates of the percentages of Jews on *Fortune*-level boards in the various studies done by previous researchers and in our more current studies using the distinctive-names technique. (Table 2.1 also includes estimates of the percentage of Jews in the population at large at these various times.)

These figures indicate that the total number of Jews with distinctive Jewish names on *Fortune* 500 boards decreased slightly from 1975 to 1985, increased from 1985 to 1995 and to 2004, and then again dipped slightly between 2004 and 2011. These figures represent 6.6 percent, 4.3 percent, 7.7 percent, 11.1 percent, and 8.7 percent, respectively, of the total number of directors of the corporations studied.[31] We were also able to determine that the presence of people with distinctive Jewish names on the boards of the biggest companies (#1 to #100) has not been consistently greater than or less than the number on the boards of the smaller companies (#401 to #500). These findings demonstrate that even though the percentage of Jews in America declined steadily throughout the twentieth century and into the twenty-first, for the most part the percentage of Jews on corporate boards

Table 2.1. Jews in the Corporate Elite

Year	Jews in the Corporate Elite (%)	Jews in the Population (%)*	Source**
1900	3.4	—	Newcomer
1925	4.3	3.4	Newcomer
1950	4.6	3.3	Newcomer
1972	6.9	2.9	Alba and Moore
1976	7.0	2.7	Burck
1976	6.0	2.7	Sturdivant and Adler
1986	7.6	2.5	McComas
1986	7.4	2.5	Bennett
1995	7.7	2.3	DJN technique
2004	11.1	2.2	DJN technique
2011	8.7	2.1	DJN technique

* The figures in this column are from the *American Jewish Yearbook* and the *Encyclopedia Judaica*; prior to 1925, the estimates included only those Jews who were members of Jewish congregations, so no figure appears for 1900. The 2011 estimate of 2.1 percent is based on Ira M. Sheskin and Arnold Dashefsky, *Jewish Population in the United States, 2011* (Storrs, CT: North American Jewish Data Bank, 2011), http://www.jewishdatabank.org/studies/downloadFile.cfm?FileID=2919), 15.
** Mabel Newcomer, *The Big Business Executive: The Factors That Made Him, 1900–1950* (New York: Columbia University Press, 1955); Richard D. Alba and Gwen Moore, "Ethnicity in the American Elite," *American Sociological Review* 47 (1982): 373–83; Charles G. Burck, "A Group Profile of the Fortune 500 Chief Executive," *Fortune*, May 1976, 174–75; Frederick D. Sturdivant and Roy D. Adler, "Executive Origins: Still a Gray Flannel World," *Harvard Business Review* (November–December 1976): 125–33; Maggie McComas, "Atop the Fortune 500: A Survey of the C.E.O.," *Fortune*, April 28, 1986, 26–31; Robert A. Bennett, "No Longer a WASP Preserve," *New York Times*, June 29, 1986.

increased, and in every case was much greater than the percentage in the population. One can only conclude that Jews are most certainly overrepresented in the corporate elite.[32]

Do Jews in the Corporate Elite Stay Jewish?

As we have indicated, the various waves of Jewish immigrants to America felt strong pressure to assimilate into the dominant Gentile culture. Many immigrants thus worked at becoming "more American" and "less Jewish." "More American" typically meant learning to speak English without an accent, dressing the way people in the new country dressed, and generally learning the cultural mores. "Less Jewish" sometimes meant decreased involvement in synagogues and other Jewish organizations, changing one's name, or having one's nose "fixed."[33]

Intermarriage patterns provide the best indicator of the extent to which American Jews have been able and willing to assimilate. Milton Gordon considers intermarriage "the keystone in the arch of assimilation"; more recently, Lipset and Raab have called it "the definitive evidence of diminished group cohesion."[34] Until the middle of the twentieth century, marriages between Jews and non-Jews were the exception rather than the rule.

In a classic study, sociologist Ruby Jo Reeves Kennedy looked at the records of more than eight thousand marriages in New Haven, Connecticut, between 1870 and 1940. She found that there had been a loosening of what she called "strict endogamy": by the end of the period, more Protestants of different denominations married one another than was the case earlier, and more Irish American Catholics married Italian American Catholics. But there had also been a strong persistence of "religious endogamy": as of 1940, the rate of in-group marriage was 80 percent for Protestants, 84 percent for Catholics, and 94 percent for Jews. Kennedy therefore proposed that the idea of America as a "melting pot" should be replaced by an alternative image, that of the "triple melting pot." Even after updating her study to include data from 1950, Kennedy argued that "cultural lines may fade, but religious barriers are holding fast."[35]

As we indicated in the introduction to this chapter, those religious barriers eventually broke down. Richard Alba's extensive research led him to conclude that "the well-known triple–melting pot thesis . . . does not seem to be holding up," and its breakdown, though demonstrable for all non-Hispanic white Americans, is "best illustrated by the marriage patterns of Jews."[36] One study of Jews who married between 1966 and 1972 revealed that 32 percent married outside the faith.[37] As of 2004, sociologists estimated the figure to be about 50 percent.[38] By 2013, the intermarriage rate had risen to 58 percent (and it was 71 among non-Orthodox Jews).[39] Almost all those who marry non-Jews remain Jewish, but only one-seventh of their spouses convert to Judaism. Slightly less than one-third of the children of these mixed marriages are brought up Jewish, and only about 10 percent of them marry Jews. Lipset and Raab wryly concluded: "The cycle is downward. There is some reason to give credence to the sour joke: 'What do you call the grandchildren of intermarried Jews? Christians!'"[40]

In the context of this larger pattern of assimilation, we found that Jews who have been successful in the corporate world have been even more likely than other Jews to assimilate, and they have done so in ways that have allowed them to fit comfortably into the power elite. As we concluded as early as 1982 in a detailed study of Jewish men and women who had been successful in the corporate world, for Jews at the top of the class hierarchy, class has come to supersede religious identity.[41]

In an interview study of graduates of the Harvard Business School, we asked both Jewish and Gentile managers about how Jews had been treated in their companies. For the most part, the respondents indicated that Jews had done well, but some were convinced that certain kinds of Jews were more likely to be successful than others. As one of the Jewish respondents put it, "If an individual is perceived as quite Jewish, into Jewish social events, it may have a negative impact. Those who have moved faster in this company are the less visible Jews." Another told us that one of his Jewish colleagues had never visited Israel because of his fear that it would have "political ramifications."[42]

The most candid comments came from one of the Gentile interviewees, who acknowledged his own prejudices as he explained his view of how things worked at his company:

> If you really want to know the way I feel, I think at the top levels, being Jewish will hurt a person's chances. But it depends on how he plays his cards. This one man I know is so polished, such an upper-class person, there's no way to know he's Jewish. I'll admit I'm prejudiced. There are certain aspects of Jewish people I don't like—they're pushy, they're loud, especially those damn New York bastards. Christ, I'm so sick of hearing about Israel. My friend is fine, however. He's an upper-class-type person, the kind who could make it to the top.[43]

Given this portrayal of the corporate world, we were not surprised to find, both in a series of systematic studies comparing Jews who were and were not corporate directors and in the interviews we conducted with Jewish directors, that Jews in the corporate elite are less likely to see Jewishness as a salient part of their identity than are other Jews. Moreover, we found that this was particularly true of those corporate directors whose parents or grandparents had also been in the corporate elite and that there were no differences in this regard between German Jews and the handful of Eastern European Jews who came from wealthy backgrounds. This was not only true in terms of marriage patterns but in terms of their interest in Israel, the likelihood of their having visited Israel, and the ways they chose to reveal (or not reveal) their Jewish identity in books such as *Who's Who in America*.[44]

Those corporate directors we interviewed who were the first in their families to make it into the corporate elite, men such as Laurence Tisch and Irving Shapiro, were still very much involved in and committed to Jewish issues. They had married Jews, for example, and had been to Israel many times. Those, however, who were of the second or third generation in their families to have been among America's economic elite—men such as Joseph Frederick Cullman III, who was the CEO at Philip Morris from 1957 to 1978, and William Wishnick, CEO at Witco Chemical from 1975 to 1991, a company started by his father—had married non-Jews and were less likely to have visited Israel. We asked those we interviewed what being Jewish meant to them. The responses of the second- and third-generation members of the corporate elite were revealing. The most telling came from one man who paused and then admitted, "It really doesn't mean anything."[45]

Our research and the work of others indicate that Jews have been successful in the corporate world and have steadily increased their presence among the corporate elite. The doors that opened at DuPont in 1973 for Irving Shapiro did indeed portend the ascent of other Jews to leadership in non-Jewish companies. It did not turn heads—it certainly did not warrant shocked front-page headlines in the *Wall Street Journal*—when, eleven years later, in 1984, the Walt Disney Company, founded by a man who had refused to hire Jews, picked as its CEO and chairman Michael Eisner, a Jew from a wealthy New York family, to save it from the threat of a hostile takeover. Nor was there much notice a few years after that when, in 1990, Richard Rosenberg, the Jewish son of a clothing salesman, became chair and CEO at the Bank of America.[46] By 2016, when Staples named Shira Goodman, a Jewish woman who is married to a rabbi and who had been very active for many years in the Boston Jewish community, as its CEO, her appointment was followed by an article in the *Jewish Daily Forward* (they were proud),[47] but little was made in the mainstream press of the fact that another *Fortune* 500 company had selected a Jew as its CEO (or even, as we will see in the next chapter, that it had chosen a white woman).

At the same time, however, because of the general pressures and temptations to assimilate, for most though not all of the Jews in the corporate elite, being Jewish is likely to become progressively less important and less important still to their children and their grandchildren. The pattern of socialization into the power elite ensures that the people who enter the higher circles do not differ significantly from those who are already there. Those who can "fit in" best are most likely to get there, and this means, at least in corporations not founded or owned by Jews, that those who put less public emphasis on their Jewishness are most likely to make it to the top. So, ironically, sixty-two years after Mills wrote his book, more Jews are in the corporate elite, but the longer their families have been there, the less likely are they to be Jewish in any meaningful sense. Whether these same patterns will reappear for other excluded groups is a key question that we explore throughout this book.

JEWS IN THE CABINET

When we looked at the cabinets of each president from Dwight D. Eisenhower through the first six months of Trump's presidency, we found that Jews had held twenty of the 300 cabinet positions (6.7 percent).[48] Strikingly, there were no Jews among the seventy-eight cabinet appointees made by Ronald Reagan and George H. W. Bush. Moreover, it was not until late in his second term that George W. Bush appointed Michael Chertoff as secretary of homeland security and Michael Mukasey, an Orthodox Jew, as attorney general.[49] All of the other presidents since 1956 appointed at least one Jewish person to their cabinets. Whereas 8.6 percent of all cabinet appointments by Democratic presidents have been Jews, only 4 percent of all cabinet appointments by Republican presidents have been Jewish.[50]

As of October 2017, Trump's cabinet included only one Jew, Steven Mnuchin, the secretary of the treasury (David Schulkin, the secretary of veteran's affairs, is also Jewish, but because some presidents have not included this position as fully "cabinet level" we have not included it in our tabulations—see note 50 for this chapter).[51]

Each of the twenty men and women married at least once, and each had at least one child. About half of them married non-Jews, which reflects the frequency of intermarriage found among Jews and especially among successful Jewish business people. Wilbur Cohen, the secretary of health, education, and welfare during the Johnson administration, married a Unitarian. Henry Kissinger, Nixon's secretary of state, married an Episcopalian. Michael Blumenthal, the CEO of the Bendix Corporation when President Carter appointed him secretary of the treasury, married a Presbyterian and, according to a profile in *Current Biography*, "he was baptized as a Presbyterian about the time of his marriage."[52] However, the story did not end there. After serving in the cabinet, he returned to the corporate world, where he became the CEO of Burroughs Corporation, which in turn merged with Sperry to become UNISYS. When Blumenthal retired as CEO of UNISYS in 1990, he worked for five years as a limited partner for Lazard Freres. He also wrote a book about Germany and the Jews, which was a "personal exploration" that told the story of his own departure from Germany at the age of twelve to spend the war years in Shanghai, two of them in a Japanese internment camp. In 1998, he accepted an offer to head the development of the Jewish Museum, Berlin, a Holocaust memorial. Thus, after many decades of ignoring his Jewish origins, he returned to his roots through the book he wrote and through his near-total commitment to a successful memorial, which opened to high praise in 2002.[53]

The other Jewish cabinet members who have married non-Jews include Harold Brown, secretary of defense under Jimmy Carter. Brown married an Episcopalian and, according to a profile in *Current Biography* written in 1977, he and his wife "now consider themselves 'unchurched.'"[54] Neal Goldschmidt, Carter's secretary of transportation, married twice, both times to non-Jews. Robert Reich, secretary of labor from 1993 to 1997 during the Clinton administration, met his wife, who is not Jewish, when he was a Rhodes Scholar in England.

These men are highly educated—seventeen of the twenty hold either a law degree or a PhD. Seven have degrees from Harvard, twelve from Ivy League schools, and all but one graduated from highly selective schools. Most came from comfortable circumstances, backgrounds that would be considered middle or upper-middle class.

But one is from much higher up than the middle or even the upper-middle class. Penny Pritzker, Obama's secretary of commerce from 2013 to 2017, is from one of the wealthiest families in the country (the Pritzkers have been near the top of the annual *Forbes Magazine* list of the wealthiest families in the country ever since it began the list in 1982). She also is unusual in that she was a major fundraiser for Obama during the primaries in 2008, and she became the national finance chair for his presidential campaign. She was ranked #315 on the 2017 *Forbes* list, with an estimated worth of 2.6 billion.

Two of those on the list were born in Germany and suffered the hardships of dislocation, but both of their families were solidly middle class. The parents of two others were immigrants who had to struggle to make ends meet. The father of one them, who died when he was eight, drove a horse and buggy around Chicago selling produce to hotels, and the other man's father worked in a factory.[55]

JEWS IN THE MILITARY ELITE

Although Jews fought on both sides during the Civil War, by the late nineteenth century it was often claimed that Jews avoided or were incapable of military service. Mark Twain, for example, wrote that the Jew "is charged with a disinclination patriotically to stand by the flag as a soldier. By his make and his ways he is substantially a foreigner and even the angels dislike foreigners."[56]

In response to such claims, in 1896, a group of seventy-eight Jewish veterans of the Union Army met in New York City and formed the Hebrew Union Veterans, a precursor to the Jewish War Veterans, an organization that sought to "uphold the fair name of the Jew and fight his battles wherever unjustly assailed" and "to gather and preserve the records of patriotic service performed by men of Jewish faith."[57] In 1984, the Jewish War Veterans opened the National Museum of Jewish History in Washington, DC.

As we have seen, by the 1920s, when virulent anti-Semitism was widespread in the United States, Jews in the military were no freer from its powerful effects than other Jews. Data for the later decades of the twentieth century are hard to come by, anecdotal, and difficult to interpret in terms of Jewish participation in the military, but it is certain that there were Jews in the most senior levels of the military establishment by the end of the twentieth century. Most striking was not merely their presence but the absence of any surprise that they were there. For many in the military, whether one is Jewish is simply no longer an issue. James Zimble, a former surgeon general of the navy who retired as a vice admiral (a three-star rank) and who at the time of our 1995 interview with him was president of the Uniformed Services University of the Health Sciences, asserted, "I have neither been victim of nor witnessed any anti-Semitism in the military. I know there are still redneck holdouts in the Deep South and elsewhere, but the military has gotten beyond that."[58]

Zimble's claims about the treatment of Jews in the military were echoed by others with whom we spoke, including Arnold Resnicoff, one of the two highest-ranking rabbis in the navy when we interviewed him in 1995. As a navy rabbi for more than twenty years, he should have been aware of serious episodes of anti-Semitism in that branch of the military. In response to our question, he said, "There is no institution—and I believe this with all my heart, I'm not just giving you some company line—that fights prejudice, anti-Semitism, racism, as much as the military. Acts of overt anti-Semitism are extremely rare, and they are punished immediately. In all my years in the military, I have seen very few cases of anti-Semitism. Those were acts by individuals, and the institution reacted swiftly and forcefully." Resnicoff may have been unduly optimistic. He was called out of retirement in June 2005 to implement the recommendations of a panel that investigated and upheld charges of religious "insensitivity" at the Air Force Academy. This insensitivity included a football coach who hung a banner in the locker room declaring the players to be part of "Team Jesus Christ," pressures on cadets to attend chapel, government e-mails that cited the New Testament, and various other forms of Christian proselytizing (including comments to Jews, made by an air force chaplain, that they would burn in hell). [59]

Even with this surge of super-Christianity at the Air Force Academy, which made many Jewish observers nervous, the general view of those with whom we spoke was that the military fights prejudice, not only against Jews but also against blacks, Latinos, and, as one of them put it, "even women." We provide support for these claims in our chapters on blacks, Latinos, and Asian Americans. However, those who assured us that the military worked to root out prejudice did acknowledge that discrimination against gay men and lesbians remained another, more difficult matter, one that we will return to in chapter 7.

Perhaps partially in response to the embarrassing revelations at the Air Force Academy in 2005, in 2008 the air force named its first Jewish chief of staff, Norton Allan Schwartz. Schwartz, the son of a typewriter salesman, and a graduate of the Air Force Academy, served as chief of staff until 2012. When he was appointed, Schwartz was one of only three Jews in senior positions in the military—the other two were Lieutenant General H. Steven Blum, who headed the National Guard from 2003 to 2008, and General Robert Magnus, the assistant commandant of the marine corps from 2005 to 2008. [60] In 2016, Obama named David Goldfein to serve as the chief of staff of the air force, and he thus became the second Jewish person to serve in that position. [61]

Moreover, not only have there been very few Jewish members of the Joint Chiefs of Staff; there has yet to be a Jewish chairman of that group. Since 1949, when General Omar Bradley became the first chairman of the Joint Chiefs of Staff, nineteen men have served in that capacity. None has been Jewish (with the exception of Colin Powell, an African American, all have been white Christian men).

For now, let us consider the appointments of two Jewish men that support the assertion put forth by Zimble and Resnicoff that being Jewish is not an issue with regard to promotion in the military, even promotion to the very highest levels of the military establishment (the first, Jeremy Michael Boorda, was in the military; the second, John Deutch, headed the CIA).

Jeremy Michael Boorda, who became the top-ranking naval officer in March 1994, turned out to be Jewish, though most people were unaware of that until it was mentioned in a long magazine profile about him that appeared in the *Washingtonian*. Boorda's parents, Herman and Gertrude Boorda, ran a dress shop in a small town in Illinois fifty miles south of Chicago. Their marriage was not a happy one, and there was so much tension in the home that Mike ran off and joined the navy in the middle of his junior year of high school.

Almost forty years later, married to a non-Jew and the father of three children, Boorda became a four-star admiral and the first Jewish member of the Joint Chiefs of Staff. At the time of his appointment, no one seemed to pay any attention to Boorda's Jewish background. In part, this may reflect the bureaucratic conformity demanded by the military. Mills noted that the military isolates its members, breaks down their previously acquired tastes and values, and thereby creates "a highly uniform type." The warlords, more than others in the power elite, according to Mills, come to "resemble one another, internally and externally."[62] In fact, in a celebrated case in the 1980s, the Supreme Court ruled that a military man did not have the right to wear a yarmulke. Such Jewish visibility, even as part of one's religious obligations, was deemed an inappropriate disruption of the uniformity of appearance required by the military.[63]

It is possible that no one paid attention to Boorda's Jewish background because of his own choice to assimilate. He ran away from a troubled and unhappy home, he married a non-Jewish woman, and even some of those who thought they knew him well were surprised to discover that he was Jewish. According to retired vice admiral Bernard M. ("Bud") Kauderer, about a year before the *Washingtonian* article appeared, Boorda was going through a receiving line that included Adm. Sumner Shapiro, the former director of naval intelligence and a Jew. When he got to Shapiro in the line, Boorda leaned over to him and whispered, "You know, Shap, I'm one of you." Kauderer told us, "This was the first inkling we had that he was Jewish. It was a source of amazement to us."[64] But in our view, the most important reason that no one paid attention to Boorda's Jewish background was that, as

Zimble and Resnicoff claimed, being Jewish is no longer an issue in the military.

The promotion of another Jewish man to a powerful position in the defense establishment provides additional support for the view that being Jewish is no longer an impediment to one's career. In March 1995, President Bill Clinton persuaded John Deutch, who had turned him down once before, to accept the nomination as director of the CIA. Deutch was born in Belgium in 1938, just thirteen months before the beginning of World War II. His family was able to escape the subsequent Nazi occupation by going first to Paris, then to Lisbon, and then, in 1940, to the United States. Deutch's father, a chemical engineer who helped invent the process for making synthetic rubber, became deputy director of the government's synthetic rubber program during the war. Deutch's mother, the daughter of diamond merchants, had a doctorate in ancient studies and allegedly spoke ten languages. Deutch attended the prominent Sidwell Friends School and received a BA from Amherst and a PhD in physical chemistry from the Massachusetts Institute of Technology (MIT). He first came to work at the Pentagon in 1961 at the age of twenty-two as one of the "whiz kids" who worked under Robert McNamara during the Kennedy administration. He left the Pentagon in 1966 to teach chemistry, first at Princeton and then at MIT. As the *New York Times* put it, since that time, "he has rotated between posts at M.I.T. and increasingly powerful positions in Democratic administrations."

In addition to his work at MIT and for the government, Deutch has also served corporations as both a board member and consultant. A lengthy profile of Deutch in the *Washingtonian* notes that, in 1992, his salary at MIT had been $207,000, but he had earned more than $600,000 from consulting and director's fees at twenty corporations, mostly defense contractors such as Martin Marietta and TRW.[65]

As was true for Boorda at the time of his appointment, Deutch's religious background received virtually no mention in the press. Although a *New York Times* profile mentioned that "he and his family fled Belgium for France and eventually came to the United States," it did not state explicitly that he was, or they were, Jewish. But Deutch is Jewish, as are the two women he has married, both of whom are from prominent German-Jewish families in the Washington area and were fellow students of his at Sidwell Friends.[66]

For a Jew to head the CIA is even more stunning a sign of acceptance than for a Jew to sit on the Joint Chiefs of Staff, for the CIA has historically been led by Christian men of impeccable upper-class credentials.[67] But Boorda's presence among the Joint Chiefs was a milestone as well, for the Joint Chiefs of Staff has also been a Gentile preserve, albeit a less socially exclusive one than the CIA. For a time during the Reagan presidency, the Joint Chiefs held "prayer breakfasts" led by one of Boorda's predecessors, the devout Roman Catholic four-star admiral James Watkins.[68]

Jews, therefore, have made it to the top of the military elite. In addition to Harold Brown, Jimmy Carter's secretary of defense, Admiral Boorda, and CIA director Deutch, numerous Jews have achieved the rank of two stars or higher (officers with a rank of two stars or higher represent only 0.2 percent of all officers).[69] Being Jewish in the military today is dramatically different from being Jewish at the Naval Academy in the early 1920s, or even from being Jewish in the military during the 1950s when Mills wrote *The Power Elite*.

Still, it must be noted that although barriers have been broken as some Jews have become part of the military elite, and there has been a dramatic decline in the levels of anti-Semitism in the military, Jews are underrepresented in the military (unlike the corporate elite, where they are overrepresented). Ted Merwin, who teaches in the Judaic Studies program at Dickinson College, writes that "According to Department of Defense statistics, Jews, who make up about 2 percent of the overall population of this country, make up less than a third of one percent of the total number of those serving in the armed forces."[70] This is in part because Jews, who tend to be economically well off, are less likely to enlist than those from working-class backgrounds.

But it is also in part because the atmosphere within the military can be decidedly Christian, and subtly or overtly, anti-Semitic. The 2005 scandal at the Air Force Academy revealed that Jewish cadets were being stigmatized and proselytized by evangelical Christians to convert. This scandal, coming on the heels of previous and subsequent scandals about widespread sexual abuse of women at the Air Force Academy, led to special investigations and lawsuits.[71]

This means that although some make it to the highest ranks, there are fewer Jews in the pipeline, and there may still be subtle or not-so-subtle forces working against Jews in the military. Moreover, aside from the possibility of being outsiders in a predominantly Christian milieu, as Rear Admiral Harold L. Robinson, a Reform rabbi who served from 1971 to 2007 as a chaplain in the navy, explained: "Admirals and generals pick aides who remind them of themselves 20 years earlier. This gives these aides an enormous advantage later on in terms of being promoted, because they understand all the workings of command."[72]

JEWS IN CONGRESS AND ON THE SUPREME COURT

The Senate

Between 1844 and 1913, six men of Jewish background served in the US Senate.[73] Then, for the next thirty-six years, when anti-Semitism was at its most virulent in the context of the large influx of Jewish immigrants from Eastern Europe, there were no Jews until Herbert Lehman, the scion of a wealthy German-Jewish family that made its fortune in New Orleans and moved to New York City, won a special election in New York in 1949 after the incumbent resigned. He came to the Senate after serving as the governor of New York for ten years and having lost a Senate race in 1946.

Since 1950, twenty-nine Jews have been elected to the Senate. Three Jewish men were elected in the second half of the 1950s, and another was elected in 1962. By 1992, there were ten Jews in the Senate, as of July 2005, there were eleven, and, as of mid-2017, there were nine.[74]

As is true for the Jews in presidential cabinets, there is a notable distinction between the two major political parties: twenty-three of the twenty-nine Jewish senators have been Democrats (five have been Republicans, and one, Bernie Sanders, is an independent who caucuses with the Democrats). But, Democrat, Republican, or independent, the presence of about ten Jews in the Senate throughout the last twenty-five years means not only that the percentage is considerably higher than the percentage of Jews in the general population, but that it also reflects a sea change in the political role played by Jews in America, who were once limited to behind-the-scenes parts.[75]

Jews who have been elected to the Senate differ dramatically from one another in the degree to which they have been involved in Judaism. At one pole is Ernest Gruening, whose father was a prominent surgeon with a summer home in Rockport, Massachusetts. Gruening went to Hotchkiss and then to Harvard, first as an undergraduate and then as a medical student. Isaacs reports that Gruening "never paid the slightest attention to things Jewish," and there is no mention of his Jewish heritage in his lengthy autobiography.[76]

At the other pole is Joseph Lieberman, an Orthodox Jew married to a woman named Hadassah, a man who, in accordance with the regulations of his faith, does not use electrical appliances or ride elevators on the Sabbath.

When Lieberman was elected in 1988 to the Senate, it was clear that things had changed, at least in Connecticut politics. In 2000, Al Gore, the Democratic nominee for president, picked Lieberman to run as his vice president.

Although commitment to Judaism, and even Orthodox Judaism, has become acceptable for those who serve in the Senate, it is neither required nor expected. This was demonstrated by one of the more consequential episodes in the political life of two Jewish senators, one that took place in the Minnesota senatorial election of 1990, a state with only 45,000 Jews, 1.5 percent of the population. The Democratic nominee was Paul Wellstone, a liberal activist and professor of political science at Carleton College who had never held political office and whose father had emigrated from Russia in 1914. (His mother was born in the United States, but her parents were Russian Jewish immigrants.) The Republican nominee and incumbent was Rudy Boschwitz, who was born in Berlin in 1930 and fled to America with his family when he was very young. Boschwitz was heavily favored, not only because he was the incumbent and Wellstone was so inexperienced but because his campaign was much more heavily financed; Boschwitz raised seven times as much money as Wellstone.

But Wellstone ran an extremely effective and resourceful campaign, drawing on more than ten thousand volunteers, many of whom had been his students. Boschwitz, meanwhile, made a series of blunders, the worst of which was described by two Minnesota journalists as "one of the most memorable pratfalls ever witnessed in Minnesota politics."[77] In an act of apparent desperation, perhaps figuring that every last vote would matter, he sent a letter to Jewish voters one week before the election to remind them of his own Jewish heritage and support for Israel and to denounce Wellstone for raising his children as non-Jews and for having "no connection whatsoever with the Jewish community or our communal life." This attack backfired, for it seemed to confirm Wellstone's claims that Boschwitz had been running a negative campaign.[78] By 1990, then, a Senate seat from a state with a very small percentage of Jewish residents could be contested by two Jews and could be decided in part by an apparent perception among voters, including many Jewish voters, that it was inappropriate for one candidate to criticize the other for the way he chose to live his life as a Jew.

Wellstone ran against Boschwitz again in 1996 and was reelected. He was campaigning for a third term, when he, his wife and daughter, three staff members, and two pilots died tragically in a plane crash in October 2002. Wellstone's Republican opponent, Norm Coleman, also Jewish, won the election against former senator Walter Mondale, who agreed to run at the last minute. Six years later, Coleman lost to yet another Jew, Al Franken (therefore four of the twenty-eight Jewish senators have been from Minnesota—more than the number from New York!).[79]

The twenty-nine Jewish senators are similar to others in the power elite in a number of ways. Almost all have been married, some more than once. All of the Jewish senators earned at least a bachelor's degree, and two-thirds have gone on to earn higher degrees (sixteen received law degrees, one a business degree, one a medical degree, and one a doctorate). They differ from Jews in the corporate community and the executive branch of government, however, in that they come from a broader range of socioeconomic backgrounds. Some were second-generation Americans who grew up in real poverty. Others had parents who owned small businesses. And some grew up in very comfortable economic settings. By the time they ran for the Senate, many had become millionaires.[80]

The House

There has been a similar increase in the number of Jews elected to the 435-member House of Representatives. In 1975, there were only ten Jewish members of the House (2.3 percent), most of whom were elected in Jewish districts in New York. By 1993, there were thirty-three Jewish men and women in the House (7.6 percent), and they served districts scattered across the country, including many in which less than 1 percent of the voting population was Jewish. In 2005, the number had dropped to twenty-six (5.9 percent), only one of whom was a Republican (the others were all Democrats, with one exception, Bernie Sanders of Vermont, a democratic socialist who has run as an independent).[81] There were twenty Jewish members of the House in the 114th Congress that served from 2015 to 2017 (4.6 percent), nineteen Democrats and one Republican, and the number of Jews in the House in the 115th Congress, serving from 2017 to 2019, increased slightly to twenty-two (5.1 percent), with eighteen Democrats and two Republicans.

The Supreme Court

One of the most prominent legal minds in American history, who came from a wealthy German Jewish family and left his practice as a corporate lawyer to fight for progressive causes, was the first Jew ever to serve on the Supreme Court. Louis D. Brandeis, who also challenged the money trust of that era in one of the most famous books ever written on corporate power, *Other People's Money—and How the Bankers Use It*, was appointed to the Supreme Court in 1916 by Democratic president Woodrow Wilson and served until 1939, often providing informal advice to President Franklin D. Roosevelt via intermediaries.[82] Since Brandeis's appointment, eight other Jews have served on the Supreme Court (as of mid-2017, 113 men and women had served on the court; therefore, 7.1 percent have been Jewish).[83]

Another Jew, Benjamin N. Cardozo, who had served as a judge on the New York Court of Appeals, joined Brandeis on the court in 1931 (he was nominated by Herbert Hoover). When Cardozo died eight years later, Franklin Delano Roosevelt named Harvard Law School professor Felix Frankfurter, who served until 1963. When Frankfurter left the court, Arthur Goldberg, the chief counsel for the AFL-CIO, replaced him and, when Goldberg left the court after only two years, his replacement was Abe Fortas, whose firm of Arnold, Fortas and Porter was one of the most influential law firms in Washington, DC (when Fortas went on the Supreme Court, it became Arnold and Porter). When Fortas resigned in 1969, there were no Jews on the court until 1993, when Clinton appointed Ruth Bader Ginsburg (the first Jewish woman Supreme Court justice) and then Stephen G. Breyer.[84] In 2010, Barack Obama appointed Elena Kagan to replace the retiring John Paul Stevens, bringing the number of Jews on the court to three (Ginsburg, Breyer, and Kagan), a striking 33 percent.[85]

Not surprisingly, these eight Jewish Supreme Court justices attended elite private schools —five attended Harvard Law School, one attended Yale, two attended Columbia, and one attended Northwestern (the total is nine because Ginsburg attended both Harvard and Columbia). They come from varied class backgrounds. Brandeis is described by a current professor of law at the Yale Law School as "a well-educated, financially prosperous son of well-educated, commercially successful immigrants who had left Germany after the failure of the liberal revolutions of 1848."[86] Cardozo was from a well-to-do New York Sephardic Jewish family that arrived in America in 1654. His father was a prominent lawyer, and the family lived in a fashionable neighborhood near Fifth Avenue.[87]

In contrast, Frankfurter's family emigrated from Austria when he was twelve and had little money. His father was descended from six generations of rabbis but was somewhat of a dreamer; after arriving in New York in 1894, he started a retail fur and silk business, which enabled the family to make it "from Seventh Street to the middle-class environs of Yorkville on

East Seventy-first Street in only five years," but the family was never secure or economically comfortable. Like many Jewish immigrants of his generation, Frankfurter attended the City College of New York (CCNY). He did so well (he graduated third in his class of 774) that he went on to Harvard Law School (where he subsequently taught, at times as the only Jew on the faculty).[88] Similarly, Goldberg and Fortas were both American-born children of Eastern European Jewish immigrants. Goldberg was the youngest of seven children born to Russian immigrant parents (his father was a peddler who drove a horse-drawn wagon), worked at odd jobs, and received scholarships to a junior college and DePaul before studying law at Northwestern. Fortas, the youngest of five children, was the son of Orthodox Jews who emigrated from England. His father "scratched out a living" at various jobs, including work as a jeweler, shopkeeper, pawnbroker, and cabinetmaker. Fortas, too, attended college on a scholarship (Southwestern University, from which he graduated first in his class), and then he graduated second in his class at Yale Law School.[89]

Ginsburg and Breyer are both the grandchildren of Eastern European immigrants. Ginsburg, born Joan Ruth Bader, was born in Brooklyn, where her parents lived in a working-class neighborhood. During her senior year of high school, her mother died of cancer and left her the "relatively large sum of $8,000 for her college tuition," which, because she had won a scholarship to Cornell, she gave to her father. Breyer grew up in San Francisco, where his father was a lawyer and his mother volunteered for the Democratic Party and the League of Women Voters. He attended Stanford and then Harvard Law School.[90] Elena Kagan grew up in New York City, where her father was a real estate lawyer and her mother was a teacher.

No matter what their class origins, most of the members of the Supreme Court end up as millionaires. According to the financial disclosures they are required to make, as of 2013 at least eight of the nine justices were millionaires (all nine might have been—because of the loose ranges that are used on the disclosure forms, Justice Kennedy, according to *USA Today*, "appears to be" below the million-dollar threshold).[91]

These eight also vary in terms of the extent of their observation of the tenets of Judaism. Brandeis grew up in a secular home and had virtually no sense of Jewish affiliation. Shortly before he became a member of the court, he stated, "I have been to a great extent separated from Jews. I am very ignorant in things Jewish." Cardozo was bar mitzvahed but did not practice Judaism as an adult (he remained a member of his Sephardic congregation but did not attend services; he referred to himself privately as a "heathen" and publicly as an agnostic). Frankfurter recounted that he went to the synaogogue during the High Holidays while he was a student at CCNY, but he "left the service in the middle of it, never to return," for Judaism "ceased to have inner meaning." Fortas always identified himself as Jewish, but Judaism had little spiritual meaning for him; according to one biographer, "he viewed his religion as a handicap to disclose rather than as a heritage to claim."[92] Goldberg was the first Jew on the Supreme Court to remain observant throughout his adult life, though (unlike, say, Joseph Lieberman) he was not Orthodox; nor did he go to a synagogue every week. He did, however, attend services on the High Holidays of Rosh Hashanah and Yom Kippur, he and his wife held seders in their house during Passover, and, shortly after he became a member of the Supreme Court, when a scheduling conflict arose, he consulted his hometown rabbi back in Chicago about whether it would be acceptable to hear arguments on Yom Kippur.[93] Breyer attended religious school, but his family was not especially observant.[94] When she approached the age of thirteen, Elena Kagan persuaded the rabbi at the Orthodox synaogogue her family attended to allow her to have a bat mitzvah. Prior to that time only boys had been bar mitzvahed, and hers was the first formal bat mitzvah at that synagogue. She now considers herself a Conservative Jew, and both she and Ruth Bader Ginsburg are members of Adas Israel, a conservative synagogue in Washington, DC.[95]

CONCLUSION

The clear evidence of representation, or overrepresentation, of Jews in the corporate elite, the cabinet, and the military elite reflects a dramatic reversal of the discrimination experienced by Jews in these arenas until the final third of the twentieth century. Although Jews may still be underrepresented in some business sectors within the corporate community, the data we have examined reveal that Jews are overrepresented overall in the corporate elite. Jews are also now overrepresented in both the Senate and the House, where they tend to be Democrats. Although they may not be overrepresented in the military elite, some certainly have made it to the highest circles. These findings lead to an important question: how have Jews been able to become part of what was formerly a Christian power elite and Congress?

They have done so in a number of ways, each of which might provide a basis of comparison in subsequent chapters as we consider the experiences of women and other previously excluded groups. First, Jews have had both the ability and the willingness to assimilate into what Alba has called the emerging ethnic category of "European Americans." Almost all Jews are white (there are almost one hundred thousand African Americans who are Jewish),[96] and all of the Jews who have moved into the power elite are white. The ethnic prejudice against Jews, therefore, was not accompanied by the added feature of race with which African Americans, Asian Americans, and others of color have had to contend. This may have made it easier for Jews to assimilate generally and, more specifically, to be accepted by those in the power elite. And this, we believe, is reflected by the dramatic increase in intermarriages between Jews and Gentiles.

A second factor is the strong cultural emphasis among Jews on academic success and the resulting overrepresentation of Jews among college graduates. This is even more the case for the most prestigious colleges and universities in America, which are golden highways to positions in the power elite and Congress. To the degree that women and people of color graduate from the same high-status schools, we should see them in the power elite and in Congress.[97]

Related to the emphasis on academic success is the fact that many Jews came to America with experience as employers or shopkeepers in their own communities.[98] Some of them or their children had achieved financial success before doors began to open for them, primarily in retailing but also in fields like investment banking. It became difficult to exclude members of the Jewish community when they had the financial wherewithal to buy their way into the corporate elite. Once in, they were asked to join other boards as outside directors. And over time, especially with the various waves of mergers and acquisitions that make it difficult to know whether a company was founded or is owned by Jews, they have simply become part of the corporate elite. Similarly, because Jews were well educated and politically active and had acquired all kinds of valuable expertise, as they became a potent group economically, more and more they began to appear in presidential cabinets and, by the 1990s, in Congress.

Alba refers to Jews as "the outstanding instance of a group that is managing to swim to some degree against the assimilatory tide."[99] This may be true when Jews are compared with other white non-Hispanic ethnic groups who are melding into European American homogeneity. But we have seen that Jews who have made it to the power elite have been likely to assimilate.

A number of factors seem to be important in understanding the successful entry by Jews into the power elite and Congress. They have light skin, and those who rise the highest are likely to have been born into relatively privileged circumstances. They have excellent educational credentials. They often have managerial skills, and they have made an effort to blend in. There is also a factor we have not mentioned: time. Second- and third-generation American Jews tend to have become fully acculturated, and non-Jewish whites seem to have become more accepting of them. In the chapters that follow, then, we shall focus on various factors, namely, class background, education, managerial experience, and color, as well as whether one was born in the United States (or one's parents were), to assess the importance of these variables in understanding why members of other previously excluded groups do or do not gain entry into the power elite and Congress.

Chapter Three

Women in the Power Elite

In November 2016, it appeared that Hillary Clinton, the twentieth woman ever to be elected to the US Senate, and the second woman to serve as the secretary of state, was going to become the first female president of the United States. Although the polls indicated that she would win, and in fact she did win the popular vote, she lost the electoral vote to Donald Trump, a man who had denigrated women for many years and throughout his presidential campaign, sometimes in the crudest of terms. Unlike in more than seventy other countries, including England, Israel, Argentina, and New Zealand, the highest office in the United States has not yet gone to a woman.

There can be no doubt, however, that much has changed since 1956, when C. Wright Mills wrote *The Power Elite*. The power elite that he identified and analyzed in the mid-1950s was, without doubt, almost exclusively a male preserve. On the opening page of *The Power Elite*, Mills states clearly that "the power elite is composed of men whose positions enable them to transcend the ordinary environments of ordinary men and women."[1] Although there were some women in the corporate, political, and military worlds, very few were in or near the higher circles that constituted the power elite. How far have women made it into these higher circles? When did they arrive, and how did they get there? What are their prospects? Do they fare better in the corporate elite, the political elite, the military elite, or the Supreme Court? These are some of the questions we will address in this chapter.

WOMEN IN THE CORPORATE ELITE

Women on Corporate Boards

In a chapter titled "The Chief Executives," Mills describes the men who owned and ran the largest corporations in the United States: "Large owners and executives in their self-financing corporations hold the keys of economic power. Not the politicians of the visible government, but the chief executives who sit in the political directorate, by fact and proxy, hold the power and the means of defending the privileges of their corporate world. If they do not reign, they do govern at many of the vital points of everyday life in America, and no powers effectively and consistently countervail against them, nor have they as corporate-made men developed any effectively restraining conscience."[2]

Who were these "corporate-made men" who occupied the "top two or three command posts" in each of the largest "hundred or so corporations"? As we indicated in chapter 2, when Mills systematically studied their backgrounds, the evidence showed clearly that they were not "country boys who [had] made good in the city" or the Horatio Alger types of popular myth; nor were they immigrants or even the sons of immigrants. Instead, Mills wrote, these executives, "today as in the past, were born with a big advantage: they managed to have fathers on at least upper-middle-class levels of occupation and income; they are Protestant, white, and American-born. These factors of origin led directly to their second big advantage: they are well-educated in the formal sense of college and post-college schooling."[3]

It went without saying that these "typical executives" were men. Although there were a handful of women on the boards of the top corporations, they were wives or daughters in family-controlled companies or presidents of prestigious women's colleges, and they were unlikely to sit in one of the few most important positions (the top two or three "command posts"). Mills virtually ignored women in the corporate elite because there were so few of them. His failure to make an issue of the absence of women in the corporate elite is evidence that he, too, was a product of his time. If Mills had seen this as an issue of importance, there can be no doubt that he would have addressed it. It was, for Mills as for most others, a given.

Mills died in 1962, a year before the publication of Betty Friedan's influential *The Feminine Mystique* and a few years before the rise of feminism on university campuses. By the 1970s, women had entered the corporate world in far greater numbers than ever before. Indeed, the sociologist Jerry

A. Jacobs wrote in the early 1990s that "the increasing representation of women among the ranks of managers in organizations in the United States is perhaps the most dramatic shift in the sex composition of an occupation since clerical work became a female-dominated field in the late nineteenth century."[4] The progress of women in the highest levels of management was of interest to many. Journalists and academics asked with some frequency whether women had made it into the corporate elite, and, if not, why not?

In 1978, *Fortune* magazine presented the results of a systematic study of women on boards of directors of the thirteen hundred companies that made up the *Fortune* 500, the *Fortune* Second 500, and the six lists of the top fifty retailers, utilities, banks, life insurance companies, transportation companies, and diversified financial companies. Drawing on the proxy-statement lists, which, as required by law, include the names and salaries of the three highest-paid officers and any board members who earned more than $40,000 in the previous year, *Fortune* found that ten of the sixty-four hundred people identified were women, representing "a measly 0.16 percent." Nor did the presence of ten women in those corporate ranks represent progress: a similar study five years earlier had "turned up" eleven women.[5]

Mills's focus, as we have noted, was on the top two or three positions in the top "hundred or so" corporations. By this rather stringent standard, only one person in the 1978 survey came close to qualifying for membership in the corporate elite: Katharine Graham was the chief executive officer of the *Washington Post* (though it was ranked only #435 on the *Fortune* list in 1978, so it was not exactly in the top "hundred or so"). As *Fortune* put it, Graham was "catapulted from housewife to president of the company after her husband's suicide in 1963."[6] This was hyperbole, however, because Graham was not just a "housewife" before her husband's death. Educated at Vassar and the University of Chicago, the daughter of the multimillionaire former owner of the paper, and an experienced journalist herself, she found that her main challenge was being catapulted into a position that had always been held by a male, not being catapulted from the role of housewife.[7]

In 1977, a women's advocacy group that had been founded in 1962, Catalyst, began a program called the Corporate Board Resource. This program was designed to draw on Catalyst's database of women of achievement "to help board chairmen carefully select and recruit female directors."[8] By the late 1970s, Catalyst was systematically monitoring the progress of women on boards and simultaneously working with boards to increase the presence of women.

Using a slightly broader sample than *Fortune* did in 1973 and 1978, one that included all directors of the top thirteen hundred companies, Catalyst found that in 1977 there were forty-six women on boards. By 1984, that figure had climbed to 367, 2.3 percent of all directors in the study.[9] In 1993, Catalyst began to publish its annual *Census of Female Board Directors* based on the top one thousand companies as a way of calling attention to how few women sit on corporate boards. Quite unexpectedly, the census provoked a large response from corporations, and by 1994 "company after company" felt the need to demonstrate that they had included women on their boards.[10]

During the next two decades, there was a slow but steady increase in the number of *Fortune*-level corporate directorships held by women, rising from 9.5 percent in 1995 to 19.2 percent in 2013. But in 2014, the Catalyst report, now based on the *Standard & Poor's* 500 instead of the *Fortune* 500, revealed that the figure was the same, 19.2 percent, and its authors added that by then the United States was lagging well behind Norway (35.5 percent), Finland (29.9 percent), and France (29.7 percent), and was only tied for tenth among nineteen other developed countries. Things were little better in 2015, at 19.9 percent.[11]

By the end of 2015, almost all of the 500 largest companies had at least one woman director, and only about 3 percent had no women on their boards. Most companies had at least two women, and 14 percent were said to be "on the path to parity" because women held half, or almost half, the board seats. Though the increases over the past few decades have been steady, clearly it will take a long time before women—who make up slightly more than half the population, and who own 48 percent of all stock—will achieve parity. Many women executives, not surprisingly, have been disappointed by these data.[12]

Who are these women, and how did they come to be corporate directors? Do they come from backgrounds similar to or different from those of the white, Protestant, American-born sons of businessmen and professionals who constituted the corporate elite in 1956? What role do they play on the corporate boards: are they tokens, or have they assumed positions of importance equal to those of their male counterparts on their boards?

A number of studies, by us and by others, have addressed these questions. Although the methods and samples in these studies differed, together they suggest some patterns and some changes over time in the characteristics of women on corporate boards.

Women directors are highly educated, better educated, in fact, than the male directors who sit on boards with them. For example, in one of our studies, based on the 4,323 directors of *Fortune* 500 companies in 2011, when we compared the educational trajectories of white male, white female, African American, Latino, and Asian American directors, the white women were more likely to have earned undergraduate degrees from prestigious schools than the white males, the Asian Americans, the African Americans, or the Latinos. The white women were also more likely than the white male directors to have earned at least one postgraduate degree (an MA, an MBA, a PhD, a law degree, or an MD), a pattern that was also true for the directors of color.[13]

The fact that so many of these women attended elite schools as undergraduates reveals not only that they presumably were well educated, but that they were likely to have come from privileged class backgrounds. That is, attending an elite school serves as an indicator that the person comes from economic privilege. As sociologist Lauren Rivera demonstrates in her book, *Pedigree: How Elite Students Get Elite Jobs*, when it comes to applying for entry-level positions at investment banks, consulting firms, and law firms, having attended an elite school signals to recruiters that the candidate is likely to be from a privileged class background and, thus, is likely to "fit in" better than candidates from less prestigious schools. As she explains:

> One of the strongest predictors of admission to elite universities is parental socioeconomic status as measured by both income and education. In fact, the positive effect of parental income on admission to prestigious colleges doubled between the 1980s and 1990s; since then, it has continued to rise. Thus, restricting competition for the highest-paying jobs to students at listed universities . . . reproduces in the labor market the significant socioeconomic barriers that students face in accessing elite education institutions.[14]

The women directors have tended to travel one of four routes to the corporate elite. The first is the business route. One study, conducted in the 1980s, found that about 40 percent classified themselves as businesswomen, but they had traveled different paths than the businessmen who sat on boards. Whereas the men had typically spent fifteen to twenty years moving up the ranks of a large corporation, the women were more likely to have been heads of non-*Fortune*-level companies. Many referred to themselves as "consultants," which was a grab bag category that included both large and small projects.[15] Some women directors had risen through the ranks of a single corporation to the level of vice president and had then been asked to join boards of firms other than the ones in which they held executive positions—they became outside directors even though they did not sit on the boards of their own firms.

The academic path is another frequently traveled route to the corporate board. Many corporate directors have been university presidents, vice presidents, or deans.[16] A 2008 survey by the *Chronicle of Higher Education* revealed that 52.1 percent of the presidents of doctorate-granting institutions sat on at least one corporate board. When Ruth Simmons left her position as president of Brown University in 2010, her salary was $576,000; she also stepped down at that time from the board of Goldman Sachs, for which she had been paid $323,539, and she received stock at the time worth $4.3 million. The pattern of senior administrators holding corporate directorships is sufficiently widespread, and sufficiently rife with conflicts of interest and bad publicity for academic institutions, that in 2016 the University of California tightened its rules for senior administrators to serve on corporate boards.[17]

Some have traveled this pathway in the reverse order—that is they have become college presidents *after*, not *before*, careers in the corporate world. Hazel O'Leary, for example, had a long career as a lawyer and a corporate executive, before she became Bill Clinton's secretary of energy from 1993 to 1997. In 2004, she became the president of Fisk University, her alma mater, and served in that capacity until 2012.[18]

A legal career can provide a third frequently traveled pathway to the corporate board. In her 1986 dissertation that looked at the class backgrounds of directors, sociologist Beth Ghiloni found that the lawyers were the least likely to have come from upper-class backgrounds ("only" 20 percent qualified as upper-class by the criteria that she used), and only a few had gone to prestigious law schools.[19]

The "volunteer career" is a fourth path that was more frequently traveled when women were first joining corporate boards. These women are especially likely to be members of the social upper class, to have attended one of the seven sister schools, and to have been in the Junior League, an exclusive service organization for women. Their experiences at the head of various nonprofit charitable and cultural organizations often put them in contact with directors and executives from the corporate world who sit on their boards of trustees. This, in turn, gives the women volunteers entrée to the corporate boards.[20]

Our look at the pathways traveled by more recent women directors indicates that all four pathways still hold, though more women are moving up through the corporations than in the past.

The Pressure to Assimilate

Obviously, a woman cannot pass as a man in the same way that a Jewish man can pass as a Gentile. A woman in the corporate world may have to find other ways to show that she is "one of the boys," even while struggling to maintain her sense of femininity.

This can put her in no-win situations. In the early 1970s, Cecily Cannan Selby, the national executive director of the Girl Scouts of America, became the first woman to sit on the board of Avon. One of the first meetings she attended was a dinner meeting, and the atmosphere was rather tense. After the meal, one of the men offered her a cigar. "When I accepted," she recalls, "I could feel them all relax."[21]

In her 1971 book, *Men and Women of the Corporation*, Rosabeth Moss Kanter suggested that the need to reduce uncertainty in large and impersonal institutions leads to the strong emphases on conformity in behavior and homogeneity in background: "It is the uncertainty quotient that causes management to become so socially restricting; to develop tight inner circles excluding social strangers; to keep control in the hands of socially homogenous peers; to stress conformity and insist upon a diffuse, unbounded loyalty; and to prefer ease of communication and thus social certainty over the strains of dealing with people who are 'different.'"[22]

A few years after Kanter's book appeared, when we interviewed black and white Jewish and Gentile men and women who had MBAs from Harvard and were in (or had been in) the corporate world, this theme emerged repeatedly. Notably, the Jewish women we interviewed agreed that being a woman posed more of a hurdle than being Jewish. A number of them, however, explained that this did not mean that their Jewishness was completely without significance. As one put it, "It's not irrelevant. It's part of the total package. Ultimately, in the fishbowl-type environment you're in, they scrutinize you carefully. It's part of the question of whether you fit the mold. Are you like me or not? If too much doesn't fit, it impacts you negatively." Another explained, "It's the whole package. I heard secondhand from someone as to how I would be perceived as a pushy Jewish broad who went and got an MBA. Both elements, being Jewish and being a woman, together with having the MBA, were combined to create a stereotype. I had to work against that stereotype from the first day." Another summed the situation up by saying, "Anything that makes you different is more likely to be a factor at senior levels because it's so much more homogeneous there."[23]

In 1990, Elizabeth Dole, then secretary of labor (and, from 2003 to 2009, a member of the Senate from her native state of North Carolina), initiated a department-level investigation into the question of whether there was a "glass ceiling" blocking women and minorities from the highest ranks of US corporations. When the Federal Glass Ceiling Commission issued the report in 1995, comments by the white male managers who had been interviewed and surveyed supported the earlier claims that upper management was willing to accept women and minorities only if they were not too different. As one manager explained, "What's important is comfort, chemistry, relationships, and collaborations. That's what makes a shop work. When we find minorities and women who think like we do, we snatch them up."[24]

One *Fortune* 500 labor relations executive used the phrase "comfort zone" to make the same point about "chemistry" and reducing "uncertainty": "You need to build relationships," she said, "and you need to be pretty savvy. And for a woman or a person of color at this company, you have to put in more effort to get into this comfort zone."[25]

Team Sports and Golf

Much has been made of the fact that men have traditionally been socialized to play competitive team sports and, until relatively recently, women have not. In *The Managerial Woman*, written in the mid-1970s, Margaret Hennig and Anne Jardim argued that the experience of having participated in competitive team sports provided men with many advantages in the corporate world. Playing on sports teams, they reasoned, taught boys such things as how to develop their individual skills in the context of helping the team to win, how to develop cooperative, goal-oriented relationships with teammates, how to focus on winning, and how to deal with losing. "The experience of most little girls," they wrote, "has no parallel."[26] Although the opportunities for young women to participate in competitive sports, including team sports such as basketball and soccer, have increased dramatically, far fewer opportunities were available when some of the women now in higher management in US corporations were young.[27] Title IX was enacted by Congress in 1972. At that time, one in twenty-seven high school girls participated in high school sports. Things changed over the next thirty years, and as of 2004, the figure was one in three. The number of girls participating in high school sports has increased every year for twenty-six years, and, as of 2015, the figure was up to 40 percent, though boys are still more likely to participate than girls.[28]

Thus, it seems likely that women born in the 1970s or later, after the effects of Title IX kicked in, have been more likely to benefit by playing competitive sports. For example, Ellen Kullman, born in 1956, the CEO at DuPont from 2009 through 2015, and who sat on the General Motors board from 2004 through 2008, was the captain of the basketball team at her prep school, the Tower Hill School, and she played for two years at Tufts. Meg Whitman, also born in 1956, the former CEO of eBay and the current CEO of Hewlett-Packard, and a member of numerous corporate boards (including Gap, Goldman Sachs, and Procter & Gamble), played three sports in high school and was on the squash and lacrosse teams at Princeton. Stephanie Streeter, born in 1958, the CEO of Banta Corp from 2001 through 2007, the CEO of Libbey, Inc. from 2011 through 2016, and a director on Goodyear Tire and Rubber since 2008 and Kohl's since 2007, was a four-year starter for Stanford's women's basketball team.

Stephanie Streeter very much believes that having played basketball and other sports taught her some important lessons that she has applied as a corporate leader. In response to a question from a reporter about advice she might give to young girls who want careers in industry, she had this to say: "I played the guard position when on the basketball [team] at Stanford and throughout all the sports I played, I learned that if you're trying new things, if you're 'leaving it all out on the field' you're going to turn the ball over. You're going to make mistakes. If you are going to be disruptive in the industry, my advice is to effectively and quickly recover from your mistakes and don't internalize them. Learn from them; move on to be better the next time."[29]

For all the presumed benefits of having participated in competitive sports, however, it may also mean that some women athletes, like some male athletes, learn to behave aggressively in ways that get them into trouble. When she was the CEO of eBay, Meg Whitman, who is six feet tall, became angry and shoved Young Mi Kim, a Korean American employee (height unknown) who was briefing Whitman for an interview. Kim threatened to sue, Whitman and Kim went through mediation supervised by a private dispute resolution service, and the company allegedly settled for "around $200,000."[30]

Despite Title IX, women have not had the debatable benefits of playing one particular team sport, football, which has been identified by some as the classic competitive and aggressive sport that prepares men for the rough and tumble (and hierarchical) world of the corporation. Another sport, golf, an individual sport, over the years has been seen to have provided advantages for men in the corporate world. Golfers can play their game, and can do so at a competitive level, but they also have the opportunity to shoot the breeze and in the process, conduct business. As Marcia Chambers showed in *The Unplayable Lie*, many golf courses, and especially the courses at many country clubs, have been as segregated by sex as the football field. Even when clubs did not bar women from joining, some did not allow them to vote, sit on their governing boards, or play golf on weekend mornings.[31] Augusta National Golf Club, the celebrated home of the Masters Tournament, after years of criticism and protests, finally in 2012 admitted two women as members—former secretary of state Condoleezza Rice and Darla Moore, a South Carolina businesswoman. As one woman commented, "It's about 10 years too late for the boys to come into the 20th century, never mind the 21st century, but it's a milestone for women in business."[32]

Many women in the corporate world have been convinced that their careers have suffered because of discrimination against them by golf clubs. In a study of executives who managed "corporate-government affairs," Denise Benoit Scott found that the women in such positions "share[d] meals with staff members and other government relations officials but never play golf." In contrast, men in such positions "play[ed] golf with a broad range of people in business and government, including legislators and top corporate executives." As one of the women she interviewed put it, "I wish I played golf. I think golf is the key. If you want to make it, you have to play golf."[33]

Similarly, when the editors of *Executive Female* magazine surveyed the top fifty women in line-management positions (in sales, marketing, production, and general management with a direct impact on the company's bottom line), they asked them why more women had not made it to the "upper reaches of corporate America." The most frequently identified problem was the "comfort factor"—the men atop their corporations wanted others around them with whom they were comfortable, and that generally meant other men similar to themselves. One of the other most frequently identified problems, not unrelated to the comfort factor, was the exclusion from "the social networks—the clubs, the golf course—where the informal networking that is so important to moving up the ladder often takes place."[34]

Based on the interviews they conducted for *Members of the Club*, Dawn-Marie Driscoll and Carol Goldberg also concluded that there is an important connection between golf and business. Both Driscoll and Goldberg have held directorships on major corporate boards. They establish their insider status at the beginning of their book: "We are both insiders. We always have been and probably always will be." In a section titled "The Link That Counts," they explain how they came to realize the importance of golf: "We heard so many stories about golf that we began to pay more attention to the interaction between golf and business. We realized the importance of golf had been right in front of our eyes all the time, but because neither of us played golf, we had missed it as an issue for executive women. But golf is central to many business circles."[35]

A few months before Bill Clinton was elected president, his future secretary of energy had some pertinent comments about the importance of fitting into corporate culture and the relevance of playing golf. "Without losing your own personality," said Hazel O'Leary, then an executive vice president at Northern States Power in Minnesota, "it's important to be part of the prevailing corporate culture. At this company, it's golf. I've resisted learning to play golf all my life, but I finally had to admit I was missing something that way." She took up golf.[36]

There is evidence that the golf anxiety expressed by women executives has its counterpart in the attitudes held by male executives: in its 1995 report, the Federal Glass Ceiling Commission found that many white male executives "fretted" that minorities and women did not know how to play golf.[37]

Whether playing golf or other sports is necessary to fit in, it is clear that women who make it into the corporate elite must assimilate sufficiently into the predominantly male culture to make it into the comfort zone. As Kathleen Jamieson points out, however, this can place them in a double bind. On the one hand, women in the corporate world are expected to be competitive and tough minded, but not too competitive or tough minded, or they risk being called ballbusters. On the other hand, women in the corporate world are expected to be feminine enough to be seen as attractive and caring, but not too feminine, lest their appearance and behavior be seen as inappropriate or as an indication that they are tender minded.[38]

We Are Family

Another factor can help smooth the way into the comfort zone for some women: family connections. Way back in 1980, when we interviewed multimillionaire Jay Pritzker for our first book, *Jews in the Protestant Establishment*, we asked him about his extremely successful and wealthy family. By the 1980s, the Pritzkers' businesses included the Hyatt hotels, Braniff Airlines, *McCall's* magazine, casinos, cable television systems, vast tracts of real estate, and hundreds of thousands of acres of timberland. At the time of our interview, various male members of the next generation had entered the family businesses, but none of the women had. Although we talked about where his children and nieces and nephews had attended high school, whether they had married Jews, and the fact that some of the sons had joined the family business, no mention was made of the daughters' doing so.[39]

Penny Pritzker, Jay's niece, was at that time a twenty-year-old senior at Harvard. After graduating in 1981 with a degree in economics, she went to Stanford, where, by 1985, she had earned both a law degree and an MBA. By the early 1990s, she had become the head of Classic Residence by Hyatt, a chain of upscale homes for the elderly, and chairman (the term she then preferred) of Coast-to-Coast Financial Savings and Loan, which managed over $1 billion in assets. After Jay Pritzker's death in 1999, she and two of her cousins emerged as those making key decisions about how to manage the $15 billion family pie; some of those decisions were successfully challenged in court by an eighteen-year-old female cousin, who, two years later, received $450 million in a settlement (as one lawyer put it, "Clearly, a divorce is taking place here").[40]

Penny Pritzker is just one of a number of nieces and daughters who by now have emerged at the top of some of America's largest corporations and financial institutions—and, as we saw in the last chapter, Pritzker is a member of the political elite as well, having become the first Jewish woman to be named to a presidential cabinet. Another daughter who has made it to the highest circles of the corporate world is Abigail ("Abbie") Johnson. Born in 1961 and holding a BA from Hobart and William Smith Colleges and an MBA from Harvard, in 2014 Johnson became the president and CEO of Fidelity Investments, a privately held company founded by her grandfather in 1946 and subsequently led by her father, who has worked at the company since 1957. As of 2016, her net worth was estimated at $12.3 billion, she ranked #16 on the *Forbes* list of the one hundred most powerful women in the United States, and she was ranked by *Inside Philanthropy* as the sixth-richest woman in the United States.[41]

Shari Redstone, the granddaughter of a wealthy grandfather and daughter of an aging tycoon, provides a third example. Her grandfather, Michael Rothstein, founded National Amusements. In 1940, at the behest of his son Sumner, he changed the family name from Rothstein to Redstone. When Michael

Redstone died, the company owned 400 theaters. Sumner went on to build the company into one of the largest media conglomerates in the country, one that owns CBS, Viacom, and Paramount Pictures. After receiving a BA from Tufts in 1975, Shari went to law school at Boston University, focusing on tax law. She worked briefly for a law firm as a defense attorney, got married, got divorced, and began to work for her father.

By 2007, it appeared that she would soon succeed her father. That year, however, Sumner and Shari battled publicly over the issue of succession, and at one point they communicated only via fax messages. In what became a long-running soap opera, with twists and turns in and out of the courtroom, Shari, various members of the Viacom board, and a fifty-one-year-old woman with whom Sumner Redstone had been living, debated whether Redstone was mentally competent, and who should control the voting stock in Viacom and CBS through the parent company National Amusement. Ultimately, according to *New York Times* business writer James Stewart, "Shari Redstone achieved almost total victory," and "she has now gained unfettered control of her father's vast media empire."[42] Whether she becomes, technically, the CEO at Viacom, one thing is certain: like Penny Pritzker and Abigail Johnson, having been born into a family of immense wealth played a key role in Shari Redstone's pathway to the corporate elite.

Women and the Buffer Zone

Aside from wanting their companies to appear diverse (especially if they cater to a diverse clientele), and wanting to pass on wealth and power not only to their sons but also to their daughters, does something more drive corporate leaders to include women in higher management and on their boards? We think there is. It has to do with the use of women to create a "buffer zone."

As part of his analysis of the transition from a pure patriarchal system, in which males hold all power, to modern capitalism, Michael Mann proposes that "a kind of compromise between patriarchy and a more gendered stratification hierarchy has emerged," both in the households and in the marketplace. In this compromise, women now occupy buffer zones between the men of their own class and the men in the classes below. This phenomenon appears at every point in the class hierarchy. Women who are part-time and unskilled manual laborers in low-income jobs, for example, serve as a buffer between the mostly male unemployed below them and the mostly male skilled manual workers above them. Secretaries and other white-collar women interact with the blue-collar workers who do maintenance jobs and deliver packages for the male managers. Women are the nurses and paralegals for physicians and lawyers. And women in the higher reaches function as a buffer between "capital and all labor" by serving as volunteers, fundraisers, and board members for a wide range of charitable and social service organizations.[43]

Drawing on this analysis, we conclude that the men who run America's corporations have women in higher management and on their boards not only to present a corporate image of diversity but to provide a valuable buffer between the men who control the corporation and the corporation's labor force (and the general public). It is not surprising, therefore, that Catalyst has found that relatively few of the women officers who hold the titles of executive vice president, senior vice president, or vice president have positions with operational responsibility for profit and loss. Instead, many are channeled into positions specializing in such areas as labor relations and public relations.[44] It is in these jobs especially that women are used as effective buffers. Because these staff jobs seldom lead to positions in top management, Ghiloni concluded her study of the velvet ghetto of public affairs in a top-fifty corporation by noting that "women can play an increasingly important role in the corporation and still not gain power."[45]

Long before women joined corporate boards or were employed in personnel and public relations, women of the upper class interceded in the social system in ways that smoothed out the hard-edged, profit-oriented impact of a business-driven economy. In the Progressive Era, some upper-class women argued for protective labor legislation, maximum hours, and more respectful treatment of labor. They came to call themselves "volunteers" as they took a hand in running health, cultural, and social welfare agencies that added a humane, socially concerned dimension to their lives of wealth and privilege. First in nonprofit institutions and now in corporations, we see the intersection of gender and class in a way that serves the power elite by providing a buffer zone between the wealthy few and the rest of society.[46]

Women as CEOs

In 1978, the futurist Herman Kahn was asked how long he thought it would take before 25 percent of the chief executives of the *Fortune* 500 were women. "About two thousand years," he replied, "but make it 10 percent, and I'll say within twenty years."[47] Kahn was not the only one in the late 1970s to predict that before the turn of the century, more than just a few women would become CEOs of *Fortune*-level companies. In 1976, *Business-Week* identified the "top 100 corporate women" and claimed that it would not be long until some became chief executive officers of *Fortune*-level companies. But when the magazine interviewed these one hundred women eleven years later, it found that their progress up the corporate ladder had been quite slow. As *BusinessWeek* summed up the situation in 1987, "Many are sticking it out, though, resigned to the idea that they may advance—but never to the highest corporate offices. Others have abandoned big companies to start their own businesses, new careers, or families."[48]

In that 1987 article, *BusinessWeek* acknowledged that "now, more than a decade later, it is clear that the optimism was overblown." Optimism, however, springs eternal in the *BusinessWeek* breast, for the very article that acknowledged the previous "overblown" optimism had a caption that read "Corporate Women: They're About to Break Through to the Top," and listed "fifty women to watch." Only one of the fifty had been on the 1976 list of one hundred. The fifty corporate women on the 1987 list, *BusinessWeek* assured its readers, were different from the hundred on the 1976 list: "These women are vastly different—better educated, more single-minded, and more confident about their prospects. They have reason to be: Their generation has achieved far greater success in the corporate world in much less time than the original 100, and many are poised at the CEO's doorway."[49]

The *Wall Street Journal* chimed in with its own prediction in 1987. In an article titled "Five Future No. 1's" the *Journal* identified five women who were likely to become CEOs of *Fortune* 500 companies within a decade: Deborah Coleman (then vice president of operations for Apple Computer), Karen Horn (then chairman and CEO-elect of Banc One Corp's Cleveland Unit), Kay Koplovitz (then president and CEO of USA Network, which was jointly owned by Time, Inc., Paramount Pictures, and MCA), Colombe Nicholas (then president of the American arm of Christian Dior), and Linda Wachner (president of Warnaco).[50]

The envelopes, please. From 1977 until 1986, Katharine Graham of the *Washington Post* was the only woman CEO of a *Fortune* 500 company. By late 1996, when we completed work on the first edition of this book, there had been four women CEOs of *Fortune* 500 companies: Katharine Graham of the *Washington Post* (she retired in 1991); Marion Sandler, co-CEO and cofounder with her husband of Golden West (#491 in 1996); Linda Wachner, president and CEO of Warnaco from 1986 to 2001; and Jill Barad, who was named CEO of Mattel (#342 in 1996) in August 1996.[51]

By 2005, another nine women had become CEOs of *Fortune* 500 companies, and as of mid-2017 there had been sixty-one women who at one time had been the CEO of a *Fortune* 500 company. Over the last decade, women have been appointed as CEOs of *Fortune* 500 companies almost every year. After the number currently in office as CEOs dropped from twenty-four on the 2015 list to twenty-one on the 2016 list, it increased again in 2017, to thirty-two, the highest it has ever been, mainly due to a flurry of new appointments, but also because a few companies that had dropped off the *Fortune* 500 list climbed back onto it. A study of women CEOs of the top 500 US and Canadian companies on the *Standard & Poor's* top 500 list indicates that the percentage of women CEOs dropped for three years in a row, from 7.3 percent in 2012, to 4.7 percent in 2013, and to 4 percent in 2014.[52] Therefore, in the last decade, what began as a slow increase in the number of women CEOs turned into a slow decrease, with yet another increase in 2017. Still, when in 1987 Herman Kahn predicted that within twenty years 10 percent of the *Fortune* 500 CEOs would be women, obviously he was wrong. On the other hand, his other prediction that it will take two thousand years before the figure is 25 percent still could be accurate.[53]

These women CEOs, like the women corporate directors described in a previous section of this chapter, are quite well educated. All but two of the sixty-one earned BAs in a variety of liberal arts disciplines, and about 40 percent went to elite schools (as with the corporate directors, they were significantly more likely to have attended elite undergraduate institutions than white male CEOs). Many earned higher degrees, especially MBAs (twenty-five of them, or 41 percent), but some earned other master's degrees, a few earned law degrees, and one a PhD. All in all, like the women who have become corporate directors, the CEOs are very well educated, better educated than the white men who have become *Fortune* 500 CEOs.[54]

Our best estimate, based on the educational and occupational backgrounds of their parents and grandparents, is that most, approximately 70 percent, have come from privileged circumstances, the upper or upper-middle class (that is, the top 15 percent of the class structure). Marion Sandler (the CEO of Golden West Financial from 1973 to 2006) was the daughter of parents who owned successful hardware and real estate businesses (she met her husband, Herb, a lawyer, vacationing in the Hamptons on Long Island). Katharine Graham (the CEO of the *Washington Post* from 1977 to 1991) was the daughter of the millionaire founder of the *Washington Post*. The father of Jill Barad (the CEO of Mattel from 1997 to 2000) was an Emmy

Award–winning television producer, and her mother was a pianist and an artist. The father of Carly Fiorina (Hewlett-Packard, 1999–2005) was a judge and a law professor, and her mother was an artist. Andrea Jung, the CEO of Avon from 1999 to 2012, had two successful professional parents: her mother was a chemical engineer and her father an architect. The father of Anne Mulcahy (the CEO at Xerox from 2001 to 2009) was an English professor who became an editor for a New York publisher. Meg Whitman, the CEO of eBay from 1998 to 2007, and the CEO of Hewlett-Packard since 2012, is the great-great-granddaughter of a US senator, and her father was a corporate executive and the founder of a financial advising company. Heather Bresch, the CEO of Mylan from 2012 to 2014, is the daughter of the former governor, and current senator, from West Virginia. The fathers of Susan Ivey Cameron (Reynolds American, 2004–2011 and 2014–2016), Patricia Woertz (Archer-Daniels, 2006–2014), Lynn Elsenhans (Sunoco, 2008–2012), Indra Nooyi (PepsiCo, 2006–present), Denise Morrison (Campbell Soup, 2011–present), and Mary Agnes Wilderotter (Frontier Communications, 2006–2015), were all bankers or corporate executives. The fathers of Angela Braly (Wellpoint, 2007–2012), Marissa Mayer (Yahoo, 2012–2016), and Jacqueline Hinman (CH2M, 2014–present) were engineers.

A much smaller percentage came from less privileged backgrounds. Cinda Hallman (the CEO of Spherion from 2001 to 2004) grew up in Texarkana, a town on the border of Texas and Arkansas. Neither of her parents graduated from college, though her father's family had been well off, and he had inherited one of a number of farms owned by his parents. Her father, who died when she was fifteen, owned a couple of small farms and, when the family needed cash, hired himself out as a carpenter. She went to college on a scholarship and worked while in college to make ends meet.[55] Eileen Scott (the CEO at Pathmark from 2002 to 2005) is the daughter of a police officer. She grew up in a large Catholic family (she is one of eleven children) and started working for Pathmark in 1969 while she was in high school as a cashier and part-time bookkeeper; she graduated from William Paterson in 1976 with a degree in business administration, moved up through the management ranks of the company, and became CEO in October 2002. Brenda Barnes (the CEO of Sara Lee from 2005 to 2010) was the daughter of a factory worker father and a homemaker mother.[56] The father of Mary Barra (the CEO of GM since 2014) was a die maker.

Lawyers and Wall Street

For the past twenty-four years, the National Association for Law Placement (NALP) has been monitoring the progress of women and minorities in law firms throughout the country. Its most recent report found that the percentage of women as full partners had inched forward. In 1993, women accounted for 12.3 percent of the partners; by 2016, that figure was up to 22.1 percent. However, the rate of increase has slowed to a crawl (up very slightly from 2015, when it was 21.5). Moreover, since 2009, the figures for associates, the pipeline to partnership in law firms, have decreased more years than they have increased. As James Leipold, the NALP executive director, puts it, "The incredibly slow pace of change continues to be discouraging."[57]

A 1996 study of the leading Wall Street investment and brokerage houses found that only about 8 percent of the managing directors were women. The study found that "the more glamorous and high paying jobs, such as investment banking and trading," were "even more of a male preserve than Wall St. itself."[58] Just how much Wall Street remained a male preserve was demonstrated in 2004 when Morgan Stanley agreed to pay $54 million to settle a sex discrimination case rather than stand trial. This was the second-largest settlement the Equal Employment Opportunity Commission had ever reached with a company. Nor was Morgan Stanley the only Wall Street firm to settle out of court for discrimination. In previous lawsuits, both Merrill Lynch and Smith Barney paid more than $200 million in settlements to women who worked in their brokerage operations. None of these firms was eager to have it said in court that it had tolerated "frat-house behavior" or to have the embarrassing numbers on compensation and promotion appear in the official court record. As the *New York Times* concluded, "Wall Street is still dominated by the white men who fill the bulk of the most powerful and highest-paying jobs in the industry."[59]

The Great Recession was a major setback for the continuation of diversity at the highest levels of the corporate world, and this was especially true for women who worked on Wall Street. In April 2013, a special section of the *New York Times* chronicled the decline of women on Wall Street due to layoffs and terminations that resulted from the collapse of the housing bubble and the subsequent financial implosion. More specifically, there was an 11 percent decline in the number of women working in the financial and insurance sectors after 2007, but only a 1.6 percent decline in the number of men.[60]

The fact that several senior women on Wall Street lost their jobs in one way or another was discussed most frankly and directly, albeit in carefully chosen words, by the (former) chief financial officer at once-mighty Citigroup, Sallie L. Krawcheck, who managed a large investment advisory firm before joining Citigroup. In the face of a "horrible downturn," she explained, "You're a CEO. You want people you have worked with for 10 years or 20 years who you can trust. These moves have led to more homogeneous leadership teams." In other words, the white males circle the wagons and exclude everyone else. As to how she lost her own job, she took the position that "we should share the losses with our clients," which led to an argument that was settled in her favor by the board of directors. However, in the process, she was no longer welcome on the executive leadership team. "In my advocacy of that position, it appeared that I really stepped across the line in terms of keeping my job. I'd say I won that client war, but it cost me my job."[61]

In the aftermath of the Wall Street fiasco and the firing of many women, another woman on Wall Street, Irene Dorner, the chief executive officer of HSBC USA, a subsidiary of a large multinational British bank, expressed her regret at not having spoken up earlier and that she had continued to climb the ladder and play by the expected rules. As she put it, "I only realized what was happening when I was 50, because there I was, making my way in the unconscious rules. I really do think the next push has got to come from the senior middle-management women who must stand up and be counted on this earlier than I did."[62]

In August 2016, in an article in *Fortune* magazine, Maureen Sherry, a former managing director at Bear Stearns, reported that only 10 percent of the professionals on the trading floor were women, and only 16 percent of all the senior executives. Although various efforts have been made, and various groups have been formed to help the women who work on Wall Street, she concluded that "the efforts can't seem to police the bro talk. . . . The result is an environment that both discourages and, yes, holds women back."[63]

We return to the prospects for further advancement for women in corporations, in law firms, and on Wall Street at the end of the chapter.

WOMEN IN THE CABINET

From Franklin Delano Roosevelt to the summer of 2017, 308 men and thirty-one women have served in presidential cabinets. Only one woman, Frances

Perkins, the secretary of labor from 1933 through 1945, served in FDR and Truman's cabinets—that is, one woman out of fifty-nine people.

Eisenhower appointed only one woman (as compared with twenty men). Of the next three presidents—John F. Kennedy, Lyndon Johnson, and Richard Nixon—not one of the seventy people who held cabinet posts were women, so the cabinet was an exclusively male club from 1955 until 1975, when Gerald Ford appointed corporate lawyer Carla Hills to be secretary of housing and urban development (HUD). Of Jimmy Carter's twenty-one cabinet members, three were women, one of whom (Patricia Harris) held two different positions. Reagan's cabinets included thirty-three people, three of whom were women. Three of George H. W. Bush's twenty appointments were women (including Elizabeth Dole, who had also served in Reagan's cabinet), and five of Clinton's twenty-seven appointments were women. Of George W. Bush's thirty-four cabinet appointments, seven were women. Eight of Obama's thirty-four appointments were women. Therefore, the number of women in presidential cabinets clearly increased since Mills wrote his book, and especially during the presidencies of Clinton (19 percent), George W. Bush (21 percent), and Obama (23.5 percent).[64]

As of late 2017, only two of Trump's fourteen cabinet appointments were women (14 percent): Elaine Chao, his choice as secretary of commerce (she previously served as George W. Bush's secretary of labor) and Betsy DeVos, as secretary of education. Chao is from a wealthy family and previously had been both a corporate executive and corporate director, as will be discussed in more detail a little later in this section. Trump's choice of DeVos follows the pattern of many of his other cabinet appointments, other than the fact that she is a woman: she is extremely wealthy, is extremely conservative, and had absolutely no previous experience in the job she was selected for. As for her wealth, DeVos is a billionaire; she was born into a wealthy Michigan family, and she married into an even wealthier family. Her father, Edgar Prince, was the billionaire founder of the Prince Corporation, a supplier of automobile parts. Her father-in-law, also a billionaire, is the cofounder of Amway. As for her conservatism, she and her husband long have been deeply involved in right-wing Christian politics, spending millions of dollars on antigay and antilabor causes, and, especially, to support candidates who endorse Christian charter schools (at one point she described education as a way "to advance God's kingdom"). As Diane Ravitch, a professor of education who has written extensively about schools in America, puts it, "DeVos is part of the Christian right royalty in the United States." Finally, as for her lack of experience, neither DeVos nor her children ever attended public schools, and DeVos has never worked in a public school or in any educational setting. Ravitch summed up DeVos's qualifications for the position in the following way: "It is hard to imagine someone less qualified to oversee the nation's schools than Betsy DeVos."[65]

Five of the thirty-one women cabinet members have served in what are considered to be the four most important cabinet positions—the secretaries of state, defense, and treasury and attorney general, all of which include "broad-ranging, multiple interests" and serve in a counseling role to the president.[66] All five were appointed by Clinton, George W. Bush, or Obama—Janet Reno, Bill Clinton's attorney general, Madeleine Albright, Bill Clinton's secretary of state during his second term, Condoleezza Rice, George W. Bush's secretary of state in his second term, Hillary Clinton, Obama's secretary of state in his first term, and Loretta Lynch, Obama's attorney general starting in 2015. In their 1981 study of women in the power structure, Faye Huerta and Thomas Lane concluded that the women of the cabinet have held the "so called 'soft issue' areas such as housing, commerce and welfare." With the appointments of three women as secretaries of state (Albright, Rice, and Clinton) and two women as attorney general (Reno and Lynch), this changed somewhat.[67]

In her study of the social backgrounds of all members of the cabinet between 1897 and 1973, Beth Mintz found that almost two-thirds (63 percent) had fathers who held professional or managerial positions, 80 percent were Protestants (48 percent were either Episcopalian or Presbyterian), and 86 percent had completed four years of college or more. Many had direct links to the business community. "Typically," she noted, "a cabinet position is one of several governmental positions held in a process of business-government interchange."[68]

The thirty-one women who have served in the cabinet since Franklin Delano Roosevelt's presidency have backgrounds similar to those that Mintz discovered. Most were born into economically secure families in which the fathers, or both parents, were well-educated professionals. The father of Oveta Culp Hobby, Eisenhower's secretary of health, education, and welfare, was a lawyer, and her husband owned the major newspaper in Houston. Both parents of Hazel O'Leary, Clinton's secretary of energy, were physicians. The parents of Barbara Franklin, George H. W. Bush's secretary of commerce, were both educators, as were the parents of Condoleezza Rice. The parents of Janet Reno were both journalists, and the fathers of Carla Hills

(Ford's secretary of housing and urban development), Elizabeth Dole (Reagan's secretary of transportation and George H. W. Bush's secretary of labor), and Ann McLaughlin (Reagan's secretary of labor) were successful businessmen. Although Ann Veneman, George W. Bush's secretary of agriculture in his first term, likes to claim, "I was born a poor little peach farmer's daughter," her father owned a successful farm with peach orchards and grapes. During Veneman's childhood, he was elected to the California general assembly, and he then became undersecretary for health, education, and welfare in the Nixon administration. "By the middle 1970s," writes Laura Flanders, "her father had become an influential man with powerful friends and he connected her to most of them."[69] Margaret Spellings, the secretary of education during George W. Bush's second term, similarly masked the privilege with which she grew up. Her official biography notes that she is one of four daughters, and that she worked in a grocery store to help pay for her college education. It does not mention that her father had a PhD in geology, and that he was an executive in the oil and gas industry. Penny Pritzker, Obama's secretary of commerce, as noted in the previous chapter, is from one of the wealthiest families in America. And, as noted above, Betsy DeVos, Trump's secretary of education, was born into great wealth, and married into even greater wealth.

Two of the thirty-one were born outside the United States. Madeleine Albright, Clinton's secretary of state, was born in Czechoslovakia, where her father was a diplomat (she grew up speaking Czech, French, and some Polish), and Elaine Chao, George W. Bush's secretary of labor and Trump's secretary of transportation, was born in Taiwan and came to the United States at the age of eight. Her father left China as an apprentice merchant seaman about the time of the Chinese revolution in 1949 and went to Taiwan. The conventional story notes that he married, had three children, came to the United States, worked three jobs, sent for the wife and children, and then started a business that became wildly successful, allowing the family to rise through the class structure, moving from Queens, to Long Island, and ultimately to Westchester County. When Chao was nominated as secretary of labor, various politicians and commentators could not say the words "American dream" often enough.[70]

But there is a bit more to the story, namely, the suggestion that James Chao had more to draw on when he arrived in the United States than the conventional version indicates. Laura Flanders provides more details about what led to this immigrant success story. Since Flanders has clearly dug deeply to find the full story on this attempted use of the Horatio Alger myth, we will quote her at some length:

> Elaine Chao was born in Taiwan in 1953, to a family who fled from Shanghai after the Chinese revolution in 1949. These were difficult years for Chinese anticommunists, but Elaine's father, James, had had the luck not only to attend one of his country's finest universities with Jiang Zemin, the future leader of the People's Republic, but also to fall in with the immensely powerful Shanghai-born family the Tungs, who shifted their operations to Taiwan for a time. The Tung dynasty is powerful in Chinese politics and business to this day. Hong Kong's first chief executive after reunification with mainland China was Tung Chee Hwa, the first child of the magnate Tung Chao Yung, in whose Maritime Trust company James Chao got his start. James Chao married into another powerful family: the Hsus (pronounced "shoe"). His wife's family would later operate a shipping empire in Hong Kong. Did James Chao arrive in the U.S. with nothing? Quite possibly, but Chao had, as one who knows his history put it, "access to plenty." Chao was connected to powerful families in Taiwan—the center of U.S.-Sino relations during the embargo against mainland China—and in trade, connections translate into freight. [71]

Both Albright and Chao, then, were born in other countries and made the difficult transition to a new culture, but each began her journey in a family with advantages.

Only three of the thirty-one seem to have come from genuine working-class origins. The father of Margaret Heckler (Reagan's secretary of health and human services) was a doorman at a New York City hotel, Patricia Harris's father was a waiter on a railroad, and Hilda Solis's parents were both immigrants, from Mexico (her father, who worked in a battery recycling plant), and from Nicaragua (her mother, who worked at an assembly line for Mattel). Heckler, Harris, and Solis were able to attend college only because they received scholarship aid. Five others were from middle-class backgrounds. The father of Shirley Hufstedler (Carter's secretary of education) was a contractor, who had to move frequently during the Depression to find work, and her mother was a teacher. The father of Donna Shalala (Clinton's secretary of health and human services) was a real estate salesman and a leader in the Syrian-Lebanese community in Cleveland, Ohio; her mother was a physical education teacher who put herself through law school at night while Shalala and her twin sister were young girls. The father of Alexis Herman (secretary of labor under Clinton) was a mortician and political activist—after suing the state's Democratic Party to secure for blacks the right to vote, he became the first black ward leader in Alabama—and her mother was a reading teacher. The father of Gale Norton (secretary of the interior under George W. Bush) learned aviation mechanics in the army and then worked for various aviation firms.[72] Loretta Lynch's father was a Baptist minister and her mother was a librarian.

It is a bit harder to categorize the class background of Juanita Kreps (secretary of commerce under Carter): her father was a "struggling mine operator" in Kentucky. Her parents divorced when she was four, and she lived with her mother until she was twelve, at which time she attended a Presbyterian boarding school. She later said of her childhood (during the Depression), "Everyone was having economic problems, and we weren't any worse off than anyone else."[73]

All thirty-one of these women graduated from college, and twenty-one did postgraduate work. Thirteen graduated from law school (two from Harvard, two from Yale, three from Stanford, with the rest from a variety of schools that include Boston College, George Washington University, Hastings, Rutgers, Stanford, and Denver University). Four did doctoral work (Kreps received a PhD in economics from Duke; Shalala, a PhD in political science from Syracuse University; Albright, a PhD in international affairs from Columbia; and Rice, a PhD in international studies at Denver University), and four attended MBA programs (McLaughlin at the University of Pennsylvania, Franklin and Chao at Harvard, and Pritzker, who earned her MBA along with a law degree from Stanford).

Kreps and Shalala came to the cabinet after rising through the academic hierarchies of large research universities (Kreps had been a vice president at Duke, and Shalala was chancellor of the University of Wisconsin). Rice, too, had been a university administrator, but she did not exactly rise through the academic ranks: after working in Washington with the National Security Council during the administration of George H. W. Bush, Rice was offered tenure at Stanford in May 1993 and became provost a month later. Margaret Heckler and Lynn Martin had served a number of terms in Congress and then been defeated in reelection bids before Republican presidents named them to their cabinets. Janet Reno had also been elected to office: she served four terms as state attorney in Dade County, Florida.

Most of the rest came to the cabinet from other government positions or from the corporate world, and some had spent time in both settings. Hills was a partner in a corporate law firm and had been working in the Justice Department; Hufstedler was a US Court of Appeals justice; McLaughlin had been the highest-ranking woman executive at Union Carbide and then worked at high-level positions in the Treasury and Interior departments; O'Leary was an executive vice president at Northern States Power, one of the largest gas and electric utility companies in the Midwest.

Chao worked as an investment banker at the Bank of America and Citicorp, served in the department of transportation while George H. W. Bush was president, and then headed the Peace Corps and United Way before joining the Heritage Foundation, a conservative think tank. Gale Norton also had worked at a conservative think tank (the Mountain States Legal Foundation) and had been attorney general of Colorado (she ran for the Republican Senate nomination in 1996 but was defeated in the primaries). Anne Veneman moved back and forth between various state and federal government positions in California and Washington and private law practice.[74] Hillary Clinton had been the senator from New York, and Penny Pritzker was a billionaire businesswoman overseeing various entities in the Pritzker empire.

Many of these women had served on major corporate boards before being nominated for cabinet positions. Before Carter nominated her to be secretary of commerce, Juanita Kreps held an endowed chair in economics at Duke University, but her income from that chair was only half what she earned as a director on boards that included R. J. Reynolds, Eastman Kodak, and J. C. Penney. In 1976, her income as a professor at Duke was $30,106, and her income from boards was $61,150.[75] When George H. W. Bush appointed Barbara Franklin to be secretary of commerce, the *New York Times* described her as "a well-connected management consultant, corporate director and Republican fund-raiser." Franklin was, at the time, a director on seven boards, which provided her with as much as $327,000 a year, depending on how many meetings she attended. Only one woman in history had served on more *Fortune* 1000 boards simultaneously, Ann McLaughlin, who was secretary of labor during Reagan's second term.[76] Before returning to Washington to work in the George W. Bush administration, Rice served on the boards of Chevron, Transamerica, and Charles Schwab.

Not surprisingly, many of these women, like the men who have served in presidential cabinets, have been asked onto boards after leaving their cabinet positions. For example, after serving in the cabinet, Carla Hills was on the boards of AOL Time Warner, American International Group, ChevronTexaco, and Lucent Technologies; Ann McLaughlin (who, after she remarried, became Ann McLaughlin Korologos) served on the boards of AMR, Fannie Mae, Host Marriott, Kellogg, Microsoft, and Vulcan Materials.[77]

As we have indicated, sitting on these boards can be quite lucrative. When it was revealed in 2003 that many charitable foundations pay their trustees quite handsomely, Juanita Kreps defended the fact that she received payment for such work. She said that she would not remain on the board of the $6 billion Duke Endowment if she were not paid to do so (in 2001, she received $132,800 plus expenses from that endowment). "I don't think we're being overpaid," she said. "We do a lot of work. We meet two full days 10 times a year in Charlotte which isn't the easiest place to get to, and there's a good bit of correspondence to deal with in between."[78]

All but Reno, Shalala, Herman, Rice, and Napolitano (Obama's secretary of homeland security) have been married. Most have had children. A few have been in major Washington power marriages. Hills's husband, Roderick Hills, also a lawyer, was head of the Securities and Exchange Commission from 1975 to 1977. Elizabeth Dole met Senator Robert Dole of Kansas while she was working in the White House Office of Consumer Affairs during the Nixon administration. They were married in 1975. During the Reagan years, some considered them "the second-most powerful couple in the nation's capital."[79] Ann McLaughlin was married to John McLaughlin, a former Jesuit priest turned Nixon speechwriter turned television talk show host. ("Father McLaughlin," we are told in one profile of Ann McLaughlin, "defended Nixon throughout the Watergate scandal, predicting publicly that the president would eventually come to be regarded as 'the greatest moral leader of the last third of this century.'")[80]

Elaine Chao is married to Mitch McConnell, senator from Kentucky, who became the majority leader in 2015. As of 2001, the two of them were considered "Washington's newest power couple," and they are even more powerful today.[81]

Patricia Harris, who died in 1985, was African American, as are Hazel O'Leary, Alexis Herman, Condoleezza Rice, and Loretta Lynch. Elaine Chao is Chinese American. The others are (or were) white. Most have been Protestants, though, as noted in chapter 2, Penny Pritzker is Jewish, and there have been at least seven Catholics (Heckler, Herman, O'Leary, McLaughlin, Martin, Sibelius, and Solis). Albright, as we have noted, was born to Jewish parents, raised a Catholic, and became an Episcopalian when she married (see chapter 2, note 50).

Overall, these women fit well with Mills's characterization of cabinet appointees in the mid-1950s. They are "quite closely linked, financially or professionally or both, with the corporate world."[82] They move smoothly and seamlessly into and out of government, and are part of the system of revolving interlocks that link the corporate community and the executive branch of the federal government. They have supplemented this ongoing pattern, not changed it.

WOMEN IN THE MILITARY ELITE

As was typically the case, Mills did not mince words when he wrote about those at the top of the military hierarchy. Mills referred in general to military men throughout history and throughout the world as "warlords," and he referred more specifically to "the men of violence: the United States warlords."[83]

In 1956, there were no women among the warlords. The only mention Mills made of women when he wrote about the military was to demonstrate the importance of rank in such an extremely hierarchical institution. Even the social lives of the women married to military men were affected by the rank of their husbands. Mills quotes the wife of Gen. George C. Marshall describing a social event for military wives between the two world wars: "At a tea such as this one you always ask the highest-ranking officer's wife to pour coffee, not tea, because coffee outranks tea."[84]

Indeed, it was not until 1967 that Congress passed legislation allowing women to be promoted to any general officer grade in the army and the air force. (The sanction of corresponding promotions for women in the navy and the marine corps took another decade.) When Gen. William Westmoreland officiated at the 1970 ceremony at which the first two women were promoted to the rank of brigadier general, he surprised everyone present. First, as he pinned the stars on Anna Hays, a twenty-eight-year army veteran who had served in three wars, he kissed her "squarely on the mouth." A few minutes later, after pinning stars on the second woman in history to become a general, he intoned, "And now, in accordance with a new Army custom—" and kissed her, too.[85]

In their 1981 study of women in power, Huerta and Lane looked at those positions in the military hierarchy mentioned by Mills for the years 1958, 1965, 1972, and 1978. Of the 478 positions they examined in the Department of Defense, the army, the navy, and the air force, they found only seven that had been occupied by women. Five of these were with the women's branches of the army and the marine corps (since eliminated by the integration of the women's corps with the formerly all-male military). The other two were positions identified as "general counsel." These findings, they concluded, were "not unexpected," given that the military is "almost universally recognized as a 'man's world.'"[86]

In large part because of the shift from conscription to an all-volunteer military in 1973, the US military has become less a "man's world," at least in terms of the number of men and women on active duty. In 1972, there were slightly fewer than 45,000 women on active duty (1.9 percent of the total force); by 2003 that number had increased to more than 210,000 (about 15 percent). The percentage of women officers was about the same as that of enlisted personnel (15 percent), but the percentage of female officers in the different branches ranged from a high of 17.8 percent in the air force to a low of 5.4 percent in the marine corps.[87]

In the years since Westmoreland instituted his new army custom (which, as far as we know, has not been repeated since), more women have been promoted in the officer ranks of the military, though the numbers remain small. In 1995, only eleven women, or 1.2 percent, had achieved the rank of general officer in the army, navy, air force, and marine corps. By 2004, of the 898 people with general officer rank, thirty-nine were women (4.3 percent). As of March 31, 2017, of the 877 people with general officer rank, sixty (6.8 percent) were women, and there were only three women among the thirty-eight who had four-star rank (7.9 percent).[88] Thus, like women on *Fortune* 500 boards, the numbers have increased, but quite slowly.

It was not until March 1996, when Clinton nominated Maj. Gen. Carol Mutter of the marine corps to be the first woman three-star general, that a woman achieved officer rank higher than two-star.[89] A few months later, Patricia Tracey became the first vice admiral in the navy; in June 1997, Claudia Kennedy became the first three-star general in the army; and in 1999, Leslie F. Kenne became the first three-star general in the air force.[90] Mutter retired in 1999, Kennedy in 2000, and Kenne in 2003, so as of July 2004, Tracey was the only woman with three-star rank in all the armed services.

In 2008, Ann Dunwoody, who had been in the army since 1975, became the first four-star general. A handful of others have since reached that status. In 2012, as Dunwoody was about to retire, Janet Wolfenbarger, who had been in the air force since 1980, became the second. Dunwoody retired in 2008, and Wolfenbarger retired in the spring of 2015. Both came from military families, and both were married to air force pilots.[91]

In July 2014, Michelle Howard, an African American, became the fourth woman, and the first African American woman, to achieve four-star status when she became the first four-star admiral in the navy.

In 2014, Lori Robinson, also in the air force, became the new commanding general of the Pacific Air Forces in Hawaii, making her the first US female four-star commander of combat forces. In 2016, President Obama named her to replace Admiral William E. Gortney as commander of US-NORTHCOM and NORAD, and, upon approval by the US. Senate, she became the highest-ranking woman in US military history.

Michelle Howard and Lori Robinson, like the women who achieved four-star rank before them (Dunwoody and Wolfenbarger) also came from military families—Howard's father was an air force master sergeant, and Robinson's father was a thirty-year air force veteran. Both also are married to military men.

In June 2015, Ellen M. Pawlikowski became a general in the air force—she replaced Janet Wolfenbarger (the second woman four-star) as she retired. Unlike those before her, she is not from a military family (though her husband is in the air force). She was in the ROTC program when she was an undergraduate at the New Jersey Institute of Technology, and she went on to earn a PhD in chemical engineering from Berkeley.

As of November 2016, of the thirty-eight people with four-star rank, three were women (Howard, Robinson and Pawlikowski). No woman has yet to become a member of the Joint Chiefs of Staff.

Two women have served as secretary of the air force, a civilian position appointed by the president with the advice and consent of the Senate. Sheila Widnell, appointed by Bill Clinton, held the position from 1993 to 1997, and another woman, Deborah Lee James, appointed by Obama, held it from 2013 to 2017.

So few women have achieved general officer rank that it is hard to draw conclusions about their backgrounds. We did, however, look at the first seventy women who became general officers and asked how they got there. All but five were white: four were African American, and one was Hispanic. Most were from middle-class backgrounds, and a disproportionate number came from the personnel field. When we asked one of these women, Brig. Gen. Wilma Vaught, president of the Women in Military Service Memorial Foundation, why this was so, she focused on what at that time had been an important issue with regard to military promotions at the highest levels: combat experience. "The types of problems you have in personnel women can handle as well as men," she told us, "and, of course, you don't need combat experience to do well in personnel." Vaught also noted that except for those who had been nurses, almost all of the seventy women had come from administrative rather than technical backgrounds.[92] In 2015, Ashton Carter, the secretary of defense, announced that the Pentagon was opening all combat roles to women ("There will be no exceptions"). Many in the military, and some members of Congress, were not happy with this decision.[93] Time will tell as to whether this leads to a dramatic increase in the number of women at the highest levels of the military, but, even if it does, it surely is not likely to happen soon.

The presence of women in the modern American military was highlighted painfully in the spring of 2004 when the world learned, with graphic and extensive photographic evidence, of the sadistic and humiliating treatment of Iraqi prisoners at Abu Ghraib prison. Three of the first seven soldiers charged with the abuse of prisoners were women: Pvt. 1st Class Megan Ambuhl, Pvt. 1st Class Lynndie England, and Specialist Sabrina Harman.

Women also served in senior levels of authority at Abu Ghraib prison. In fact, two of the twelve women generals in the army played prominent roles. The prison was directed by one of the nine one-star generals, Brig. Gen. Janis Karpinski. Karpinski, who served in the Special Forces and holds a bronze star, was in charge of three US-British–led prisons, eight battalions, and thirty-four hundred army reservists. Karpinski was first suspended from her command; then, after an internal army review found that she had been derelict in "all aspects of command responsibilities," she was demoted to the rank of colonel. In addition, one of the army's three women who held two-star rank, Maj. Gen. Barbara Fast, was the top intelligence officer in Iraq, in charge of the interrogators at Abu Ghraib. The allegations of dereliction of duty against Fast were found to be "unsubstantiated."[94]

The presence of women in both junior and senior positions at the prison demonstrated quite clearly that the mere addition of women to a previously all-male culture does not necessarily change the culture. As writer and commentator Barbara Ehrenreich put it, lamenting "a certain kind of feminist naiveté" that assumes that the presence of women in leadership roles automatically changes the nature of the organization they lead, "Women do not change institutions simply just by assimilating into them."[95]

There are, then, very few women in the military who have made it to what Mills considered warlord status, and prospects are not good for more than token presence in the highest military circles for a long time. The percentage of women officers remains quite small, the system of promotion remains riddled with biases against women, and there continues to be extensive evidence of sexual harassment against women. Jeanne Holm, the third woman promoted to the rank of general and the first in the air force, concluded in the 1992 revised edition of her 1982 book *Women in the Military*, "It would be unrealistic to believe that a system still so heavily weighted toward operational experience of the kind as yet available on only a limited basis for women will be able to operate in an unbiased fashion."[96] Laurie Weinstein and Francine D'Amico, who have written extensively about women in the military, are more direct than Holm in their condemnation of the ways that military culture works against women: "When American women enter the United States military institution, they enter hostile territory: it is, quite literally, No-*Woman's*-Land."[97]

The climate for women in the military and the number of sexual assaults continue to be serious problems. When Senator Kirsten Gillibrand (D-NY) proposed a measure to shift prosecutions for sexual assaults from the chain of command, as has been the case in the past, to military lawyers, because the evidence was quite clear that victims fear retaliation for reporting assaults, it was defeated by five votes in 2014, by ten votes in 2015, and in 2016 it was neither debated nor voted upon.[98] In March 2017, a report was released that showed that in the previous year the number of sexual assaults had increased dramatically at two of the three military academies (the Naval Academy and West Point).[99] That same month, it was revealed that an online, invitation-only, Facebook page that had more than 30,000 active duty and veteran marines on it, included thousands of naked and private photographs of marine corps women.[100]

WOMEN IN CONGRESS AND ON THE SUPREME COURT

The Senate

Forty-four women have served in the Senate since 1950. They fall into three eras: those who served in the Senate before 1978, mostly women who initially were appointed to replace deceased husbands; from 1978 to 1992, when women were elected to the Senate, but only one or two at a time; and after 1992 ("the year of the woman"), when there has been a steady increase in the number of women in the Senate.

From the time Mills wrote *The Power Elite* until 1972, only one woman served in the US Senate: Margaret Chase Smith (R-ME).[101] Smith's husband, a Maine politician "who ran for office 48 times in his lifetime without a defeat," was a member of the House from 1937 to 1940.[102] He became gravely ill and, dying, asked his constituents to elect his wife, a former teacher and newspaperwoman. They did, and she served in the House for eight years before successfully running for the Senate in 1948.

During her long tenure in the Senate, Smith had some female company, but it tended to be brief, and it was invariably the result of the death of a male senator during his elected term of office.[103] Several of them were widows appointed to take the place of their deceased husbands, and they did not serve for long. Maurine Neuberger (D-OR), widow of the senator from Oregon, won a special election to complete his term and won the seat in the regular election in 1960; she then chose not to run again in 1966. When Smith was defeated in her bid for reelection in November 1972, in large part because of her support for the war in Vietnam, the Senate was again, for six years, an all-male club.[104]

Nancy Landon Kassebaum's (R-KS) election to the Senate in 1978 represented a genuine breakthrough, for she was the first woman to be elected who did not replace a deceased male. Kassebaum was not, however, without valuable political connections. Her father, Alf Landon, had been governor of Kansas and had run for president against Franklin Delano Roosevelt in 1936. The *New York Times* asserted in an editorial that if her "middle name were Jones her campaign would have been a joke."[105] In addition to a name familiar to the voters of Kansas, she had something else that helps one become a member of the Senate—a net worth of millions of dollars that enabled her to finance her campaign.

Two years later, the number of women senators doubled when Paula Hawkins (R-FL) was elected from Florida. Hawkins had run for the Senate in 1974 and for lieutenant governor in 1976. She lost both of those races, but she won the Republican primary in 1980 and was elected as part of the Reagan landslide that year. Six years later, Governor Bob Graham defeated her. Another woman senator was elected in 1986, Barbara Mikulski (D-MD), who had previously served five terms in the Maryland House of Representatives, so there continued to be two women in the Senate (Kassebaum was the other).

In 1992, four women were elected to the Senate, tripling the number of women in that body from two to six. This major increase, whether by coincident or not, followed closely on the heels of the Clarence Thomas confirmation hearings, which captivated the nation and demonstrated quite persuasively to many TV viewers and newspaper readers that the Senate Judiciary Committee (and, by extension, the US Senate) consisted of white men determined to ignore and denigrate the testimony of a black woman lawyer, Anita Hill, who had endured sexual harassment by the nominee when she was employed at the Equal Employment Opportunity Commission (EEOC).

Due to this electoral success, Kassebaum and Mikulski were joined by Carol Moseley-Braun (D-IL), the first African American woman ever to be elected to the Senate; Barbara Boxer (D-CA), who had served five terms in the House; Dianne Feinstein (D-CA), the former mayor of San Francisco; and Patty Murray (D-WA), a former preschool teacher, state legislator, and self-described "mom in tennis shoes."[106]

In June 1993, the number of women in the Senate climbed to seven when Kay Bailey Hutchison (R-TX), a Republican, won a special election after Clinton selected Lloyd Bentsen, a Democratic senator from Texas, as secretary of the treasury. In November 1994, when Maine elected Olympia Snowe (R-ME), who had been an aide to Senator William Cohen when he served in the House, she became the eighth woman in the Senate.[107] When Bob Dole resigned from the Senate in May 1996 to pursue his quest for the presidency full-time, the Republican governor of Kansas selected Sheila Frahm (R-KS), a moderate, pro-choice Republican, to replace him, increasing the number of women in the Senate to nine, but she soon lost any chance of continuing when Sam Brownbeck, an antiabortion ultraconservative defeated her in the Republican primary (Brownbeck served in the Senate until 2011, when he became the governor of Kansas). In that 1996 election, Mary Landrieu (D-LA) was elected to the Senate from Louisiana. Like Nancy Kassebaum, who had been elected to the Senate eighteen years earlier (and who chose not to run for reelection in 1996), Landrieu was the daughter of a successful politician whose name was well-known throughout the state: her father, Moon Landrieu, had been mayor of New Orleans and secretary of housing and urban development in the Carter administration. Susan Collins (R-ME), also elected in 1996, had worked for more than a decade as adviser on business affairs to William Cohen when he served in the House of Representatives.

In the years since 1996, another twenty-four women have been elected to the Senate, eighteen Democrats and six Republicans. The 115th Congress, beginning its work in January 2017, reached a high point of twenty-one women, one more than the previous (114th) Congress. This small increase of course did not lead to celebrations on the part of those who support diversity in the halls of power. As Debbie Walsh, director of the Center for American Women and Politics at Rutgers put it, "The small increases . . . are nothing to dance in the streets about."[108] That is, the situation seemed more like stasis than an advance because there had been at least fifteen women in the Senate since 2007.

In this third era, since 1992, the women elected have been well educated and they have tended to come from economically privileged backgrounds. The twenty-one women currently serving in the Senate all graduated from college, three-fourths have postgraduate degrees, and many attended elite schools (for example, Feinstein went to Stanford, Lisa Murkowski (R-AK) went to Georgetown, Shelley Moore Capito (R-WV) went to Duke, Amy Klobushar (D-MN) went to Yale, Kirsten Gillibrand (D-NY) went to Dartmouth, Tammy Baldwin (D-WI) went to Smith, and Maggie Hassan (D-NH) went to Brown). Notably, although only two of the first twenty-seven women elected to the Senate had law degrees (Carol Moseley-Braun and Kay Bailey Hutchinson), eleven of the twenty-one currently in the Senate do (and eight of the last eleven elected). This may reflect a pattern in which the more recently elected women are more likely than those who preceded them to come from privileged backgrounds, though it may also indicate that more women with political aspirations have come to understand that a law degree is the one best avenue to a political career (or it may indicate both).

Most (fifteen of the twenty-one, or 71 percent) of those currently in the Senate come from either upper- or upper-middle-class backgrounds. This includes a few whose fathers or mothers were politicians (Lisa Murkowski is the daughter of former US Senator and governor of Alaska, Frank Murkowski—he appointed her to replace him in the Senate; Shelly Capito's father, Arch Moore, served three terms as the governor of West Virginia). It also includes women whose parents were physicians (e.g., Feinstein and the newly elected Kamala Harris, D-CA), lawyers (e.g., Gillebrand), scientists (Baldwin), or successful businesspeople (Joni Ernst, R-IA).

The other 29 percent came from either working- or middle-class backgrounds. Maria Cantwell (D-WA), for example, grew up in a working-class Irish neighborhood, and was the first in her family to earn a college degree. Patty Murray's father ran a local five-and-ten-cent store on the main street of the small town in which she grew up, one of seven children. Elizabeth Warren's (D-MA) father was a janitor who had a debilitating heart attack when she was young, and the family faced difficult economic circumstances. Mazie Hirono's (D-HI) father was a veterinarian, but also an alcoholic and a compulsive gambler. When Mazie was four years old, her mother divorced him and, a few years later, fled Japan for Hawaii, where she raised Mazie and her two brothers, working as a typesetter during the day and three nights a week for a caterer.

The four women most recently elected to the Senate reveal two of the patterns just described (all are from economically privileged backgrounds, and all four are lawyers), but they also reflect a striking new pattern in that they are quite diverse ethnically. Tammy Duckworth (D-IL) has an American father and a Thai mother (she was born in Thailand when her father was working for the United Nations and for various multinational corporations). Kamala Harris (D-CA) is the daughter of a physician born in India (her mother) and an economist born in Jamaica who teaches at Stanford (her father). Catherine Cortez Masto (D-NV), the first Latina elected to the Senate, is the daughter of a Mexican American lawyer who became the head of the Las Vegas Visitors Authority (and a good friend of Senator Harry Reid, the person she replaces in the Senate); her mother's family is Italian. The fourth, Maggie Hassan (D-NH), who defeated the incumbent Kelly Ayotte in New Hampshire, is a white woman whose father, a political scientist at MIT, later became the president of the University of Massachusetts, and briefly served in Lyndon Johnson's cabinet as secretary of housing and urban development. Perhaps this is the beginning of a fourth era of women in the Senate.

These women currently serving in the Senate are from heterogeneous religious backgrounds. There are eight Catholics, two Methodists, two members of the United Church of Christ, one Baptist, one Evangelical Lutheran (Joni Ernst), one Jew (Dianne Feinstein), one deist (Tammy Duckworth), and one Buddhist (Mazie Hirono); the others simply list "Protestant."

The House

Although the numbers of women elected to the House have increased, slowly, over the last few decades, there was a decline from the 114th Congress to the 115th (those elected in November 2016): the number of women dropped from eighty-four to eighty-three, sixty-two Democrats and twenty-one Republicans. Women, therefore, make up about 19 percent of the House of Representatives.

A systematic look at these eighty-three women who were in the House as of January 2017 indicates that almost all have college degrees, though a few only "attended" college and one has an AA degree. They went to a wide range of schools (some elite, some not so elite). Slightly more than half (57 percent) earned postgraduate degrees, with about half of those earning law degrees, and the others mostly earning master's degrees (with a few who earned PhDs). As a group, they are well educated, though less likely than the women in the corporate elite, presidential cabinets, and the Senate to have done postgraduate work or to have attended elite schools. They are also somewhat less likely to come from privileged backgrounds: whereas we estimated that three-fourths of the women in the Senate came from the top 15 percent of the class structure, we estimate that "only" about 40 percent of those serving in the House come from that level of privilege (about the same number come from middle-class backgrounds, and about 20 percent come from working-class backgrounds).

The Supreme Court

Only four women have been appointed to the Supreme Court. The first was Sandra Day O'Connor, an Episcopalian appointed in 1981 by Ronald Reagan, who had promised during the 1980 campaign that, if elected, he would appoint a woman to the Supreme Court. O'Connor grew up on a huge, 160,000-acre ranch in southeastern Arizona founded by her grandfather in 1880, thirty years before Arizona became a state, on land that the United States had obtained from Mexico (after the Mexican American War of 1846–1848) through the Gadsden Purchase. By the time Sandra was born, in 1930, it was, as she and her brother describe it in their jointly written memoir, "the largest and most successful ranch in the region." Because of the ranch's isolation, she went to live with her grandmother in El Paso, where she attended the Radford School for Girls, an exclusive private academy, and then the local high school. After she graduated from high school at the age of sixteen, she went to Stanford for her bachelor's degree (in economics) and then for law school.[109]

While in law school, she briefly dated her future Supreme Court colleague, William Rehnquist, a fellow law school student, but she married another fellow law school student, John Jay O'Connor III, the son of a physician from a wealthy San Francisco family. After they spent a few years in Germany (he was a lawyer in the army), they settled in her native state of Arizona, where he joined a "prosperous and prestigious Phoenix law firm," and she raised three sons. As one biographer described this period in her life, "O'Connor maintained her contacts with the legal world through the traditionally female vehicle of community volunteer work. She was president of the Phoenix Junior League and active in a variety of civic organizations." In addition, and perhaps most importantly for her future career, she became active in Republican Party politics, including working as a precinct organizer for Barry Goldwater in his presidential bid in 1964. She was appointed to the state senate and then won reelection, and she cochaired the statewide committee to elect Richard Nixon in 1972.[110] She then was elected as a judge, was appointed to the Arizona Court of Appeals, was chosen by Reagan in 1981, and was on the court until 2006.[111]

In 1993, Bill Clinton appointed a second woman, Ruth Bader Ginsburg, to the court. She is now known by many as The Notorious RBG due to a popular book that, based on her outspoken presence on the court, compared her to a well-known rapper, The Notorious B.I.G.[112] Ginsburg is the daughter of Russian Jewish immigrants who lived in a working-class neighborhood in Brooklyn. She earned a scholarship to Cornell, and then began law school at Harvard. When her husband accepted a job in New York City, she transferred to Columbia (she was on the Law Review at both Harvard and Columbia). Her husband, who died in 2010, was a professor of law at Georgetown.

Seventeen years later, Barack Obama appointed the third woman ever to sit on the Supreme Court, Elena Kagan. As noted in the previous chapter, she, like Ginsburg, is Jewish. She grew up in New York City, where her father was a lawyer and her mother a teacher. She majored in history at Princeton, and was editor of the student newspaper. After a year studying at Oxford in England, she earned her JD from Harvard and embarked upon a legal career that included clerking for Thurgood Marshall, teaching law at both the University of Chicago and Harvard, and becoming dean of the law school at Harvard.[113]

In 2009, Obama appointed another woman, Sonia Sotomayor, to the court. Sotomayor is the first justice of Hispanic heritage, and the first Latina. She was born in the Bronx to Puerto Rican parents. Her father, who had a third-grade education, died when she was nine, and her mother, a nurse, raised Sonia and her brother. She attended Catholic schools, and then won scholarships to attend Princeton and the Yale Law School. She was married and divorced and has no children.[114]

CONCLUSION

The power elite is no longer the all-male enclave it was in the 1950s. The presence of women has increased most clearly and steadily in the corporate world and cabinets, but the percentage of women on corporate boards is still less than 20 (far lower than in many other countries); in recent presidential cabinets it has approached, and slightly exceeded, 20 percent, though there were fewer women in Trump's initial cabinet. Although there has been a slow but steady increase in the number of women holding general officer rank, and there now have been a few women appointed as four-star generals, there has yet to be a woman among the highest-ranking military officers, the Joint Chiefs of Staff. The women in the corporate and military elites, and presidential cabinets, are thus very much still in the minority, even though some clearly have attained positions of real power.

The participation of women in Congress increased dramatically after 1978, with the strongest surge coming in the 1990s. Still, women make up only about 20 percent of the Senate and the House. About three-fourths are Democrats, a gap that has increased, not decreased, over the past decade (there are fewer Republican women in the House now than there were a decade ago).

To put the slow progress of women in electoral office in the United States into a larger perspective, a study by the Pew Research Center found that the percentage of women in Congress ranks eighty-third out of 137 countries. The United States fell well behind such countries as Rwanda, Cuba, Sweden, South Africa, Bolivia, and Andorra. In order to increase the pace by which women are represented electorally, some countries have enacted legislation guaranteeing a certain number of positions to women (some countries have done the same thing for corporate directorships).[115]

Unlike Jewish men, who, over the generations, can become virtually indistinguishable from the Christian men in the power elite, the women in the power elite and Congress remain identifiably different. Still, the more similar they are to the men who have long dominated the power elite in terms of attitudes and values, class background, and education, the more acceptable they are, and the more likely to move into the higher circles. The women who have been elected to Congress have come from more varied backgrounds, as have both the women and the men who have gone the furthest in the military.

Despite the gains that women have made in the corporate world, the hopeful projections made over the years by corporate leaders and magazine editors about continuing advances are not borne out. Such optimism flies in the face of several sobering realities, beginning with the fact that the extreme gender segregation of the occupational structure has not improved since the early 1990s. Even the occupations that have more women, such as management, law, and medicine, remain highly segregated in terms of specializations and functions. There is also the fact that women still earn only 80 percent of what men earn for the same work.[116] The same Jerry A. Jacobs who was quoted earlier in this chapter concerning the dramatic increases of women in management amended his view to acknowledge that changes in gender segregation and wage differentials did not come as rapidly as he thought they would: "Indeed, the closer you look within nominally integrated occupations, the more segregation you find. Men and women are segregated by occupation, by firms within occupation, and by jobs and specializations within firms. There are 'men's jobs' and 'women's jobs' at all levels of education, skills, and experience, and at each level, the women's jobs tend to be paid less."[117]

Experts argue over the varying weights to assign to the several factors that perpetuate this situation, but they usually begin with the inflexible way in which work is structured and the long hours demanded of executives and professionals. This deadly combination forces women to choose between career advancement and their families because they remain the primary caregivers at home. There is also the fact that women soon see the preference that male colleagues and clients have for associating with other men ("homophily"), leaving them outside the information and contact networks that can lead to business deals or better jobs. They also have to suffer the ongoing coarseness of the male-centered "culture" that prevails in many corporations and on Wall Street. They face insinuations about their femininity, putting their self-images on the line. Finally, they often must endure negative remarks about the capabilities of women, as well as outright discrimination.[118]

The idea that the chief problem for women in the corporate elite is the nature of the workplace, not an allegedly temporary lack of supportive female colleagues, is reinforced by the fact that men who are tokens in female-dominated work settings do not suffer the same kinds of problems as women who are tokens in male-dominated work settings, as would be expected if the cause were essentially being a part of a small minority. According to Christine Williams, a sociologist who has studied both women who do traditionally men's work and men who do traditionally women's work, "Discrimination is not a simple by-product of numbers: The social organization of work tends to benefit certain groups of workers over others, regardless of their proportional representation in an occupation. Consequently some groups (like women) suffer because of their minority status; other groups (like men) do not."[119]

So, as long as the social organization of work benefits men but creates impossible choices and unpleasant personal experiences for women, few women will make it to the top because many of the most likely candidates will have been driven out. This problem was demonstrated once again by the resignations of several high-level women executives at Ford Motors in 2004. These women explained to a reporter that the company had an almost militaristic structure in which there was little or no cooperation or sense of decency: "Aside from the long hours, frequent moves and disruptive work schedules that seem to come with a job in a global industry, there are complaints about the fear of retribution, temper tantrums, and a general lack of humanity and understanding that you have to have a life outside the office. As one . . . put it, 'How can people with master's degrees scream at each other?'" [120]

More recently, a series of interviews with women who almost became CEOs but didn't, indicates that the barriers that prevented them from getting to the top were many, and often subtle. Women are perceived as less dependable, as less visionary, as less able to promote themselves, and as more likely to be penalized for stumbles. As one explained, "For years I thought it was a pipeline question. . . . But it's not. I've been watching the pipeline for 25 years. There is real bias, and without the ability to shine a light on it and really measure it, I don't think anything's going to change." [121]

However, the series of gauntlets that keep very many women from becoming CEOs does not mean that women will cease to have a key function within the power elite. Indeed, they now seem to have the ideal role from the traditional male point of view. They serve as tokens, buffers, and experts until they reach their early forties or fifties; then, they become the consultants and advisers who are the role models and instructors for the new generation of buffers. They will, for the most part, continue to follow the pathways to boards of directors in the same ways they have since the 1970s, sometimes but relatively rarely as CEOs of major corporations but more often as university presidents, partners in law firms, officers in public relations firms, former political appointees and elected officials, and heads of high-status charitable organizations.

Thus, whether or not very many women make it to the innermost corporate circles, we believe that the corporate world is strengthened by their presence. They take some of the sting out of an impersonal business system that can be hard on workers at the lowest levels (and those beneath them who cannot find work). In addition, their presence helps to legitimate the system because it feeds into the Horatio Alger mythology that anyone who works hard can rise to the top. A close look at the class backgrounds of those women who have made it to the top, however, demonstrates that the upper classes are overrepresented by a factor of about ten or fifteen to one.

It also seems unlikely that the military will become a more open pathway of advancement for women into the power elite. The premium on extensive combat experience and command of combat troops (arenas that only very recently have been opened to women) is just too great. We therefore think that the main avenue for women into seats of power will be within the political arena, where they have more control over the pace and timing of work. The increasing number of women serving in city governments and state legislatures will mean a growing number of able and experienced women candidates who will have credibility with voters and financial support from women in business and the professions. We think that members of the Democratic Party will continue to lead the way in this regard but that the Republicans will have to follow suit to some extent, just as they have in the past.

Chapter Four

Blacks in the Power Elite

In the spring of 1963, attorney general Robert F. Kennedy, the brother of the president, asked the writer James Baldwin to invite a group of African Americans to talk about how the Kennedy administration might deal with the increasing unrest in the country's urban ghettos. According to the singer Lena Horne, who was there that day, Bobby Kennedy said that "he thought a Negro would be President within 40 years."[1] Close. Forty years later, in 2003, there had been no black president, and no one was predicting that there would be one soon, but, just five years later, in 2008, Barack Obama was elected the nation's forty-fourth president.

In the late fall of 2016, as his eight years in the presidency were about to end, Obama looked back on his having been elected in the following way: "A President who looked like me was inevitable at some point in American history. . . . It might have been somebody named Gonzales instead of Obama, but it was coming. And I probably showed up twenty years sooner than the demographics would have anticipated. And, in that sense, it was a little more surprising. The country had to do more adjusting and processing of it. It undoubtedly created more anxiety than it will twenty years from now."[2]

Five years later than Bobby Kennedy predicted, or twenty years earlier than the demographics might have predicted, how did this happen? What does the election of the country's first black president in 2008 reveal about the role of blacks in the power elite? To address these questions, we need to return to the early 1960s, which was a time of many firsts for blacks—as corporate directors, as cabinet members, as senators, and as members of the Supreme Court. These appointments were clearly the result of the civil rights movement, the Civil Rights Act of 1964, the Voting Rights Act of 1965, and the continuing marches, demonstrations, and confrontations, the early signs of which had led Bobby Kennedy to ask James Baldwin to help him bring the group of African Americans to meet with him (at Kennedy's parents' fancy New York apartment).

But none of these appointments would have been possible if there had not been a large number of patient and determined black Americans who were ready, willing, and more than able to fill the positions that were offered to them, and it is to these future members of the power elite and Congress that we now turn.

BLACKS IN THE CORPORATE ELITE

About a year after the New York meeting hosted by Bobby Kennedy, on June 23, 1964, a headline on the business page of the *New York Times* read, "Negro Lawyer Joining U.S. Industries Board." The subject of the story was Samuel R. Pierce Jr., a graduate of Cornell University, where he had been a Phi Beta Kappa student and a star halfback on the football team. When Pierce joined the board of U.S. Industries, he became the first black to sit on the board of a *Fortune* 500 company.[3]

The same week that Pierce joined the board of U.S. Industries, another African American, Asa T. Spaulding, became a member of the board of W. T. Grant, a nationwide chain of more than one thousand general merchandise stores. Spaulding was the president of the North Carolina Mutual Life Insurance Company of Durham, the largest black-owned business in the country.[4]

Obviously, the appointment of two black men to corporate boards in 1964 was a product of the civil rights movement, but why these particular companies at this particular time? The chairman and chief executive officer of U.S. Industries, John I. Snyder Jr., was both atypical and ahead of his time. The *New York Times* described him the following way: "Soft spoken and scholarly, Mr. Snyder presented a rather contradictory picture of a millionaire businessman. He was an industrialist who cared deeply about labor. He was a staunch Democrat among Republicans. He believed strongly in the union shop as a necessity for good labor-management relations."[5] Or, as *Business-Week* rather scornfully described Snyder a few years later, comparing him unfavorably to his more profit-oriented successor, "he dabbled in liberal politics, engaged in civil rights work, and argued that private business should try to fulfill its 'social responsibilities.'"[6]

The reason for the integration of the W. T. Grant board was as obvious as it was vigorously denied. The company had been under attack because many of its Southern stores operated segregated lunch counters. There had been both picketing and sit-ins at Grant lunch counters, and neither had been good for business. Although the chairman of the board claimed that Spaulding's appointment had nothing to do with the "lunch counter policy," it was clearly an effort to defuse an embarrassing and potentially costly situation.[7]

Has it been more typical for boards to integrate because of socially conscious CEOs or as a reaction to protest? According to sociologist Sharon Collins, who has conducted extensive interviews with black executives, most were hired not because of a commitment to equality and diversity on the part of senior management, though some senior managers may have had such a commitment, but because of pressures of one kind or another on their companies. In addition to the specific protests against individual companies for particular policies, such as the refusal of some W. T. Grant stores to serve blacks at their lunch counters, federal laws created general pressures to integrate the higher levels of management. Not only did companies have to deal with overt protests, or the threat of them, but they had to adhere to newly legislated guidelines in order to obtain government contracts. Most of Collins's interviewees attributed the opportunities that opened for them to both overt protests and federal policies against discrimination. As she puts it in *Black Corporate Executives*, the black executives she interviewed "believe that new job opportunities emerged because of this federal affirmative action legislation and because of community-based political pressures, including urban violence."[8]

Our look at the first dozen companies to add black directors to their boards leads us to conclude that the same pattern Collins observed at the senior executive levels held for board appointments. In some cases, like U.S. Industries, what Collins calls a "moral commitment" drove the boards, but more often, as was the case with W. T. Grant, the companies were responding to external pressures.[9]

But what led the boards of those first two companies, U.S. Industries and W. T. Grant, to choose Samuel R. Pierce Jr. and Asa T. Spaulding from among the many possible candidates for integrating the American corporate elite? As was the case for the first Jews asked to join all-Christian boards and the first women to join all-male boards, the two men selected were not likely to make those already in the boardroom uncomfortable: they were highly educated, they were assimilated into the mainstream (that is to say, white) culture, and they were not prone to rock the boat.

Samuel Pierce grew up in comfortable circumstances on Long Island. His father had parlayed a menial job at the elegant Nassau Country Club into a valet service for members of the club; subsequently, he opened his own dry-cleaning store, began to buy real estate, and became a devoted Republican, an affiliation that he passed on to his son. In 1943, midway through his undergraduate work at Cornell, the younger Pierce dropped out to join the army, serving in North Africa and Italy during World War II. After the war, he returned to Cornell, where he completed his bachelor's and law degrees. By 1955 he was working in the Eisenhower administration, and by 1959 the governor of New York had appointed him to fill a vacancy as a judge. Two years later, he became the first black partner of a major New York law firm, Battle, Fowler, Stokes & Kheel. Theodore Kheel, a well-known labor arbitrator who did work for U.S. Industries, was a close friend of CEO John Snyder. Aware of Snyder's willingness to add a black to the U.S. Industries board, Kheel, who had served with Pierce on the New York State Banking Board, suggested Pierce to Snyder.[10]

As for Asa Spaulding, who was sixty-two when he joined the W. T. Grant board, his father owned a farm in rural North Carolina and also ran a general store, cut timber, and operated a still that produced both turpentine and rosin.[11] His great-uncle, A. M. Moore, was a physician who lived in Durham and founded a small insurance company. Dr. Moore realized that Asa was proficient in math, so he persuaded Asa's parents to let their son move to Durham, where the schools were better. After receiving a bachelor's degree from New York University and a master's degree in mathematics and actuarial science from the University of Michigan, he returned to Durham in 1932 to be the actuary at North Carolina Mutual. In 1959, Spaulding became president of the company after the death of his cousin Charles C. Spaulding, who had been the president for some thirty years.

A 1967 *New York Times Magazine* profile of Spaulding stressed his "cautious way of life," contrasting him to the militant Black Power types prone to demonstrations and boycotts. "No, sir, I didn't get out and picket or demonstrate anywhere during the civil-rights drive," Spaulding told the reporter. "I felt I could contribute much more toward racial advancement in other ways. . . . We mustn't get impatient. We've made progress, though not everyone is satisfied."[12]

U.S. Industries and W. T. Grant did not exactly open the floodgates, but by mid-1971, there were a dozen blacks on *Fortune* 500 boards. A closer look at some of those who were among the first dozen to join *Fortune* boards (in the late 1960s and early 1970s) reveal that they were, like Pierce and Spaulding, highly educated, many were from families that were economically comfortable or even quite wealthy, and some had developed valuable political connections. For example, Clifton R. Wharton Jr., who joined the board of Equitable Life in 1969, came from a highly educated family. His father, a lawyer, was the first African American to pass the Foreign Service Exam, and in the early 1960s, he became the country's first black career ambassador when he was named ambassador to Norway.[13]

After receiving an MA in international affairs from Johns Hopkins and a PhD in economics at the University of Chicago, Wharton worked in the nonprofit world, and then became the first black president of a major American university when he assumed that post at Michigan State. After eight years there, he became chancellor of the State University of New York from 1978 to 1987; in 1988 he was appointed the CEO of a large corporation, TIAA-CREF, the country's largest private pension fund.[14] At the time of his CEO appointment, and as chairman of the company's board of directors as well, he was a member of five *Fortune*-level corporate boards (Ford Motor Company and Burroughs in 1973, Time, Inc., in 1983, Federated Department Stores in 1985, and TIAA-CREF in 1986), so he was already a well-known and proven figure in the corporate community.[15]

The first eleven black corporate directors had one characteristic in common: they were all men. By early 1971, there was much speculation about which *Fortune*-level board would be the first to name a black woman and which woman would be named. Many assumed the woman would be Patricia Roberts Harris, who had served as ambassador to Luxembourg. Indeed, in May 1971, it was announced that Harris had agreed to join the boards of Scott Paper and IBM. The following year, she went on the board of Chase Manhattan.[16]

The daughter of a waiter on a Pullman railroad car, she bristled at her 1977 confirmation hearing when William Proxmire, the liberal senator from Wisconsin, himself from a wealthy background, suggested that she might not be able to defend the interests of the poor. "You do not seem to understand who I am. I am a black woman, the daughter of a dining-car worker. I am a black woman who even eight years ago could not buy a house in parts of the District of Columbia. I didn't start out as a member of a prestigious law firm, but as a woman who needed a scholarship to go to school. If you think I have forgotten that, you are wrong."[17]

After graduation from Howard University summa cum laude in 1945, and after working as program director of the YWCA in Chicago, she returned to Washington and worked first with the American Council on Human Rights and then with Delta Sigma Theta, a sorority. In 1955, she married a Howard law professor and decided to attend law school at George Washington University.

After law school, Harris worked in the Department of Justice, then left to teach law at Howard. John F. Kennedy appointed her cochairwoman of the National Women's Committee for Civil Rights, and in May 1965, Lyndon Johnson, whose nomination she had seconded at the 1964 Democratic convention, selected her to be ambassador to Luxembourg. As a law professor and former ambassador, Harris was an unsurprising choice as the first black woman to join a corporate board, though some were surprised at how long it took the corporations to ask her.

One intriguing exception exists to the general early pattern of blacks named to corporate boards. Unlike his mostly well-educated, well-off, and in some cases well-connected predecessors, this corporate director came from an impoverished background and attended a nonelite college in West Virginia. He was also a minister who had led public boycotts as a means of confronting large corporations. Yet, he was named to the board of the largest company in the world. This might not have come about if not for a racist slip of the tongue.

By January 1971, blacks had joined the boards of seven major corporations, but none was as major as General Motors (GM), ranked number one by *Fortune* since the magazine began publishing its list of the top five hundred companies in 1955. At the annual GM stockholders meeting in spring 1970, an antimanagement group attacked the company for its minority-hiring policies and its lack of corporate responsibility.[18]

They managed to place some proposals on the annual shareholder ballot, including one that would have added three public representatives to GM's board and another that would have created a one-year Shareholders' Committee for Corporate Responsibility. None of the proposals garnered support on more than 3 percent of the ballots cast, but at that stockholders meeting, James Roche, CEO and chairman at GM, who had been on his feet for most of the troubled six-and-a-half-hour meeting, made an embarrassing slip of the tongue. He was challenged by a young minister from Dayton, Ohio, about

GM's failure to send a representative to a television station in Dayton to respond to some of the criticisms of GM. Was GM not, the minister asked, a "public corporation"? Roche responded by claiming, "We are a public corporation owned by free, white—" At this point, as some people in the audience gasped and others laughed at his use of a well-known racist phrase, Roche lamely added, "umm—and—and—and black and yellow people all over the world." Though Roche later tried to downplay any meaningfulness to the slip and asserted that he simply had become confused by the audience's laughter, it was clearly an embarrassing episode in a long and difficult day.[19]

A few months later, with unhappy memories of the annual stockholders meeting and well aware that the Rockefeller Foundation and other institutional stockholders were watching closely, Roche called Leon Sullivan, an activist minister in Philadelphia, who grew up poor in Charleston, West Virginia, the son of divorced parents, who attended college on a football scholarship to West Virginia State University, only to injure his knee during his sophomore year and lose the scholarship. He was able to stay in school by working in a steel mill, and, at the same time, became the minister for a small Baptist congregation in Charleston. The following year, learning that the New York politician and minister Adam Clayton Powell Jr. was coming to town on a lecture tour, Sullivan invited him to speak to his congregation. Powell accepted and was so impressed with Sullivan that he offered him a job in New York after he graduated. Two years later, Sullivan became an assistant minister at Powell's church. He also worked on Powell's initial campaign for Congress and earned a master's degree in sociology from Columbia and a divinity degree from the Union Theological Seminary.[20] In 1950, Sullivan became the pastor of the Zion Baptist Church in North Philadelphia, and embarked upon two decades of activism in which his church grew tremendously and he set up a job training program for high school dropouts that soon spread to seventy cities.

Roche's decision to pursue Sullivan for the GM board therefore is quite revealing, for Sullivan certainly differed from the other early black corporate directors both in his academic background and in his professional and political experience. It is likely that Roche and the GM board assumed that naming a highly visible and politically active minister would serve as an effective response to those shareholders who were protesting various of the company's policies. In 1964, W. T. Grant could name a sixty-two-year-old African American who was willing to tell a *New York Times* writer that "we mustn't get impatient," but General Motors in 1971, facing vociferous and embarrassing shareholder protests, needed to make a stronger statement as it integrated its board.

One of Sullivan's first acts as a board member was to vote against the entire board on a controversial resolution. In its coverage of GM's 1971 shareholders meeting, the *Wall Street Journal* reported, "The meeting's dramatic highlight was an impassioned and unprecedented speech by the Rev. Leon Sullivan, GM's recently appointed Negro director, supporting the Episcopal Church's efforts to get the company out of South Africa. It was the first time that a GM director had ever spoken against management at an annual meeting."[21] This challenge to boardroom hegemony may have been just what Roche needed to demonstrate GM's willingness to tolerate criticism. As *Forbes* magazine explained, "Such public dissent is rare in big business, and it certainly didn't harm GM's reputation."[22]

By June 1972, GM had started the General Motors Minority Dealer Development Academy, part of a program to encourage and provide support for minority members to become automobile dealers.[23] Years later, the guidelines that became known as the Sullivan Principles were used by many institutions, especially universities, when they decided whether to divest the holdings of companies that did business in South Africa.[24]

Blacks on *Fortune*-Level Boards

In the early 1970s, with doors to some boardrooms finally opened, more and more *Fortune*-level companies added black directors to their boards, though few companies added more than one. When *Black Enterprise* magazine ran an article in September 1973 on black directors, there were sixty-seven black men and five black women on the boards of slightly more than one hundred "major U.S. companies." As the article noted, with approximately fourteen thousand directors on the boards of the one thousand companies that appeared on *Fortune*'s annual list, black directorships represented less than 1 percent of the total.[25] By 1981 there were seventy-three. In percentage terms, African Americans had gone from zero prior to 1964 to less than 1 percent in 1981.

Nor was there a dramatic increase in the number of black executives moving up the corporate ladder. In 1980, the *Wall Street Journal* summarized the findings of two studies that demonstrated how few blacks had moved into the higher ranks of management. In one, a survey by Korn/Ferry International, only three of seventeen hundred senior executives were black. In the other, only 117 blacks out of 13,000 managers were ranked as "department head" or higher in Chicago companies.[26] George Davis and Glegg Watson wrote in their 1982 book, *Black Life in Corporate America*, that after three years of extensive interviewing, "We heard of only a few of the [*Fortune*] five hundred that had a Black in what could be considered senior management."[27] Also in the early 1980s, John Fernandez reported that in his study of more than four thousand managers drawn from twelve large corporations, he had found only four blacks at the five highest levels.[28] Similarly, in a study of more than one thousand business executives promoted to the positions of chairman of the board, president, or vice president of leading corporations during the fiscal year 1983–1984, Floyd Bond, Herbert Hildebrandt, and Edwin Miller found that 99.2 percent were white, and only 0.2 percent were black (the other 0.6 percent were Hispanic, "Oriental," or "other").[29]

It is therefore important to keep in mind the distinction between *inside directors*, those who move up through the corporate ranks and become directors of the companies they work for, and *outside directors*, those who are asked onto a board based on visibility they have achieved outside the company. The first African Americans to sit on major corporate boards were outside directors, though a few had been successful businessmen in black-owned companies.

In chapter 3, we presented data on women directors of *Fortune* companies tabulated by Catalyst. During the 1990s, an organization called Directorship monitored the presence of various minority groups on corporate boards. The data they gathered show a steady increase in the presence of blacks on *Fortune* 1000 boards from 118 in 1992 to 220 in 1999, an increase from 1.6 percent to 3.4 percent of all the *Fortune* 1000 directors.

Directorship no longer monitors the number of African Americans on corporate boards, but a study was done of African American directors on *Fortune* 500 boards in 2004 for the Executive Leadership Council (ELC), an organization of African Americans who hold senior executive positions in *Fortune* 500 companies. This study found that among the 5,572 board seats on *Fortune* 500 companies, African Americans held 449 (or 8.1 percent).

As was true for our update on Jews and women, we then did our own study of black directors of all of the *Fortune* 500 companies in 2011. Of the 4,323 directors, 291, or 6.7 percent, were African Americans (most of these, 5.2 percent, were men, and the other 1.5 percent were women).[30] The *percentage* of African American corporate directors therefore has not increased, and might have declined, in the last ten years. This very much fits with the broader patterns we have found about diversity in the power elite—dramatic gains in diversity resulted from the protests of the 1960s, and these gains now have been followed by stasis and decline—about which we will have more to say in the final chapter.

Far more seats were held by blacks than there were blacks who held those seats—that is to say, many sat on more than one board. In fact, on average, blacks who sat on *Fortune* 1000 boards in the 1990s sat on two of them, which put them in the category of "interlocking directors," meaning those who serve to link corporations together. Interlocking directors make the idea of a corporate community more concrete and visible, but the corporate community is also, and perhaps more importantly, knit together by common stock ownership among the wealthy, the fact that they share the same corporate law firms, accounting firms, and investment bankers, and the important social-psychological ingredient of "common enemies," such as labor unions, environmentalists, and consumer activists.

A breakdown by sex reveals that black men who were directors sat on an average of 1.9 boards, and black women who were directors sat on an average of about 2.4 boards. For example, eleven of thirty-four 1994 interlockers were women, and seven of the twenty-eight interlockers in 2011 were women. Though Patricia Roberts Harris, who served on a number of corporate boards, was referring to her appointment as ambassador to Luxembourg and not to her corporate directorships, a comment she made may help to explain why so many corporate boards, seeking to appear diversified, select black women: "When I'm around, you get two for the price of one—a woman and a Negro."[31] Building on the sentiments expressed by Harris's comment, women of color in any highly visible positions in the corporate or political worlds became generally known in the corporate community and the business press as "twofers."

Male or female black corporate directors became major interlockers, some serving on as many as ten or eleven boards once they had proven to be sensible and useful participants in board meetings. As if to underscore this point, we found that blacks were more likely than whites to have three or more directorships in both 1994 and 2011, and black women more than black men. In addition, they tended to come from economically advantaged or highly prestigious backgrounds, and almost all had excellent educations, often with one or more degrees beyond a college BA. One of the top interlockers in 1994, former congressman William H. Gray III, sat on seven boards, including those for Chase Manhattan, Warner-Lambert, and Westinghouse.

His father and grandfather were clergymen; his father had also been a college president, and his mother taught high school. Another big interlocker from 1994, Barbara Scott Preiskel, a graduate of Wellesley and Yale Law School, sat on five boards, including those for General Electric and the *Washington Post*. Her father was a lawyer who became a real estate broker, and her mother taught high school chemistry.

Or to take a prominent example from 2011, John W. Rogers Jr., a major donor to Obama's presidential campaigns, sat on three *Fortune* boards (Aon, Exelon, and McDonald's). In doing so he followed in the footsteps of his mother, Jewel LaFontant, who sat on many corporate boards, including TWA, Mobil, and Revlon. She was also a prominent Republican lawyer (and she herself was the daughter of a prominent lawyer), and gave the seconding speech for Richard Nixon at the 1960 Republican National Convention. Rogers's father, also a lawyer, was a former Tuskegee Airman, and for many years served as a judge. On the other hand, Joyce Roche, who became the first female African American vice president at Avon, and who sat on three boards in 2011 (AT&T, Dr. Pepper, and Macy's), demonstrates that not all of the biggest interlockers came from privileged backgrounds. Her father, a farmer, was killed in a hit and run accident when she was two, and thereafter her mother, a domestic, struggled to make ends meet.

Pathways to the Corporate Elite for Black Directors

To determine the career pathways that blacks have taken to the corporate elite, we focused on the first cohort of one dozen African American directors between 1964 to 1971, the thirty-four interlockers in 1994, and the twenty-eight interlockers in 2011, sixty-nine women and men in all. Eight different routes emerge, some more prevalent in the 1960s, and others prevalent in more recent times. The first pathway was via the academic hierarchy, starting as a researcher or professor and then becoming a senior administrator (most likely a college president), as was the case for Clifford Wharton and ten others. Some followed a second pathway, the same one that Asa Spaulding traveled: they founded, or rose to the top of, black businesses.

Some followed a third path—they had successful careers in the world of nonprofits, especially civil rights organizations, before they were asked to join corporate boards, such as Leon Sullivan, one of the original dozen corporate directors. Others followed a fourth path, the one that Samuel Pierce had traveled: they were lawyers who had experience in high-powered corporate law firms and in government. C. Wright Mills and others have noted that it is not unusual for members of the power elite to move from one of the higher circles to another and back again. Indeed, Mills wrote that "the inner core of the power elite" included men "from the great law factories and investment firms, who are almost professional go-betweens of economic, political and military affairs, and who thus act to unify the power elite."[32] To give one example, Aulana Peters, one of the five people who were interlockers in both 1994 and 2011, worked for a decade for a major Los Angeles corporate law firm after finishing law school, spent four years working for the US Securities and Exchange Commission during the Reagan administration, and in 1988, returned to the Los Angeles law firm. By 1994 she sat on four major corporate boards (Mobil, Merrill Lynch, Minnesota Mining and Manufacturing [3M], and Northrop Grumman).

The fifth pathway is working as a management consultant, whether in economics, finance, management, or public relations. For example, Arthur Brimmer, a Harvard-trained economist who became president of Brimmer and Company, an economic and financial consulting firm, sat on eight boards in 1994.

By 1994, and certainly by 2011, two additional pathways had opened that were not available in the past: a rise through the ranks of white corporations, and being the child of someone who founded a major corporate enterprise. A. Barry Rand, one of those who worked his way to the top, was the only child of college-educated, middle-class parents in Washington, DC. Rand went to work for Xerox at the age of twenty-four, shortly after he graduated from American University with a degree in marketing. He worked for Xerox for thirty-one years, moving steadily up the corporate ranks. By 1992 he was executive vice president, one of the four most senior executives at the company.

By 2011, a number of the interlockers had taken this pathway to the corporate elite—in fact, it was the most frequently traveled pathway by 2011. Eight of the twenty-eight interlockers had risen through the ranks in the corporate world, sometimes at one company, sometimes at more than one. In a few cases, they had started at entry-level positions. One particularly impressive example is Donna A. James, a single teenage mother whose parents had divorced when she was a child. After she received a BA degree in accounting from North Carolina A & T, she started in an auditing position with Coopers & Lybrand. A few years later, she was recruited as an accounting specialist by Nationwide, where she soon became a special assistant to the company's CEO. She then became a vice president of the human resources division, a senior vice president with responsibility for 290 employees and a $35 million budget, and in 2000 she became executive vice president.[33] In 2011, she sat on the boards of Coca-Cola, Conseco, and Limited Brands.

The road to the top began at birth for Linda Johnson Rice. She graduated from the University of Southern California (USC) with a degree in journalism, and then earned an MBA from Northwestern University. At the age of twenty-nine, she became the president and chief operating officer of Johnson Publishing Company, founded in 1942 by her parents. Rice's father is one of only a handful of blacks to have appeared on the annual list published by *Forbes* magazine of the four hundred richest Americans.[34]

Still another pathway had emerged by 2011, that of the military career. At least three of the interlockers had spent a key segment of their careers in the military before they became corporate directors. For example, Lester Lyles, a graduate of Howard University where he was in the Air Force ROTC program, had a long career in the air force, culminating with the rank of general, vice chief of staff. After he retired in 2003, just like so many generals before him, he was asked onto a number of corporate boards, especially those with large defense contracts, and in 2011 he sat on the boards of General Dynamics, KBR, and Precision Castparts.

Although there are now more pathways to major corporate directorships, this does not necessarily mean that more blacks will be appointed as corporate directors. We discuss this issue in a later section of this chapter after a careful look at the many black men and one black woman who became CEOs of *Fortune* 500 companies around the turn of the twenty-first century.

Black CEOs of *Fortune* 500 Companies

In 1991, we predicted that "it seems unlikely that more than two or three blacks will make it to the very top of a *Fortune*-1000 corporation in the next two decades, even with the cultural capital of prep school and Ivy League educations."[35] Were we right? No. By the end of 2001, there had been five black CEOs of *Fortune* 500 companies, starting with two appointed in 1999 and, by the end of 2005, another four. More than a decade later, as of mid-2017, there had been seventeen.[36]

Another way to look at this is to ask how many African American CEOs there were in any given year. There were six African American *Fortune* 500 CEOs in 2005, the number rose to seven in 2007, and then dropped to around five or six most years. As of mid-2017, there were only four. This decline is, we believe, another sign that the heyday of diversity in the corporate world has come and gone.[37]

A look at these seventeen African American CEOs reveals some clear patterns. First, and most obviously, there were no women among them until Ursula Burns was appointed CEO at Xerox in July 2009 (she stepped down as CEO in 2016 when the company split into two companies—she continued as chair of the board). It is noteworthy that there have been so many more African American men who have become CEOs than African American women, just as there have been more African American male corporate directors and interlockers, because African American women are more likely, not less likely, than African American men to graduate from college, to earn MBAs, or to earn law degrees. Clearly gender works against African American women as they move upward through the corporate ranks.[38]

Second, it is striking that these seventeen CEOs have been better educated than white CEOs, with five lawyers, eight who earned MA or MBAs, and one who has a PhD. Five attended Harvard, either as undergraduates or for law degrees or MBAs (or both), and others attended such prestigious schools as Williams, Bowdoin, Johns Hopkins, the University of Michigan, and Stanford.

Third, about half grew up in families that faced difficult economic circumstances, far higher than is the case for white CEOs. The father of Franklin Raines (the CEO of Fannie Mae from 1999 to 2004) was a custodian for the city of Seattle, and his mother worked as a cleaning woman; at one point, when his father fell ill, the family was on welfare for two years. The father of Lloyd Ward (the CEO of Maytag from 1999 to 2000) was a letter carrier by day who also worked a night job as a janitor at the local movie theater in a small town in southern Michigan (he died when Ward was eighteen). The father of Stanley O'Neal (CEO at Merrill Lynch from 2002 to 2007) worked on a farm in Alabama, and his mother worked as a domestic; as a boy, O'Neal contributed to the family finances by delivering newspapers and picking corn and cotton. When he was twelve, his family moved to a housing project in Atlanta, and his father found work at a General Motors factory. The father of Clarence Otis (CEO at Darden from 2005 to 2014) was a custodian for the city of Los Angeles and worked a second full-time job cleaning the office of a local dentist; his mother took care of the children of friends and neighbors who worked during the day. John W. Thompson (CEO of Symantec from 1999 to 2009), whose father was a postal worker who liked to hunt and whose mother was a teacher, still tells people that he is just a "country boy."[39] Kenneth Frazier, who has been CEO of Merck since 2011, is the son of a Philadelphia janitor. Marvin Ellison, the CEO of J. C. Penney's since 2015, is the son of sharecroppers.[40]

In sharp contrast, some of these CEOs grew up in quite comfortable circumstances. The father of Kenneth Chenault (CEO of American Express since 2001) was a dentist, and the parents of Barry Rand (CEO of Avis from 1999 to 2001) were "college-educated." Roger W. Ferguson Jr., the CEO of TIAA-CREF since 2009, is the grandson of an architect, and the son of a US Army mapmaker (also described as an "avid investor"). Before attending Harvard (as an undergraduate, for a PhD in economics, and for a law degree), Ferguson went to prep school at Sidwell Friends, the elite prep school in Washington, DC, that Chelsea Clinton, Al Gore's son, and the Obama daughters attended. Notably, however, a higher percentage of the black CEOs came from working- or lower-class backgrounds than was the case for the first black directors, or for the 1994 and 2011 interlockers.[41]

It is even more revealing to contrast the backgrounds of these seventeen men with the fifty-five women who are or have been CEOs of *Fortune* 500 companies. As we showed in chapter 3, most of the women who have become CEOs have come from privileged backgrounds.

Fourth, no matter what their circumstances at birth, whether they went to public or private high schools, Ivy League colleges or state universities, these African American CEOs seem to have developed what a friend of one them called "smoothness." They appear to be, as she put it, "entirely at ease with white people."[42] In an ethnographic study of African American executives at a "major financial service corporation in center city, Philadelphia," sociologist Elijah Anderson observed that the black executives at the highest ranks appeared to be "utterly polished." "Their demeanor in the presence of whites," he wrote, "seems almost casual and certainly confident. During such interactions, they leave no doubt that they are the social and intellectual equals of their white counterparts."[43] When Anderson wrote those words in 1999, the country had not yet experienced Barack Obama as its president, but his comment seems to capture just how "utterly polished" and how "casual and certainly confident" Obama was as president.

A fifth pattern emerges as one looks at the backgrounds of these men: many were excellent athletes who participated in team sports. Franklin Raines was the quarterback of his high school football team, and Lloyd Ward attended Michigan State on a basketball scholarship. Barry Rand was all-metropolitan in the Washington, DC, area in football, basketball, and track and told one interviewer that he went to Rutgers expecting to become a professional football player. Richard Parsons (the CEO of Time Warner from 2001 to 2007) was an all-around athlete in high school and played freshman basketball at the University of Hawaii. Kenneth Chenault played three sports in high school and ran track and played soccer at Bowdoin. Clarence Otis played both football and tennis in high school. [44]

There is, of course, much debate about whether the amount of time young African American males devote to playing and watching sports detracts from the quality of their educations. As sports sociologist Harry Edwards and others have argued, many young African Americans end up with nothing when their athletic careers come to an end, and the athletic careers of most young athletes end long before they ever receive a paycheck as a professional athlete. [45] Indeed, as of 2000, there were only fourteen hundred black athletes playing professional basketball, football, and baseball (compared to more than thirty-one thousand black physicians and surgeons, thirty-three thousand black lawyers, and five thousand black dentists). [46] Lloyd Ward's story is particularly revealing in this respect because when he played basketball at Michigan State, he had to reject pressures from his coaches not to take courses such as organic chemistry and calculus but instead to take Mickey Mouse courses ("We're paying you to be a basketball player"). [47]

Whatever the merits of athletic participation for most young black students, the fact that at least six of the African American CEOs participated in athletics at the high school or collegiate level suggests that having been good athletes and playing on teams did not hurt them and probably helped them in their adult careers. Perhaps it taught them leadership skills; perhaps it taught them to compete against and play alongside white teammates; perhaps it taught them self-confidence. Or, as Barry Rand noted, perhaps it taught them how to be in the limelight. As he said of his high school athletic career, "I was used to being at the center of athletic attention." [48]

It is also noteworthy that many former professional athletes have become very successful businessmen. Their route, of course, is quite different from that of the CEOs we have discussed, for they accumulated considerable economic capital as professional athletes, as well as valuable contacts and name recognition. When we did a study of the African American directors of the most successful black-owned corporations, the list included a number of former professional athletes. For example, basketball players Dave Bing and Julius Erving and NFL defensive lineman Charlie W. Johnson were founders of three of the largest African American–owned corporations in the United

States. Similarly, when we looked at the African Americans who sat on S&P 1500 boards in 2004, the list included a number of former professional football players (Willie Davis sat on many boards, but also on the list were Calvin Hill and Lynn Swann) and former professional basketball players (including Dave Bing, Julius Erving, and Wayne Embry). These men are part of what the *Wall Street Journal* has called the "growing fraternity of athletes-turned-entrepreneurs."[49]

Are the Barriers Coming Down and for How Many?

As the data we have presented make clear, much has changed since the first African Americans joined corporate boards in 1964. At the same time, blacks (like women, but not Jews) remain underrepresented on corporate boards. Although blacks accounted for about 11 percent of the US population in 1964 and about 13 percent in 2016, the percentage of seats held by blacks on *Fortune* 500 boards rose from zero to 6.7 percent in 2011. Studies indicate that since that time the number of African Americans on boards has stayed even or declined. For example, a study of the top 200 *Standard & Poor's* companies showed that the percentage of African American directors had dropped from 9 percent in 2006 to 8.6 percent in 2015.[50]

But what about the pipeline? Are other younger blacks moving through the ranks? In the early 1980s, there were very few blacks at the higher levels of management in the largest companies. A 1990 study by the executive search firm Korn/Ferry International indicated that the number of blacks in "high-level management positions" had increased during the previous decade, but only from 0.2 percent to 0.6 percent.[51]

In its July 2002 feature story titled "50 Most Powerful Black Executives," *Fortune* asserted that there are "more on the way." The article noted that the Executive Leadership Council (consisting of senior black executives in *Fortune* 500 companies who are "no more than three steps away from CEO") had 275 members as of that date, compared with nineteen members when it was founded in 1986. There are, however, several thousand executives within three steps of the top in *Fortune* 500 companies, so the 275 represented less than 5 percent of the total.[52]

As part of our study of African American CEOs, we looked at the photographs of 3,062 men and women who served on the "leadership teams" of 262 of the *Fortune* 500 companies in 2010 that included photos of those senior executives—that is, those who were one step from the CEO office at those corporations. We found that ninety-one, or 3 percent, were African American, with three times as many men as women.[53]

Thus, there are blacks in the pipeline, though they seem to be leaving at higher rates than others, and those who remain represent a percentage that is well below that of blacks in the larger population. Sociologist Sharon Collins has demonstrated how the very forces that led to the hiring of many African Americans—a federal commitment to affirmative action and the enforcement of equal opportunity guidelines—fell by the wayside in the 1980s and 1990s.[54]

Collins concluded in 1993 that "the gains blacks have made over 25 years may be in jeopardy." And, indeed, we believe that these gains would have been in even greater jeopardy were it not for a new set of private-sector programs that begin in elementary schools in some areas of the country and continue through to corporate internships for black college students. These efforts, which we discuss further in chapter 8, have been funded primarily by the major corporations. Essentially, the corporations have gone into partnerships with various educators who have come to them for funding to help prepare students of color for prep schools, elite colleges, and the corporate world. The corporations and their foundations, we believe, have been motivated by the threat of lawsuits for racial discrimination in the workplace, the increasing purchasing power of black consumers, and the need for diverse management teams in an increasingly globalized economy.[55]

The decreased support from the government and the increased support from the corporate world were demonstrated when the George W. Bush administration fought affirmative action in cases that challenged the admissions policies at the University of Michigan Law School, but briefs from *Fortune* companies, as well as one from military officers, supported the university and argued that affirmative action was necessary. Moreover, the majority decision, written by Sandra Day O'Connor, expressly mentioned these briefs from members of the power elite. She wrote,

> Major American businesses have made clear that the skills needed in today's increasingly global marketplace can only be developed through exposure to widely diverse people, cultures, ideas, and viewpoints. High-ranking retired officers and civilian military leaders assert that a highly qualified, racially diverse officer corps is essential to national security.[56]

Therefore, there are black CEOs, there are black directors, and there are blacks in the corporate pipeline, though the numbers are small and show either no increase, or a decline, in these categories. It is likely that for the foreseeable future, many of the blacks in the corporate elite will have arrived there from the outside, though more in recent years have risen through the ranks of major corporations. Many African Americans in the corporate elite, however, will continue to be outside directors who are lawyers, university presidents (or the deans of medical schools or business schools), successful in businesses founded by blacks, or "management consultants."

There is evidence, however, that the legal pipeline has been shrinking for blacks. A 2017 study of black partners in major law firms by the National Association for Law Placement indicated that except for a small increase in 2016, the percentage of African American associates has been in decline. According to the report, "Representation of Black/African-Americans among associates has fallen every year from 2010 to 2015. Despite a small increase in 2016 to 4.11%, representation of Black/African-American associates remains below its 2009 level of 4.66%."[57]

A diverse array of blacks seems to have the potential to join the corporate elite. The first twelve black directors included both conservative Republican lawyers such as Samuel Pierce and longtime liberal activists such as Leon Sullivan, and the 1994 group of interlocking directors included conservative Republicans and liberal activists, although, in both groups, the traditionalists far outnumbered the activists. As we indicated, Sullivan was an exception, for the general tendency has been to select directors who will not rock the boat too much. Even the few activists who have been asked and agreed to join corporate boards are likely over time to have become part of the establishment. In a 1993 profile in *Current Biography*, Vernon Jordan's willingness to join corporate boards was explained in the following way: "During his ten years at the helm, he greatly expanded the influence of the National Urban League by enlisting the cooperation of some of the largest corporations in the United States. As part of the effort, he began serving on the boards of directors of such corporate giants as J. C. Penney, Xerox, and American Express."[58] In addition, though, Jordan was also expanding his own influence, and by 1995, as a partner in a major Washington, DC, law firm, wearing shirts "custom-made in London," a confidant and golfing buddy of the president, and a director of ten corporations, Jordan had become an influential insider rather than an outsider activist.[59]

BLACKS IN THE CABINET

Before Bill Clinton's election in 1992, only five blacks had served in presidential cabinets. Clinton's cabinets included five blacks. Four African Americans served in George W. Bush's administrations, and five in Obama's. As of late 2017, only one, Ben Carson, had served in the Trump administration. Therefore, the total number of blacks who have been in presidential cabinets is twenty.

The first of the five blacks who served in the cabinet before the Clinton administration was Robert Weaver, who in 1966 became Lyndon Johnson's secretary of housing and urban development. Weaver grew up in a suburb of Washington, DC, in one of the few black families among some three thousand neighbors. His white neighbors went to nearby all-white schools, but he and his brother had to commute forty-five minutes each day to attend black schools in the city. "Their one ambition," Weaver said of his parents, "was to send us to New England schools."[60]

Weaver went to a New England school, Harvard, where he earned a BA, an MA, and a PhD. (He was not the first in his family to attend Harvard; his grandfather had gone there.) He then went to Washington, DC, to be a part of Roosevelt's New Deal, serving in a variety of positions as adviser to agency heads on minority issues. He was the architect and leader of the "black cabinet," a group of blacks who lobbied for and assisted in the integration of the federal government.[61]

After World War II, Weaver held teaching positions at Northwestern, Columbia, and New York universities. When John F. Kennedy was elected president, he named Weaver to head the Housing and Home Finance Agency, at the time the highest federal administrative position ever held by an African American. Five years later, during Lyndon Johnson's presidency, the agency, with its name changed to the Department of Housing and Urban Development, achieved cabinet status, and in 1966, Weaver became the first African American to hold a cabinet position.[62]

But following that breakthrough, there were no black cabinet members for another seven years when President Gerald Ford selected William T. Coleman Jr., a corporate lawyer with impeccable educational, professional, and social credentials. Coleman, one of the first African American corporate directors, was from a solidly middle-class family that claimed six generations of teachers and Episcopal ministers on one side and numerous social workers on the other. Coleman grew up outside Philadelphia, where his father was the director of the Germantown Boys Club. After graduating from the University of Pennsylvania summa cum laude in 1941 and the Harvard Law School in 1946 (interrupted by a stint in the army air corps during the war), Coleman became a law clerk to Supreme Court Associate Justice Felix Frankfurter.

One of Frankfurter's other law clerks was Boston Brahmin Elliot Richardson, whom Coleman had met when they both served on the editorial board of the *Harvard Law Review*. Each morning, before turning to their legal work for Justice Frankfurter, Coleman and Richardson spent about an hour reading poetry together. Richardson became the godfather to Coleman's daughter. When his clerkship ended, Coleman joined the prestigious New York law firm of Paul, Weiss, Rifkind, Wharton & Garrison; a few years later, he returned to his hometown to join a prominent Philadelphia law firm, where he soon became a partner. As a high-powered and socially connected Republican corporate lawyer, Coleman was an unsurprising choice when corporate boards sought to integrate in the late 1960s and early 1970s. Over the years he sat on many boards, including Penn Mutual, Pan Am, International Business Machine (IBM), Chase Manhattan, PepsiCo, the American Can Company, AMEX, and INA. Coleman was such a successful corporate lawyer and had served on so many boards that when he agreed to become secretary of the treasury under President Ford, his income dropped dramatically: he sold shares of stock, gave up all his directorships, and accepted a salary that was one-fifth what he had earned in private life. [63]

The third black in a presidential cabinet, Patricia Roberts Harris, was also the first black woman, just as she had been the first black woman appointed to a *Fortune* 500 board. In fact, she held two successive cabinet positions during Carter's presidency: first, from 1977 to 1979, she was secretary of housing and urban development (HUD), and from 1979 to 1981 she was secretary of health, education, and welfare (HEW).

George H. W. Bush's only black cabinet appointee was Louis Sullivan, a physician whom Barbara Bush had come to know well when she joined the board of trustees of the Morehouse School of Medicine, where Sullivan was dean. After Sullivan gave a speech introducing her at the Republican National Convention in August 1988, Barbara Bush successfully lobbied for his appointment as secretary of health and human services.

Clinton was the first president to appoint more than one black to his cabinet. His initial cabinet included three: Ron Brown, the former chair of the Democratic National Committee; Mike Espy, a former congressman from Mississippi, who was one of the first black leaders to endorse Clinton's presidential candidacy; and Hazel O'Leary, the corporate vice president discussed in chapter 3. After his reelection in 1996, Clinton appointed Alexis Herman to replace Robert Reich as secretary of labor and Rodney Slater to replace Frederico Peña as secretary of transportation. After growing up in Alabama, where her father, a mortician, was the first black elected to the Democratic Party organization, Herman began her career working for a nonprofit (Catholic Charities), and then she worked in the Carter administration. She founded her own consulting firm in 1981 and sat on various *Fortune* 500 boards before she became Clinton's secretary of labor from 1997 to 2001. When she left her cabinet position, she again became a corporate director for a number of corporations, including Coca-Cola, Cummins, and MGM.

There were four African Americans in George W. Bush's cabinet: Colin Powell, secretary of state from 2001 to 2005; Roderick Paige, secretary of education from 2001 to 2005; Alphonso Jackson, who replaced Mel Martinez as secretary of housing and urban development in 2004 and served through 2008; and Condoleezza Rice, Bush's replacement for Powell as secretary of state.

Obama appointed five African Americans to his cabinets, though only one was among his initial appointees in 2009: Eric Holder, the attorney general from 2009 to 2015. After he was elected to a second term, Obama appointed two more African American men, Anthony Foxx as secretary of education, and Jeh (pronounced "Jay") Johnson as secretary of homeland security. When Holder left to return to the private sector (he returned to his former law firm, Covington and Burley), Obama appointed an African American woman, Loretta Lynch, to replace him, and when Foxx stepped down at education, Obama chose another African American, John B. King Jr., to replace him. Trump's initial cabinet included one African American, Ben Carson, a neurosurgeon, who became secretary of housing and urban development, even though he had no knowledge or experience in relation to housing or housing policy.

Twelve of the twenty African Americans who have been cabinet members (that is, 60 percent) were born into economically comfortable circumstances. This is a higher percentage than was the case for the first twelve black directors on *Fortune* boards (about 50 percent), the 1994 black interlockers (about 40 percent), and the 2011 black interlockers (about 25 percent).

Four of the twenty, Patricia Roberts Harris, Rodney Slater, Alphonso Jackson, and Ben Carson, came from poverty. As noted in chapter 3, Harris's father worked as a waiter on a railroad. Slater grew up picking cotton and peaches in Marianna, Arkansas. Jackson was the youngest of twelve children—his father did not graduate from high school and, as Jackson explained, he "juggled three jobs to keep food on the table."[64] Carson's father, a World War II veteran who worked in a Cadillac plant, was twenty-eight years old when he married Carson's mother, who was only thirteen. They separated when Carson was eight, and Carson lived with his mother and various other relatives in a number of homes in Detroit.

But all twenty, whether poor or well off, went to college, nine to prestigious "white" schools and five to prestigious "black" schools. Thirteen of the twenty went to law school, two went to medical school, and three completed doctoral work—in economics, physical education, and political science.

BLACKS IN THE MILITARY ELITE

In chapter 2, we told of the Jewish midshipman Leonard Kaplan's being "sent to Coventry" in the 1920s, which meant that no one spoke to him during his entire four years at the Naval Academy. Benjamin O. Davis Jr., the first black to graduate from the US Military Academy in the twentieth century, had a parallel experience during his four years at that institution in the 1930s. After he had been at West Point for a short time, there was a knock on his door announcing a meeting in the basement in ten minutes. Davis painfully recalled that meeting and its long-term effects in the autobiography he wrote almost sixty years later:

> As I approached the assembly where the meeting was in progress, I heard someone ask, "What are we going to do about the nigger?" I realized then that the meeting was about me, and I was not supposed to attend. I turned on my heel and double-timed back to my room.
>
> From that meeting on, the cadets who roomed across the hall, who had been friendly earlier, no longer spoke to me. In fact, no one spoke to me except in the line of duty. Apparently, certain upperclass cadets had determined that I was getting along too well at the Academy to suit them, and they were going to enforce an old West Point tradition—"silencing"—with the object of making my life so unhappy that I would resign. Silencing had been applied in the past to certain cadets who were considered to have violated the honor code and refused to resign. In my case there was no question of such a violation; I was to be silenced solely because cadets did not want blacks at West Point. Their only purpose was to freeze me out.
>
> Except for the recognition ceremony at the end of plebe year, I was silenced for the entire four years of my stay at the Academy.[65]

Davis stuck it out at West Point and graduated near the top of his class. Even after graduation in 1936, his classmates (among them William Westmoreland, who commanded US troops in Vietnam from 1964 to 1968 and came from a wealthy textile family in South Carolina) continued their silent treatment of him for years. In fact, for the next fifteen years, as his assignments took him to different locations in the United States and around the world, not only did his classmates continue to give him the silent treatment, but they and their wives also shunned Davis's wife.[66]

Davis was to become the second black to hold the rank of brigadier general (and the first to hold that rank in the air force). The first was his father, whose military career spanned a fifty-year period from the Spanish American War to World War II. The senior Davis enlisted in the cavalry in 1899, soon passed the tests to become an officer, and over the years rose through the military ranks, with various stints teaching military science at Wilberforce University in Ohio and the Tuskegee Institute in Alabama.

Pioneers such as the Davises helped prepare the way for a military that some have called a model of integration. According to Charles Moskos and John Sibley Butler in *All That We Can Be*, "By the mid-1950s, a snapshot of 100 enlisted men on a typical parade would have shown twelve black faces; integration had become a fact of Army life. At a time when Afro-Americans were still arguing for their educational rights before the Supreme Court and marching for their social and political rights in the Deep South, the Army had become desegregated with little fanfare."[67]

By 1985, of the 1,067 men with general officer rank, thirty-six, or 3.4 percent, were black. By 1995, there were still only thirty-six blacks with general officer rank, but there were fewer generals overall, so the percentage of blacks was a bit higher at 4.0 percent.[68] In May 1996, when Bill Clinton nominated Vice Adm. J. Paul Reason to become a four-star admiral, he became the first black four-star in that branch of the service. (The air force had promoted a black to four-star rank twenty years earlier, and the army had done so in the mid-1980s; the marine corps as yet had not.)[69] By September 2004, of the 898 men and women with general officer rank, forty-seven, or 5.2 percent, were black. A 2011 report to the Pentagon revealed that the blacks made up 8 percent of those with general officer rank, and data provided to us by the Department of Defense indicated that as of March 31, 2017, the number of blacks with general officer rank had dropped, to 7.5 percent; three of the thirty-eight men and women who had achieved four-star rank were African American (two men and one woman). Thus, after a slight increase from 2004 through 2011, over the past six years there has been a decline in the percentage of blacks with general officer rank, and blacks remain underrepresented at the highest levels of the military.[70] In fact, concerned that blacks were "virtually absent" from leadership in combat units, which function as the main avenue to the highest ranks, in 2014 the army expanded its recruiting efforts in large metropolitan areas.[71]

An indication of the future of African Americans in the military elite can be seen in the number of graduates from the three military academies, which produce a disproportionate number of generals and admirals. At West Point, the number of black graduates increased from an average of two or three a year between 1955 and 1967 to an average of seventy per year from 1990 through 1994. The class of 2008, which had 1,235 entering students, included seventy-two African Americans (5.8 percent). The starting point was even lower at the Naval Academy, which graduated fewer than two a year until 1967, but the average was seventy-seven a year from 1990 through 1994. The class of 2007, which started with 1,227 students, included sixty-nine African Americans (5.6 percent). At the Air Force Academy, there were, on average, fewer than two black graduates a year until 1967, but the figure reached sixty-two between 1986 and 1989. The Air Force Academy's entering classes of 2005 through 2009 included a total of 6,570 students, 295 of whom (4.5 percent) were African Americans. Although data for all of the academies are not available for every year, we do know that at West Point, the class of 2016 included 105 African Americans among the 1,150 entering students, or 9.1 percent.[72] The entering class of 2020 at the Naval Academy included seventy-five African Americans in the class of 1,177 students (or 6.4 percent). At the Coast Guard Academy, there were only three African Americans out of 186 students in the class of 2016 (or 1.6 percent).[73] Thus, it seems safe to conclude that African Americans continue to be underrepresented at these academies.[74]

Moreover, when the *Air Force Times* did a study based on six years of statistics on air force promotions, it concluded that "if you're a minority, your odds of being tapped for promotion . . . are not as good as they are for white airmen." These data helped to explain "the gradual—but noticeable—whitening of the Air Force as airmen progress higher up the ranks."[75]

One might expect that those relatively few blacks who have achieved general officer status, almost all of them men, would become, at the time of their retirement, prime candidates for senior corporate positions. As Mills pointed out back in the 1950s, there was "increased personnel traffic . . .

between the military and the corporate realms" because of "the great cultural shift of modern American capitalism toward a permanent war economy."[76] As a result, Mills added, "Get me a general" became the slogan of corporate recruiters. But Moskos and Butler found, much to their surprise, that this has not been the case for black generals. In numerous interviews with retired generals over the years, they found that "even the most qualified black generals" have not been hired as consultants and have not been asked onto corporate boards. "This is particularly puzzling," they write, "considering that most of these retired generals once had responsibility for thousands of soldiers and oversaw logistic systems of enormous cost and complexity. . . . It is difficult not to conclude that the discrimination these people overcame in the military overtakes them again when they return to civilian life."[77]

Still, a retired black general became one of the best-known and most admired Americans. It was a major breakthrough in 1989 when Colin Powell was named chairman of the Joint Chiefs of Staff. And, indeed, Powell's ascendance to the top of the military hierarchy has had as much impact for civilians as for soldiers. According to Moskos and Butler, "The elevation of Colin Luther Powell to the chairmanship of the Joint Chiefs of Staff in 1989 was an epic event in American race relations, whose significance has yet to be fully realized."[78]

Powell's parents were both Jamaican immigrants, a fact he makes much of, and so will we when we explore the reasons for the success and failure of minorities in the United States in chapter 8.[79] While a student at the City College of New York, Powell joined the Reserve Officers' Training Corps (ROTC), and when he graduated in 1958, he was commissioned as a second lieutenant. Powell has emphasized that he "found himself" in ROTC: "Suddenly everything clicked. . . . I had found something I was good at. . . . For the first time, in the military I always knew exactly what was expected of me."[80] Equally important, the military had become a place where blacks could do well. "I had an intuitive sense that this was a career which was beginning to open up for blacks," says Powell. "You could not name, in those days, another profession where black men routinely told white men what to do and how to do it."[81]

Starting out as a junior officer in Vietnam, Powell rose quickly through a series of command and staff jobs, and then received a big boost when he became a White House Fellow in 1972.[82] Four years later, when Jimmy Carter appointed the African American corporate lawyer Clifford Alexander as secretary of the army, the number of black generals tripled over the next four years while he held that position. One of them was Colin Powell, appointed in 1979 at the age of forty-two. By 1987 he had become national security adviser under Reagan, and in 1989, under George H. W. Bush, he became the first black—and the youngest man ever—to be chairman of the Joint Chiefs of Staff. After the Gulf War, polls consistently indicated that Powell was among the most admired people in America.[83] However, Powell's image took a hit when, under intense pressure from George W. Bush and Dick Cheney, in February 2003 he testified to a plenary session at the United Nations that there was "no doubt" in his mind that Saddam Hussein had biological weapons and the capacity to produce nuclear weapons, claims that were subsequently proven false. In a television interview two years later, Powell acknowledged: "It will always be a part of my record. It was painful. It's painful now."[84]

"THING IS, I AIN'T THAT BLACK"

Throughout the twentieth century and into the twenty-first, scholars have demonstrated that a disproportionate number of black professionals have been light skinned, and that blacks with darker skin are more likely to be discriminated against. Horace Mann Bond found, for example, that many "early Negro scholars" were "light-complexioned" individuals from families that had been part of the antebellum "free colored population" or born to "favored slaves." He explained their success in the following way: "The phenomenon was not due, as many believed, to the 'superiority' of the white blood; it was a social and economic, rather than a natural selection. Concubinage remained an openly sustained relationship between white men and Negro women in the South for fifty years after the Civil War; the children of such unions were more likely to have parents with the money, and the tradition, to send a child to school, than the former field hand slaves who were now sharecroppers and day laborers."[85]

The authors of the 1995 report of the Glass Ceiling Commission argued that "gradations in skin color" had continued to affect the career chances of men and women of color. They write,

> *Color-based differences* are inescapable but nobody likes to talk about them. These are complicated differences because they are not exclusively racial and not exclusively ethnic. The unstated but ever-present question is, *"Do they look like us?"*

Though it is mostly covert, our society has developed an extremely sophisticated, and often denied, acceptability index based on gradations in skin color.
It is not as simple a system as the black/white/colored classifications that were
used in South Africa. It is not legally permissible, but it persists just beneath
the surface, and it can be and is used as a basis for decision making, sometimes
consciously and sometimes unconsciously. It is applied to African Americans,
to American Indians, to Asian and Pacific Islander Americans, and to Hispanic
Americans, who are described in a color shorthand of black, brown, yellow,
and red. [86]

Although this issue is generally not commented upon directly, some accounts of African Americans in positions of power allude to it indirectly. For
example, Patricia Roberts Harris is described as follows in *Current Biography*: "Among her ancestors were Negro slaves, Delaware and Cherokee Indians, and English and Irish settlers. . . . In some of her facial features she
resembles Sophia Loren." [87]

Not surprisingly, therefore, when we looked at photographs of those
black Americans who had made it into the power elite, we noted that they
were lighter skinned than many other black Americans. We were able to
confirm this observation more systematically by asking two raters, working
independently, to use the Skin Color Assessment Procedure, a skin-color
rating chart developed by two psychologists, to rate the skin color of many of
those we had identified as members of the power elite and various control
groups of other black Americans. The differences were powerful: the blacks
in the power elite were rated as lighter skinned than the blacks in the control
groups, and this was especially true for the black women in the power elite,
who were rated as lighter than any of the other groups. [88] In fact, when the
raters scored the photographs in *Ebony* magazine's 1996 list "100 Most
Influential Black Americans and Organization Leaders," Hazel O'Leary had
the lowest score (and was thus seen as the lightest) of anyone on the list.

More recently, we conducted a similar study based on the skin color of
the African American men who had become CEOs of *Fortune* 500 companies. We asked a group of students to rate their skin color on a 1-to-10 scale,
and also to rate the skin color of a sample of twenty men who were the
presidents of historically black colleges and universities (HBCUs). The black
CEOs were rated as significantly lighter than the college presidents. [89]

These findings not only make sense in terms of the earlier research on
skin color among eminent black Americans, but they are also consistent with
our findings on Jews and women in the power elite. As we have indicated in

the previous two chapters, those Jews who have made it into the power elite are likely to have been highly assimilated in the first place. The longer they have been in the power elite, especially the corporate and military elites, the less distinguishable they become from their Gentile counterparts. Similarly, the women who have made it into the corporate elite are those who fit in the best, and though it is certainly easy enough to distinguish them from men in terms of their appearance, they tend to be (or to become) quite similar to the men surrounding them in terms of class background, values, and behaviors. In chapter 3, we quoted a woman executive who explained to us that although she perceived her gender to pose the most substantial obstacle to her advancement in her career, this did not mean that being Jewish was irrelevant. "It's part of the total package," she told us. "It's part of the question of whether you fit the mold. Are you like me or not? If too much doesn't fit, it impacts you negatively."[90]

In the same way, being black makes it hard to "fit the mold," and being a dark-skinned black makes it even harder. This is not the only factor operating in terms of what can make one different, but it contributes to whether "too much doesn't fit." This may explain why light skin is more prevalent among black women in the power elite than among black men, for black women are already different from the white male power elite norm because of their sex. It is as if one can accumulate only so many points of difference from the norm, and a combination of gender points and skin-color points can exceed the acceptable limit. This same preference for lighter skin, now typically referred to as "colorism," and based upon a substantial body of research, will appear again in the chapters on Latinos and Asian Americans. It is found not only in the ways that whites react to people of color, but within the African American, Latino, and Asian American communities, including immigrants from South Asia.

Colin Powell captured the essence of skin color's role in the broader context of not being too different from, and thus threatening to, whites. In a lengthy *New Yorker* profile, Henry Louis Gates Jr. asked Powell to explain polls that showed him having greater appeal among whites than among blacks. Powell, described by Gates as "light-skinned and blunt-featured," cut through sociological jargon and the need for statistical analyses:

> One, I don't shove it in their face, you know? I don't bring any stereotypes or threatening visage to their presence. Some black people do. Two, I can overcome any stereotypes or reservations they have, because I perform well. Third thing is, *I ain't that black.* . . . I speak reasonably well, like a white person. I

am very comfortable in a white social situation, and I don't go off in a corner. My features are clearly black, and I've never denied what I am. It fits into their general social setting, so they do not find me threatening. I think there's more to it than that, but I don't know what it is.[91]

BLACKS IN CONGRESS AND ON THE SUPREME COURT

The Senate

The first three blacks to have served in the US Senate in modern times represent three eras. Indeed, if Edward Brooke, born in 1919, was a product of the old black middle class of the mid-twentieth century, and Carol Moseley-Braun, born in 1947, was a product of the race-conscious 1960s, Barack Obama, born in 1961, is a product of the increasingly biracial and bicultural world of the 1980s and 1990s.[92]

Edward Brooke was a Republican who represented the state of Massachusetts from 1967 until 1979. His father was a lawyer, and Brooke grew up in upper-middle-class neighborhoods in the Washington, DC, area. The family lived mostly in black neighborhoods, though for a while they lived in a white neighborhood that was so rigidly segregated that blacks who did not live there could not pass through the neighborhood without a note from a white person. According to one account, "He spent his boyhood summers on his mother's family plantation in Virginia, where his grandparents told the light-skinned youth that he was a descendant of Thomas Jefferson and of a British admiral, Sir Philip Bowes Brooke, and that he was related to Rupert Brooke, the English poet."[93]

After graduating from Howard in 1941 and serving in the army during World War II, he attended Boston University Law School, where he edited the *Law Review*. After he graduated in 1948, he started a one-man law practice outside Boston, and a few years later, he entered state politics. In 1948 and again in 1952, he ran for the state legislature both as a Democrat and as a Republican (it was then legal to do so); both times he lost the Democratic nomination but won the Republican one, then lost in the general election. In 1960, he ran for secretary of state as a Republican, losing by fewer than twelve thousand votes. Two years later, he won the election for attorney general, the second-highest office in the state. (He gained the Republican nomination on the second ballot over Boston blue blood Elliot Richardson.) In 1966, he ran for the US Senate and won, defeating the former governor, Endicott ("Chub") Peabody.

In running for state attorney general, Brooke downplayed his race. He was, he asserted, an American first, a Republican second, and "a black incidentally." He declared, "I'm not running as a Negro. I never have. I'm trying to show that people can be elected on the basis of their qualifications and not their race."[94] A few years later he remarked, "I am not a civil rights leader and I don't profess to be one."[95]

Brooke lost his bid for a third term in the Senate when he was ensnared in a set of allegations about financial impropriety, fueled by bitter divorce proceedings with his wife, an Italian he met during the war. Although he was never convicted of a crime, his reputation suffered, and he lost that election to Paul Tsongas. He subsequently worked as a consultant and lawyer for various Washington, DC, law firms and real estate developers. According to one account, in the early 1990s he was living in Virginia with his second wife and son and describing himself as a "retired country gentleman."[96]

Carol Moseley-Braun, the second African American elected to the Senate in modern times, was never prone to downplay race. As a teenager in Chicago in the 1960s, she staged a one-person sit-in at a restaurant that would not seat her, refused to leave an all-white beach even when whites threw stones at her, and marched with Martin Luther King Jr. in a demonstration calling for open housing in an all-white neighborhood. She describes her upbringing in the following way: "They raised us in a world that did not acknowledge or legitimize racism. Ethnic pride was part and parcel of that world—my maternal grandparents had been Garveyites and Muslims, 'race men' as they were called at the time."[97]

Born to a middle-class family on the South Side of Chicago—her father was a policeman and her mother a medical technician—Moseley-Braun received a BA from the University of Illinois at Chicago and a JD from the University of Chicago Law School.

Six years after graduating from law school she was elected to the Illinois House of Representatives, and a decade later, she was elected Cook County recorder of deeds. When, four years later, she decided to run for the US Senate, entering the Democratic primary against the incumbent, Alan J. Dixon, who had voted to confirm Clarence Thomas, few at first thought she had a chance. As one account puts it, Moseley-Braun's candidacy "appeared so unpromising that political organizations created to provide seed money to women's campaigns across the country gave her nothing or just token contributions late in the race."[98] Nonetheless, she defeated Dixon, and when she won the general election, she became one of seven women in the Senate (see chapter 3) and the only African American. She was defeated in 1998 in her attempt for a second term, and, once again, the Senate had no African American members.

Barack Obama's mother, a white woman born in Kansas, met his father, a Kenyan, in 1959 when they were students at the University of Hawaii. When Obama was a toddler, his father left Hawaii to do graduate work in economics at Harvard (the scholarship he won was not big enough to enable him to take his wife and son with him), and upon completing his doctoral degree, he returned to Africa.

His parents divorced, and a few years later, Obama's mother met and married an Indonesian. She and six-year-old Barack moved to Jakarta, where Barack lived for four years before returning to Hawaii to live with his maternal grandparents (his grandfather first managed a furniture store and then sold insurance and his grandmother was one of the first two women to be appointed as a vice president at the bank she worked for). Despite his grandparents' relatively modest middle-class standing, his grandfather was able to convince his employer, an alumnus of Punahou, the most elite private school on the islands, carefully modeled after the best New England prep schools, to accept young Barack. He entered as a fifth grader, and graduated eight years later, having accumulated elite social connections and upper-class manners and style ("cultural capital") in the process.[99]

He began college at Occidental before transferring to Columbia, from which he graduated in 1983. After three years working in Chicago as a community organizer, he went to the Harvard Law School, where he became the first black editor of the *Harvard Law Review*. After graduating from law school in 1991, and before returning to Chicago, he spent a year working on the book that was to become *Dreams from My Father*, a memoir that describes his growing up in Hawaii and Indonesia and his search as a young adult to learn more about his father, his family in Kenya, and his own racial identity.[100] He returned to Chicago, practiced civil rights law, and taught at the University of Chicago Law School. When the opportunity arose, he ran for and was elected to the state senate representing a district that included both Hyde Park (home of the university) and some of the most impoverished ghettos on the South Side.[101]

Seven years after his election to the state senate, Obama burst upon the national scene in March 2004 when he beat six others to win the Democratic primary for Senate (he won 53 percent of the vote). With no Republican opponent to worry about back in Illinois due to a series of embarrassing

Republican mistakes, Obama traveled to Boston in July 2004 to deliver an electrifying keynote address at the Democratic National Convention. Revealing what a *Chicago Tribune* reporter described at the time as his "raw ambition, so powerful that even he is still coming to terms with its full force," Obama remarked to this reporter as he was about to take the stage for his historic speech, "I'm LeBron, baby. I can play on this level. I got some game."[102]

Obama's popularity with whites, which not only contributed to his election as a senator from Illinois, but to his successful campaigns for the presidency in 2008 and 2012, results in part because he is so comfortable among them. As he said about himself: "I was born to a white mother, raised by a white mom and grandparents who loved me deeply."[103] And as he said about the white voters from rural areas and small towns who voted for him, first as a senator and subsequently for president: "I know those people. Those are my grandparents. The food they serve is the food my grandparents served when I was growing up. Their manners, their sensibility, their sense of right and wrong—it's all totally familiar to me."[104]

Whites are also comfortable with him, in part for the same reasons they are comfortable with Colin Powell. His biracial and multicultural background (and his light skin) insulate him from the stereotypes they hold of African Americans, and, as a result, like Powell, he is perceived as nonthreatening.[105] But Obama is not just popular with many middle-level whites because he knows their style and is biracial. He is well liked by many whites in the power elite (with the glaring exception of the ultraconservative Southern whites and Northern racists, who demonize him) because they know a suave, well-educated, prep school graduate when they interact with one. Seven years at Punahou led to a very gracious style and an abundance of cultural capital.

Five more African Americans now have served in the Senate, four Democrats and one Republican. Roland Burris, a longtime Democratic politician in Illinois, was appointed as a seventy-one-year-old caretaker to fill the Senate position left open when Barack Obama was elected president, and did not run in 2010, which meant that there were again no African Americans in the Senate. Tim Scott, a Republican, was appointed by the governor of South Carolina to fill the seat vacated by Jim DeMint when he resigned in 2013 to become president of the ultraconservative Heritage Foundation. Scott was then elected in a special election in 2014, and reelected in 2016 to a full term, which made him the first black Republican senator since Edward Brooke (who served from 1967 through 1979), and the first black senator from either party to win a Senate seat in a Southern state since 1881. Scott was joined by Democrat William Maurice Cowan when he was appointed in 2013 to replace the senator from Massachusetts, John Kerry, when he became secretary of state (Cowan decided not to run in 2014), and by Cory Booker, a Democrat, who won a special election held in 2013 to replace Frank Lautenberg, the senator from New Jersey, who had died in office. Booker then won the regular Senate election scheduled for 2014, making him the first black senator ever to serve from that state. The black male senators were then joined by a woman of Jamaican American and Indian American ancestry with the election of the California attorney general, Kamala Harris, to the Senate.

These three senators of African American heritage in the Senate as of mid-2017 (Scott, Booker, and Harris) rather dramatically reflect the diversity within the black community in the early twenty-first century. To begin with, the Republican, Scott, grew up in the South in what might be called "working poverty"—his parents divorced when he was seven, and he and his two brothers were raised by his mother, a nurse's assistant, who worked long hours to keep the family afloat economically. Scott went to Presbyterian College in Clinton, South Carolina, on a football scholarship, but after one year transferred to Charleston Southern University, from which he graduated with a BS in political science. He is unmarried and is an evangelical Christian. He was one of the few prominent blacks who supported Donald Trump for president in 2016. As the *New York Times* reported, a few weeks before the election, "He has repeatedly stated that he will vote for Mr. Trump, even as he has characterized some of his statements and actions as 'disgusting,' 'indefensible' and 'racially toxic.'"[106]

Cory Booker's background and politics are quite different from Scott's. The son of two of the first black executives at IBM, he grew up economically privileged. He went to Stanford, where he played football (he was a tight end), was senior class president, and won a Rhodes Scholarship. After two years at Oxford, he went to Yale Law School. He was elected to the Newark City Council, and then became mayor of Newark before he was appointed to the Senate to replace Frank Lautenberg. Like Scott, he is unmarried. Although he has admitted that as a teenager he himself hated gays, and there have been rumors that Booker is gay, he has refused to respond to these on principle. In 2013, he explained his stance in the following way: "And people who think I'm gay, some part of me thinks it's wonderful. Because I want to challenge people on their homophobia. I love seeing on Twitter when someone says I'm gay, and I say, 'So what does it matter if I am? So be it. I hope you are not voting for me because you are making the presumption that I'm straight.'"[107]

The newest African American senator, Kamala Harris, was elected in November 2016. She, too, grew up in economic privilege, though her parents divorced when she was young. Her father, Jamaican born, teaches economics at Stanford; her mother, a Hindu who emigrated from India, was a physician (she died in 2009). She is thus the first Indian American, and the second black woman, to serve in the Senate. Raised in Berkeley, Oakland, and then Montreal, Quebec, when her mother accepted a job doing research and teaching at McGill after the divorce, she attended Howard for her BA, and then Berkeley for her JD. Before her election to the Senate she served as the state's attorney general. In 2014, she married Douglas Emhoff, the managing partner at a large Los Angeles law firm.

The House

In the November 1990 election, twenty-five blacks were elected or reelected to the House; in 1992, that number rose to thirty-eight, and it stayed at about that number until the 2016 elections, when it reached forty-seven (10.8 percent); twenty-eight were men (60 percent), and nineteen were women (40 percent). The large majority (forty-five of the forty-seven, or 96 percent), were Democrats, and the other two (4 percent), were Republicans.[108] Therefore, although African Americans are not proportionally represented in the House of Representatives, they do constitute 10.1 percent of that body, a figure that is certainly higher than the figures we have cited for blacks on boards of directors, in the higher ranks of the military elite, and in the Senate (prior to Trump's initial cabinet, most recent presidential cabinets have had a higher percentage).

When we looked more systematically at the forty-seven blacks who were in the House as of mid-2017, some revealing patterns emerged. First, as noted, only two are Republicans.[109] Second, although all but one graduated from college, relatively few did their undergraduate work at elite colleges or universities. Although two went to Harvard, one to Yale, and one to Princeton, far more went to HBCUs including Fisk, Howard, Morehouse, Tougaloo, and Tuskegee, to state schools—more often branch locations, not the flagship location—or to various schools that many Ivy Leaguers would have trouble locating (e.g., Concordia, Central State, Thomas Edison State College). Most of these forty-seven men and women earned postgraduate degrees. Of those who earned higher degrees, the largest number earned law degrees (nineteen), followed by master's degrees (eleven), MBAs (two), MSWs (two), and PhDs (two).

The schools attended suggest that, as a group, the black men and women who have been elected to the House have come from less privileged backgrounds than those who have been appointed to *Fortune*-level boards of directors or presidential cabinets. We were able to corroborate this by looking at the family backgrounds of those about whom we could find information.

Slightly more than one-fourth of them grew up in economically comfortable backgrounds (this is less than the figure of 40 percent for the 1994 interlocking directors, but about the same as for the 2011 interlocking directors, whom we looked at earlier in this chapter). This includes a few who are the children of men who themselves had served in the House of Representatives. It also includes the two Harvard graduates, both of whom had fathers who were physicians. It also includes one whose father was a college president and whose mother was the head librarian at the college.

About half are from stable working-class families. These include men and women whose fathers were coaches, letter carriers, grocers, salesmen, and labor organizers, and whose mothers were social workers, librarians, nurses, and teachers. About one-third came from real poverty, some of them raised by single mothers, or, after their parents divorced or died, by grandparents, and some grew up in housing projects. For example, when her mother died when she was young, Brenda Lawrence (D-MI) was raised by her grandparents. Similarly, when Marc Veasey's (D-TX) parents divorced when he was ten, he was raised by his grandparents.

In the final chapter, we will explore the many ironies related to the increase in diversity that has taken place in the power elite. Here we wish to underscore an irony related to the dramatic increase in the number of black members from the South who were elected to the House of Representatives in 1992—the number more than tripled, from five to seventeen. This increase was the result of what one white civil rights lawyer called an "unholy alliance" between black leaders in the South and those in power at the highest levels of the national Republican Party.[110] This unlikely partnership was made possible by amendments enacted a decade earlier to the Voting Rights Act in 1982, followed by a favorable Supreme Court amendment that in effect made it legal (and in some cases mandatory) to create majority-black, majority-Latino, and majority-minority voting districts.

The alliance (unholy or not) was primarily the result of the work of Lee Atwater, the manager of George H. W. Bush's successful 1988 presidential campaign.[111] In a coldly calculating way, Atwater advocated reversing the efforts that had been made during the Reagan administration to hamper the expansion of black rights within the political arena. Instead, the plan Atwater and the Republicans proposed would give more power to black voters in some districts. At the same time, the carefully redesigned districts would make it possible for Republicans to defeat the incumbent white Southern Democrats, partly by giving the incumbents new white constituents who did not know them, and partly by taking away the loyal black Democratic voters the white Democratic incumbents were dependent upon. The result was likely to be more blacks elected, but also more Republicans elected in the Southern states.[112]

In order to implement this plan, Atwater and the Republicans needed the votes of black Democrats in state legislatures because, understandably, Southern Democratic incumbents at the state and federal levels fiercely opposed the plan. Ultimately, the black legislators agreed to the plan, and, as a result, the Southern Republicans in the House "went from being a perennial minority party to being the majority party" in the "span of just two elections," 1992 and 1994. They gained nine seats in 1992 and sixteen in 1994, and for good measure they "added another seven seats to their delegation" in 1996.[113]

Thanks for the most part to the Southern Republican successes in those first two elections after reapportionment and redistricting, the national party suddenly had the majority in the House. Moreover, Newt Gingrich, an ultra-conservative from the white suburbs of Atlanta, now known by many people primarily as an incendiary talking head on television, became Speaker of the House (as Gingrich walked from his former seat to the front of the House to assume the speakership, one of his Republican colleagues shouted, "It's a whole new world!").[114]

When the Republicans took control, twenty members of the Congressional Black Caucus lost their committee and subcommittee chairmanships, which seemed ironic and self-defeating to some observers. For example, Lani Guinier, the biracial daughter of a black father who was a union organizer and a Jewish mother who was a pro-integration activist, a former civil rights lawyer for the NAACP Legal Defense Fund and now a Harvard Law School professor, warned that "proponents of black voting rights have won the ballot, but may be losing the war."[115] She may have been right. In the concluding chapter, we return to this Atwater-inspired alliance and its long-term effects within a larger theoretical context that may explain why many Southern black Democrats very much wanted to have as many black representatives in Congress as possible, despite the risks for the national Democratic Party in the House.

The Supreme Court

Just as the few African Americans to have served in the Senate provide a study in contrasts and reveal the tenor of the times, so, too, do the two African American men to have served on the Supreme Court, Thurgood Marshall and Clarence Thomas. Marshall, appointed by Lyndon Johnson, a Democratic president, in 1967, was from a stable home, was politically liberal, and was tall and light skinned. Thomas, appointed in 1991 by George H. W. Bush, a Republican president, grew up in a very unstable home, is extremely conservative, and is short and dark skinned.

Marshall grew up in Baltimore. His father, a "pale-skinned blue-eyed man," dropped out of elementary school and worked as a railroad porter. His mother, also light skinned, was a college graduate and, like her mother before her, was a teacher. After graduating from Colored High and Training School, he attended Lincoln University and then graduated from Howard University School of Law. As the chief counsel for the NAACP, Marshall had won the landmark *Brown v. Board of Education of Topeka, Kansas* decision in 1954 that forced the desegregation of the country's public schools. John F. Kennedy named him to the US Court of Appeals, and in 1965, Lyndon Johnson named him to the office of US Solicitor General before nominating him two years later for the Supreme Court.[116]

Thomas was born to a teenage mother in Pin Point, Georgia, eleven miles down the coast from Savannah, an unincorporated community originally founded by freed slaves, and with a population of fewer than 400 people. His early childhood was one of hardship and abandonment, and he never really knew his father. However, he was raised after the age of six in comfortable circumstances by his grandparents—his grandfather was a leading business figure in the black community. (Thomas later revealed to colleagues that his well-off grandfather rarely spoke to him as a boy except to order him to do chores, whipped him with an electrical cord, and locked him in a closet when he misbehaved.) Raised a Baptist, his grandmother had converted to Catholicism, and Clarence was able to attend Catholic schools, first a school run for black children by Franciscan nuns, and then a seminary. He attended Holy

Cross (his acceptance was clearly the result of the college's late-1960s commitment to affirmative action) and then Yale Law School (also the result of affirmative action).

After graduating from Yale, Thomas worked first for the wealthy heir John Danforth, the grandson of the founder of Ralston Purina (and at the time the state attorney general in Missouri) and then as a corporate lawyer in the pesticide and agricultural division of Monsanto Company. When Danforth won a Senate seat, Thomas went to Washington, DC, to be his legislative aide. After attending a conference for black conservatives, he came to the attention of Ronald Reagan, who appointed him assistant secretary for civil rights in the Department of Education. Not long thereafter, Reagan appointed him to head the Equal Employment Opportunity Commission, where he did everything he could to dismantle the agency, much to the dismay of its staff and the African American community across the United States. George H. W. Bush nominated Thomas to the US Court of Appeals in Washington, DC, in 1990, and then, a year later, when Thurgood Marshall announced his retirement, Bush nominated Thomas to the Supreme Court. This turned out to be one of the most controversial Supreme Court appointments in history (the final vote in the Senate was 52–48, the most votes ever cast against a successful nominee).[117]

Whereas Marshall was so light skinned that he was once called a "tall, yeller nigger" by a redneck sheriff in Tennessee, Thomas was quite dark skinned. As one woman who attended elementary and junior high school with him said, "He was darker than most kids, and in that generation, people were cruel. He was teased a lot, they'd call him 'Nigger Naps' . . . and a lot of girls wouldn't want to go out with him." Another childhood friend said, "Clarence had big lips, nappy hair, and he was almost literally black. Those folks were at the bottom of the pole."[118]

Marshall married twice. His first wife was an African American from a middle-class family (when they met, she was a student at the University of Pennsylvania). After she died, he married one of the secretaries in the NAACP office, Cissy Suyat, born in Hawaii of Filipino parents.[119] Thomas also married twice. His first wife, from whom he is now divorced, was a light-skinned black woman (one of her four grandparents was Japanese), and his second wife, Virginia ("Ginni") Lamp, is a white woman from a well-to-do, Republican, Nebraska family who works for the right-wing Heritage Foundation (they were strong Goldwater supporters in 1964).[120]

Marshall ridiculed Thomas and other black conservatives as "the goddam black sellouts." According to African American journalist Carl Rowan, "Marshall would shake his head in wonderment that a black man who grew up in Jim Crow Georgia, and who had benefited from a thousand affirmative actions by nuns and others, and who had attended Yale Law School on a racial quota, could suddenly find affirmative action so destructive of the character of black people."[121]

CONCLUSION

Three patterns emerge from our examination of blacks in the power elite and Congress that we also found for Jews and women. First, it is apparent that social background is important. Although some have authentic stories to tell of going from rags to riches, as do a smaller percentage of whites in the power elite, most are from either working-class or middle-class families, and many are from economically privileged backgrounds. Whether one is white or black, the advantages of being born into privilege are apparent.

Second, education is important. As we have seen repeatedly in this chapter, the blacks who have made it into the power elite and Congress are quite well educated. This not only underscores the importance of education, which we also found to be the case in the chapters on Jews and women, but reinforces the oft-heard claim that blacks have to be better educated than whites to get ahead.

Third, the same pattern holds for blacks that held for Jews and women in the cabinet and Congress. Cabinet members tend to be from families higher in the socioeconomic spectrum than elected officials, and they include Republicans as well as Democrats. In keeping with their lower social-class origins, almost all of those who have been elected to Congress have been Democrats.

However, we also found two differences that were not present for Jews and women. The first is that the increasing involvement of Jews and women of all faiths in the power elite does not seem to have been the case for African Americans. The number of African Americans in the corporate elite (both corporate directors and CEOs), in the political elite (cabinets and Congress), and in the military elite has leveled off or even declined.

A second issue at play for blacks but not Jews or women is colorism. As we have noted in our discussion of the skin color of CEOs, various cabinet members, and Colin Powell ("Thing is, I ain't that black!"), whether an

African American is light skinned or dark skinned seems to be a factor in whether that person is likely to make it to the power elite. We note this not only to point out a distinction between Jews, white women, and African Americans, but because, as will be seen in the next few chapters, colorism is part of the story for Latinos and Asian Americans.

Chapter Five

Latinos in the Power Elite

When Roberto Goizueta left his native Havana, Cuba, in 1949 to begin his freshman year at Yale University, he had no idea that by the 1980s he would be running one of the largest corporations in the United States. Basque and Spanish in racial and cultural heritage and a member of the wealthy upper class in Cuba, he returned home to Havana after he had earned a degree in engineering, and from 1954 to 1960, he worked for the Coca-Cola subsidiary in Cuba.

But Goizueta and other wealthy young Cubans did not count on the actions of another Cuban-born son of a successful Spanish immigrant, Fidel Castro, who turned his back on his father's large ranch and his own elite education to create the revolutionary army that overthrew Cuban dictator Fulgencio Batista in January 1959. By the early 1960s, Castro was threatening major capitalist enterprises, leading Goizueta and more than 380,000 other Cubans to emigrate to the United States by 1980.[1] In 1960, Goizueta became assistant to the senior vice president of Coca-Cola in the Bahamas, and by 1964, he was assistant to the vice president for research and development at the company's headquarters in Atlanta.

It took only a few years before Goizueta became a vice president for engineering; shortly thereafter, he was a senior vice president, then an executive vice president. He was named president and chief operating officer in 1980 and became chairman of the board and CEO in 1981. When he died in October 1997, he was one of the most powerful corporate chieftains in the United States, atypical though he may be of most of the 56.6 million people identified as of October 2016 as Hispanic Americans.[2]

129

Vilma S. Martínez, born to Mexican American parents in 1943 in San Antonio, Texas, had a very different experience. As a young girl, she was bitter about the discrimination she experienced. She recalls that her junior high school counselor recommended that she go to a vocational or technical high school, her high school counselor would not advise her about applying to college, and her father, a construction worker, was skeptical about the usefulness of college for a woman, saying that she "would not complete school, that she would get married and have children." But she insisted on an academic high school, graduated from the University of Texas in two and a half years, and did not have the first of her two children until 1976, nine years after she had earned a law degree from Columbia University.[3]

Martínez practiced civil rights law as a staff attorney for the NAACP Legal Defense Fund from 1967 to 1970 and for the New York State Division of Human Rights after that. After two years as a labor lawyer with the Wall Street firm of Cahill, Gordon & Reindel, she became one of the prime movers in establishing the Mexican American Legal Defense and Education Fund (MALDEF). In 1973, she became MALDEF's general counsel and president. Three years later, the liberal Democratic governor of California, Jerry Brown, surprised everyone by appointing Martínez, only thirty-two years old, a regent of the University of California, where she rubbed elbows with a cross-section of the California corporate rich and lobbied for greater diversity in the faculty and student body. In May 1982, she joined the Los Angeles law firm of Munger, Tolles & Olson, where her clients have included Pacific Telephone, Blue Cross, and Allstate Insurance.[4] She has been on the boards of a number of *Fortune* 500 corporations: Anheuser-Busch, Burlington Northern Santa Fe, Fluor, and Shell Petroleum. In 2009, Barack Obama chose her to be the ambassador to Argentina, a position she held until 2013.

But not all Latinas from the Southwest are liberal enough to work for the NAACP or MALDEF. Those from New Mexico, whose ancestors were sometimes landholders before the American conquest of the territory, are often quite conservative. Patricia Díaz, born in Santa Rita, New Mexico, in 1946, was the daughter of an army sergeant who was transferred frequently. She spent her teenage years in Japan, graduated from a high school in Santiago, Chile, and received her BA in 1970 from UCLA and a law degree in 1973 from Loyola University in Los Angeles. After three years with a large corporate firm in Los Angeles, she became a management attorney specializing in labor disputes, first with Pacific Lighting and then with ABC in Hollywood. She was working for ABC in 1983 when Ronald Reagan unexpectedly named her as a "Democratic" appointee to the National Labor Relations Board, the second female and first Latina member in its forty-seven-year history. There she joined the majority in a wide range of decisions that were extremely damaging to labor organizing.[5] In 1986, she became a member of the Federal Communications Commission (FCC). After an equally conservative three-year tenure as an FCC commissioner, she returned to the private sector as a corporate lawyer for U.S. Sprint. In 1992, George H. W. Bush tried to improve his appeal to Mexican Americans in the Southwest by appointing Díaz as assistant secretary of state for human rights and humanitarian affairs. When Bush lost his bid for reelection, Díaz joined the Washington, DC, office of the venerable Wall Street law firm of Sullivan & Cromwell and became a director of Telemundo, the second-largest Hispanic radio and television corporation in the United States. Married to Michael Dennis, a lawyer, and going by the name of Patricia Díaz Dennis, she left Sullivan & Cromwell to become senior vice president and general counsel for SBC Pacific Bell/SBC Nevada Bell (now part of AT&T). Her being a conservative Democrat has served Díaz Dennis—and the Republicans—extremely well.

Goizueta, Martínez, and Díaz Dennis are prime examples of why social scientists stress that it is very risky to generalize about the Hispanic or Latino experience in the United States. The approximately two million Cuban Americans, many of whom were quite well off in Cuba, have one story, while the approximately five million immigrants from Puerto Rico usually have another. (Actually, a few of the Puerto Rican immigrants are also wealthy, but most arrived poor.) Similarly, people of Mexican descent in New Mexico, many of whom have ancestors who have lived in the area for more than one hundred years and who sometimes call themselves "Spanish Americans," are different from the Mexican American immigrants to Texas and California. Moreover, the Mexican Americans of the Southwest range from middle-class entrepreneurs to migrant farmworkers, and they vary greatly in color and appearance as well because of a history of intermarriage with the indigenous Indian populations of Mexico. The Latino population in the United States also includes some immigrants from Spain and various Latin American countries.

There has been considerable debate and disagreement among scholars and political activists about what general name, if any, should be used to characterize a group whose main common heritage is the Spanish conquest and the Spanish language. The term *Hispanic* has been favored by some, especially on the East Coast; others prefer *Latino*, especially on the West Coast. As

Ramon Gutierrez explains in an essay titled "What's in a Name? The History and Politics of Hispanic and Latino Panethnicities," whatever term is used, the label emerged as part of a concerted push for panethnicity, a process that brings together disparate people with shared experiences:

> Immigrants and long-time residents hailing from such divergent places as Mexico, Puerto Rico, and the Dominican Republic began celebrating their unity as "Latinos" in the 1970s, just as persons from such distinct places as China, Japan, and Korea came to call themselves "Asian Americans" in the United States. As new panethnic groups, they protested their marginalization and the toxic legacies of racism, militated for political recognition, and petitioned the state for compensatory remedies, demonstrating not only broader levels of interaction among their different national groups but also a heightened sense of oppositional consciousness in relation to the state. [6]

In a 2013 report by the Pew Research Center on Latino self-identification, however, it was found that only 20 percent of those in a national survey called themselves "Hispanic" or "Latino." The majority indicated that they thought of themselves as "Mexicans," "Puerto Ricans," "Cubans," or whatever their country of family origin. [7] Given the complex history of the two terms, we will continue to use the terms *Latino/Latina*, *Hispanic American*, and *Hispanic* interchangeably when a general term is needed. When possible, we will use specific ethnic identifications, such as Mexican American or Cuban American. [8]

Underlying this diversity of national origins and the tendency to identify primarily with one's own subgroup, there are nonetheless two factors that powerfully shape the degree of acceptance and assimilation of all Latino immigrants. The first is their religion. The 70 percent who are Catholics can blend in easily with the largest single church in the United States (69.5 million strong, making up 22 percent of the US population in 2015). Their Catholic heritage is an important piece of cultural capital because it provides entrée into new social circles as they attain education or a higher-status occupation. True, local parishes are sometimes differentiated by status and income levels, but new social connections can be made through new parishes if a person is climbing the social ladder. [9]

The second major factor influencing the fate of Hispanic Americans is skin color and facial features. As various sociological studies have noted, there is great variation in the appearance of Latinos, ranging from a pure "European" look to a Native American look. [10] In most Latin American countries, the lighter-skinned and more European-looking people tend to be in the higher social classes, and the darker-skinned and more Indian-looking people in the lower classes, and there are consistent patterns of discrimination against those with darker skin.[11] As for the people of African descent in these countries, virtually all of whom are descendants of slaves, they are fewer in number and more completely ostracized and isolated than in the United States. As the extreme case of Mexico reveals, Afro-Mexicans primarily live in rural areas and are hesitant to venture very far from their towns and villages of origin.

As we shall show, our own study of the skin color of Hispanics in the corporate elite leads to the same conclusion: it is advantageous to be light skinned.

LATINOS IN THE CORPORATE ELITE

As was the case with African Americans, there was a dramatic increase in the number of Latinos in the corporate elite after the year 2000, with a subsequent leveling off or decline (depending on whether one looks at data on corporate directors or CEOs). We reached this conclusion for corporate directors based on past studies and on the 2011 database that we have used in the previous chapters on Jews and women.

These results revealed that the number of Hispanic directors on *Fortune* 500 boards increased from forty-seven people with sixty-two board seats in 1998 to fifty holding fifty-eight seats in 2001, followed by a big jump in 2005 to sixty-nine people with ninety-five seats. Then, when we looked at the 4,323 men and women who sat on the boards of *Fortune* 500 companies in 2011, we found that there were 107 Latinos (2.4 percent) and twenty-nine Latinas (0.7 percent). Therefore, the proportion of Latinos climbed, slowly, to 3.1 percent in 2011, and there were more than three times as many Latinos as Latinas.

These patterns reveal that although the percentage of Latino *Fortune* 500 directors slowly increased from 1998 to 2011, this was less impressive when one takes into account the fact that Latinos made up about 12 percent of the population in 1998 and now make up about 16 percent. Even though this increase in the general population includes many immigrants and young people who are not likely to be corporate directors, it is clear that Latinos were, and continue to be, underrepresented in terms of corporate directorships.

These findings based on our 2011 data set are in line with the findings of large-scale studies published in recent years by the Alliance for Board Diversity, an organization that includes four important advocacy groups for corporate diversity, one for women (Catalyst), one for African Americans (the Executive Leadership Council), one for Latinos (the Hispanic Association for Corporate Responsibility, or HACR), and one for Asian Americans (the Leadership Education for Asian Pacifics, or LEAP). Their research has looked at *Fortune*-level directors over the years. In their most recent report, they found that the percentage of Latino *Fortune* 500 directors was about 3.3 in 2012 and 3.5 in 2016, with far more Latinos than Latinas. They concluded, as have we, that "African Americans, Hispanics/Latinos and Asian Pacific Islanders have made only small gains or experienced losses in corporate boardroom representation." More generally, they conclude that "the pace at which *Fortune* 500 boards are becoming more diverse is slow."[12]

Although we have considerable confidence in our findings (and those of the Alliance for Board Diversity), it is important to stress that they are not perfect. Deciding who is and who is not Hispanic is not an exact science. As with Jews, names can be misleading. When a reader of *Hispanic Business* wrote to complain that John Castro, the CEO of Merrill Corporation, had been omitted from a list of corporate executives published in the January 1995 issue (along with the list of the "boardroom elite"), the editors replied that "company officials tell us he is not Hispanic."[13] Similarly, Arthur Martinez, the seemingly Latino CEO of Sears, Roebuck from 1992 to 2000, is mostly Irish. As a company spokesperson explained to us when we inquired, "He is mostly of Irish descent. A family member married someone from Spain generations ago, and that is where the name comes from."[14] There are also Hispanics whose names do not reveal that they are Hispanic: in 1994, H. B. Fuller Company selected Walter Kissling, born and raised in Costa Rica, as its CEO.[15]

We also have analyzed the social, educational, and career backgrounds of the ninety-six Latinos and Latinas who sat on *Fortune* 500 boards in 1998, 2001, 2004, and 2005, and the 133 who sat on *Fortune* 500 boards in 2011 (thirty-three of the 2011 directors were already on the earlier, 1998–2005, list, so the new total was 196 rather than 229). The gender difference was large: 158 of the 196, or 81 percent, were men, and thirty-eight, or 19 percent, were women. But, as is the case for African Americans, the Hispanic women were more likely to sit on multiple boards than the men (for the 2011 directors, 34 percent of the women sat on two or more boards, but only 24 percent of the men).

Although the available biographical information is not complete in all cases, almost 60 percent of the men and women on our list seem to have been raised in at least middle-class circumstances in either the United States or elsewhere, slightly lower than the case for white women and Jewish corporate directors, but slightly higher than for African American corporate directors. At least one-third were born outside the United States, and this is more the case for the 2011 directors than those who sat on boards previously, indicating the effects of globalization (the highest number were from Cuba and Mexico, followed by Brazil and Puerto Rico). Only a minority of those on the list of directors could be considered genuine bootstrappers, making their way to the top of corporations without the benefit of family backing or an elite education.

As might be expected from our account of Roberto Goizueta's appointment as CEO at Coca-Cola and the large number of Cuban Americans among the wealthiest Hispanics, many of the *Fortune* 500 directors on our list were either born in Cuba or born into Cuban American families. Most, though not all, of the Cuban Americans had the advantage of being born to parents who were wealthy, well educated, or both. This was true, for example, for Roberto Mendoza, who, like Roberto Goizueta, was born in Cuba and educated at Yale and who became the head of mergers and acquisitions at Morgan Guaranty Trust in 1987, earning him a seat on the board.

And it was also true for Alfonso Fanjul. He and his brother José manage a fifth-generation, privately held family business, Flo-Sun, with cane fields in Florida and Puerto Rico, a leading sugar producer in the United States and the Dominican Republic. Forced to relocate to the United States when Castro came to power, the Fanjuls have by far the worst labor record of any sugar-producing company in the country, frequently violating minimum wage and labor laws with their predominantly Latino migrant labor force. In brushing off criticism of the Fanjuls back in the 1990s, a New York friend of theirs said, "They are completely accepted by society [in Palm Beach]—they hang out with all the best people."[16] As of 2004, the family was estimated to be worth more than $500 million, with an estimated $65 million of its income each year due to government subsidies (and "untold hundreds of millions" from price supports).[17]

In 1996, the *New York Times* reported that, despite his permanent residency in the United States, Alfonso Fanjul (known as "Alfy") had Spanish citizenship. Some critics suggested that he preferred having Spanish citizenship to avoid US estate taxes, but a flap over his large campaign finance donations—Alfy is a major donor to the Democratic Party—led him to claim that he was applying for American citizenship. His brother José (known as "Pepe") contributes to the Republicans (according to the Center for Responsive Politics, the Fanjuls gave millions of dollars to politicians and political committees between 1990 and 2009; they were among the biggest financial supporters of Marco Rubio in his senatorial and presidential campaigns). Though they describe themselves as having political differences, political analysts attribute their donations to both parties simply as a calculated strategy to make sure that, no matter who is elected, they will have political clout.[18]

With the death of Roberto Goizueta, Armando Codina became the most prominent Cuban American in corporate America. He, too, was born to privilege in Cuba—his father was the president of the Senate prior to the revolution—but Codina's route to the corporate elite was more difficult than Goizueta's. Codina's parents, who had divorced when he was young, were able to arrange for him to leave the island in the early 1960s as part of a program run by the Catholic Church called "Operation Peter Pan" (fourteen thousand youngsters participated in this program). He was sent to an orphanage in New Jersey, where he reports that he had a difficult time mixing with children from troubled backgrounds (when he arrived, he recalls, with "fine English flannel suits" that had been made specially for him by a tailor his mother had taken him to in Cuba, many of the other kids gave him a very hard time).[19]

He spent a few years in a foster home in New Jersey and then began college at Jacksonville University in Florida. His mother, who spoke no English and had never worked, was able to leave Cuba, and she came to live with him in Florida. In order to support the two of them, he dropped out of school, worked two jobs, and, with $18,000 that he borrowed from the Small Business Administration, he started a small business, a computer company that handled billing and processed forms for doctors. The business did well; he sold it in 1978 for $4 million and started the Codina Group, a real estate development company that was to be his ticket to the big time.[20]

Active in Republican politics, he became the chairman of the 1980 Bush campaign in Florida. After Bush lost that campaign and became Reagan's vice president, he asked Codina to hire his son, Jeb, as president of his company, which Codina did. Subsequently, as Jeb Bush ran for various offices in Florida—successfully for secretary of commerce and unsuccessfully for governor—he worked intermittently for the firm. While he worked for Codina, however, he made a lot of money. As William Finnegan wrote in the *New Yorker*, "people in Miami say, 'Codina made Jeb a rich man.'"[21] When Jeb Bush won the governorship in 1998, Codina paid him a bonus of $630,000.[22]

Codina continued to support the Bush family—a fundraiser at his house for George W. Bush as he geared up for the 2004 campaign netted $2 million, and he was a key backer in Jeb Bush's failed bid for the Republican nomination in 2016. He also has served on numerous *Fortune*-level boards, including Winn-Dixie, BellSouth Corp, American Airlines, Florida Power and Light, and General Motors. By 2011, however, Codina, at sixty-five years old, no longer sat on any *Fortune* 500 boards.[23]

Several directors are Spanish Americans from New Mexico. These include Katherine Ortega, whose paternal grandparents settled in New Mexico in the late 1880s. Her father owned a café, then a furniture business. Because her father was a lifelong Republican, Ortega likes to say she was "born a Republican."[24] After graduating from Eastern New Mexico State University in 1957 with a degree in business, she started an accounting firm with her sister, which the family turned into the Otero Savings and Loan Association in 1974.

Ortega moved to California in the late 1960s, working first as a tax supervisor for the accounting firm of Peat, Marwick, Mitchell & Company and then as a vice president for Pan American Bank, where her bilingualism was valuable in working with the local Latino community. In 1975, she gained visibility as the first woman president of a California bank, the Latino-owned Santa Ana State Bank. Four years later, she returned to New Mexico as a consultant to her family's saving and loan association, and in 1982, Reagan named her to his Advisory Committee on Small and Minority Business Ownership.[25] From 1983 to 1989, she served in the Reagan administration in the largely ceremonial position of treasurer of the United States. That office gave her the public stature to give one of the keynote speeches at the 1984 Republican presidential convention. In 1989, she left her government position and marketed herself as a corporate director who could provide both Hispanic and female perspectives. By 1995, she sat on no fewer than six boards: Diamond Shamrock, ITT Raynier, Kroger Company, Long Island Lighting, Paul Revere Insurance Group, and Ralston Purina (by 2005, she was only on one *Fortune* 500 board: Kroger).

There are some rags-to-riches stories among the Latino directors. Most of them concern Mexican Americans. Edward Zapanta, for example, was told by his high school counselor that he should become a mechanic like his father, but he went on to earn a BA from UCLA and an MD from USC. He founded a medical clinic in a predominantly Mexican American neighborhood near where he grew up, and he was on the boards of Southern California Edison and the Times Mirror Company. William S. Davila provides another example. Neither he nor his parents graduated from college. Davila started as a stock boy at Von's Markets in 1948 and ended up CEO of the company in 1987 at the age of fifty-six. He retired from the position in 1992 but continued to serve as a director at various companies, including Home Depot, Hormel Foods, and Pacific Gas and Electric; he died in 2014.

Luís Nogales provides another example of a Mexican American rags-to-riches story. Nogales was born in 1943 in the central valley of California, where his parents were farmworkers, albeit farmworkers who bought books on literature and history, in both English and Spanish, and "traveled with their own small library."[26] Nogales attended San Diego State University on a scholarship and graduated from Stanford Law School in 1969. After working for three years as Stanford's liaison to Mexican American students, he went to Washington, DC, as a White House fellow and then became assistant to the secretary of the interior. He returned to the West Coast in 1973 to work for Golden West Broadcasting, owner of the California Angels baseball team as well as radio and television stations. In 1983, he became executive vice president and in 1985 president of United Press International (UPI). When UPI was sold in 1986, he went to work in Spanish-language television for Univision. After negotiating the sale of Univision to Hallmark in 1988, he formed his own investment and consulting company, Nogales Partners, and served on the boards of two *Fortune* 500 companies: KB Home, Inc., and Edison International.

But not all of the Mexican Americans in the sample started at the bottom. Shortly after his graduation from Notre Dame in 1947, Ignacio E. Lozano Jr. became the assistant publisher of *La Opinión*, the highly successful newspaper his father founded in 1926. Now retired, he has served as a director of Bank of America, Walt Disney Company, Pacific Mutual Life, and Pacific Enterprises. His son, José, became the publisher of the paper, and his daughter, Monica, became first the managing editor of the paper (in 1987) and then the president and chief operating officer. In late 2003, the Los Angeles–based *La Opinión* merged with the New York–based *El Diario/La Prensa*, bringing the country's two largest Spanish-language newspapers under one umbrella company called ImpreMedia. At the time of the merger, José became vice chairman and executive vice president of ImpreMedia, and Monica became senior vice president. At that time, she also became the publisher and CEO of *La Opinión*. She has served on the boards of Disney, First Interstate Bank of California, Fannie Mae, and Tenet Healthcare.

Similarly, Enrique Hernández Jr. and Roland Hernández are Mexican Americans who had the advantage of being raised in a well-to-do family. Enrique Hernández Sr., a former police officer, created Inter-Con Security Systems, a company with offices in twenty-five countries that employs more than twenty-five thousand workers. Enrique Jr., a graduate of Harvard, has been on the boards of five *Fortune* 500 companies: Chevron, McDonald's, Nordstrom, Tribune Company (of Chicago), and Wells Fargo. Roland, also a Harvard alumnus, has been a director at Wal-Mart and MGM Mirage.

Latino CEOs and the Corporate Pipeline

The first Latino CEO, Cuban American Roberto Goizueta, became the head of Coca-Cola in 1981, several years before the appointment of the first Asian American CEO (1986), the first woman CEO whose parents did not own the corporation (1986), and the first African American CEO (1999). But it was another fourteen years before the next Latino became a *Fortune* 500 CEO. When Goizueta died in 1997, there were only two. Over the next few years, however, there was the same dramatic increase that occurred for women and African Americans, and by 2005 there had been fourteen Latino CEOs. A year-by-year look at the Latino *Fortune* 500 CEOs in office reveals that the number peaked in 2008 at thirteen. Although the cumulative number continued to increase (as of mid-2017 it was up to twenty-nine), the number in office each year from 2009 through 2014 hovered between nine and twelve; in 2015, it again matched the 2008 peak of thirteen, but in 2016, with four of these CEOs having stepped down, the number dropped back to nine.

Strikingly, there had yet to be a Latina *Fortune* 500 CEO until March 2017, when Geisha Williams, a Cuban-born woman who came at the age of six to the United States when her parents left Cuba in 1967 and trained as an engineer at the University of Miami, was named CEO at PG&E (#166 on the 2016 *Fortune* list). By this time, there had been fifty-one white women, four Asian American women, and one African American woman *Fortune* 500 CEOs.

And, of course, as previously noted, the percentage of Latinos in the national population has increased dramatically in recent years, faster than any other ethnic or racial group. According to the Bureau of the Census, more than 17 percent of the population is Latino, making them the largest ethnic or racial minority group.[27] Therefore, as the Latino population has been growing, the number of Latino CEOs for the most part has stayed flat and recently has declined. At the same time, however, the percentage of whites in the working-age population will begin to decline within the next two decades, and native-born Latinos are increasing their share of good jobs, defined as the top one-quarter of all jobs.[28]

When we conducted a study of the skin color of the new CEOs, a study similar to one that we did on Latino corporate directors for the previous editions of this book, we found that the Latino CEOs were quite light skinned. In fact, based solely on their photographs (but not their names), raters were unable to identify some of them as Latino.[29] This is not news to the Latino CEOs themselves. As Enrique Salem, the CEO of Symantec from 2009 through 2012, told a reporter for *Financial Times*, "To be honest, most people can't tell I'm Hispanic."[30]

Also noteworthy is the fact that eighteen of the twenty-nine Latino CEOs were born outside the United States (six were born in Cuba, three in Spain, two in Mexico, and the others in a range of Spanish-speaking countries). In this respect, they reflect the effects of globalization on the corporate elite, and they are not alone among CEOs in being foreign born (a number of *Fortune* CEOs were born in India, and others were born in Turkey, England, Germany, Morocco, Egypt, and elsewhere).

Below the CEO level, the numbers of Latino executives remain small. As mentioned in chapter 3, for our research on new CEOs we studied the pipeline of those who might be on their way to the CEO office by examining the "leadership teams"—those who report directly to the CEO—using a sample of 307 executives from twenty-five companies on the 2010 *Fortune* 500 list. By far, the majority were white men (66 percent), with white women the next largest group (19 percent). Latinos, like African Americans, were quite underrepresented: only 4.2 percent were Latinos, almost all of whom were men.[31] These figures, along with the recent decline in the number of Latinos serving as CEOs of *Fortune* 500 companies, provide further evidence that diversity is no longer increasing within the power elite.

It is clear that Latinos in the corporate world came a long way in recent decades: there has been a steady, though slow, increase in the number of corporate directors; some Latinos are or have been CEOs of *Fortune*-level companies, though this number is in decline; and there are some who are moving through the pipeline. Latinos, however, remain very much underrepresented in the higher levels of the corporate world.

LATINOS IN THE CABINET

There have not been very many Latinos in presidential cabinets. In some cases, they have been last-minute appointments to help win forthcoming elections, and at times Latinos have been named to positions traditionally not in the cabinet, but given cabinet status (such as the Small Business Administration), apparently to give the impression of greater diversity at the cabinet level.

As of mid-2017, there had been thirteen Latinos in presidential cabinets.[32] Six were appointed by Republicans (Reagan, the two Bushes, and Trump), and seven by Democrats (Clinton and Obama). All except one have been men. Eight of the thirteen have been Mexican Americans, three have been Cuban Americans, one a Dominican American. Eight of the thirteen have been lawyers,

It was not until the very end of Reagan's second term, in 1988, that the first Latino was named to a presidential cabinet, and the appointment was an unexpected and unlikely one at that. On the eve of the Republican convention that year, as his eight years as president were about to end, Ronald Reagan's sudden announcement of Lauro Cavazos, a Democrat and college president, as the new secretary of education may have seemed a bit unusual to the casual eye. But his friend George Bush, who was then vice president, was struggling in his campaign for president at the time, especially in Texas. Because the Democratic nominee for vice president, Lloyd Bentsen, was a popular senator from Texas, the Republicans feared that Bush would lose the state and its many electoral votes. Since Bush had already proclaimed that he would become "the education president" and that he would appoint a Latino to his cabinet, Reagan decided to help matters along with a person who just happened to be a registered Democrat from Texas. In the words of Alicia Sandoval, a spokeswoman for the National Education Association, the appointment of Cavazos was "just a ploy to help get Bush elected and carry Texas . . . a classic case of tokenism."[33] Bush did carry Texas on his way to victory, and he reappointed Cavazos, who served until December of 1990, when he was forced to resign because Bush's advisers considered him ineffectual.[34]

Cavazos grew up on an eight-hundred-thousand-acre ranch, where his father worked for forty-three years as a foreman in the cattle division. He was educated in a one-room schoolhouse for the children of the ranch's Mexican laborers until, when he was eight years old, his father persuaded reluctant officials in a nearby town to let his children attend what had been up to that time an all-Anglo school. After graduating from high school in 1945, Cavazos served for a year in the army, then began what was to become a lengthy and conventional climb through the ranks of academe. First, he received a BA and an MA in zoology from Texas Technological College (now Texas Tech University) and a PhD from Iowa State. After teaching at the Medical College of Virginia for ten years, he left to become professor and chairman of the anatomy department at the Tufts University School of Medicine. He rose through the administrative ranks over the next sixteen years, becoming the dean in 1975. He left in 1980 to return to Texas Tech as president, the position he held when Ronald Reagan came calling.

In January 1993, two Latino men, Henry Cisneros and Federico Peña, became members of Bill Clinton's cabinet. There are some striking similarities between the two. Both were born in Texas in the spring of 1947 into stable middle-class families (Cisneros's father was a civilian administrator for the army, and Peña's father was a broker for a cotton manufacturer). Both attended Catholic schools, received BAs from universities in Texas, went on to earn postgraduate degrees (a doctorate for Cisneros, a law degree for Peña), became the first Latino mayors of the cities in which they lived in the early 1980s (Cisneros of San Antonio in 1981, Peña of Denver in 1983), were reelected throughout the 1980s, and, by the early 1990s, were partners in private investment companies (Cisneros in Asset Management, Peña in Investment Advisors, Inc.). By spring 1995, both were out of the investment business and were being investigated by the Justice Department, Cisneros for allegations that he misled federal investigators during his prenomination interviews about payments he made to a former mistress and Peña in connection with a contract awarded in 1993 to an investment firm he had just left.[35]

In 1996, Janet Reno appointed an independent counsel to look into the accusations against Cisneros. After the election, he resigned from the cabinet and became president of Univision, the largest Spanish television broadcaster in the United States. Although he initially faced eighteen felony counts for having lied to the FBI about the payments he made to his former mistress, in

September 1999 the case was settled when he pleaded guilty to one misdemeanor count of lying to the FBI about the payments; he was fined $10,000 (Clinton pardoned him as he was leaving office). In August 2000, he left Univision to run a newly formed housing company, American-City Vista, that would build affordable housing in downtown urban areas, a company that changed its name to CityView, which he chairs.[36] He is also a partner in an investment banking firm. He sat on the board of Countrywide Financial, one of the major mortgage lenders caught up in the subprime scandal of 2008 (and subsequently sold "at a fire-sale price to Bank of America").[37]

Peña continued as secretary of transportation throughout Clinton's first term and became the secretary of energy at the beginning of Clinton's second term. He resigned from that position after eighteen months, joining Vestar Capital Partners, a New York– and Denver-based investment firm. He became a managing director with Vestar in 2000, and then a "senior adviser" at that firm until October 2016. He joined the board of Wells Fargo in 2011, and as of December 2016 still sat on the board of that company (a company that has paid millions of dollars for violations of federal regulations).[38]

George W. Bush appointed three Latinos to his cabinets: Melquiades ("Mel") Martinez as secretary of housing and urban development, Carlos M. Gutierrez as secretary of commerce, and Alberto Gonzales as attorney general. In December 2003, at the urging of White House strategists, the Cuban-born Martinez resigned from his cabinet position so that he could run for the open Senate seat in Florida (created when Bob Graham sought the Democratic nomination). Martinez won the primary and then won a close race against Betty Castor, the Democratic nominee.

Shortly after the 2004 election, when Bush's secretary of commerce, Donald Evans, announced his resignation, the president named Carlos M. Gutierrez, one of the Latino CEOs discussed earlier in this chapter, as his replacement. As we have noted, Gutierrez was from a wealthy family in Cuba: his father was an exporter of pineapples, and his family was part of what he refers to as "Cuba's high society." When Bush named him, he had been president and CEO at Kellogg since 1999.[39]

Bush's third Latino cabinet appointment, attorney general Alberto Gonzalez, who is also a genuine rags-to-riches story, turned out to be his most controversial. The son of a migrant worker, he received his undergraduate degree from Rice and a law degree from Harvard. He became a partner at what the *New York Times* calls "one of the premier law firms in Texas" before he became general counsel to Bush when he was governor of Texas, and he was counsel to him when he became president in 2001. But his advice to the president about the treatment of prisoners and about torture made him a controversial appointee. In one memo, for example, he advised the president that the Geneva Conventions did not apply to Al Qaeda or Taliban soldiers in Afghanistan or to the prisoners at Guantanamo; along the same lines, he solicited and participated in the preparation of another memo that redefined torture in such a narrow way that it only included physical abuse that produced the kind of pain that accompanies "serious physical injury, such as organ failure" or death. Despite editorial opposition, the Senate confirmed Gonzales.[40] Notably, Gonzalez is the only Latino of the thirteen who have been in the cabinet to hold what political scientist Thomas Cronin considered one of the more important "inner cabinet" positions (state, defense, treasury, and attorney general).[41]

During the first term of his presidency, Barack Obama continued the tradition of appointing Latinos who were atypical, at least as the term usually applies. The first was Ken Salazar, a man with a Spanish heritage dating back to the sixteenth century, who was secretary of the interior from 2009 through 2013. Born in Colorado and raised on the ranch his father, Enrique, had inherited from his father, Salazar attended St. Francis Seminary in Ohio, did his undergraduate work at Colorado College, and then went to law school at the University of Michigan. The other Latino in Obama's cabinet during his first term was Hilda Solis, secretary of labor from 2009 through 2013. She had a considerably different history. Her father, originally from Mexico, worked in a battery recycling plant, and her mother, who was from Nicaragua, was an assembly-line worker. Prior to serving in the cabinet (as the first Hispanic woman ever), she had served five terms in the House of Representatives as a Democrat from California.

When both Salazar and Solis left their positions, there was a period in 2013 when there were no Latinos in the cabinet. Under considerable pressure to diversify his cabinet, Obama then appointed Tom Perez, the son of Dominican parents, to replace Hilda Solis as secretary of labor. Perez, a graduate of Brown and Harvard Law School, was born in Buffalo, New York, where his father was a doctor (his mother's father had been the Dominican ambassador to the United States).[42]

Obama's fourth Latino appointment was Julian Castro, a Mexican American, who became secretary of housing and urban development (HUD) in July 2014. Castro, a three-term mayor of San Antonio, was born in Texas to Mexican American parents. His father was a math teacher, and his mother a political activist who helped establish the political party La Raza Unida. He is the identical twin of Joaquin Castro, a member of the US House of Representatives. Thus, as his second term came to an end, three of Obama's fifteen cabinet members were Latinos (and four of his thirty-two cabinet appointments had been Latinos).

As of late 2017 Trump had appointed one Latino, Alexander Acosta, as secretary of labor. Acosta's parents left Havana for Miami when they were teenagers. According to a story in the *Miami Herald*, as he was growing up, both parents worked while his grandmother took care of him. As of 2004, his father was working in a cellphone store and his mother as a paralegal at a law firm.[43] He attended a prep school in Miami, skipped his senior year, and then went to Harvard for both a BA and law degree. After law school, he clerked for Supreme Court Justice Samuel Alito when Alito was on the US Court of Appeals for the Third Circuit. He had served on the National Labor Relations Board (NLRB), led the Justice Department's Civil Rights Division, was the chairman of the board of U.S. Century Bank, and, at the time of his appointment, was the dean of the law school at Florida International University College of Law.

The majority of the thirteen Latinos who have been in presidential cabinets have come from working- or middle-class backgrounds, but three of the thirteen come from economically privileged backgrounds.

LATINOS IN THE MILITARY ELITE

Although the number of Latinos has been increasing in the military (in 2013, Latinos made up 11.4 percent of active-duty military forces, and about 17 percent of new recruits), the number of Latinos of general officer rank in the armed forces of the United States has remained flat over the last decade. Of the 1,067 people who held that rank in 1985, only two were Latinos (one in the navy, the other in the air force)—at that time, therefore, it was close to 0 percent. By 2004 the number had climbed to 1.7 percent. Thirteen years later, as of March 31, 2017, the percentage was exactly the same: of the 877 who held general officer rank, only fifteen were Latinos—1.7 percent (twelve Latinos, three Latinas). Moreover, there were no Latinos among the thirty-eight men and women who held four-star rank.[44]

There has been only one Hispanic four-star general: Richard E. Cavazos, a Puerto Rican American, who grew up in Texas, the son of a foreman of a ranch in San Antonio. Cavazos joined the army, fought in Korea and in

Vietnam, and rose through the ranks. According to Colin Powell, in 1982, after receiving a poor evaluation, he was considering leaving the army but was talked out of it by Cavazos.[45]

As we did with African Americans in chapter 4, we considered the longer-term prospects for an increasing Latino presence in the top levels of the military by looking at the makeup of current classes at the three major service academies. At West Point, approximately 6.4 percent of the members of the entering class of 2008 were Hispanic; at the Naval Academy, approximately 9 percent of the members of the entering class of 2007 were Hispanic; and at the Air Force Academy, 6.3 percent of the entering classes of 2005 to 2009 were Hispanic.[46] Therefore, although the number of Hispanics in the military has increased dramatically in recent years, this increase has not been matched by corresponding increases in their enrollment at the three major service academies, nor has there been an increase in the last decade of those holding general officer rank. As is the case for women and blacks, the military does not appear to be a great avenue to the power elite for Latinos.

LATINOS IN CONGRESS AND ON THE SUPREME COURT

Due to a concentrated population base in the state of New Mexico and in some congressional districts, Latinos have gradually developed a small amount of political representation in Congress. The story could begin with those few who were elected from the territories of Florida and New Mexico in the nineteenth century or with those elected to the House from Louisiana or New Mexico after 1912, but we will restrict ourselves to the eight senators elected since 1935 and the twenty-seven members of the House first elected after 2005.

The Senate

Until the 2004 elections, there had been only two Latino senators, Dennis Chávez and Joseph Montoya. Both were from Spanish families that had lived on the land in New Mexico since the seventeenth century, and both were lawyers who had gone to Georgetown University. Chavez was appointed to office in 1935 after the elected senator died in a plane crash; he served until 1962, when he died in office. Shortly thereafter, Montoya was elected to the Senate in 1964 after four terms in the House. He was defeated in 1976 after a series of newspaper articles detailed alleged improprieties involving a shopping center he owned in Santa Fe, claiming that he had received "special treatment" from the IRS, whose budget was reviewed by a committee he headed.

After Montoya's defeat in 1976, there was no one in the Senate who could be called a Latino for twenty-eight years, until 2004, when two Latinos were elected. The first was Cuban American Mel Martinez (R-FL), who won a Senate seat in Florida when he left his position as George W. Bush's secretary of housing and urban development to win a close race against the Democratic nominee, a politically moderate former state education commissioner. However, just five years later he resigned from the Senate, and two weeks later he became a lobbyist for an international firm. The other, Ken Salazar (D-CO), was more in the mold of Chavez and Montoya because his family of Spanish descent had been in the Southwest for four centuries; he resigned eight months earlier than Martinez to join the Obama cabinet as secretary of the interior.

Three more Latinos, all men with Cuban backgrounds, have been elected to the Senate since 2004. In January 2006, House member Bob Menendez (D-NJ) became a senator when Jon Corzine, the previous senator, was elected governor of New Jersey and appointed Menendez. At the end of his one-year appointment, Menendez then ran for the office in November 2006 and won reelection. He has a working-class background (his father was a carpenter and his mother a seamstress). Both parents left Cuba in 1953, moving first to New York City and then to New Jersey. Menendez is the first in his family to attend college.

Marco Rubio (R-FL) was elected to the Senate in November 2011. He, too, had previously served in the House of Representatives. His parents left Cuba in 1956 during Batista's regime for better economic opportunities. His father worked for many years as a bartender, and his mother worked at various jobs in retail and in the service industry. After he graduated from high school in Miami, Rubio attended Tarkio College in Missouri for a year on a football scholarship. He then attended a community college in Santa Fe, transferred to and graduated from the University of Florida, and earned a law degree from the University of Miami. He has been called "the crown Prince" of the Tea Party movement. He ran for president in 2016, and, when defeated by Donald Trump, he claimed he was not going to run again for the Senate. He changed his mind, however, and won another term.

The third Cuban American is Ted Cruz (R-TX), who was elected in November 2012. Cruz was born in Canada, where his Cuban American father and American-born mother had settled after leaving Cuba in 1957, two years before Castro came to power (his father had fought for Castro at the age of fourteen, and later became a staunch opponent). In Canada Cruz's parents owned a seismic data processing firm for oil drillers (his father graduated from the University of Texas; his mother graduated from Rice University with a degree in mathematics). Cruz himself is a graduate of Princeton and Harvard Law School, and Cruz, like Rubio, is a Tea Party favorite. Cruz, too, had an unsuccessful bid for the Republican presidential nomination in 2016. His wife, Heidi Cruz, is an investment manager at Goldman Sachs, the controversial investment bank turned commercial bank (as part of his attacks on Cruz during the 2016 presidential campaign, Trump also attacked Heidi Cruz).

In November 2016, the first Latina was elected to the Senate: Catherine Cortez Masto (D-NV), the former attorney general in the state of Nevada, was elected to replace the retiring minority leader, Harry Reid. The daughter of a prominent Mexican American attorney in Las Vegas (her mother is Italian), Masto earned a BA from the University of Nevada, Reno, and a JD from Gonzaga. When Harry Reid decided not to run in 2016, he endorsed Masto, who had served two terms as the Nevada attorney general (Reid was old friends with her father). She won a close race against a Trump supporter who was funded extensively by the conservative billionaires Charles and David Koch.

Therefore, there have been eight Latinos in the Senate, seven men and one woman, five Democrats and three Republicans (all three Republicans have been Cuban Americans, though one, Cruz, was born in Canada). But, as of 2017, there were only three in the Senate, so there is no trend indicating a growing Latino presence in that body.

The House

In 2005, there were twenty-three Latinos in the House. By 2017, the number had increased to thirty-five (a rise from 5.3 to 8.0 percent). The large majority were male (77 percent) and Democrat (also 77 percent). Almost one-third were born outside the United States, with three born in Mexico, three in Puerto Rico, two in Cuba, one in the Dominican Republic, and one in Guatemala. Most went to public high schools, and the few who didn't went to private Catholic schools. All attended college, and most graduated. The large majority went to state schools for their undergraduate work, though one went to Yale, one to Harvard, one to Dartmouth, and two to Stanford. About half (seventeen of the thirty-five) did graduate work, most frequently a law degree (and mostly at state schools, though three went to Harvard). One, Raul Ruiz (D-CA), elected to the House in 2013, has an MD from Harvard (he is the son of farmworkers, and did his undergraduate work at UCLA).

We don't have evidence on the class backgrounds for each one, but based on those for whom we do have information we estimate that about three-fourths grew up either in working- or middle-class homes (their parents, for example, were farm laborers, worked in factories or restaurants, or were schoolteachers), The other one-fourth came from either upper- or upper-middle-class families (that is, families that we estimate to have been in the top 15 percent of the class structure). In some cases their parents were professionals (for example, Michelle Lujan Grisham, D-NM, is the daughter of a dentist, and Filemon Vela Jr., D-TX, is the son of a judge); some of the parents of others were successful politicians.

The Supreme Court

The most striking Latino addition to the power elite in the past decade was the appointment in 2009 of Sonia Sotomayor to the Supreme Court. Sotomayor, born in the Bronx to Puerto Rican parents, is the first person of Latino origin to sit on the Supreme Court, and the third of four women, with three of those four women serving on the court as of mid-2017. Her father, who had only a third-grade education, and who had a serious alcohol problem, died when she was nine, and she was raised by her mother, who worked as a telephone operator and as a practical nurse. In addition to the death of her father and being raised by a single mother, she was a childhood diabetic (as she puts it in her moving memoir, *My Beloved World*, "The challenges I have faced—among them material poverty, chronic illness, and being raised by a single mother—are not uncommon, but neither have they kept me from uncommon achievements"). After graduating from Cardinal Spellman High School as valedictorian, she attended Princeton on a full scholarship and graduated summa cum laude; she then graduated from Yale Law School, where she was the editor of the law review.[47] (Eight of the nine members of the court in 2014 were graduates of either the Yale or Harvard Law Schools; the ninth is a graduate of Columbia Law School.)

Sotomayor worked in the district attorney's office in New York for four years after her graduation, and then joined a corporate law firm, becoming a partner in 1988. She left the firm in 1992 after her appointment to the US District Court for the Southern District in New York by Republican president

George H. W. Bush. She gained the enduring gratitude of baseball fans across the United States in 1995 by ending a lengthy Major League Baseball strike with an injunction against the team owners, which stopped them from unilaterally instituting a new collective bargaining agreement and using replacement players. When Democratic president Bill Clinton nominated her to the US Court of Appeals in 1998, Senate Republicans tried to block her appointment. She was eventually confirmed, and President Obama appointed her to the Supreme Court in 2009.

Until the death of Antonin Scalia and the appointment of Neil Gorsuch (raised a Catholic but now a member of an Episcopal church), Sotomayor was one of six Catholics on the court, but she has voted with the three Jewish members, two of whom are women, especially when there is a liberal-conservative split on social issues. However, along with most other members of the court, five of whom (like Sotomayor) worked as corporate lawyers early in their careers, she usually supports the US Chamber of Commerce position when issues concerning corporations are brought before the court.[48] In that regard, the corporate community is well served by a strong majority on the Supreme Court, whatever their political background, ethnicity, religion, or gender.

CONCLUSION

Hispanic Americans are part of the corporate community and will continue to be included, especially those with light skin, high-status social backgrounds in their ancestral countries, or both. Such people are racially and culturally similar to the Europeans who came directly to the United States. However, due to their origins in several different Latin American countries, they add an international flavor to the American power elite in an age of increasing corporate globalization. In the case of Cuban Americans, they build on a strong immigrant business community in southern Florida that will continue to generate a disproportionate number of new members in the corporate elite.

The acceptance of light-skinned Hispanic Americans into American society in general and the corporate elite in particular can be seen most clearly in the marriage partners of three of the women corporate directors we have highlighted in this chapter. Vilma Martínez married Stuart Singer, a fellow lawyer, in 1968. Patricia Díaz married Michael Dennis, also a lawyer, also in 1968, and she goes by the surname of Díaz Dennis. Katherine Ortega also married a lawyer, Lloyd Derrickson, in 1989.

The military has not been as important an avenue of upward mobility for Latinos and Latinas as it has for African Americans, but it has not been notable for discrimination against Latinos in the past either. As for participation in the political arena, our conclusions are more tentative because there have been so few cabinet appointees and elected officials to study. As with the other groups, though, appointed officials tend to come from higher socioeconomic backgrounds and to be present in both Republican and Democratic administrations. Elected officials, on the other hand, with the important exception of Cuban Americans, tend to come from the middle and lower levels of the society and to be Democrats. It is likely that Mexican Americans from the labor movement will play an increasing role in the Democratic Party, forcing the Republicans to redouble their efforts to recruit well-to-do Hispanics of all ethnic backgrounds to maintain their claims to diversity and inclusiveness.

Mostly, though, our updated look at Latinos in the power elite indicates that they have lost ground. In some cases, such as Latino CEOs of *Fortune* 500 corporations, the numbers have declined. Even when the numbers have increased somewhat (as in the percentage of Latino corporate directors), this must be considered in the context of their being the fastest-growing group in the country—in 1980 Latinos made up 6.5 percent of the population, and by 2014 that figure was up to 17.3 percent.[49] Moreover, with the exception of the appointment of Sotomayor to the Supreme Court and Geisha Williams as CEO of PG&E, most of the newly arrived Latinos in the power elite have been men, not women. Finally, given the consistently negative things Donald Trump had to say during his campaign for the presidency about Mexican Americans, and more generally about all immigrants, when combined with the fact that a large majority of Latinos voted for Hillary Clinton, it may be a while before Latinos increase their presence in the power elite in a meaningful way.

Chapter Six

Asian Americans and South Asians in the Power Elite

The label *Asian American* is every bit as ambiguous, and problematic, as *Hispanic* or *Latino*. The immigrant groups from a wide range of Asian countries included under that label do not share a common language, national heritage, or immigration pattern. The term *Asian American* first appeared in 1968 in an effort to develop some pan-Asian organizations in order to resist discrimination and ensure a fair share of social services at the local level. However, these different groups often remain wary of one another because of historic enmities between their native countries. [1]

Moreover, we have concluded that our previous use of the umbrella term *Asian Americans* to include people from many cultural backgrounds was even more limited than we realized. Further research, and the unforeseen rise of new "Asian American" groups, reveals that "South Asians," mostly from India, but also from Pakistan, Bangladesh, and Sri Lanka, must be analyzed and treated as a separate group. They had a very different migratory path several thousand years ago, from west to east, and remained distinct from the Asian migrants to their east. As a result, they have cultural backgrounds that are quite different from the Chinese Americans, Japanese Americans, and Korean Americans who were central to the Asian American category that was created in the late 1960s and widely used for the next several decades. In fact, the relatively sudden rise of South Asians to positions of importance in the early twenty-first century, almost all of whom arrived in the United States after they had finished their BA degrees in other countries, has added yet another new and unique dimension to American diversity because of their centuries of speaking English in their native countries, all of which were British colonies. In addition, many of them went to British-style universities that were part of their countries' colonial heritage or to elite universities in Great Britain itself. Although there were a few immigrants to the United States as early as 1820, there were only 12,000 Indian Americans in 1960, and there was no real growth until changes in immigrations laws in 1990 attracted a stream of educated urban young people who now make up the second-largest immigrant group after Mexicans. Then, too, India is now second only to China in sending foreign students to American universities. In this chapter, therefore, we will use a large umbrella term, *Asian Americans and South Asians*, and within that term there are two categories, Asian Americans (mostly Chinese, Japanese, and Korean Americans) and South Asians (mostly Indians born in the United States or who immigrated).

There are four generalizations that hold for at least the three groups that were traditionally considered Asian Americans in our work and the work of others—Japanese Americans, Chinese Americans, and Korean Americans. First, they are very highly educated, either in their country of origin or in the United States.[2]

Second, and not fully appreciated in understanding the acceptance of Asian Americans by white Americans, based on a 2012 survey of Asian Americans by the Pew Research Center, 48 percent of Asian Americans identify themselves as Christians, more than any other category of responses (26 percent said they were unaffiliated, and only 14 percent said they were Buddhists, followed by Muslims at 4 percent). Thus, the seeming cultural "gap" between Euro Americans and immigrants from Asian countries is not so great when it comes to this intimate and important cultural issue, which provides a collective way to deal with anxiety-arousing transitions (birth, arrival to adulthood, marriage, and death). Christianity is strongest among Korean Americans, whose families in Korea began to adopt the religion at the turn of the twentieth century as a reaction to pressures from China and Japan. Japanese Americans and Chinese Americans also attend Christian churches founded by Korean Americans.[3]

Third, many Asian Americans historically have been "middlemen" in the United States in more ways than one, owing partly to their educational backgrounds, partly to their concentration in small businesses. Asian Americans in California, for example, say that in both large corporations and government agencies they often become middle managers, taking orders from white bosses and giving orders—and termination notices—to Hispanic and African

American workers; some of them cynically call themselves a "racial bourgeoisie."[4] But Asian Americans also often end up as middlemen in a second and more traditional sense, as small-business owners providing services and retailing in or near ghettoes and barrios, marketing the products of big corporations in areas where companies such as Safeway, Sears, and Revco do not wish or dare to tread. This role has been especially common among Korean Americans in major cities such as New York and Los Angeles, and this has led to some highly visible confrontations with African Americans and Mexican Americans.[5]

Fourth, there is evidence that many Asian Americans have faced difficulties in advancing to the highest levels of large organizations. They are stereotyped as lacking in "interpersonal" and "leadership" skills and in their written or spoken English. Thus, despite high levels of educational attainment and considerable evidence of their general acceptance by white Americans, it is likely to be very difficult for very many of them to reach the highest levels of the power structure.[6]

ASIAN AMERICANS AND SOUTH ASIANS IN THE CORPORATE ELITE

Corporate Directors

When we looked at Asian American corporate directors for the previous editions of this book, using various strategies to identify them, our estimate was that the number of Asian Americans represented less than 1 percent (we used not only the *Fortune* 500, but also the *Fortune* 1000, and the *Standard & Poor's* 1500).[7] For this edition of the book, we drew on the sample of 4,323 men and women who sat on the boards of directors of *Fortune* 500 companies in 2011—the same data set we have used in the previous chapters on Jews, women, blacks, and Latinos. In this sample, 104, or 2.4 percent, were either Asian Americans or South Asians (eighty-five were men; nineteen were women). Slightly over half of these, fifty-eight, were Chinese (thirty-nine), Japanese (fifteen), or Korean (four), so 1.34 percent of the total number of directors were Asian Americans; the remaining forty-six were South Asians, thus 1.06 percent of the total, and most of these were from India (thirty-four). Therefore, the percentage of both Asian and South Asian *Fortune* 500 corporate directors had increased somewhat by 2012, but not a great deal. Moreover, it must be kept in mind that, according to the 2010 US census, there were 17.3 million Asian Americans, 5.6 percent of the total population (up from 4.2 percent in the 2000 census). Therefore, although Asian Americans and South Asians have increased their presence among corporate directors, they still are quite underrepresented when compared with their presence in the larger population.

Population data indicate that within the Asian American population, the largest groups were Chinese (3.79 million, or 22 percent of the Asian American population), Filipino (3.41 million, or 20 percent), Indian (3.18 million, or 18.4 percent), Vietnamese (1.73 million, 9.8 percent), Korean (1.7 million, 9.8 percent), and Japanese (1.3 million, 7.5 percent). When we compare the percentages of corporate directorships within the Asian and South Asian group of 104 with the population data, we find that the Chinese Americans were overrepresented, at 36.6 percent, as were the Indian Americans, at 33 percent, and the Japanese Americans, at 14 percent, but the Filipinos (only 1 percent), Vietnamese Americans (only 1 percent), and Korean Americans (3.8 percent) were underrepresented.

These patterns are even clearer when we look at the seventeen Asian American and South Asian men and women who sat on more than one corporate board in 2011. Eight of the seventeen were Indian Americans, six were Chinese Americans, two were Japanese Americans, and one was from Pakistan. As six of the seventeen were, or had been, CEOs of *Fortune* 500 companies, let us turn to a more careful look at the patterns that emerge when we look at the Asian American and South Asian CEOs, and then we will look at just who some of these CEOs are.

Similarly, there is evidence that Asian Americans are underrepresented not only on boards, but within the companies at the highest ranks. A 2012 study found that Asian Americans held only 1.5 percent of the corporate officer positions at all *Fortune* 500 companies, and a much-publicized 2015 study of five major Silicon Valley firms (Google, Hewlett-Packard, Intel, LinkedIn, and Yahoo) found that the higher one went in the company, the lower the percentage of Asian Americans (the opposite pattern was the case for women). This has led some to refer to a "bamboo ceiling," and to claim that the bamboo ceiling is "worse than the glass ceiling effect that's been identified for women."[8]

CEOs

Although there had been only thirteen Asian American and South Asian CEOs a decade ago when the previous edition of this book was published, the number is now up to twenty-nine. When we look not at the total number who have been CEOs (a number that, obviously, can only increase), but the number who were serving as CEO each year, some clear and revealing patterns emerge. The first striking observation, one that corresponds to previous findings for African Americans, Latinos, and, in the last few years, white women, is that the number of Asian American and South Asian CEOs reached its peak a few years ago—in this case, in 2011. There were eight in 2000, a number that increased steadily until 2011, when there were thirteen. Since that time, the number dropped: there were still thirteen in 2012, but eight in 2013, nine in 2014, ten in 2015, and ten at the end of 2016.

A second pattern has to do with which groups were represented among the CEOs, and when. Two of the first three were Chinese Americans (and three of the first nine), but only one of the last ten. In contrast, none of the first three Asian American CEOs was Indian born or of Indian background, and only one of the first six, but six of the last ten have been Indians.

Almost all, twenty-five of the twenty-nine, are men (86 percent), and only four are women. Similarly, almost all, twenty-three of the twenty-nine (79 percent), were born abroad—twelve in India, five in either Shanghai or Taiwan, two in Canada, one in Pakistan, one in Kenya, one in South Korea, one in Sri Lanka, and one in Bangladesh. They are quite well educated. Most, but not all, have bachelor's degrees (two dropped out as undergraduates—Sanjay Kumar, CEO of Computer Associates from 2000 to 2004, and Wayne Inouye, CEO of Gateway from 2004 to 2006), and they have among them thirteen master's degrees, eleven MBAs, and six PhDs. Many attended elite schools in their home countries (for example, in India, the Indian Institute of Technology), and many attended, either as undergraduates or for postgraduate work, elite schools in the United States (including Harvard, Yale, Princeton, Columbia, MIT, the University of Chicago, Berkeley, and Stanford).

We don't have sufficient information for all twenty-nine of them about their parents' occupations and educational backgrounds, but for those for whom we do have information (twenty of the twenty-nine), we conclude that about 80 percent come from either upper-class or upper-middle-class backgrounds. For example, the father of Fred Hassan, the CEO of Pharmacia and then Schering Plough from 1997 to 2009, is the son of the first ambassador from Pakistan to India. Andrea Jung, the CEO of Avon from 1999 to 2012, is the daughter of a chemical engineer (her mother) and an architect (her father). The father of Vikram Pandit, the CEO of Citigroup from 2007 to 2012, was the executive director of Sarabhai Chemicals. Only four were from middle- or working-class backgrounds, and two of the four were Japanese Americans (Ko Nishimura, the CEO of Selectron from 1992 to 2003, whose father started at Berkeley, but was interned during World War II and ended up working in a fruit stand, and Wayne Inouye, former CEO of Gateway, whose parents also were interned; after they were released, they bought a farm, which did well in some years, but not so well in other years).

As of mid-2017, the longest-serving CEO from either an Asian American or South Asian background was Indra Nooyi, who became CEO of PepsiCo in 2006. Nooyi is the only woman among the six people of Indian background who were *Fortune* 500 CEOs in 2016. Born in Madras, Nooyi spent her first twenty-three years in India. She received a BA from Madras Christian College, and then an MBA from the India Institute of Management in Calcutta before she came to the states to study at the Yale School of Management. As a Brahmin from a traditional family, she was surprised that her parents allowed her to study in the states. As she says, "It was unheard of for a good, conservative, south Indian Brahmin girl to do this. It would make her an absolutely unmarriageable commodity." After she received an MA degree from Yale, she worked for Boston Consulting Group, then Motorola, and then, beginning in 1994, PepsiCo, where she rose through the ranks to become president and chief financial officer.

In 2010 Ajay Banga, born in India to a Sikh family, became the CEO of MasterCard. We realized that things had really changed at the top of the corporate elite when he was appointed. In our earliest studies of the women and the men of color who had become directors of major corporations, we emphasized the need for identity management. There are various ways that potential corporate directors can signal that they are willing and able to work effectively with the white men they are about to join on boards of directors. We drew on some memorable anecdotes that described such behavior: as we have noted in chapter 3, one woman director told a story about how she had smoked cigars with the guys at her first board meeting as a way to let them know she was one of them, and another explained that when she became a senior executive at an energy company she realized that she had to take up golf. In terms of appearance, we concluded that African Americans were unlikely to wear dashikis and Jews were unlikely to wear yarmulkes.[9]

Banga, the son of a general in the Indian army, received his bachelor's degree in economics from Delhi University and an MBA from the elite Indian Institute of Management. He worked for Nestlé, and then PepsiCo, before joining Citigroup. While at Citigroup, he managed the company's overseas credit card and banking businesses, and he oversaw the bank's operations in Asia. Given that seven other Indians had become *Fortune* 500 CEOs, and given his considerable experience with Citicorp, Banga's appointment did not surprise us. We did, however, take careful notice of his photograph in the *New York Times*, which showed him wearing a turban. As the *New York Times* explained, Banga is "a Sikh and wears the turban that distinguishes worshipers of his religion"[10] His appointment, therefore, suggested another breakthrough at the top, one that signaled that appearance no longer needed to conform quite so rigidly to the dominant white male (and Christian) model to which we had become so accustomed.

The reason that Ajay Banga's strikingly atypical appearance was more acceptable to the MasterCard board became clear later that year. Just one day after India announced that it planned to give identity cards to its 1.2 billion citizens, Banga arrived in Mumbai in the hopes of securing a contract for the company to implement such a massive undertaking. Born, raised, and educated in India, and, as we have noted, having previously held management-level jobs in that country at Nestlé and PepsiCo, Banga knew the country and the culture. Although there was no guarantee that MasterCard would get this lucrative contract, as the *New York Times* explained, "MasterCard hopes that Mr. Banga's ability to glide among cultures, languages and borders gives it an edge."[11]

In addition to the identity card account, Banga hoped that millions of middle-class Indians would choose MasterCard for their credit cards, prepaid debit cards, or other mobile payment systems. He was aware that future business growth for MasterCard was going to depend on winning battles for the growing middle classes in countries such as India. As he noted, estimating the size of the emerging global middle class over the next five years, "Whether it's 200 million or 400 million, it's a lot of millions."[12]

Banga, perhaps more than any of the other Latino, Asian American, and South Asian CEOs, demonstrates the increasingly global nature of the *Fortune* 500 and the potential benefits of appointing a new CEO who is "not from around here."

The Asian American and South Asian directors and CEOs, therefore, tend to be male, foreign born, well educated, and generally from privileged backgrounds. The Chinese Americans and Indian Americans are overrepresented, although, as our findings on CEOs indicate, there has been a decided shift over time toward those with Indian backgrounds.

ASIAN AMERICANS AND SOUTH ASIANS
IN THE POLITICAL ELITE

There now have been four Asian Americans in presidential cabinets, but it was not until 2000 that the first one was named. In the final months of his second term, President Clinton nominated Norman Y. Mineta, a Japanese American, to be secretary of commerce. After the Supreme Court finally settled the 2000 election, George W. Bush named Mineta to be secretary of transportation. In addition, as we noted in the chapter on women, Bush named Elaine Chao to be his secretary of labor.

Mineta, born in 1932, was ten years old when he and his family were taken from their home in California to an internment camp in Wyoming. After graduating from Berkeley, he joined the army, where he served as an intelligence officer in Korea and Japan. He returned home to San Jose, California, where he worked in his father's insurance agency until he became active in politics, rising from city council, to mayor, to the US Congress, in which he served from 1976 to 1995. While in the House, he helped to pass legislation that granted $20,000 to every Japanese American who had been interned during World War II. He resigned from the Congress in 1995 with a year to go in his term to become a senior vice president at Lockheed Martin (a decision that made many of his Democratic colleagues and constituents unhappy, especially when a Republican was chosen in a special election as his replacement). After five years in the corporate world, he joined Clinton's cabinet in 2000, and was secretary of transportation until 2006.[13]

As we explained in chapter 3, Elaine Chao, a Chinese American, was born in Taiwan and came to the United States when she was eight. Hers is a classic Chinese American success story: her parents were well educated and well connected, and after leaving China and then Hong Kong, her hard-working father came to the United States and built a thriving international shipping and trading business. Chao received a BA from Mt. Holyoke and an MBA from Harvard. She became an investment banker with Citicorp from 1979 to 1983 and then spent 1983 and 1984 in Washington, DC, as a White House Fellow during Reagan's first term. She then took a job as a vice president for syndications at the Bank of America and, while working for the bank in California, became more involved in Republican politics, chairing a national committee of Asian Americans for George H. W. Bush and Dan Quayle in 1988. This earned her appointments as deputy administrator of the Maritime Administration and later as deputy secretary of the Department of

Transportation before she became the director of the Peace Corps, a position she held for less than a year, and then, from 1992 to 1996, the president of the United Way of America (and a director at Dole Foods). In 1993, she married Kentucky senator Mitch McConnell, the very conservative Republican who has been a senator from Kentucky since 1985 and the Senate majority leader since 2015. Prior to her appointment to the cabinet she had become an expert on philanthropy at the Heritage Foundation, a right-wing think tank. She was secretary of labor from 2001 through 2009, and then returned to the Heritage Foundation and was a commentator on Fox News. She has been on the boards of Citigroup, Dole Foods, News Corp, Wells Fargo, and Vulcan Materials. When Trump chose his cabinet and named her secretary of transportation, she was one of the few people he nominated who was not a wealthy white Christian male. [14]

Obama named two Asian Americans to his cabinets: Steven Chu, a Chinese American, as secretary of energy, and Gary Locke, a Chinese American, as secretary of commerce. Obama also named Eric Shinseki, a Japanese American, as secretary of veterans' affairs, but as we noted in chapter 2, because of the inconsistency across presidencies with this and some other cabinet-level appointments, we have not included it as a cabinet position.

Chu, a Nobel Prize–winning physicist, served as Obama's secretary of energy from 2009 through 2013. His parents both were born in China, the children of educators (Chu's grandfather was a college professor before becoming the president of Tianjin University). His parents came to the United States where his father earned a PhD in chemical engineering and his mother studied economics. Steven was born in St. Louis (his father was teaching at Washington University), went to high school there, did his undergraduate work in math and physics at the University of Rochester, and then earned a PhD in physics at Berkeley. He worked at Bell Labs, where he and some coworkers did the research on "laser cooling" that was to earn him the Nobel Prize. He left Bell in 1987 to teach physics at Stanford, and in 2004 moved to a joint appointment at the Lawrence Berkeley National Laboratory and the University of California, Berkeley, physics department.

Although Eric Shinseki held a cabinet-level position but not a traditional cabinet post, we will describe him and his background in some detail because there have been so few Asian Americans in cabinets, and because of the prominent role he has played in both the military and the political elite. Shinseki became known to many Americans because of his rise through the military elite. When he retired as a four-star general, he was the highest-ranking Asian American in military history. He grew up in Hawaii, and attended public schools. His father managed a Ford dealership, and his mother was a beautician. An excellent student, a fine athlete, and a student leader at Kauai High School, he won an appointment to the US Military Academy at West Point and later earned a master's degree in English literature from Duke University.

During his thirty-eight-year career in the army, he won two Purple Hearts for life-threatening injuries in Vietnam, commanded NATO soldiers in Germany and in Bosnia-Herzegovina, and spent four years on the Joint Chiefs of Staff. His years on the Joint Chiefs of Staff were marked by disagreements with the civilian leadership in the Pentagon, especially George W. Bush's secretary of defense, Donald Rumsfeld. Because Shinseki had already challenged Rumsfeld on earlier decisions, Rumsfeld was particularly annoyed when Shinseki and other military men publicly differed with his confident assertion that the United States needed no additional troops to stabilize Iraq after the initial invasion. In fact, Shinseki drew rebukes from Rumsfeld and other administration officials when he told a congressional committee that the United States would need as many as two hundred thousand troops as a peacekeeping force in Iraq. In a speech that Shinseki gave at his retirement ceremony in June 2003, he did not mention Rumsfeld by name (he did not have to) as he warned against arrogance: "You can certainly command without that sense of commitment, but you cannot lead without it. Without leadership, command is a hollow experience, a vacuum often filled with mistrust and arrogance."[15]

In 2009, Obama appointed Shinseki as secretary of veterans' affairs, a department that was plagued with decades-long problems that included overwhelmed facilities and management failures. Shinseki served until his resignation in 2014 in the aftermath of a scandal that involved ongoing questions about substandard care and long waits for care, but also, and most troublesome, false records that covered up these problems.[16]

Obama also appointed Gary Locke, a Chinese American, as the secretary of commerce. Locke was born in Seattle; his father was a sergeant in the army in World War II, and then ran a grocery store. His mother was born in Taiwan. Locke spent his early years in a housing project. After high school (and becoming an Eagle Scout), he won a scholarship that allowed him to attend Yale as an undergraduate, and he earned a law degree from Boston University. He then moved back to Seattle, won election to the state house, where he served for eleven years, and became governor of Washington (the first Chinese American governor in the country). He served as secretary of commerce until 2014, when Obama appointed him the ambassador to China.

No South Asians have been appointed to presidential cabinets. However, early in his presidency Donald Trump appointed a South Asian, Nikki Haley, then the governor of South Carolina, who was born in South Carolina to parents who had emigrated from India, to be the ambassador to the United Nations. At birth, Haley was named Nimrata Randhawa; her father is a college professor and her mother a lawyer-turned-businesswoman. A graduate of Clemson, with a degree in accounting, Haley worked in her mother's multimillion-dollar international clothing business before she won a seat in the South Carolina House of Representatives in 2004, and was elected governor of South Carolina in 2010. Although a staunch Republican conservative on issues such as abortion, immigration, and tax reform, after the mass shooting in a Charleston church Haley changed her previous position and supported removing the Confederate flag from the statehouse grounds. [17]

ASIAN AMERICANS AND SOUTH ASIANS IN THE MILITARY ELITE

In spite of the aspersions cast upon their patriotism and their bitter internment experience, Japanese Americans volunteered for service in World War II and fought courageously throughout Europe. Two future Democratic senators from Hawaii, Daniel Inouye and Spark Matsunaga, both decorated for bravery on the field of battle, used veterans' organizations in Hawaii as their political base in winning elections. Japanese Americans also served in such important roles as intelligence officers and interrogators of prisoners in the war with Japan. Nonetheless, the military has never been a major avenue of mobility for Japanese Americans, and none had reached the highest levels of the military elite until Eric K. Shinseki became army chief of staff, and, thus, a member of the Joint Chiefs of Staff.

A 2012 report by the military indicated that 3.7 percent of all active-duty members of the military were Asian (this report did not separate out Asian Americans and South Asians), and 4.4 percent of all "active-duty officers" (there were 238,861 total, 10,291 of whom were Asian). As of March 31, 2017, nineteen of the 877 men and women who held general officer rank were Asian Americans, or 2.2 percent. Seventeen of the nineteen were male, and as of mid-2017, only one of the thirty-eight men and women who held four-star rank was Asian American (a male, Admiral Harry B. Harris Jr., who was born in Japan to a Japanese mother and a father who was a chief petty officer in the US Navy).[18]

Just as Eric Shinseki became known for the leadership he provided in the military elite (before holding a cabinet-level position, and thus becoming a part of the political elite), another Asian American, a Filipino general named Antonio Taguba, became known to many outside the military during the Iraq war. Taguba was born in Manila, and his family moved to Hawaii when he was ten. After graduating from Leilehua High School and from Idaho State University, he, too, joined the army and followed in the footsteps of his father, Tomas, a career military man (Tomas was captured and tortured by the Japanese when they invaded the Philippines in 1941). Taguba rose through the ranks, accumulating three master's degrees as he did so, emerging as an acting director of the army staff during the Iraq war. He was appointed to inquire into the activities of the police brigade at the Abu Ghraib prison. The report that he issued chronicled a long list of "sadistic, blatant and wanton criminal abuses," including "egregious acts and abuses of international law." Seymour Hersh, in a *New Yorker* article, referred to Taguba's report as "devastating" and praised Taguba for "fearlessly" taking issue with orders that were given at the prison by various people in charge, including three-star general Ricardo Sanchez. A retired army major general interviewed by Hersh explained that Taguba's report flew in the face of pressures from the Pentagon: "He's not regarded as a hero in some circles of the Pentagon. He's the guy who blew the whistle, and the Army will pay the price for his integrity. The leadership does not like to have people make bad news in public."[19] A few years later, in 2008, Taguba wrote the preface to a report by the Physicians for Human Rights on the abuse of prisoners at Abu Ghraib and in Afghanistan. In that preface, he pulled no punches when it came to the issue of torture and war crimes committed by the Bush administration: "There is no longer any doubt that the current administration committed war crimes. The only question is whether those who ordered torture will be held to account."[20]

As noted above, as of March 31, 2017, there were nineteen Asian Americans with general officer rank (2.2 percent). This could increase over time, as there has been an increase in the number of Asians at the three service academies. Recent data indicate that about 9–10 percent of those entering the Naval Academy, West Point, and the Air Force Academy were of Asian background.[21] Despite the reputation of the armed forces as the most diversified institution in America and the recent increase in the number of students at the three service academies, there is little evidence that the military represents a likely route to the power elite for very many Asian Americans. As one writer put it, "Asian Pacific Americans are at the bottom of the totem pole in the military ranks."[22]

ASIAN AMERICANS AND SOUTH ASIANS IN CONGRESS

The Senate

There now have been eight Asian Americans or South Asians in the Senate. All of the first five, whose time in the Senate spanned from 1959 through 2013, were Asian Americans (three Japanese Americans and two Chinese Americans); all were men; four were from Hawaii and one was from California. Then, in the 2012 election, a Japanese American woman was elected (also from Hawaii), and in 2016, two more women, one with Thai in her background, the other with some Indian ancestry, were elected, one from Illinois, and one from California. Therefore, as of late 2017, there were three Asian or South Asian Americans in the Senate—all women. They very much reveal the changing nature of those who are providing diversity in the power elite.

The first Asian American elected to the US Senate was Hiram Fong of Hawaii, a Chinese American. His father had been an indentured servant on a sugar plantation and his mother a maid. Fong (who changed his name early in his adult life from Yau Leong to Hiram) earned a BA at the University of Hawaii in 1930 and, in 1935, a law degree from Harvard. He then returned to Hawaii to begin his political career. He won his first political race in 1938 for a seat in the Territorial House of Representatives. By 1959, when Hawaii entered the Union as the fiftieth state and Fong won one of the two Senate seats, he had amassed a fortune.[23]

The second Asian American senator was Daniel Inouye, a Japanese American born in Honolulu in 1924, and, as noted earlier, a decorated military World War II hero. He served in the House for four years and, in 1963, became the first Asian American Democrat elected to the Senate. His father was a file clerk. Following his service in World War II, where he lost his arm in the fighting in Italy, Inouye earned a bachelor's degree from the University of Hawaii and a law degree from George Washington University, then entered the political arena, where he remained for the rest of his life. He was reelected for the ninth time in 2010, but two years later, in December 2012, he died at the age of eighty-eight (his last word was "Aloha").[24]

The third Asian American senator, Spark Matsunaga, from a poor immigrant Japanese family, worked many different jobs as a teenager, then graduated from the University of Hawaii in 1941 and served in World War II. After his highly decorated war service, he used the GI Bill to earn a law degree at Harvard and returned to Hawaii to serve as a Honolulu prosecutor and involve himself in Democratic Party politics. He won a seat in the House in 1962 and defeated Hiram Fong in 1976 to join Inouye in the Senate. When Matsunaga died in 1990, a fourth Asian American, Daniel Akaka, of Hawaiian and Chinese heritage, won his seat. Akaka, whose father had a third-grade education and worked in a machine shop, went to the University of Hawaii on the GI Bill, earning his BA in education, and worked as a teacher, principal, and program specialist for the state's Department of Education before winning a seat in the House in 1976 with 80 percent of the vote. He became the first native Hawaiian in Congress (native Hawaiians, who constitute 20 percent of the population, are defined as those with indigenous ancestors who lived in the islands before the US Marines toppled the monarchy in 1893).[25]

The fifth Asian American senator, and the only one from a mainland state, would have to be classified as atypical whatever his social or ethnic background, and he was not born in the United States. S. I. Hayakawa, a one-term Republican senator from California from 1975 to 1981, was born in 1906 in Canada, where his well-to-do Japanese parents had an import-export business. Hayakawa completed his BA and MA in Canada, and then came to the United States to earn a PhD in English and American literature at the University of Wisconsin in 1953. He somehow developed a fascination with pseudoscientific claims about "general semantics," and in 1949, he wrote a best-selling popular book, *Language in Thought and Action*. Hayakawa taught at San Francisco State University starting in 1955 and became a vice president there in 1968. His confrontational stance toward antiwar and civil rights protesters made him a conservative celebrity. His theatrics led to his elevation to the presidency of the campus. He switched his registration from Democratic to Republican and won his Senate seat in 1974, receiving little support from Japanese American voters. He was an abysmal failure as a legislator, falling asleep at inopportune moments, making inappropriate remarks, and generally ignoring the details of his position. Voters rejected him for a Democrat in 1980, despite the general Republican sweep that year.

After Inouye's death in 2010, followed by Daniel Akaka's announcement in March 2011 that he was not going to run for a fourth term in 2012, there was a dramatic change in Asian American representation in the Senate. In November 2012, Hawaii became the first state to elect a female Asian American senator, Mazie Hirono, a Japanese American. She was also the Senate's first Buddhist, and, at the time, the only Asian American in the Senate (Brian Schatz, one of nine Jews in the Senate, was appointed to replace Daniel Inouye).

Hirono was born in Japan. Her father, a veterinarian, was an alcoholic and a compulsive gambler, and her mother left him when Mazie was four years old. A few years later, Mazie's mother and her maternal grandparents moved to Hawaii, and lived in genuine poverty in their early years in the country. She attended public schools, the University of Hawaii (where she was Phi Beta Kappa), and Georgetown for a law degree. She then returned to Hawaii and practiced law. She moved through the political ranks in Hawaii, serving in the state house and as lieutenant governor before running for and winning a seat in the House that she held from 2007 to 2013, when she ran for and won Akaka's Senate seat.[26]

Mazie Hirono was the only Asian American in the Senate from 2013 through 2016, but in November 2016 two women with at least some Asian or South Asian American background were elected: Tammy Duckworth (D-IL) and Kamala Harris (D-CA). Duckworth was born in Thailand to a Chinese mother and an American father. Her father was a marine who went on to work for international companies and for the United Nations on issues related to refugees and housing. The family moved to Hawaii, her father lost his job, and the family relied on food stamps to make ends meet. She earned a BA at the University of Hawaii, and an MA in international affairs at George Washington. She then moved to Illinois to pursue a PhD and joined the Illinois National Guard. Her unit was deployed to Iraq, and, on November 12, 2004, the helicopter she was copiloting was hit. She survived, but she lost both legs and the use of one arm. She rehabbed at Walter Reed Hospital, and was invited by Senator Dick Durbin to attend the State of the Union Address in 2005. She subsequently ran for Congress in Illinois, and lost a close contest; she was appointed to oversee the Department of Veterans' Affairs in Illinois, was appointed by Obama to be assistant secretary of veterans' affairs, then ran for Congress again and won. After serving in the House from 2013 through 2016, she ran for, and won, the Senate seat.[27]

If Duckworth's story—a biracial woman, injured in combat—reflects the changing nature of diversity in the Senate, so, too, does that of Kamala Harris. She was born in Oakland, California; her father is a Jamaican economist who teaches at Stanford and her mother, born in India, was a physician who specialized in breast cancer (she died of breast cancer in 2009). Her parents divorced when she was young, but before they did they lived in a black neighborhood and Kamala and her sister sang in a choir at a local black Baptist church. Her mother moved to Montreal to do research and teach at McGill University, and Kamala graduated from high school in Montreal. She then went to Howard as an undergraduate and to Berkeley for law school. After working for more than a decade in the district attorney's office, in 2003 she was elected the district attorney for the city and county of San Francisco. In 2010 she became the attorney general for the state, and was reelected in 2014. In 2016 she won the Senate seat previously held by Barbara Boxer.

Harris, therefore, like Duckworth (and like Barack Obama), is biracial, though perhaps multiracial is a better term—she is part African American (her father is Jamaican, and she grew up, for a while, in a black neighborhood), and part Indian (her mother was born and educated in India), and she spent some of her formative years in Quebec. These two women represent the complexity of ethnic identity, and the geographic fluidity of some of those who are becoming corporate and political leaders. They certainly reveal the changes that have taken place in terms of who "represents" Asian and South Asian Americans, especially when contrasted to the five Asian American men who were elected to the Senate between 1959 and 1990 (Hiram Fong, Daniel Inouye, Spark Matsunaga, S. I. Hayakawa, and Daniel Akaka).

The House

Twenty-one Asian Americans have been elected to the House, starting in the late 1950s. The first was Daniel Inouye (D-HI) who served in the House for two terms, from 1959 through 1963 before he became a senator. The large majority, seventeen of the twenty-one (81 percent), have been Democrats, and fourteen of the twenty-one (67 percent) have been male. Seven have been elected in California, nine in Hawaii, and the other five in various states around the country.

In addition to the twenty-one Asian Americans, there have been twelve people with South Asian backgrounds elected to the House. The first, Dalip Saund (D-CA) was of Indian ancestry. He was elected to the House two years before Inouye, and served until 1963. It was not until 1980 that another Indian American was elected (Mervyn Dynally [D-CA], born in Trinidad, was of mixed Indian and African heritage), and another twenty-four years before the third, Bobby Jindal, an Indian American, was elected in 2004 in Louisiana.

In 2017, three Indian Americans and a Vietnamese American were elected to the House, all Democrats, two men and two women, from states across the country.

When we combine the presence of Asian Americans and South Asians in the House, a rather striking pattern emerges. In 2006, there were five serving in the House, four men and one woman. A decade later, in mid-2017, that number had more than doubled to thirteen. Not only had the number increased, but so too had the percentage of women—seven of the thirteen were women. Six of the thirteen were Japanese Americans, four were Chinese Americans, and the other three included one Filipino, one Samoan, and one Indian.

As another way to show the growth in the numbers of Asian Americans and South Asians in the House, two were elected for the first time in the 1950s, two in the 1960s, three in the 1970s, two in the 1980s, three in the 1990s; however, seven were elected between 2001 and 2009, and fifteen have been elected since 2010. The more recently elected members are from a range of backgrounds—they include not only Japanese and Chinese Americans but also men and women who are from, or whose parents were from, Samoa, Vietnam, and Bangladesh. Notably, although only one Indian American was elected between 1960 and 2000, five have been elected since that time.

As is true of most of those in the power elite, and especially the other Asian Americans and South Asians in the power elite, those who have served in the House are quite well educated. The thirteen who are currently in the House all graduated from college, many from elite schools (two from Harvard, one from Princeton, one from Chicago, one from Stanford, one from Georgetown, one from UCLA, and another from Berkeley), eleven have postgraduate degrees, including six who have law degrees (Harvard, Yale, Georgetown), one who has a PhD, and one who has an MD.

About two-thirds are from upper- or upper-middle-class backgrounds. This includes a few whose parents were local politicians (Tulsi Gabbard [D-HI] and Grace Meng [D-NY]), and others whose parents were successful businesspeople (e.g., Ami Bera [D-CA] and Pramilla Jayapai [D-WA]), engineers (e.g., Ro Khanna [D-CA]), and academicians (e.g., Raja Krishnamoorthi [D-IL]). Four of the thirteen came from working- or middle-class backgrounds, including Colleen Hanabusa (D-HI) whose parents ran a gas station.

As was the case for the most recently elected Asian Americans to the Senate, the five who were elected to the House in November 2016 reveal the changing makeup of Asian representation. Three are of Indian background (Ro Khanna, Raja Krishnamoorthi, and Pramila Jayapai), and all three are from economically privileged backgrounds. Khanna's father was a chemical engineer, Krishnamoorthi's father a college professor, and Jayapai's father a marketing executive (and her mother is a writer). The other two are Japanese and Vietnamese, and both come from working- or middle-class families. As noted above, the parents of Colleen Hanabusa ran a gas station. The other, Stephanie Murphy (D-FL) is a Vietnamese American who left Vietnam with her parents when she was one year old. Her parents then worked blue-collar jobs during the day and cleaned office buildings at night to support the family.

CONCLUSION

The patterns among the Asian Americans and the South Asians show cleavages similar to those found among Latinos. Wealthier and better-educated immigrants, such as Chinese Americans and Indians, tend to be the corporate directors and appointees in Republican administrations. Those from immigrant families that came to the United States from less privileged socioeconomic backgrounds, such as Japanese Americans, are more likely to be elected officials. Moreover, Japanese Americans, with their history of communal sharing to establish small farms and small businesses and with their common experience of arbitrary incarceration during World War II, tend to defend civil liberties and tend to be Democrats.

From the point of view of the power elite, successful Asian Americans and South Asians have had a number of functions. First, some among the Asian Americans have served as "middlemen" in corporate management and in selling corporate products in low-income communities through small retail businesses. Second, some Asian Americans have been "ambassadors" for their corporations to Asian countries. Third, like some of the Latinos discussed in chapter 5, Asian Americans and South Asians have added a further international dimension to the power elite. Fourth, because both Asian Americans and South Asians are an especially well-educated group of men and women, they have provided much-needed scientific and technical expertise in corporations, research institutes, engineering schools, and science departments.

The economic and political achievements we have described in this chapter are such that old-line members of the power elite can claim that their circles are now diversified in terms of Asian Americans and South Asians as well as women, African Americans, and Hispanic Americans. But does the increase in diversity in the power elite that we now have documented in the previous chapters on Jews, women, blacks, and Latinos, and in this chapter on Asian Americans and South Asians, extend to differences in sexual orientation and gender identity? We turn to that complex question in the next chapter.

Chapter Seven

LGBT People in the Power Elite

Attitudes and laws have become far more favorable for sexual and gender minority people than anyone could have imagined just fifteen years ago. Many celebrities, news broadcasters, film and television stars, and athletes have come out as gay, lesbian, or bisexual. There are also well-known transgender people who are frequently in the news (one of them, Caitlin Jenner, the former male Bruce Jenner, is a much-quoted Republican). In 2010, President Obama signed the Don't Ask, Don't Tell, Repeal Act, which paved the way for lesbians, gay men, and bisexuals to serve openly in the military. In June of 2015, the Supreme Court (a court with a 5–4 conservative majority) ruled that state-based bans on same-sex marriage were unconstitutional, and that same-sex couples should receive the same benefits as different-sex couples. Since 2010, polls have indicated that most Americans support these changes.

Many, especially religious conservatives, however, strongly oppose these changes, and the legal protections for lesbian, gay, bisexual, and transgender (LGBT) individuals still seem quite fragile, especially with the election of Donald Trump, with a Republican majority in both the House and the Senate, and with a majority of conservatives on the Supreme Court. Moreover, whether or not these dramatic changes in the larger culture are undermined, the improved climate for sexual minority people in the last decade[1] does not mean that people will feel comfortable allowing their sexual identity to be known.

Moreover, in recent decades more people have come to realize that many individuals do not fall into the binary categories of "gay" or "straight." A number of acronyms have appeared to suggest a broader range of sexual identities, including LGBQQ and LGBTQ+ (with the *Q*'s standing for Queer or Questioning and the + suggesting a spectrum of unspecified sexualities).

Whatever terms are used, sexual and gender minority people have not become highly visible in the power elite—based on appearances, and what they tell us, almost all of those who hold positions that place them in the power elite are heterosexual and cisgender (a person whose identity and gender correspond with the sex assigned at birth). That is to say, as is true for Jews, we can't tell just by looking at them (as is usually the case when it comes to identifying women, African Americans, Asian Americans, and South Asians in the power elite). We therefore are not focusing here on actual sexual or gender identities, but on the extent to which people are willing to be open about their sexual minority and gender minority identities if they are in, or close to being in, the corporate, political, or military elite.

One more thing. People tend to assume that gay men, lesbians, and bisexuals are either "in the closet" or "out" (and thus "open"), but, in reality, there are many shades in between. A study in 1995 of hundreds of lesbian and gay people in the corporate world found that most of those who remained closeted had disclosed their sexual orientation to some of their coworkers. Many told the researchers that although they were out at work, they still did not want their real names published.[2] So, as of slightly more than twenty years ago, there were lesbian and gay people in the corporate world who disclosed their sexual orientation to certain colleagues, or even to most of their colleagues, but this information was not public in the sense that it was accessible to researchers trying to understand the extent to which the power elite had diversified. At that time, there were virtually no openly sexual or gender minority people in the power elite.

Our interest has not been to "find" those in the power elite who are members of sexual minority groups, but rather to explore whether people in the power elite are willing to be public about their minority sexual or gender identities. That is, we are interested in determining the extent to which continuing prejudices and barriers, whether inside or outside of elite circles, prevent sexual and gender minority people from rising to the top. We will explore the extent to which they have in this chapter.

LGBT PEOPLE IN THE CORPORATE ELITE

In the introductory letter that he wrote for the 2017 Corporate Equality Index, an annual rating of major corporations done by the Human Rights Campaign (HRC), Chad Griffin, the president of the HRC, noted that despite ongoing and even "unprecedented" attacks on the LGBT community, "progress toward greater equality" in the corporate world had not just remained steady, "it had sped up." In addition to more companies receiving higher scores on their ratings, more companies had included "transgender-inclusive health care coverage."[3] And based on many studies, there can be no doubt that the experiences of sexual and gender minority people who work for *Fortune* 500 companies these days are different from those of their counterparts in the 1950s, or even the early 1990s.[4]

A study in the early 1990s based on interviews with lesbian and gay graduates of the Harvard Business School found that none of those interviewed even mentioned the lack of domestic-partner benefits. When asked, they said that they did not think it was likely that such benefits would be provided in very many companies in the foreseeable future.[5] By 1995, however, not only had various West Coast companies already known for progressive corporate policies—Lotus, Apple Computer, and Levi Strauss, for example—added domestic-partner benefits, but even the Walt Disney Company, known throughout the years for its conservatism, had done so.[6] By the end of 2004, 216 of the *Fortune* 500 (43 percent) offered domestic-partner benefits for same-sex couples (a tenfold increase since 1995), and by 2017, 81 percent of the *Fortune* 500 companies offered domestic-partner benefits.[7]

In spite of these changes in domestic-partner benefits, and the changes affecting LGBT individuals that took place throughout the culture and the legal system, considerable evidence demonstrates that sexual and gender minority people continue to encounter prejudice and discrimination in the corporate world. Moreover, there is reason to believe that the higher one moves in the executive ranks, the greater the importance placed on either cisgender heterosexuality or the appearance of cisgender heterosexuality. This was found to be the case in research done in 1990, in 1995, and, more recently, in 2014.

For a 1990 doctoral dissertation that he wrote for the Annenberg School of Communications at the University of Pennsylvania, James Woods traveled around the country interviewing seventy gay men who worked as professionals, many (but not all) in law firms and corporations. (His was a snowball sample, in which an initial group of friends and contacts put him in touch with others.) Woods concluded, "They learn to control and monitor outward appearances, to distort them when necessary. They learn to dodge. For many the result is a calculating, deliberate way of approaching social encounters. One can say . . . that they *manage* their sexual identities at work."[8]

A few years later, in 1995, Friskopp and Silverstein published a study that they conducted based on the experiences of lesbian and gay graduates of the Harvard Business School. Themselves graduates of the business school (where they were members of the Gay and Lesbian Student Association), they mailed a survey to more than one hundred people who were on the mailing list of the Harvard Gay and Lesbian Alumni Association; sixty-seven were returned. They also interviewed more than one hundred people, including some who had indicated on their returned surveys that they were willing to be interviewed.[9] They found that "discrimination in the form of a hostile atmosphere, corporate cowardice, and unequal benefits is rampant." As a result, they wrote, "the fear of the lavender ceiling looms large for many," especially at "conservative" *Fortune* 500 companies.[10]

Citing the fear of discrimination, many of their respondents reported that they had remained closeted: "Those employed by America's most prominent conservative companies almost universally believed they would be discriminated against in some fashion if they were completely open about their gay identity in their current work environment. These professionals include those working for *Fortune* 500 manufacturers (both industrial and consumer products companies) and in construction, energy, real estate, transportation, investment banks, and utilities. To a lesser degree this fear is shared by those employed by large banks, insurance companies, pension funds, and major consulting firms."[11]

More recently, in 2014, a study by the Human Rights Campaign, based on a survey of 1,700 employees, concluded that the majority of LGBT employees in large corporations, both executives and employees at lower levels, remained closeted at work. In another study, done about the same time, 83 percent of those surveyed reported that they hid aspects of their sexual identity at work, frequently because they believed that their bosses expected them to.[12] This conclusion is not unlike the one we have drawn about Jews and blacks in the corporate world: they are much more accepted now than in the past, but they are still expected not to appear too different from the predominantly white Christian males around them (for example, by wearing a yarmulke or a dashiki).

For women, African Americans, Latinos, and Asian Americans, we have been able to make some rough estimates of who sat on boards, and who was in the corporate pipeline, based on appearance; in addition, for Jews, and for some other ethnic groups, we have used the Distinctive Name Technique to make such estimates. However, we have no way to make even rough estimates of how many sexual and gender minority people are in the higher management ranks of the corporate world or sitting on boards of directors of *Fortune* 500 companies. According to Out Leadership, a strategic advisory firm that advises multinational corporations on LGBT issues, as of 2016, there were "fewer than 10 openly LGBT directors on the boards of *Fortune* 500 companies," and "only two *Fortune* 500 boards include[d] sexual orientation and gender identity in their definition of board diversity."[13]

There are about 7,000 directors on *Fortune* 500 boards, so the "fewer than 10 openly LGBT directors" represents less than one-tenth of 1 percent. Clearly, openly LGBT directors on *Fortune* boards are extremely rare. Over the past few decades, however, there have been a few highly publicized anecdotal cases of senior executives, founders of companies, or CEOs who have been outed. These anecdotal cases can be helpful in understanding the changing nature over time of the degree of acceptance, or the lack thereof, when it comes to deviating from the heterosexual norm that continues to prevail in the higher circles of corporate America.

In 1996, Allan Gilmour, a retired top executive at Ford Motors, decided to reveal his gay sexual orientation in an interview in *The Advocate*, a magazine that addresses issues of relevance to sexual and gender minority communities. Gilmour had served for thirty-five years as the company's chief financial officer and as vice chairman of the board, and on two occasions he was considered for, but not chosen as, CEO. Still, he waited until two years after he retired to come out publicly. The son of a Vermont cattle dealer, a graduate of both Harvard and the University of Michigan, and a lifelong conservative Republican, he was still on the boards of Prudential Insurance, Dow Chemical, Detroit Edison, U.S. West, and Whirlpool when he did the interview with *The Advocate*.

Gilmour made clear that he chose to wait until he was no longer working at Ford to reveal his sexual orientation. In fact, he noted, he did not even take phone calls at work from his thirty-four-year-old partner until a few months before he retired. As Gilmour put it, "I perceived the risk of coming out in the business world as fairly substantial."[14]

Notably, however, none of the chairmen of the boards on which Gilmour sat asked him to leave those boards. He contacted each one after the story broke, and, he said, "I was told uniformly that it makes no difference." He spent the next few years actively involved in fundraising for lesbian and gay causes, including overseeing an investment fund that supported lesbian and gay groups.

A few years later, in June 2002, after Ford had lost $5.5 billion the previous year, and with increasing concerns on Wall Street about the company, Gilmour suddenly was asked, at age sixty-seven, to once again become the chief financial officer to help turn the company around. The decision to ask a now highly visible gay man to return as the CFO was made by Bill Ford, forty-five years old, who had become CEO the previous October. He knew that Gilmour was the person for the job. As one Ford executive put it, "Gilmour's return is like Yoda coming back to Earth."

Ford's stock shot up when Gilmour was rehired. According to *Newsweek*, "Previously bearish Wall Street analysts issued buy recommendations." As for the larger implications of his return, Gilmour acknowledged that "this is much less controversial now" but added that we as a society "have some good distance to go." In his view, opportunities and acceptance had improved for lesbian and gay people in corporate America, but not enough and not in all segments: "It depends on the company and the nature of the industry. The newer companies and industries pay much less attention to these issues." He worked for two more years and then retired again in 2005. In 2011, at the age of seventy-six, Gilmour was named the president of Wayne State University in Detroit, and served in that capacity until 2013. [15]

Obviously, if Out Leadership is accurate that there were "fewer than 10 openly LGBT directors" in 2016, the floodgates have not exactly opened since Gilmour left the corporate world in 2005. However, one CEO of a major corporation, and a second person who was the founder of a company that is now in the *Fortune* 500, have come out in recent years, though only after they had been outed by others. Their stories, too, help to demonstrate the pressures on gay men in the corporate world, and the changes that have taken place in the last decade.

In the first case, Tim Cook, the CEO of Apple since 2001 (Apple was #35 on the 2011 *Fortune* list, #5 in 2014, and #3 in 2017), was accidently outed in June 2014 by the host of a CNBC news show during a conversation about gay CEOs of "major companies." The host's gaffe was met with silence, hems, and haws by the other participants, and the segment became a major topic of conversation on business sites and in Silicon Valley for a few days.[16]

A few months later, in October, Cook wrote an article in *Bloomberg BusinessWeek* in which he came out as a gay person ("I'm proud to be gay, and I consider being gay among the greatest gifts God has given me"). Although Cook no doubt mentioned God out of sincerity, invoking the deity could not help but to deflect criticisms from many centrists and conservatives, and perhaps even some ultraconservatives.

That Cook is gay was no surprise to some people. As he pointed out in his article, he had been open with many people about his sexual orientation, and many of his colleagues at Apple knew he was gay (and, of course, he had been outed on CNBC a few months earlier). Still, he had not publicly acknowledged that he was gay until he wrote the column in October, and this generated front-page attention in media across the nation and throughout the world.[17]

That it took so long for a CEO of a *Fortune* 500 company to come out reveals just how slowly corporate America adjusts to major social trends in the larger culture. As we have indicated, the first African American *Fortune* 500 CEO was appointed in 1999, more than thirty years after the height of the civil rights movement (Martin Luther King gave his "I Have a Dream" speech in 1963, and Congress passed the Civil Rights Act in 1964). So, too, has corporate America lagged behind as dramatic changes have taken place in the larger culture's treatment of sexual minority people.

Given the historic and still ongoing resistance to sexual and gender minority people in the corporate community, and the virulent antigay materials put out by ultraright advocacy groups supported financially by ultraconservatives in the corporate community, at times sexual and gender minority people have decided to start their own businesses, some of which have become so successful that they have become influential supporters of people in the political elite. At times the businesses they started became *Fortune*-level companies or have been bought out by *Fortune*-level companies. Some of these entrepreneurial innovators have emerged as rich and influential people, and some have been asked onto *Fortune*-level corporate boards. We will use two such people as examples, one a Democrat and one a Republican.

The Democrat is the billionaire media executive David Geffen, who grew up in a three-bedroom apartment in a Jewish-Italian section of Brooklyn. His mother ran a brassiere and corset shop while his father "read a lot," recalls Geffen, because he wasn't successful or ambitious. "There were times that kids said to me, 'What does your father do?' and I had to make something up because I actually didn't know what he did."[18]

After an undistinguished record in high school, Geffen enrolled at the University of Texas at Austin, dropped out after one semester, and headed to California, where he held a number of jobs before landing a lowly but coveted position in the mailroom of the William Morris talent agency. He told his employer that he was a graduate of UCLA, then intercepted the expected reply from UCLA denying this claim, steamed open the envelope, and replaced it with a bogus letter that he had prepared on UCLA stationery, stating that he had graduated.[19]

Desperately wanting to be an agent, he followed the astute advice of a more experienced William Morris agent, who told him that, rather than trying to persuade established stars to work with a mailroom boy in his early twenties, he should seek to represent some of the undiscovered musical talent of his own generation.

He became the agent for a singer and songwriter, Laura Nyro, who wrote a series of hits for herself and various other artists. When her publishing company, half-owned by Geffen, was sold to CBS in 1969, he received $2 million in CBS stock at the age of twenty-five. Within a year, he had started his own record company, Asylum, which put out records by Joni Mitchell, Jackson Browne, Linda Ronstadt, and the Eagles, among others, and five years later he sold the company to Warner Communications for $7 million.

In 1980, he started Geffen Records, which was extremely successful, and he branched out to invest in theater. By 1990 he was ready to move toward conglomeration. He sold his company to MCA for $550 million worth of stock, rather than accepting various lucrative cash offers, because he figured that MCA itself would be sold in the near future. When the Japanese company Matsushita bought MCA, Geffen, as MCA's largest shareholder, received a check for an estimated $670 million.[20] A 1990 article in *Forbes* described him and his wealth in the following way: "This 47-year-old chap given to blue jeans, T shirts and a fashionable, day-old stubble, will be worth nearly $900 million. David Geffen is well on his way to achieving his well-known ambition of becoming Hollywood's first billionaire. And he's a bachelor to boot."[21]

He was indeed a bachelor, but not an eligible one in the conventional sense. Geffen had not yet gone public about his sexual orientation, but over the next few years, he became increasingly involved in fundraising for the battle against AIDS, and he told a reporter for *Vanity Fair* that he was bisexual. Then, both frightened and energized by the venomous language at the 1992 Republican National Convention, especially a speech in which Patrick Buchanan claimed that there was "a religious war going on in this country for the soul of America," Geffen became involved in Clinton's presidential campaign. Even before the Republican convention ended, he had called Clinton's campaign director, Mickey Kantor, an old friend from Kantor's days as a Los Angeles lawyer. Geffen became a major contributor and fundraiser.[22]

In late November 1992, just a few weeks after Clinton's election, in a speech to six thousand people at Commitment to Life VI, a benefit for AIDS Project Los Angeles, Geffen disclosed publicly that he was gay. "As a gay man," he told the crowd, "I have come a long way to be here tonight." This declaration generated considerable publicity. *The Advocate* named Geffen "Man of the Year."[23]

In chapter 2, we noted that, several decades ago, Laurence Tisch advised young Jewish men interested in business careers to avoid the large "Gentile" companies because they would only get "bogged down." Geffen, when asked a week after the AIDS fundraiser whether being gay had influenced his decision to pursue a career in show business rather than another business, said that it had been a key consideration: "When I realized as a teenager that it was possible that I might be gay—I wasn't sure until my twenties—I thought, *What kind of career can I have where being gay won't make a difference?* I thought about it a lot, and I decided that the entertainment business was a profession in which being gay was not going to be unusual or stand in my way."[24]

The other, and in some key ways opposite, example of a gay male entrepreneur who has used his wealth to try to influence a political campaign is Peter Thiel. He was born in Germany; his peripatetic father, a chemical engineer, brought his family to the United States when Thiel was an infant. After graduating from high school in San Mateo, California, where he first read (and was much taken with) the novels of Ayn Rand, he went to Stanford for both a BA and a law degree.

After working for a firm as a securities lawyer, then as a derivatives trader, and then as a speech writer for a former conservative Republican secretary of education, Thiel returned to the Bay Area in 1996 during the dotcom boom. He raised $1 million from friends and family, started Thiel Capital Management, and hit pay dirt right away when one of the groups he backed started PayPal, which netted him $55 million when it was sold to eBay. He invested some of that money in Facebook, and by 2016 he was listed #246 on the Forbes 400, with an estimated worth of $2.7 billion. He was chair of the board at PayPal and on the board at Facebook, and, therefore, he was not just rich but by our operational definition, he was in the corporate elite.

Along the way, in 2007, Thiel was outed by a California magazine called *Valleywag*, owned by *Gawker*. The story they ran, titled "Peter Thiel Is Totally Gay, People," so incensed him that in 2016 he secretly funded a lawsuit by the wrestler Hulk Hogan against *Gawker* (*Gawker* had posted a video of Hogan having sex with a friend's wife). The $140 million settlement that Hogan won drove *Gawker* into bankruptcy. By that time, Thiel had publicly acknowledged his gay sexual orientation—in 2011, he was named as one of eight openly gay innovators by *The Advocate*.[25]

He then gained even more media attention when he contributed $1.25 million to Trump's presidential campaign, and then spoke for him at the Republican convention. Thiel was only the third openly gay person ever to speak at a Republican convention. In 1996, Stephen Fong, the head of the San Francisco chapter of the Log Cabin Republicans, gave a one-minute speech, and in 2000, Jim Kolbe, a gay congressman from Arizona, who came out in the mid-1990s when some gay rights activists threatened to out him for voting for the Defense of Marriage Act, endorsed George W. Bush. Neither Fong nor Kolbe made any mention of their sexual orientation in their speeches (despite this, in 2000 some delegates from Texas bowed their heads in prayer during Kolbe's speech). Thiel, however, told the almost all white, almost all straight, crowd, one that had supported antigay legislation for many years, "I am proud to be gay. I am proud to be a Republican."[26]

Apparently fearful of chaos in America, or a possible worldwide pandemic, Thiel became even more well-known in 2016 when it was revealed that he had become a citizen of New Zealand in 2011, although he did not fulfill the residency requirement, and had no intention to move there immediately. He was granted citizenship in 2011 "in the public interest" after he said that he had "found no other country that aligns more with my view of the future than New Zealand," and that being a citizen would help him mobilize the country's entrepreneurs. In 2015, he bought a 477-acre lakefront estate in that country for $10 million.[27]

Given what an uphill battle it continues to be in the corporate world for sexual and gender minority people, and especially with the conservative national climate reflected by Trump's 2016 victory and a Republican-dominated Congress, we think that in the foreseeable future those who start at large corporations and do manage to rise through the ranks are likely at some point to go off on their own. They may start companies or else find work in more comfortable environments. This has been the case for a while, and is likely to continue.

Consider, for example, Kathy Levinson, a 1977 graduate of Stanford, an economics major, and the university's only three-sport varsity athlete (field hockey, basketball, and tennis). Levinson held various senior executive positions with Charles A. Schwab & Company, helping that company to become one of the first major corporations to offer domestic-partner health insurance coverage. After thirteen years with Schwab, she left in 1996 to work for E*TRADE Group, where she was president and chief operating officer from 1999 to 2000. She made enough money to give Stanford $1 million in 1998, and she was named one of the most influential businesswomen in the San Francisco Bay Area. In recent years, she has been a managing director at Golden Seeds, an investing group that invests in woman-owned or -founded companies. Married and the proud biological mother of two daughters, she has been active in the Gay and Lesbian Leadership Council and several Jewish organizations. She has served as a member of the California Democratic Central Committee and in 2012 was a cochair of the National Finance Committee for President Obama's reelection campaign.[28]

Similarly, David Bohnett, a self-described electronics geek from the suburbs of Chicago, worked for Arthur Andersen after he graduated with a bachelor's degree in business administration from USC and an MBA from the University of Michigan. Of being a gay man at Arthur Andersen, he said, "It wasn't going to be easy. I would have had to push down who I was, and that didn't seem right to me." So he left the corporate world, worked for a while for a software company, and then, using his life savings and $386,000 in life insurance money he had inherited when his partner died of AIDS, he created Beverly Hills Internet, the first ever World Wide Web video camera (it overlooked Hollywood and Vine). The idea caught on, the company expanded, the name was changed to GeoCities, and within four years, the first-quarter revenues were almost $8 million. In 1999, GeoCities merged with Yahoo! ("Right company, right culture, right price, right time," said Bohnett). Bohnett's profit from the deal: $350 million.[29]

Bohnett started the David Bohnett Foundation, which as of 2016 had contributed more than $100 million to various causes, including LGBT issues, AIDS related issues, voting rights and voting registration, animal research and animal rights, and gun control. Bohnett has been on numerous cultural, political, and corporate boards, including NCR Corporation (#409 in 2016). He is a strong supporter of the Democratic Party, and in 2012 President Barack Obama appointed him as a trustee of the John F. Kennedy Center for the Performing Arts.

It is our guess that the pathways followed by Geffen, Thiel, Levinson, and Bohnett will appeal more to the next generation of sexual and gender minority people than the more confining pathway traveled by Allan Gilmour. Gilmour was willing to put up with the segmentation of his work and private lives. As Bohnett's comments about working for Arthur Andersen suggest ("I would have had to push down who I was, and that didn't seem right to me"), younger sexual and gender minority people may not be willing to do so. Perhaps they will either find niche settings in the corporate world that accept them or they will go out on their own.

LGBT PEOPLE IN THE POLITICAL ELITE

Like everyone else, sexual and gender minority people mostly reflect and express their social and educational backgrounds, as well as their occupational training and experience. They can be from backgrounds up and down the class structure. Thus, a wealthy ultraconservative such as Phyllis Schlafly can have a gay son; an army brat such as Newt Gingrich can have a lesbian half-sister; a psychoanalyst such as Charles Socarides, who claimed that he could "cure" one-third of the homosexuals he treated, could have a gay son, Richard, who served in the Clinton administration as the White House liaison to the Labor Department; and former vice president Dick Cheney can have an openly lesbian daughter.[30] In fact, many prominent sexual and gender minority people are from comfortable socioeconomic backgrounds, have had excellent educations, and have experienced considerable success in the professions, academia, and business.

There are LGBT Democratic clubs and LGBT Republican clubs across the country, but only the Republicans are organized by a national centralized office. The umbrella group is called the Log Cabin Republicans—the name refers to Abraham Lincoln, who is alleged to have grown up in a log cabin and who supported individual rights (but whose father actually was a skilled carpenter and farmer who owned two farms of six hundred acres each and several town lots, as well as horses and livestock).[31] Membership skyrocketed after Buchanan's speech at the 1992 convention, when many formerly closeted gay Republicans decided they had to become more involved in order to combat the antigay views of the religious right. The then president of the Texas Log Cabin Republicans, Paul von Wupperfeld, the son of a Goldwater Republican certain that it would be "unnatural" for him to vote Democrat, claimed that the state organization's membership had more than tripled in the twelve months ending in December 1992, an increase that he attributed in no small part to the Republican convention.[32] That year, the Log Cabin Republicans decided they could not endorse the Bush-Quayle ticket.[33] Twelve years later, in 2004, it was, as Yogi Berra might have put it, déjà vu all over again when, after George W. Bush supported a constitutional amendment denying legal recognition of same-sex marriages, the board of the Log Cabin Republicans voted overwhelmingly against endorsing the Bush-Cheney ticket. According to the group's political director, Bush's endorsement of the marriage amendment had led to the group's doubling in size.[34] Despite Peter Thiel's endorsement of Trump, the Republican platform included strongly antigay positions, and those Trump had mentioned as possible Supreme Court nominees had anti-LGBT records, so in 2016, the fourteen-member board of the Log Cabin Republicans voted against endorsing Trump.[35] They probably had reason. Though Trump's appointee, Neil Gorsuch, has many gay friends who vouch for his personal openness toward gay marriage, and he worships with his wife and two daughters at an Episcopal church in Boulder that has gay and lesbian parishes, he has taken legal stances on some LGBT issues that are deeply concerning within the LGBT community.[36]

Some Republicans are sexual and gender minority people, and so, too, are some staff members who work in the offices of elected Republican officials. This at times has created anguish for those closeted staffers of particularly homophobic congressmen. Some have found themselves preparing antigay briefings for their bosses during the day and returning to their same-sex partners at night. As one explained, "How would you like to turn on your television and see your boss, or your boss's cohorts, telling you what a horrible person you are every other day? Happens to me all the time." Still, most have chosen to say nothing, and most have remained closeted at work, for to do otherwise would be to risk their own jobs or the jobs of their partners. Furthermore, they do not want to hurt what they see as the more important cause: conservatism. As one openly gay Washington, DC, consultant, who worked to gain the support of gay voters for George W. Bush, put it, "They believe in the cause, the president, and the ideals of the Republican party," and to come out might mean they would no longer be seen as "part of the team" or, worse, would be "labeled a liberal."[37]

Some sexual and gender minority true believers in the conservative movement not only have stayed in the closet but have used homophobic issues to further the right-wing cause. The first famous right-wing gay man who was well-known for his support of gay-baiting was Roy Cohn, assistant to Senator Joseph McCarthy (McCarthy made a reputation for himself by pursuing "Communists" and "queers" in the State Department). Cohn became infamous all over again in 2016 when the *New York Times* featured a long story on what he had taught Donald Trump as one of his lawyers in the late 1970s and early 1980s ("What Donald Trump Learned from Joseph McCarthy's Right-Hand Man"). His advice to Trump when he was challenged for not renting to African Americans became Trump's general approach: "Tell them to go to hell and fight the thing in court."[38]

Another closeted man with internalized antigay attitudes, Terry Dolan, became a right-wing activist in his teens and worked on the 1972 Nixon reelection campaign. In the mid-1970s, he was a cofounder of the National Conservative Political Action Committee (NCPAC), along with the later provocateur and Trump adviser, Roger Stone, which had an impact during the Reagan years. NCPAC was hostile to all things liberal, and its shrill fundraising letters railed against feminists and "gay activists" ("Our nation's moral fiber is being weakened by the growing homosexual movement," read one). Dolan, like Cohn, died of AIDS; unlike Cohn, who refused to acknowledge that he had AIDS, Dolan endorsed gay rights before he died in 1986.[39]

As late as 2012, he was still being listed in a "Hall of Shame" by a gay author at Salon, whose article was titled "LGBT's Worst Foe: The Closet Monster."[40] However, NCPAC faded away a few years after his death.

But the gay conservative ideologue who has been of greatest use to the right wing has been political consultant Arthur Finkelstein. Finkelstein previously guarded his private life with care, but, apparently, the attractions of marriage were too great for him once the possibility existed, thanks to the efforts of liberal gay people: despite the horrors that the thought of same-sex marriage creates for most of his conservative clients and for conservative voters, he married his same-sex partner of forty years in Massachusetts in April 2005, which, of course, generated considerable (risky) publicity. Before his marriage, Finkelstein had been a major political strategist for over twenty-five years for a range of conservatives and conservative causes, including former North Carolina senator Jesse Helms (whose use of homophobia outdid that of all other Republicans in the 1990s). Although he came to describe himself as a pro-choice, pro-same-sex-marriage libertarian, his polling organization included the authoritarian right-wing prime minister of Hungary among his clients, and in 2016 he did polling for the Republican Jewish Coalition, whose major benefactor is casino owner Sheldon Adelson, the second-richest man in the world at the time.[41]

So, just as diehard liberals at times endorse politicians with whom they differ on specific issues because they agree with the overall liberal position, so, too, do diehard conservatives who are members of sexual and gender minority groups allow their belief in the overall conservative ideology to override the more specific issues related to sexual orientation, even though such a stance seems to go against their self-image and their self-interest. As Martin Duberman, a historian who has written extensively about gay issues, explained, by about 2005 being a gay Republican was no longer the contradiction that he and others previously assumed it was. Writing about the George W. Bush administration, he observed that "a number of gay people approve of the administration because they are militaristic, they are jingoistic, and they may have grown up in fundamentalist families."[42]

Nonetheless, most sexual minority people vote Democratic, and they, too, like the Log Cabin Republicans, have organized politically. In 1977, the Municipal Elections Committee of Los Angeles was formed. Its bland generic name made it difficult to know immediately that it was a lesbian and gay political action committee, the first in the country, and made it easier for politicians to accept money from the group without having to acknowledge support from lesbian and gay people. The adviser to this early gay political action committee was David Mixner, a very different political consultant from Arthur Finkelstein. Fifteen years later, Mixner emerged as Bill Clinton's liaison to lesbian and gay people during the 1992 campaign.[43]

Mixner was a baby boomer born in 1946; his father managed the workers on an absentee-owner farm. After graduating from the local public high school in 1964, Mixner attended three different colleges before finally dropping out of Arizona State to work in Eugene McCarthy's 1968 presidential campaign, in which he became one of the organizers, and then one of the four organizers of the Vietnam moratorium in October 1969. He later met Bill Clinton at a gathering of antiwar liberals at Martha's Vineyard, and the two twenty-five-year-olds, one a Yale Law School student, the other a college-dropout political activist, hit it off. They kept in touch because of their shared political aspirations. Fast-forwarding to October 1991, Mixner arranged a meeting in Los Angeles between Clinton, by then governor of Arkansas, and a small group of wealthy Southern Californians known as Access Now for Gay and Lesbian Equality. The group was impressed by Clinton, in part because he was comfortable with their agenda, which included an end to the ban preventing sexual minority people from serving in the military.

As the word spread, Mixner was able to rally considerable support from LGBT communities for Clinton, with Patrick Buchanan's hair-raising speech at the Republican convention making this task much easier. As Mixner said to one interviewer, "Support crystallized overnight with Pat Buchanan's speech. It created a voting bloc and tripled the money."[44] According to Mixner, lesbian and gay people contributed $3 million of the $25 million Clinton raised.[45]

In spite of the money Mixner raised and assurances by Clinton of access to decision makers with regard to lesbian and gay issues, Mixner and other activists were frozen out and treated badly by most members of Clinton's inner circle, a sordid story that Mixner tells in his book, *Stranger among Friends*. Clinton's youthful and arrogant aides, Rahm Emanuel and George Stephanopoulos, both from white ethnic groups that had been discriminated against in the past, were the worst offenders. In May 1996, when Clinton said he would support a Republican bill denying recognition of same-sex marriages, Mixner called the decision "nauseating and appalling" and an "act of political cowardice."[46]

Although Mixner's public criticisms of Clinton led Rahm Emanuel, at one point, to declare Mixner "persona non grata," by 2002, when Emanuel was running for Congress in a Chicago district with a large sexual and gender minority population, the two had nicer things to say about one another. Emanuel claimed his conflict with Mixner was a learning experience and that he hoped to bring people together "for the good of the country." Mixner responded, "Rahm and I will never be friends, but he's running a great campaign, doing all the right things working with and for the gay community."[47] Mixner, like Geffen, has rallied sexual minority peoples' support for various Democratic politicians, just as the Log Cabin Republicans have raised money and gotten out the more conservative gay vote. As a longtime admirer of Bernie Sanders, he gave the Sanders campaign a monthly contribution from its early stages, but he endorsed Hillary Clinton as soon as it became clear that she would win the nomination, claiming that he had "never viewed her as anything other than a progressive" and therefore she "has earned our support."[48]

LGBT INDIVIDUALS IN THE MILITARY

Almost immediately after he entered office, in 1993, Bill Clinton blundered into a firestorm over gay people's participation in the military. After initially taking a clear and principled stand, based at least in part on his pledge to Mixner and the donors he brought into the Clinton campaign, he crumbled in the face of opposition led by a traditional Southern Democrat, Senator Sam Nunn of Georgia, then chairman of the Senate Armed Forces Committee. This was yet another example of what had been true since 1939—Southern Democrats were pivotal in both the Senate and the House because of their alliance with Northern Republicans on many issues that were of key concern to union leaders and liberals. In his opposition to sexual and gender minority people serving in the military, Nunn also had other support outside Congress, including the Joint Chiefs of Staff and the entire religious right. Colin Powell was also against allowing openly lesbian, gay, or bisexual men and women in the military, although he later tried to sugarcoat his vigorous opposition by telling Henry Louis Gates Jr., "I never presented the case in terms of there being something wrong, morally or any other way, with gays. I just couldn't figure out a way to handle the privacy aspect." (As journalist Clarence Page pointed out, Powell's argument that sexual minority people in the military would threaten "discipline, good order, and morale" was the very same language that Gen. Dwight Eisenhower had used in the 1940s to justify maintaining racial segregation in the army.)[49] Others in the military were much more blunt, and crude, about their opposition to sexual minority people in the military: Adm. Thomas Moore, former chairman of the Joint Chiefs of Staff, once referred to homosexuality as "a filthy, disease-ridden practice."[50]

The result was Clinton's endorsement of an ambiguous policy generally referred to as "don't ask, don't tell," which went into effect in November 1993, whereby sexual minority people could be in the military as long as they did not acknowledge their sexual orientation. It did not take long for many to conclude that things had gotten worse, not better, for sexual minority people in the military. In Mixner's view, by mid-1995, "it was clear to everyone, except perhaps the President and his staff, that the 'Don't Ask, Don't Tell' policy was a disaster." As he went on to note, the number of dismissals of lesbian, gay, and bisexual people from the military had not, as intended, decreased but instead had increased.[51]

The pattern of increased dismissals continued until 2001. Whereas 617 service members had been dismissed for their sexual orientation in 1994, by

2001 that number had more than doubled to 1,273. Then, clearly because the country was at war, first in Afghanistan and then in Iraq, and because meeting goals for new recruits had become more and more difficult, the numbers declined, first to 902 in 2002, then to 787 in 2003, and to 653 in 2004 (the same decline in discharges for lesbian, gay, and bisexual people occurred in World War II and during every war since then). Despite this decline based on military needs, a government study revealed that more than three hundred foreign-language specialists considered critical in the war on terrorism had been dismissed since 1993 because of their sexual orientation, including fifty-four who spoke Arabic; another four hundred or so with critical skills, such as specialists in code breaking and air traffic controllers, were also dismissed.[52]

By late 2003, on the tenth anniversary of the policy, nearly ten thousand service members had been dismissed. The Servicemembers Legal Defense Network, a group that has monitored the policy since its inception, held a news conference at which three retired military officers, two generals and one admiral, criticized the policy as ineffective and demeaning and disclosed that they had been forced to hide their sexual orientation from family and friends.[53] And by 2005, critics of the policy had gained new allies, including conservatives, in part because of the cost of recruiting replacements (according to the Government Accountability Office, it cost nearly $100 million to replace those dismissed between 1993 and 2003, and this did not count the costs of investigating them, providing counseling for them, or handling legal challenges).[54] Others, like Wayne Gilchrest, a conservative Republican member of the House from Maryland, said that he had changed his views on the policy out of respect for gay marines with whom he had served in Vietnam and for his gay brother.[55]

Even though Clinton later came to regret the policy—in 1999, while still in office, he acknowledged that the implementation of the policy was "out of whack," and in 2000, after the election, he simply referred to it as that "dumb ass policy"—it remained in effect until the end of 2010. Finally, after numerous lawsuits, despite ongoing opposition from the heads of the marine corps, army, and navy, and after attempted filibusters, both the House and the Senate passed the Don't Ask, Don't Tell, Repeal Act of 2010. Implementation began in mid-2011. In February 2015, Ashton Carter, the secretary of defense, named Eric Fanning, an openly gay man, as his chief of staff. Fanning, a graduate of Dartmouth, had never served in the military—he worked for CBS National News, for two strategic communications firms, and then in various administrative roles in the navy, air force, and army, before his appointment. In September of that same year, Obama named Fanning as secretary of the army, making him the highest-ranking openly gay member of the Department of Defense. He served in that capacity until January 2017.[56]

In April 2017, Trump, after his first nominee (a billionaire owner of a professional hockey team) had to withdraw because of financial conflicts of interest, nominated Mark E. Green, a Tennessee state legislator, to replace Fanning. Green previously referred to being transgender as "a disease." This nomination was vehemently opposed by LGBT advocates, and he withdrew his name in May 2017. Still, that Trump would nominate a man with such views, plus the appointment of Jeff Sessions as attorney general and Tom Price as the secretary of health and human services—both men have been rabid opponents of legislation supporting the LGBT community—indicated that, during a Trump administration, the government is unlikely to be a friend to the LGBT community, and much will depend on decisions in the court system.[57]

Shortly after the don't ask, don't tell policy was repealed in December 2010, Tammy Smith, who had been in the army since 1986, came out to her military colleagues. In April 2012, when she was promoted to brigadier general, she became the first openly lesbian general officer. At the ceremony, when her wife, Tracey Hepner, pinned the star on her, it was a long way from General Westmoreland kissing the first woman general on the lips at her promotion ceremony (see chapter 3). In 2015, Smith took command of the ninety-eighth training division at Fort Benning, Georgia, and in 2016, she became a major general.[58]

Similarly, in 2015, Brigadier General Randy S. Taylor, who had been in the service for twenty-seven years, at a Pentagon ceremony introduced his husband ("My husband Lucas is sitting right up there"). He also served as the master of ceremonies at the Pentagon's Fourth Gay Pride Celebration.[59]

That there is now at least one openly gay general, and at least one openly lesbian general, and that each year there is a gay pride celebration at the Pentagon, speaks volumes about the dramatic and previously unimaginable changes that took place within the military over the space of about twenty-five years, with the pace greatly accelerating after 2010. Still, there are very few LGBT individuals who serve in the military at the highest military ranks, even though doors have been forced open by activists who have risked their careers.

LGBT PEOPLE IN CONGRESS, BUT NOT IN THE CABINET

As yet, no openly LGBT individuals have been appointed to presidential cabinets. However, openly gay men, lesbians, and one bisexual person now have run for and been elected to the House of Representatives and the Senate.

There have been two eras in which sexual and gender minority people have been in the House or the Senate: the first, in which gay men either were elected, outed, and then came out publicly, or they came out publicly only after they had left office, and the second, in which lesbian, gay, and bisexual people have disclosed their sexual orientation before the campaign, and were elected (as yet, no openly transgender people have been elected to the House or the Senate). The first era included Democrats such as Barney Frank (D-MA), who served from 1981 to 2013, and Gerry Studds (D-MA), who served from 1973 to 1997, and Republicans such as Steve Gunderson (R-WI), who served from 1981 to 1997, Jim Kolbe (R-AZ), who served from 1985 to 2007, and Mark Foley (R-FL), who served from 1995 to 2006. Much has been written about how and why they were outed, and how it affected their political careers.[60]

The second era began in 1998 when Tammy Baldwin, the first openly lesbian member of the Wisconsin Assembly, ran for and won a seat in the House. She served in that capacity from 1999 through 2013, when she successfully ran for the Senate against the Republican governor of Wisconsin, Tommy Thompson. She was, and continues to be, the only openly lesbian, gay, or bisexual person in the Senate.

Baldwin's parents divorced shortly after her birth in 1962, and she and her mother moved in with her maternal grandparents (both grandparents worked at the University of Wisconsin, her grandfather as the chair of the biochemistry department and her grandmother as a costume designer for the theater department). When she was nine, her mother married again, this time to an African American. Baldwin graduated first in her class at Madison West High School and then went to Smith, where she completed a double major in political science and math. She returned to Wisconsin, and just two years later, she was elected to the first of four terms on the Dane County Board of Supervisors. During her first two terms, she also completed a law degree at the University of Wisconsin. In 1993, she won election to the Wisconsin state legislature, thus becoming the first openly lesbian, gay, or bisexual member of that body.[61]

As of March 2017, there were five openly gay men and one openly bisexual woman in the House, all of whom are Democrats: Jared Polis (D-CO), elected in 2008; David Cicilline (D-RI), elected in 2010; Sean Patrick Maloney (D-NY), elected in 2012; Mark Takano (D-CA), elected in 2012; Mark Pocan (D-WI), elected in 2012; and Kyrsten Sinema (D-AZ), elected in 2012.

These six members of the House received undergraduate degrees from prestigious schools (Princeton, Brown, the University of Virginia, Harvard, the University of Wisconsin, and Brigham Young), and among them they hold two law degrees and a PhD. They range in age from forty-one (Sinema) to fifty-seven (Takano). They come from varied backgrounds, including one whose parents owned a successful business (Polis), another whose father was a prominent attorney (Cicilline), one whose parents were interned during World War II (Takano), and one whose parents divorced when she was young and who lived for two years in an abandoned gas station with no running water or electricity (Sinema).

CONCLUSION

The gay liberation movement, like the women's movement of the late 1960s, was emboldened by the civil rights and antiwar movements. As the movements of the 1960s took on various forms, they affected one another and, to varying degrees, contributed to cracking the monolithic nature of the power elite.

The problem facing openly sexual and gender minority people as they move closer to the power elite, while unique in some ways, is, at a deeper level, similar to the problems facing others who were previously excluded. They, too, will have to find ways to enter the comfort zone of the upper- and upper-middle-class, Ivy League–educated, white, cisgender, heterosexual males at the center of the power elite. They will have to do so by asserting as many similarities as possible and by managing differences that might rekindle discomfort. Most of all, for the foreseeable future they apparently have to behave in traditionally masculine or feminine ways.

Woods makes this point about identity management when he asserts that while many in the corporate world "don't care if someone's gay or not," they do care "how effeminate you are."[62] It is likely that a similar problem faces lesbians in making sure they do not appear too "masculine." As we concluded in chapter 3, this is a key issue for heterosexual women as well.

Our assumption is that there are, and have always been, sexual minority people in the power elite, but to stay there, they have had to "manage" their image by remaining closeted. Whether openly LGBT people will become more than a token presence in the power elite in the coming decades remains to be seen. For now, the fact remains that sexual and gender minority people, who are relatively few but increasing in number, especially among younger people, have made gains against overwhelming odds because they come from all classes and religious backgrounds, including closeted, outed, and open members of the upper-middle and upper classes with the wealth and connections to support a movement energized by indefatigable activists.

Chapter Eight

The Ironies of Diversity

As the preceding chapters have shown in detail, the power elite and Congress are more diverse than they were before the civil rights movement, and the social movements that followed in its wake brought pressure to bear on corporations, politicians, and government. Although the power elite is still composed primarily of Christian, white men, there are now Jews, women, blacks, Latinos, Asian Americans, South Asians, and a few openly gay men and lesbians on the boards of the country's largest corporations; presidential cabinets are far more diverse than was the case sixty years ago; and the highest ranks of the military are no longer filled solely by white men. In the case of elected officials in Congress and the Supreme Court, there is much more diversity now than in the past. At the same time, we have shown that the incorporation of members of the different groups has been uneven.

In this final chapter, we look at the patterns that emerge from our specific findings to see if they help explain the gradual inclusion of some groups, the continuing or near exclusion of others, and, for some groups, either stasis or a notable drop-off in their presence in the power elite. We also discuss the impact of diversity on the power elite and the rest of American society. We argue that most of the effects were unexpected and are ironic. The most important of these ironies relates to the ongoing tension between the American dream of individual advancement and fulfillment ("liberal individualism") and the class structure: we conclude that the racial, ethnic, and gender diversity celebrated by the power elite and the media actually reinforces the unchanging nature of the class structure and increases the tendency to ignore class inequalities. We also wonder if the stasis and drop-off in diversity in these higher circles signal the twilight of further diversification of the power elite.

WHY ARE SOME INCLUDED?

The social movements and pressures for greater openness at the higher levels of American society led to some representation for many previously excluded groups, but some have been more successful than others. Four main factors explain why some people come to be included: higher-class origins, elite educations, a lighter skin color, and the ability to make oneself acceptable to established members of the power elite through a process that we call "identity management."

The Importance of Class

Those who have brought diversity to the power elite have tended to come from business and professional backgrounds, like the white, Christian males C. Wright Mills studied more than sixty years ago. We estimate that about 70 percent of the women who have become corporate directors or CEOs of *Fortune* 500 companies grew up in privileged economic circumstances—the top 15 percent of the class structure (often called the upper-middle and upper classes, with the upper class also being an ownership class that depends on profits for most of its income and hence also a "capitalist" class).[1] Similarly, many of those born in other countries were born to privilege. For example, most of the Cuban Americans and Chinese Americans who became part of the power elite came from displaced ruling classes, far from the conventional image of immigrants who start with nothing. Some of the South American immigrants who rose to the top at a few corporations in recent years also came from high-status backgrounds, and even more so for a number of South Asians who came from privileged backgrounds in India, usually accompanied by a British-style education.

On the other hand, the Jews and Japanese Americans in high positions have mostly been the products of two- and three-generational climbs up the social ladder. The first African American members of the corporate elite and the cabinet tended to come from the small black middle class that predated the civil rights movement. Although there is no systematic information on the social backgrounds of gay and lesbian leaders, who are treated in most studies as if they have no class origins, our anecdotal information suggests that many visible activists and successful professionals have come from business and professional families as well.

A high-level social background, of course, makes it easier to acquire the values, attitudes, and styles that are necessary to hire, fire, and manage the work lives of employees with blue, white, and pink collars. This point can be extended to include even those from more modest circumstances, like Lauro Cavazos, whose father was a ranch foreman, or Katherine Ortega, Sue Ling Gin, and David Geffen, whose families owned small businesses, or David Mixner, whose father was in charge of minority farmhands on a farm he did not own. Most of those we studied, in other words, learned firsthand that a few people boss the majority or have independent professions based on academic credentials and that they, too, were expected to be part of those who give orders and have professional careers.

When we compare the newly arrived members of the power elite with their counterparts in Congress, however, two further generalizations emerge. First, members of the power elite tend to come from more privileged social backgrounds than elected officials. Second, the elected officials are more likely to be Democrats than Republicans. These two findings suggest that there are class and political dimensions to our findings on the differences between the power elite and Congress that cut across gender and ethnic lines. Now that the power elite is housed almost exclusively in the Republican Party and the liberal-labor coalition has become more important within the Democratic Party, the country's traditional regional, racial, and ethnic politics is being replaced by a more clear-cut class-and-race politics, with both the Republicans and Democrats able to say that they are diverse in terms of leaders and candidates from all previously excluded groups. (Even the Republican Party can claim gay and lesbian members thanks to the Log Cabin Republicans, although many conservative Republicans would prefer not to.) And as everyone knows, the number of African Americans who are Republicans is very small, but they are important to the success of the party with centrist white voters because they "prove" that the party is trying to be inclusive of everyone. [2]

The Importance of Education

Class by no means explains all of our findings, however. Education also matters a great deal. The members of underrepresented groups who make it to the power elite are typically better educated than the white males who are already a part of it. This is seen with the European American women and

African Americans on corporate boards and in presidential cabinets, as well as the successful Asian American and South Asian immigrants. Education seems to have given them the edge needed to make their way into the power elite. In the case of many of the African Americans, new educational programs in elite private high schools, created in response to the disruptions of the 1960s, were more than an edge. They were essential. In effect, these scholarship programs in part compensated for the wealth they did not have, providing both the social and cultural capital that usually requires considerable wealth and family connections.[3]

Moreover, it is not merely having academic degrees that matters but also where those degrees are from. Again and again, we saw that a significant number were from the same few schools that educate Christian, white, male leaders, such as Harvard, Yale, Princeton, and MIT on the East Coast, the University of Chicago in the Midwest, and Stanford on the West Coast. Whether it was Bill Clinton or George W. Bush in the White House, Hillary Clinton in the Senate and as secretary of state, Joseph Lieberman in the Senate from Connecticut, or Clarence Thomas on the Supreme Court, they all went to Yale in the 1960s.

These elite schools not only confer status on their graduates but also provide contacts with white male elites that are renewed throughout life at alumni gatherings and on other special occasions. School connections, in turn, lead to invitations to attend exclusive social events and join expensive social clubs, which extend the newcomers' social networks even further. With success in business or a profession comes invitations to serve on boards of trustees of elite foundations and universities, and the circle is completed.

In short, they have acquired the full complement of networks of friends and contacts that provides access to jobs, financial capital, and marriage partners of high social standing, which are the essence of social capital. The newcomers thereby become part of the ongoing institutional framework that defines and shapes the power elite in the United States, even though only a few of them are likely to reach the very top. The individuals in the power elite may come and go, and they may diversify in gender, race, ethnicity, and sexual orientation, but there is stability and continuity in terms of the types of people who are fed into the set of institutions that define the power elite and dominate the American social structure.

As was true of social class origins, there is a difference in educational attainment between those in the power elite and those in Congress: the men and women elected to Congress are not as likely as those in the power elite to have attended elite colleges and universities or to have earned postgraduate degrees.

The Importance of Color

Just as class alone cannot explain all of our findings, neither can the combination of class and education: skin color also matters. African Americans and darker-skinned Latinos find it more difficult than others to use their educational credentials and high-class social capital as passports to occupational success. This can be seen poignantly in our skin-color comparisons of successful blacks and Latinos. Even among those who had achieved some level of prominence, those who had made it into the power elite were lighter skinned than those who had not. On this score, our data simply reinforce both earlier and subsequent work by others. As the Glass Ceiling Commission concluded twenty years ago, a conclusion that still holds, "Our society has developed an extremely sophisticated, and often denied, acceptability index based on gradations in skin color."[4]

Julia Alvarez, a writer whose novels have captured the difficulties of leaving one's Latin American home and coming, with far fewer material resources, to the United States to start anew, understands well the importance of one's class background in the old country and of light skin in the new country. In an essay about leaving the Dominican Republic and coming to the United States as a young girl, Alvarez acknowledges the advantages her family had over other immigrant families because they were well educated, had access to money, and (as she says, "most especially") were light skinned:

> My family had not been among the waves of economic immigrants that left their island in the seventies, a generally darker-skinned, working-class group, who might have been the maids or workers in my mother's family house. We had come in 1960, political refugees, with no money but with "prospects": Papi had a friend who was a doctor at the Waldorf Astoria and who helped him get a job; Mami's family had money in the Chase Manhattan Bank they could lend us. We had changed class in America—from Mami's elite family to middle-class spics—but our background and education and most especially our pale skin had made mobility easier for us here.[5]

Alvarez's perceptive and honest assessment of the advantages she had (so different from the public relations stories put out by many corporate chieftains), coupled with the findings we have described on color discrimination, may help to explain why it is still the case that so few people of color have made it into the power elite. The failure of American society to accept darker-skinned citizens, especially African Americans, is the most difficult issue that needs to be understood by social scientists. We return to this issue in the next section, "Why Are Some Still Excluded?"

Although colorism in the United States is primarily a product of two centuries of slavery and a century of Jim Crow, it is also a worldwide phenomenon, as true in India as it is in the United States or the Dominican Republic. This predisposes immigrants from all over the world to adapt quite easily to the American version of colorism, and in the process to become as exclusionary toward African Americans as white Americans. [6]

Identity Management

Finally, we have seen that the newcomers who join the power elite have found ways to demonstrate their loyalty to those who dominate American institutions—straight, white, Christian males. They know how to act and interact using the manners, style, and conversational repertoire of the already established elite, and they can hold their own in discussing the fine points of literature and the arts; that is, they have the "cultural capital" that comes from high-class origins or an elite education. When William T. Coleman recited great poetry with his fellow law clerk, Boston Brahmin Elliot Richardson, he was not only sharing a mutual love of poetry with a colleague and friend; he was demonstrating his elite educational background. Reading between the lines of traditional stereotypes, we can imagine Jewish and black executives being properly reserved, Asian American executives acting properly assertive, gay male executives behaving in traditionally masculine ways, and lesbian executives acting in traditionally feminine ways. Within this context of identity management, we also can see why Cecily Cannan Selby decided to reduce tension at a dinner meeting with the previously all-male Avon Products board by lighting up a cigar and why Hazel O'Leary decided she had to learn to play golf if she wanted to advance in her corporate career. In all these ways, the newcomers are able to meet the challenge of moving into a "comfort zone" with those who decide who is and who is not acceptable for inclusion. They have shown that they are willing to pay the price to join the in-group.

At the same time, in chapter 3 we drew on research on the sociology of organizations to stress that the demand for demonstrations of outward conformity by established leaders is not primarily a matter of personal prejudice or cultural heritage. It is, instead, the need for trust and smooth working relationships within complex organizations that lead to the marked preference for women and people of color who think and act like the straight, Christian males running those organizations. Such demonstrations may be especially important when there are suspicions that the newcomers might have lingering loyalties to those they have left behind. The social movements that arose in the 1960s rocked the boat enough to open some space for nontraditional leaders, but not enough to change the way in which work is structured and institutions are managed. Unless, and until, changes are made in work structure and institutional cultures, underrepresented groups will be at a disadvantage in climbing the managerial hierarchy, even though they are now able to enter the competition.

In summary, class origins, an excellent education, and the proper appearance, especially in terms of lighter skin tone, and identity management through deft and timely displays of cultural and social capital, are the building blocks for entry into the power elite, with identity management as the final step, the icing on the cake.

WHY ARE SOME STILL EXCLUDED?

How is the continuing exclusion of African Americans and Latinos who are darker skinned to be explained? From the power-structure perspective that we favor, the answer is to be found in the economic and political domination of darker-skinned people that began when European settlers took North and South America from the Native Americans and imported an estimated ten to twelve million slaves from Africa in order to make the southern United States, the West Indies, and parts of Latin America highly profitable to them. This economically driven subjugation, which unfolded in brutal fashion shortly after 1492 in ways that are all too familiar, burgeoned in the United States in the late seventeenth century and created the "racial hierarchy" that persists to this day based on a jumble of prejudices, cultural stereotypes, strategies of exclusion, and feelings of superiority on the part of those who come to be defined as, and are accepted as, white.

The fact that both indigenous Indians and African slaves were conquered and subjugated in the United States is less visible today because there are so few Native Americans left. They are now often regarded positively as brave and heroic warriors, but until fairly recently, they were treated as less than human due to the first (and most successful, along with that in Australia) large-scale ethnic cleansing by a modern democracy. Their numbers dropped from millions in the pre-Columbian era in what is now the United States to 237,000 in 1900, in good part due to lack of immunity to European diseases in the first few hundred years, and then to murder for another two or three hundred years, at which point they were no longer a threat to the land hunger of the white settlers.[7] Today, most of the approximately 1.5 million self-identified Native Americans not living on reservations are of mixed white and Indian heritage, and 59 percent of those who are married are married to whites.[8]

In the United States, then, and unlike many Latin American countries, where both Indians and former African slaves mostly occupy the bottom rungs of society or are complete outcasts, the brunt of the persistent sense of group superiority on the part of Euro Americans is on the significant percentage of the population—about 13 percent, as we noted earlier—who are descendants of slaves (and slave masters in some cases). In this country, being "black" means being stigmatized because the dishonored status of being a slave became identified with the racial features of "blackness." In particular, skin color became the major means by which enslaved and conquered groups could be identified and stigmatized for purposes of keeping them subordinated. However, hair texture and facial features were also part of the subordinating racial stereotyping, and are playing an increasing role as darker skin also becomes a marker of immigrant groups who are somewhat less stigmatized.[9]

In addition to carrying the legacy of slavery, which stripped people of any group or personal identity, rendered them subject to constant surveillance and violence, and regularly broke up roughly one-third of all nuclear families as a way to destroy feelings of kinship, African Americans also continued to endure subordination to white Americans in the post-slavery era. In the South, that subordination began with the exploitative system called "tenant farming," which left African Americans with little more than their freedom, a mule, and a few farm implements.[10] In the North, African Americans were kept out of the best-paying construction jobs, often with the use of violence by white workers, despite their having the necessary skills. They encountered cross burnings, race riots, and racial covenants in deeds of trust when they tried to live in white neighborhoods, which meant they were excluded from predominantly white public schools and forced to pay higher prices for housing that depreciated in value because whites would not live nearby.[11] They were also less likely to receive any benefits from the government programs that carried many blue-collar workers into the middle class, such as federal housing financial loans and the GI Bill, a form of government subsidy that has long been forgotten by those who think of themselves as having made it exclusively on their own.

Until the 1960s, it was rare that any but a small number of African Americans could accumulate any wealth at all. Although the civil rights movement brought formal equality and voting power to African Americans, which in turn led to improved treatment in many social spheres and better jobs, especially with the government, the fact remains that it has been impossible for African Americans to close the socioeconomic gap with whites. According to detailed work on wealth accumulation by sociologist Thomas Shapiro, based on his own interviews in several cities, along with national surveys and government statistics, as of about ten years ago the typical African American family had only one-tenth the wealth of the average white family (a net worth of $8,000 versus $81,000 for whites). This was because whites were able gradually to accumulate wealth throughout the twentieth century with the help of the aforementioned government-backed mortgages, large tax deductions on home mortgages, the GI Bill, and other programs that were available to very few, if any, African Americans at the time. Moreover, whites were able to pass down this wealth to their children through inheritance, not only at the time of death, but also in the form of what Shapiro calls "transformative assets," which include help with college tuition, down payments on new homes (which then appreciate in value), and gifts or loans to survive unexpected crises that cause a temporary drop in income. According to more recent work, the gap is even more pronounced now.[12] Even when the focus is on income, not wealth, a study of the black-white income gap between 1967 and 2015 shows there has been no change in the substantial advantage that whites have had over blacks, at any level of the income distribution, over that forty-eight-year period, except for a soaring increase in the last decade in the gap between whites and blacks in the top 1 percent of earners.[13]

The historic legacy of income and wealth discrimination means that African Americans lack similar transformative assets. In addition, more black wealth goes to helping relatives and friends in need and to taking care of aging parents, so the little wealth African Americans do accumulate is less likely to be given to young adult children as transformative assets or eventually inherited by them. Even when blacks and whites are at the same level in terms of earnings, they are at different starting points in terms of wealth, making it impossible to close the gap through earnings. Racial inequality is growing worse, not better, because of both the initial advantages enjoyed by whites and their greater capacity to pass on these advantages as transformative assets. As Shapiro concluded in 2017: "The phrase 'toxic inequality' describes a powerful and unprecedented convergence: historic and rising levels of wealth and income inequality in an era of stalled mobility, intersecting with a widening racial wealth gap, all against the backdrop of changing racial and ethnic demographics."[14]

This huge wealth differential is compounded further by continuing discrimination and exclusion on the part of whites, especially in the area of employment, where many whites wrongly think there is now color-blind fairness.[15] Although the official racist ideology of the past is now gone, or at least not as likely to be verbalized in public, there is strong evidence that more covert forms of racism still persist that make many blacks feel uncomfortable or unwanted in white settings. In covert racism, which also has been called free-market and color-blind racism, traditional American values, especially those concerning the fairness of markets, including labor markets, are blended with antiblack attitudes in a way that allows whites to express antagonism toward blacks' demands ("Blacks are getting too demanding in their push for civil rights") or resentment over alleged special favors for blacks ("The government should not help blacks and other racial minorities—they should help themselves") without thinking of themselves as racists. White Americans say they simply want everyone to be treated the same, even though most of them know that African Americans are not treated equally and, if life is thought of as a race from birth to death, African Americans start the race many yards behind the usual starting point for whites.[16]

Then, too, more subtle forms of racial discrimination are uncovered in various kinds of social psychology experiments that have revealed "aversive racism," in which whites express egalitarian beliefs but also hold unacknowledged negative feelings about blacks. The resulting ambivalence means that they avoid blacks, especially when the norms are conflicting or ambiguous. The evidence for aversive and other subtle forms of racism is important because it reveals the persistence of cultural stereotypes about blacks and demonstrates that these stereotypes affect behavior, often at an unconscious level. These stereotypes, in turn, convey to African Americans that they continue to be seen as "different." They come to feel that they are not respected, which naturally breeds resentment and hostility, which is then sensed by whites and said to be groundless in this day and age.[17] It is a vicious circle in which the victims are blamed for the poverty into which they have been collectively forced, with only a relative handful able to escape each generation.

This cycle of discrimination, exclusion, resentment, and mutual recrimination is very different from what happens to most of the groups who come to the United States as immigrants from Europe, Asia, or Latin America. Immigrants usually arrive with a sense of hope, often as families or in extended kin networks, and with an intact culture; these combine to enable them to endure the discrimination and exclusion they often face at the outset. As they persist in their efforts, the dominant majority grudgingly accepts some of them. As a recent National Academy of Science Report by sociologists and social psychologists has found, the "new" immigrants since the 1970s from Latin America and Asia are going through this process at exactly the same pace as did "white immigrants" in the late nineteenth and early twentieth centuries (many of whom were not considered "white" when they arrived).[18]

To make matters more complex, as we have noted, most recent immigrant groups bring similar negative attitudes toward African Americans from their home countries, as in the case of nonblack Latinos, or soon adopt them once they are in the United States, as seen in the case of some Asian American groups. They often claim that African Americans do not see the "opportunities" that lie before them and do not work hard. Thus, most immigrants come to share the stereotypes and prejudices of the dominant white majority.

This point is demonstrated for Mexican Americans in an analysis of information in the 1990 Latino Political Survey, where 60 percent of all Mexican Americans felt "warmly" toward whites on a "feeling thermometer scale," compared to only 36 percent who felt that way toward African Americans; those with lighter skin or born outside the United States expressed even less warmth toward African Americans.[19] Similar findings are reported in a study of attitudes toward African Americans on the part of both Latinos and Asian Americans in Los Angeles.[20]

The difference between the fates of subjugated minorities, such as Native Americans and African Americans, and immigrant Americans of all backgrounds, can be seen in the two most revealing indicators of acceptance by the dominant group: residential patterns and rates of intermarriage.

The classic study on residential patterns, based on census data from 1970, 1980, and 1990, demonstrated that African Americans continued to live in predominantly black neighborhoods, but this is not the case for Latinos or Asian Americans. In *American Apartheid: Segregation and the Making of the Underclass*, sociologists Douglas Massey and Nancy Denton revealed just how persistent residential segregation has been in the United States. Massey and Denton looked at the thirty metropolitan areas with the largest black populations. Based on two different measures ("black-white segregation" and "spatial isolation"), they concluded that the 1970s showed virtually no increase in integration, "despite what whites said on opinion polls and despite the provisions of the Fair Housing Act."[21] Moreover, they did not find that degree of segregation for Hispanics and Asian Americans. "In fact," Massey and Denton concluded, "within most metropolitan areas, Hispanics and Asians are more likely to share a neighborhood with whites than with another member of their own group." In turn, this residential distancing from African Americans comes to be shared by Latinos and Asian Americans, as seen in a study that asked Latinos and Asian Americans to construct their "ideal" neighborhood, which included no African Americans for 33 percent of Latinos and 40 percent of Asian Americans.[22]

In the final chapter of their book, which included 1990 census data, Massey and Denton concluded that "there is little in recent data to suggest that processes of racial segregation have moderated much since 1980. . . . Racial segregation still constitutes a fundamental cleavage in American society."[23] This conclusion still held based on data from the 2000 census, which showed only a slight decline in residential segregation for African Americans, along with increasing segregation for everyone along class lines.[24]

And, for the most part, it still held in 2016, twenty-three years after *American Apartheid* was first published. In a 2016 article, Massey acknowledged that "racial attitudes have thus evolved such that whites no longer insist on segregation in all circumstances and are willing to share social space with black Americans under certain limited conditions," such as metropolitan areas where blacks "are relatively affluent." However, he went on to say, where blacks make up a large portion of the population, and have high rates of poverty, they "continue to experience high levels of segregation."[25]

However, it was not simply that most whites wanted to exclude blacks from their neighborhoods. In fact, in the 1920s and 1930s residential segregation laws were passed in many cities and states, not just in the South, but also outside the South.[26] As a result, it was even more difficult for upwardly mobile blacks to raise their children in higher-class neighborhoods. As Mary Pattillo-McCoy showed in her 1999 book, *Black Picket Fences: Privilege and Peril among the Black Middle Class*, even those blacks who had made it into what Bart Landry a decade earlier had called "the new black middle class" were likely to live in black middle-class neighborhoods that were contiguous with lower-income black neighborhoods. As her subtitle suggests, the privilege of their middle-class experience was up against the pressures and the perils that came from living so close to lower-income, higher-crime areas, as it would be for the well-insulated white middle class as well.[27]

In her 2007 book, *Blue Chip Black: Race, Class, and Status in the New Black Middle Class*, Karyn Lacy found that even blacks in the predominantly black upper-middle-class neighborhoods in the Washington, DC, area that she studied—which were not contiguous with lower-income black neighborhoods—had to make constant efforts to assert their class standing in white public spaces. She looked especially at their experiences when shopping, when working in predominantly white settings, and when dealing with real estate agents. They use a variety of strategies to communicate their status, and their cultural capital, to the whites with whom they interacted, which she calls constructing public identities. This includes the use of "exclusionary boundary work" (showing they are different from lower-class blacks) and "inclusionary boundary work" (showing that they are similar to the middle- or upper-middle-class whites with whom they are interacting). For the most part it is successful, but it takes a great deal of energy and had its costs. As she put it, "Even when such strategies pay off, they can be tiring and irritating, exerting a potential psychological toll."[28]

Lacy's valuable study therefore makes clear that the black middle class is not monolithic, and the experiences of those in the black middle class can vary considerably. The high-income neighborhoods that she studied are atypical in the fact that they are not bordered by lower-income neighborhoods. As another sociologist, Patrick Sharkey, showed, using census data from 2000, there were only ninety-two census tracts that were predominantly black and surrounded by other relatively affluent neighborhoods (only 1.6 percent of all majority-black neighborhoods).[29] Lacy's findings, therefore, are even more striking in that they reveal just how challenging it is for those who live in the small percentage of more privileged upper-middle-class black neighborhoods that are not contiguous with lower-income neighborhoods to face the daily task of preempting the stereotypes and possible discrimination of the whites they encounter.

There have been dozens of studies focusing on the marriage patterns of underrepresented groups. All of them point to increasing intermarriage occurring between the large white population and each previously excluded immigrant group. Importantly, this increasing intermarriage is most striking among those who are the American-born children of immigrant parents, which shows how rapidly assimilation can occur if people live in common neighborhoods, go to common schools, and share common cultural traditions, anywhere from the Christian religion, a love of baseball, or a devotion to a favorite musical group. For example, drawing on data from the 1990 census, Jerry Jacobs and Terry Labov found that Filipino Americans, Native Americans, Cuban Americans, Chinese Americans, Japanese Americans, Puerto Rican Americans, and Mexican Americans all were quite likely to marry non-Hispanic whites (the percentages ranged from 66 percent to 28 percent), but this was not the case for African Americans (only 5 percent of the males and 2 percent of the females married non-Hispanic whites).[30]

More recent data indicate that the frequency of black-white intermarriage has increased, though blacks are still much less likely to intermarry than Asian Americans or Latinos. A study based on 2015 census data found that from 1980 to 2015, the percentage of Asian Americans intermarrying had dropped from 33 to 29, and the percentage of Latinos intermarrying had increased from 26 to 27; the percentage of African Americans intermarrying had increased from 5 to 18. In addition, the percentage of whites intermarrying had almost tripled during that thirty-five-year period, from 4 percent to 11 percent. However, whites were least likely to marry blacks: whereas 42 percent of the newlywed intermarriages were between whites and Hispanics, and 15 percent were between whites and Asians, only 11 percent were between whites and blacks (with far more black men marrying white women than white men marrying black women).[31]

Whites in the United States are less likely to marry those of African descent than whites in other countries. As Sheryll Cashin, a law professor at Georgetown who has written extensively about race, explains in her 2017 book, *Loving: Interracial Intimacy in American and the Threat to White Supremacy*:

> In the market for long-term partners, the United States remains an outlier in terms of the prominent racial barrier between those with visible African ancestry and those without it. Canada, France, Germany, Great Britain, and the Netherlands, for example, all have higher rates of unions between whites and second generation immigrants of African descent. . . . Canada, which never adopted antimiscegenation laws against Afro-Canadians or had much African slavery, provides a pointed contrast. . . . In a comparison of married or cohabiting couples aged twenty-five to thirty-four in metropolitan areas, one study

found that 62 percent of black men and 49 percent of black women in Canada have a white partner, compared with 16 percent of black men and 7 percent of black women in the United States.[32]

Although younger whites are more likely to intermarry or live with black partners than older whites, and although they hold attitudes showing that they are more likely to accept integration than do older whites, Cashin concludes that "frankly, all nonblacks have the most reluctance to integrate with blacks," more than with other nonwhite groups.[33] Therefore, although there has been an increase in intermarriage generally, and an increase in the frequency of intermarriage between whites and blacks, we conclude that the same pattern Jacobs and Labov found based on 1990 census data still holds: whites are the group least likely to intermarry, and, when they do intermarry, they are least likely to marry African Americans.[34]

Still, the demographic trends showing an increase in intermarriage, including between blacks and whites, and the trends on black-white biracial identities, provide some evidence that points in a different direction. These data suggest that there is now much less stigma related to black-white intermarriage than in the past. Moreover, the percentage of biracial children with one black and one white parent has increased dramatically. It was not until 2000 that the US Census first allowed respondents to choose that they were multiracial. As demographer William Frey has shown in his book *Diversity Explosion*, the number who identified as both black and white doubled during that ten-year period, to 1.8 million. Moreover, Frey breaks these data down by age, and shows that the numbers are far greater for young people than older people. In 2010, whereas only one in one hundred African Americans over the age of forty were identified as both black and white, it was one in fifteen for those under the age of five. As Frey argues, "These trends foreshadow a continued blurring of racial divisions at the household and personal levels that would have been unimaginable even a decade ago."[35] If the frequency of black-white intermarriage, and thus the frequency of biracial children born to black and white parents, continues to increase at the dramatic rate of the decade between 2000 and 2010, it would be a major indication that the castelike barriers that have held back African Americans can be broken down.

The power of our earlier comparison between the treatment of subordinated groups such as African Americans and immigrant groups is demonstrated in studies of the different course of events for most dark-skinned immigrants of African heritage, as examined most carefully in the case of West Indians.

Based on their experience of their home countries, where there are few blacks at the top and few whites at the bottom, they expect to encounter obstacles in occupational advancement due to what is called "structural racism" by sociologist Mary Waters,[36] who conducted revealing interviews with West Indians, African Americans, and their white supervisors at a food service company in New York. Despite their expectations about structural racism, however, West Indian immigrants arrive hopeful and with positive attitudes toward whites as individuals, leading to pleasant interactions with most of the whites they encounter. But their initial hopeful attitudes are gradually shaken by the unexpected "interpersonal racism" they encounter in some of their interactions with whites. They are also made wary by the degree to which everything is "racialized" in the United States. Although most of them retain a hopeful stance, they develop greater sympathy for what they see as the more defensive stance toward whites taken by African Americans.

As black immigrants come to realize the depth of the problem they face, they strive to preserve their accents and try to retain their "foreign" identities in an attempt to avoid the stigmatization applied to African Americans. They also attempt to socialize their children so that white Americans do not see them as African Americans. Earlier generations of West Indian immigrants, for example, sent their children back to the Caribbean to be educated. More recently, West Indians in New York who arrive from middle-class backgrounds have founded private schools that are based on the educational system "back home" in the islands. These schools often emphasize that their teachers have been trained in the West Indies, the curricula are rigorous, the students wear British-style school uniforms, and there is strict discipline.[37]

But these strategies are not always successful. Although some children of middle-class West Indians are able to resist racialization and end up among the blacks of African descent at the most selective universities in the United States (where as many as 25 percent of the black students have at least one parent who is foreign born), many others, as well as the children of other black immigrants, begin to view American society the same way working-class African Americans do because they face the same situation: high rates of unemployment, lack of good jobs, and not-so-subtle racism.[38] Treated like African Americans, many black West Indians, black Puerto Ricans, black Dominicans, and black Cubans come to see themselves subjectively as African Americans. As Waters concludes, "It is in the second generation that this process of rapid cultural change is most evident. The children of these immigrants do grow up exhibiting the racialism their parents are concerned with preventing. Indeed, the rapidity of the change in attitudes about race between parents and children is quite dramatic."[39]

Those white Americans who say that racism is a thing of the past and blame African Americans for creating problems for themselves by dwelling on it often point to their good interpersonal relations with immigrant groups, including West Indians, as evidence for their claim. However, as Waters demonstrates, the persisting racial discrimination practiced (and denied) by whites is in fact the root of the problem, generating the tensions that whites attribute to African Americans:

> It is the continuing discrimination and prejudice of whites, and ongoing struc-
> tural and interpersonal racism, that create an inability among American, and
> ultimately West Indian, blacks to ever forget about race. The behavior and
> beliefs about race among whites, and the culture of racist behaviors among
> whites, create the very expectations of discomfort that whites complain about
> in their dealing with their black neighbors, coworkers, and friends. That expec-
> tation is not some inexplicable holdover from the long-ago days of slavery, but
> rather a constantly re-created expectation of trouble, nourished by every taxi
> that does not stop and every casual or calculated white use of the word "nig-
> ger."[40]

Based on the findings on how differently black and nonblack immigrants are treated, it seems likely to us that, over time, the overwhelming majority of the children and grandchildren of nonblack immigrants to the United States will blend together with non-Hispanic whites into a common cultural pool and then sort themselves out along class and educational lines, using ethnic and racial identities for mostly symbolic and strategic purposes. On the other hand, Americans of African descent, whether African Americans or immigrants, will find themselves struggling to hold on to whatever class standing they are able to attain. Race, as well as class, will continue to determine their life chances.[41] We therefore agree with those who argue that people of African descent have been treated very differently from all other previously excluded groups. In making this point, we are fully aware that other groups have suffered many forms of discrimination and exclusion, and we do not want to diminish the depth of personal anguish that such mistreat-ment has caused, but the fact remains that people of African heritage are the only ones to experience the combined effects of race, slavery, and segrega-tion.[42] This confluence is unique because the "dishonored" or "stigmatized" status attached to slavery everywhere it has been practiced cannot easily be overcome or forgotten when there are the constant reminders of African descent, such as skin color, hair texture, and distinctive facial features. These findings point to a stark possibility: the United States continues to be a country based on class but with elements of caste that are present at all class levels.

Based on our analysis that includes the distinction between subordinated and immigrant minorities as well as skin color, we can see why the gains made by African Americans since the civil rights movement are in constant peril in a context where they have not been able to accumulate sufficient wealth to help their children or provide support in times of crisis. Given the ongoing discrimination and accumulated disadvantages, it may be that even the current rate of entry into the power elite will be difficult to maintain. Our data on the number of African American CEOs and corporate directors support this view. Upwardly mobile black Americans could continue to be the exception rather than the rule without the strong support of affirmative action laws and programs at the federal level.[43] But such laws and programs have been trimmed back since the new conservative era began in the 1980s, making further progress problematic.

WHY DID BLACKS IN THE SOUTH JOIN AN "IMPROBABLE PARTNERSHIP"?

These stark conclusions may also provide a larger perspective for understanding why many (but not all) African American leaders in the South were willing to work with the Republicans on the redistricting plan in the early 1990s (discussed in chapter 4), which ultimately led to Republican control of the House in 1994 and most of the years since then. In the first three decades after the Civil War, twenty African American Republicans served in the House, but all were gone by 1901 (in a defiant farewell address, one of them admonished: "This is perhaps the Negroes' temporary farewell to the American Congress, but let me say, Phoenix-like, he will rise up some day and come again").[44] Ten more African Americans, all in the North, joined the House before 1970, the first of whom was elected from an inner-city neighborhood in Chicago in 1928, followed by black colleagues from similar neighborhoods in New York (1944), Detroit (1954), and Philadelphia (1958), and then six others during the ferment created by the civil rights movement in the 1960s.

But no African Americans were elected from the eleven "Southern states" traditionally defined as by political scientists (Alabama, Arkansas, Florida, Georgia, Louisiana, Mississippi, North Carolina, South Carolina, Tennessee, Texas, and Virginia) until 1972, when two were elected.[45] One was Andrew Young, a highly regarded minister and civil rights leader who had worked closely for several years with Martin Luther King Jr. Young won his seat in a heavily black (but not majority-black) district in Atlanta, and served two terms before accepting an appointment from President Jimmy Carter to be the first African American to serve as the US ambassador to the United Nations. His seat in the House was taken by a white moderate Democrat who defeated John Lewis, the former president of the Student Nonviolent Coordinating Committee (SNCC) and one of the young black heroes of the civil rights movement. The other successful candidate, Barbara Jordan, was a rising leader in a Houston district that was mostly black, but partly Latino. She was a practicing attorney and the first African American to be elected (in 1966) to the Texas Senate since 1883. Harold Ford Sr., a prominent, well-to-do funeral director in the African American community in the increasingly black city of Memphis, narrowly defeated the white Republican incumbent to join Young and Jordan in 1974.

For the next nine years, there were no additional Southern blacks elected to the House. Despite having won the right to vote through the Voting Rights Act of 1965, African Americans were kept out of office, not only in the House of Representatives, but also at the local and state levels, through a variety of resistance strategies. This began with the elimination of districts in favor of citywide and countywide elections, which diluted the strength of the black vote, and also included the gerrymandering of state legislative districts. In the years between 1965 and 1989 in the eight Southern states that were most carefully watched by the Department of Justice and the federal courts for illegal actions in relation to voting, "black office-holding was practically nonexistent in council districts that were less than 40% black," and it usually took districts that were over 50 percent black for African Americans to win local elections.[46] As for the state level, African Americans won less than 1 percent of any of those eight states' legislative voting districts if the districts were less than 50 percent black.[47] Moreover, as the number of black elected officials at the local and state levels grew in the relatively few predominantly black districts, blacks in more racially mixed districts were even less likely to be elected, which indicated that most white Southerners were not willing to vote for blacks.[48]

In the face of the infrequency of the election of blacks at any level of government, several amendments to the Voting Rights Act in 1982 and a very supportive Supreme Court decision in 1986 strengthened the hands of the Department of Justice, federal courts, civil rights organizations, and civil rights lawyers. Although the Reagan administration attempted to water down and delay the implementation of the legislation and the Supreme Court ruling, there was a profound increase in black representation at the city and county levels due to the "virtual" elimination of at-large elections in all but the smallest cities. These changes, however, did not affect racially polarized voting, so there had to be "close federal supervision of boundary drawing."[49]

The most important impact of the many legal and activist initiatives at the congressional level in the early 1980s was the creation of two majority-black districts in which black candidates were soon successful. The first was a relatively uncontroversial augmentation of the inner-city district in Atlanta, where this time John Lewis was elected. There was also a lengthy court battle that forced the creation of a rural majority-black district in Mississippi won by Mike Espy, who, as we noted in chapter 4, subsequently became the secretary of agriculture in the Clinton administration. Their victories immediately doubled the number of Southern blacks in the House, which had been stuck at two since 1977.

Despite the efforts of black activists, there were still only four blacks from the South in the House as the 1980s ended. It is within the context of this very meager level of black representation (not only in the House, but at every level of government in the South), that many African American leaders decided to join the "improbable partnership" with Lee Atwater and other Republican leaders that created twelve new majority-black districts in eleven Southern states, even though it also created more districts in which Republicans could defeat white Southern Democrats.[50] As a result of this unlikely alliance, the number of African Americans from the South in the House skyrocketed from two in 1983 to seventeen in 1993. However, this dramatic increase did not continue. Twenty-four years later, as of mid-2017, there were only twenty-one African Americans from the South in the House, one of whom is a biracial Republican from a San Antonio suburb who was an undercover CIA operations agent in Pakistan for several years, where he learned the native language. He relies on the 15–20 percent of white voters to pull him through in a Texas district with a very small black population and a very large majority of Latinos that tends to have a very low turnout percent.[51]

As the South continues to gain House seats through reapportionment due to population shifts (especially in Texas and Florida), it seems likely that the Republicans, who dominate in almost all of the eleven traditional Southern states, will continue to shape districts to increase their majority. If the past twenty years are any indication, they will make sure that their computer-aided reconfigurations of districts do not eliminate any majority-black, majority-Latino, or majority-minority districts. For example, after wrangling for three years with Democrats (after the 2000 census gave two new House seats to Texas), the Republicans reconfigured six districts in which they felt confident they could defeat white Democrats. In the face of this reality, one conservative white Democrat switched his allegiance to the Republicans a year before the next election was held, and the Republicans won five other seats.

As a result, the Texas delegation to the House in 2005 consisted of twenty-one Republicans and eleven Democrats, a reversal of the situation just two years before, when there were seventeen Democrats and fifteen Republicans.[52] In addition, they added more black voters to a relatively new majority-minority district, which helped a black challenger defeat the white incumbent in a Democratic party primary and win election to Congress in 2004. This stratagem also provided the Republicans with "cover" for any legal challenge they might face based on their overall redistricting plan.[53]

Many of the Southern black leaders of the 1980s, most of them veterans of the early civil rights movement, may have had high hopes for black-white voting coalitions based on nonracial issues. This seems to have been the case for John Lewis, who said that African Americans in the South "should embrace the consequences of the Voting Rights Act" because they involved "a natural development of American politics and society" to one in which there could be "minority-led biracial and multi-racial coalitions."[54] Some perhaps concluded, in the face of the ongoing castelike political system in the South, that they would rather have a presence in the House than depend on occasional favors from white Southern Democrats. This approach would provide recognition for the black community and fulfill the personal ambitions of black politicians as well. Still others may have hoped to create enough of a black Southern presence in the House to aid an increasingly large biracial, multiethnic coalition in the Democratic Party outside the Southern states.

Whatever their motivations, African American leaders in the South and the many other pro-integration Americans of all colors, along with social scientists who study race relations, seem to have underestimated the determination of the great majority of those who now define themselves as "white" to shape the nation's future in their own image. Using both racial and nativist appeals, mixed with a conservative strain of Christianity, the white supremacists who now have substantial influence over the Republican Party have been able to fashion a message that resonates with a majority of white Christians in the North and an even larger majority of white Christians in the South. This does not augur well for the inclusion of all potential voters in the political arena, or for the acceptance of diversity in neighborhoods, schools, and workplaces.

CORPORATE SUPPORT FOR DIVERSITY

The American system of class stratification, mixed as it is with castelike exclusions of African Americans and of some darker-skinned immigrants, is not accepted by those who are forced to live on the margins of society. The result is ongoing resistance in the form of alleged "deviant" behaviors as well as periodic disruptions and new social movements led by young activists, which often begin with police confrontations that lead to the injuries or deaths of young black males. In this context, people and organizations within the power elite continue to support the kinds of programs founded during the uprisings and riots in inner cities in the 1960s. In doing so, they have been able in part to offset a small part of the Republican-led decline in government support for equal opportunity. In particular, they have supported a set of corporate-sponsored programs designed to identify and educate academically talented African American youngsters who can be groomed for elite universities and possible incorporation into the power elite. These programs begin in elementary school in some areas of the country, then carry through to private high schools, Ivy League universities, and corporate internships. These programs are also financed by donations from the large charitable foundations that the corporate rich in turn influence through financial donations and directorship positions, as well as by a myriad of small family foundations that donate a few hundred thousand to a few million dollars each year. Since we have written about these programs elsewhere, with a special emphasis on the first and largest of them, A Better Chance, founded in the early 1960s by a handful of New England boarding school headmasters with help from the Rockefeller Foundation, we will provide only three examples here.[55]

The Black Student Fund in Washington, DC, places students in more than fifty private schools in Maryland, Virginia, and the District of Columbia with the help of foundation grants and personal gifts. Since its founding in 1964, it has served thousands of students, the large majority of whom have gone on to earn at least a BA. The Steppingstone Foundation, which started in Boston and added programs in Philadelphia and Hartford, has a program for children in the fourth and fifth grades, who are prepared through two six-week summer sessions, Saturday classes, and after-school classes once a week for acceptance into both private and elite public schools that will see them through their high school years with the help of scholarship support. At its founding in 1990, the program served fourteen students; in 2015, at the time of its twenty-fifth anniversary, it provided assistance to more than 1,600 students. Many of the Steppingstone graduates have attended prestigious schools (in 2016, Steppingstone students were accepted at Columbia, Johns Hopkins, MIT, and Yale).

Prep for Prep in New York City may currently be the largest and most comprehensive of these programs. Created in 1978 as a pilot project under the auspices of Columbia University's Teachers College just as the full-scale attack on affirmative action was beginning, it takes in fifth through seventh graders in New York City each year for a fourteen-month program to prepare them for placement in private day schools and boarding schools. Like the Steppingstone program, it includes two intensive, seven-week summer programs, as well as after-school classes one day a week and Saturday classes during the school year. It sponsors a leadership institute and offers counseling services. Its program of summer job placements is meant to introduce students to the business and professional worlds. Alumni participate in a summer advisory program to help create what is called the "Prep Community," a support group that provides a sense of group identification.

As of October 2016, 4,521 Prep for Prep students had graduated from day schools, boarding schools, or specialized high schools like the Bronx School of Science (another 719 were currently enrolled at those schools), and the large majority went on to graduate from college. Many of those college graduates had attended schools characterized as "most selective" on the annual list published by *U.S. News & World Report*. On its website, Prep for Prep provides the numbers of its alumni who, as of 2017, had attended Ivy League schools: Harvard (174), Yale (160), Penn (155), Columbia (131), Brown (100), Princeton (86), Cornell (88), and Dartmouth (54). It also included the most frequently attended schools for graduate work: Columbia (124), NYU (116), Harvard (75), Penn (73), Fordham (38), and Yale (34).

Wall Street lawyers, financiers, and corporate executives direct the program. For example, its chairman, Scott L. Bok, is the CEO at Greenhill and Co. Others on the board work at powerhouse corporations like Blackstone, Bank of America, Merrill Lynch, Turner Broadcasting Systems, and Deutsche Bank, at major law firms, and investment banks. There are two emeritus chairmen, John L. Vogelstein, a senior limited partner at the investment bank E. M. Warburg, Pincus, & Company, and Martin Lipton, a partner at Wachtel, Lipton, Rosen & Katz.

Once African American students are in college, there are programs that encourage any interest they may have in going to law school or business school. A joint program between major corporations and the Harvard Business School is one good example of how African Americans are recruited for the business community. For thirty-five years, the Harvard Business School has sponsored the Summer Venture in Management Program, a weeklong residential program designed to expose talented minority students to management in the business world. The participants are "underrepresented minority U.S. citizens" who have completed their junior year of college, been hired as interns during the summer by sponsoring companies (generally *Fortune*-level companies), and been nominated by those companies to spend a week at the Harvard Business School learning what a high-profile business school is like. Participation in the program does not guarantee subsequent acceptance into the Harvard Business School, but it does allow the school to identify and encourage applications from highly qualified individuals.

Taken as a whole, this elementary-to-graduate-school pipeline may produce several thousand potential members of the corporate community each year, if successful graduates of public high schools who receive business and law degrees are added to the prep school graduates. However, these programs are not large enough to provide opportunities for more than a tiny fraction of all African Americans without much more help from the government at the national, state, and local levels. They are primarily a way to provide some highly educated Americans of African descent with the educational credentials to rise in the corporate community.

THE MANY IRONIC IMPACTS OF DIVERSITY

The impetus for greater diversity, as we have stressed, did not come from within the power elite but was the result of external pressures brought to bear by the civil rights movement. The fact that the American power elite was in competition with the Soviet Union for access and influence in previously colonized Third World countries also played a role, but that factor can easily be exaggerated in historical hindsight. Faced with the possibility of continuing massive disruption and rioting in the inner cities of major urban areas, most members of the power elite reluctantly accepted integration, and later diversity, as a goal.

Their willingness to take major steps to quell more rioting is best demonstrated in the case of the affirmative action programs originally designed to create more job opportunities for African Americans. Despite hesitation among pro-integration Americans about breaking the taboo on quotas and preferences, including on the part of the social psychologists and black activists who had been working toward integration for decades, affirmative action policies were hurriedly adopted by political and business elites in 1967. These leaders within the power elite acted in haste in the face of the estimated 329 major disturbances in 257 cities between 1964 and 1968, which resulted in 220 deaths, 8,371 injuries, and 52,629 arrests.[56] At the urging of first President Kennedy and then President Johnson at off-the-record meetings with the Business Council, at the time the most central organization in the power elite, corporate CEOs took the lead in calling on all businesses to provide more jobs for African Americans as quickly as possible. They thereby helped legitimize what they knew was preferential hiring because job programs were seen not only as the fastest and surest way to restore domestic tranquility but also as a means of avoiding larger government programs and expanded welfare benefits as well. Moreover, it was the corporate-backed Nixon administration in 1969 that created the stringent guidelines for hiring by government contractors (under the guise of "good faith" efforts at meeting numerical "targets"), which were soon attacked by ultraconservatives as a "quota" system once the upheavals and the burning of cities had subsided.[57]

Once the concern with urban unrest declined, however, the elite origins of the plan were soon ignored. It was at this point, too, that Nixon abandoned his guidelines, and ultraconservative Republicans began to attack affirmative action as unfair to whites and unconstitutional—a mere experiment by liberals and professors. The fear of disruption was gone, so now the rewriting of history could begin, along with attempts to capitalize on the increasing backlash among white workers, whose race-based voting in 1968 provided the margin of victory for Nixon's election and initiated an era of antiunion activities that soon helped to undermine those in the white American middle class who did not have college degrees. Thus, in the first of the many ironies arising from the saga of diversity, African Americans and white liberals, who had been very hesitant about preferential hiring in the beginning, ended up defending a program created and endorsed by white male elites in a time of crisis.[58] In a related irony, the successful ultraconservative Republican campaign to place the "blame" for the affirmative action program on African Americans and white liberals helped in the ongoing effort to dislodge frustrated whites from the Democratic Party, blue collar and white collar, union and nonunion, and, in the process, make it possible for antiunion forces to destroy the union movement.[59]

Although it was African Americans and their white allies who created the disruption and pressures that led to government programs, including affirmative action, other previously excluded groups soon became eligible for consideration and benefited greatly, perhaps even more than African Americans in terms of higher-level jobs.[60] This change, which was gracefully accepted by most African American leaders, and even seen by some of them as a way to expand their coalition, ended up marginalizing African Americans within the programs they created. It also added to the opposition by middle-American white males, who deeply resented the increased competition they had to face for good blue-collar and government jobs from African Americans, other people of color, and women of all colors.

In response to this growing resentment, defenders of the program in and around the corporate world began to talk in the latter half of the 1970s about the need for "diversity" in management circles and to emphasize its importance for business reasons rather than social-justice goals. At this point, the focus shifted to such business advantages as having managers who could interact with an increasingly heterogeneous set of lower-level wage earners. Proponents of diversity also emphasized that a "multicultural" management team would be essential for competing in the many non-European countries that were part of the rapidly expanding global economy, and in increasingly diverse domestic retail markets as well. But for all the changes in rationale and the emphasis on bottom-line business objectives, the actual practices of the corporations (and universities and large nonprofit organizations) remained about the same, based on the procedures and programs initially established by social movements and government laws.[61]

Although African American management consultants were part of this effort to redefine the affirmative action programs as diversity programs and thereby fend off the right wing of the Republican Party, a further irony developed: diversity no longer needed to include African Americans. The new goal was to have a high percentage of nonwhites and women. And it was not long before foreign-born executives and professionals, even those who came to the United States as young educated adults from foreign universities, were included in the statistics, driving the numbers even higher.[62]

In what may be the greatest and most important irony of them all, the diversity forced upon the power elite may have helped to strengthen it. Diversity has given the power elite a set of people who can serve, however inadvertently, as ambassadors, buffers, and tokens. This is an unintended consequence that few insurgents or social scientists foresaw. As a number of subsequent social psychology experiments show and experience confirms, it often takes only a small number of upwardly mobile members of previously excluded groups, perhaps as few as 2 percent, to undermine an excluded group's definition of who is "us" and who is "them," which contributes to a decline in collective protest and disruption and increases striving for individual mobility. That is, those who make it are not only "role models" for individuals, but they are safety valves against collective action by aggrieved groups.[63]

Tokens at the top create ambiguity and internal doubt for members of the subordinated group. Maybe "the system" is not as unfair to their group as they thought it was. Maybe there is something about them personally that keeps them from advancing. Once people begin to ponder such possibilities, the likelihood of any sustained group action declines greatly. Because a few people have made it, the general human tendency to think of the world as just and fair reasserts itself: since the world is fair, and some members of my group are advancing, then it may be my fault that I have been left behind. As liberal and left-wing activists have long known, it is hard to sustain a social movement in the face of "reforms," which has led to long-standing and unresolved debates about how activists should proceed.[64]

DO NEW MEMBERS OF THE POWER ELITE
ACT DIFFERENTLY?

Perhaps it is not surprising that when we look at the business practices of the members of previously excluded groups who have risen to the top of the corporate world, we find that their perspectives and values do not differ markedly from those of their white male counterparts. When Linda Wachner, one of the first women to become CEO of a *Fortune*-level company, the Warnaco Group, concluded that one of Warnaco's many holdings, the Hathaway Shirt Company, was unprofitable, she decided to stop making Hathaway shirts and to sell or close down the factory. It did not matter to Wachner that Hathaway, which started making shirts in 1837, was one of the oldest companies in Maine, that almost all of the five hundred employees at the factory were working-class women, or even that the workers had given up a pay raise to hire consultants to teach them to work more effectively and, as a result, had doubled their productivity. The bottom-line issue was that the company was considered unprofitable, and the average wage of the Hathaway workers, $7.50 an hour, was thought to be too high (that year, Wachner herself was paid $10 million in salary and stock, and Warnaco had a net income of $46.5 million). "We did need to do the right thing for the company and the stockholders," explained Wachner.[65]

Nor did ethnic background matter to Thomas Fuentes, a senior vice president at a consulting firm in Orange County, California, a director of Fleetwood Enterprises, and chairman of the Orange County Republican Party. Fuentes targeted fellow Latinos who happened to be Democrats when he sent uniformed security guards to twenty polling places "carrying signs in Spanish and English warning people not to vote if they were not U.S. citizens." The security firm ended up paying $60,000 in damages when it lost a lawsuit stemming from this intimidation.[66] The Fanjuls, the Cuban American sugar barons, had no problem ignoring labor laws in dealing with their migrant labor force, and Sue Ling Gin, an Asian American corporate director, explained to an interviewer that, at one point in her career, she had hired an all-female staff, not out of feminist principles but "because women would work for lower wages." Linda Wachner, Thomas Fuentes, the Fanjuls, and Sue Ling Gin acted as employers, not as members of disadvantaged groups. That is, members of the power elite of both genders and of all ethnicities practice class politics. In our study of those we call "new CEOs"—white women and CEOs of color—we looked at whether the companies that had appointed them as CEOs had scored higher on five different ratings that assessed the treatment of employees: "The 100 Best Companies for Women" (published by *Working Mother* magazine); "The 100 Best Corporate Citizens" (published by *Corporate Responsibility* magazine); the "Corporate Equality Index," or CEI (published by the Human Rights Campaign's Workplace Project); "The 100 Best Companies to Work For" (published by *Fortune* magazine); and "NAFE 50 Top Companies for Executive Women" (published by the National Association for Female Executives, or NAFE). When we compared the companies that had hired new CEOs with a sample of companies that had hired Jewish CEOs and another sample of companies that had not hired either new CEOs or Jewish CEOs, we found that the companies that had hired new CEOs did no better on the ratings. In fact, the only statistically significant finding was that the companies that had hired new CEOs did worse on the ratings by *Working Mother* magazine.[67]

The issue of the ethnic and gender makeup of corporate leadership and whether greater diversity at the top actually improves the lives of employees is, of course, more complex. Various researchers have sought to determine the effects of a company having women and minorities in senior positions, and there is evidence that it can increase opportunities for women and minorities at lower levels in those corporations. For example, companies that appoint women to senior management positions are more effective in recruiting, hiring, and advancing women.[68] In a 2014 study of *Fortune* 500 companies from 2001 through 2010, Alison Cook and Christy Glass, two social scientists at Utah State University, explored the extent to which the presence of minority or women CEOs, and minority or women on their boards of directors, was related to the companies' equity and diversity policies. Using outcome measures such as whether the companies had progressive policies for work-life benefits (such as flexible hours), progressive policies for LGBT employees, and programs focused on hiring and promoting, and whether the company used minority- and women-owned businesses for its purchasing and contracting, they found that whether the CEO was a woman or a minority had no effect. However, the makeup of the boards was meaningful, especially when it came to certain of their outcome variables. They concluded that they found little evidence for "the power of one thesis," but "stronger support for the power in numbers thesis." That is, a single woman or minority CEO did not seem to make a difference on the measures they assessed, but having multiple women and minority members of the board did.[69]

Cook and Glass also note that some scholars have expressed skepticism about corporate diversity practices in general, and about the actual enforcement of policies, asserting that they primarily serve to protect the company from assertions of bias and discrimination, and serve to protect the company's image. "Despite the existence of formal policies," they acknowledge, "compliance remains low and uneven, bias continues to shape everyday practice and interaction for women and minorities, and managers responsible for implementing diversity programs face nominal accountability for their impacts. . . . More recent scholarship on the impact of diversity policies suggests that such efforts may even reinforce bias and exclusion toward members of underrepresented groups"[70]

In a study published in 2011, Frank Dobbin, a sociologist at Harvard who now has been studying affirmative action, diversity, and diversity programs for decades, along with two of his colleagues, looked at 816 corporations over a twenty-two-year period. They found that fewer than one-third of the corporations had any form of diversity program beyond equal opportunity advertising programs, which had been around since the late 1960s. They looked at six different kinds of diversity programs. Four of them (equal employment advertising, diversity training for managers, diversity training for the general workforce, and the creation of affinity networks for the various underrepresented groups) had no effect on the subsequent diversity of management. Only two types, task forces, which bring together a wide range of people from different departments to generate new ideas to promote diversity, and mentoring programs, which pair members of underrepresented groups with higher-level executives who might be of help to them, were found to have any impact. However, only 15 percent of the companies in the sample had task forces and only 10 percent had mentoring programs, which suggests to us that whatever usefulness they may have has not been widespread.[71]

Reaching back to the early years of trying to increase diversity, when it was still called affirmative action, Frank Dobbin and Alexandra Kalev found that companies that hired diversity officers, or created new diversity departments in the 1960s or 1970s, "saw increases in diversity"; on the other hand, the "bureaucratic hiring and promotion systems" advocated by personnel experts "may have done more harm than good, institutionalizing patterns of inequality rather than challenging them." Overall, then, after about fifty years of trying a variety of programs, this is not a record that bodes well for the future of diversity in the corporate world, even though some programs seem to have worked.[72]

Nancy DiTomaso, a sociologist at Rutgers who has studied diversity in corporations for many years, and who conducted a large interview study of attitudes about race and class in white non-Hispanics, notes that she has long been "dissatisfied with the content of the training provided by diversity experts, both in the university and in corporations."[73] In her view, many of these programs have not worked because white participants see others, not themselves, as the problem. As she writes: "I found, as others did, that corporate interest in and talk about race and diversity either puzzled whites who were forced to attend diversity training programs or, alternatively, assured them because they did not believe themselves to be prejudiced or to be someone who engaged in the use of stereotypes. But I also found that diversity training frequently made them mad and, not infrequently, resistant to the overall message regarding the value and benefits of diversity."[74]

Most of the 246 whites from New Jersey, Ohio, and Tennessee that she interviewed for her study saw themselves and most other whites as committed to color-blindness and equal opportunity. They were therefore surprised that there has not been greater progress toward equality. They thus overlooked the neighborhood, school, and workplace segregation that lead to unequal opportunity and a lack of familial and group financial resources, as well as the exclusion of African Americans from informal job-information networks.

Due to their inability to see the larger sociological and economic forces that shape everyone's lives, white Americans explain the lack of racial equality as caused by lack of effort, responsibility, or hope on the part of African Americans.[75] DiTomaso's empirically based analysis of why there can be continuing exclusion without active white racial animosity contains many of the same elements that were summarized as "blaming the victim" in a classic study by William Ryan.[76] As DiTomaso puts it in what she calls her "bottom line" summation: "The search for 'racists' provides legitimacy or 'cover' for the dynamics of power and makes possible the opportunity hoarding that enables whites to receive advantages or privileges without being racists."[77]

In what may be yet another irony, recent research indicates that the very existence of diversity policies can conceal and delegitimize racial discrimination. A series of studies found that when objective information indicated that racial discrimination in fact had taken place, both whites and racial minorities perceived organizations that had policies in place that emphasized a celebration of diversity as more fair than those that did not. As the authors write, "The results suggest an irony of multicultural diversity structures: They can create a false fairness effect that conceals and delegitimizes discrimination."[78] Along these same lines, a number of researchers have found that diversity programs at elite schools can contribute to students at those schools endorsing beliefs in the importance of individual merit and downplaying the importance of institutional or systemic barriers to advancement.[79]

Therefore, because the pressure from most social movements has declined or been safely routinized, because there has been a dollop or two of diversification, and because so many corporations have made a nod or two toward diversity programs (effective or not), the pressure from below has diminished. As a result, diversity in the corporate elite generally has slowed or declined. Consider, for example, CEOs of *Fortune* 500 companies. There does seem to have been a slow but steady increase in the number of white women CEOs over the last decade: the numbers climbed, ever so slowly, almost every year from 2000 to 2014, when there were twenty-six, dropped the following two years, to twenty-one in 2016, but rose again in 2017, to thirty-two. For the other groups we have looked at, the data do not show this general pattern of increase over the decade. The number of African Americans peaked in 2007, at six, and, as of late 2017, there were four (a number that will drop to three in February 2018 when Kenneth Chenault, the CEO of American Express, steps down); the number of Asian American and South Asian CEOs peaked in 2011, at thirteen, and, as of late 2017, was eleven; the number of Latino CEOs peaked in 2008 at thirteen, and as of late 2017 was eleven. We also found patterns of stasis or decline in the political and military elites.

CONCLUSION

The black and white liberals and progressives who challenged Christian, white, male homogeneity in the power structure starting in the 1950s and 1960s sought to do more than create civil rights and new job opportunities for men and women who had previously been mistreated and excluded, important though these goals were. They also hoped that new perspectives in the boardrooms and the halls of government would spread greater openness throughout the society. The idea was both to diversify the power elite and to shift some of its power to underrepresented groups and social classes. The egalitarian social movements of the 1960s wanted a more open and less hierarchical society.

They were strikingly successful in increasing the individual rights and freedoms available to all Americans, especially African Americans, even though African Americans remain disadvantaged due to backlash and ongoing stigmatization. As we have shown, the social activists also created pressures that led to openings at the top for individuals from groups that had previously been ignored. But as some individuals made it, and as the concerns of social movements, political leaders, and the courts gradually came to focus more on individual rights and individual advancement, the focus on "distributive justice," general racial exclusion, and social class was lost. The age-old American commitment to individualism, reinforced by tokenism and reassurances from members of the power elite, won out over the commitment to greater equality of income and wealth that had been one strand of New Deal liberalism and a major emphasis of left-wing activism in the 1960s.

Despite the best efforts of the early activists, and many of those who followed their example, we must conclude that the increased diversity in the power elite has not generated any changes in an underlying class system in which the top 1 percent of households received 23.8 percent of all income in 2016, an increase from just over 10 percent in 1992, and almost as much as the 26.5 percent received in 2016 by the next 9 percent combined. By contrast, the bottom 90 percent received 49.7 percent, a sharp decline from their 59 percent in 1989, the first year in which this detailed, interview-based survey was carried out by a unit of the Federal Reserve Board. The share of net worth possessed by the top 1 percent of households in 2016 was even higher, 38.6 percent, which was slightly larger than the 38.5 percent held by the next 9 percent. This means that just 10 percent of households owned 77.1 percent of all net worth in that year, leaving only 22.8 percent for the bottom 90 percent, a very large decline from the 33.2 percent it held in 1989.[80]

The values of liberal individualism embedded in the Declaration of Independence, the Bill of Rights, and American civic culture were renewed by vigorous and courageous activists in the years between 1955 and 1975, but the class structure and the virtual exclusion of Americans of African descent and many of the darker-skinned immigrants from Latin America remain a major obstacle to individual fulfillment for the overwhelming majority of Americans. The conservative backlash that claims to speak for individual rights has strengthened this class structure. It creates obstacles that thwart advancement for most individuals from families in the bottom 80 percent of the wealth distribution, and even more so for those who face castelike exclusions. This solidification of class divisions in the name of individualism is more than an irony. It is an ongoing dilemma. It has been accelerated by the decline of diversity and is likely to be further exacerbated by the elections of 2016 and their aftermath.

Furthermore, the many racial, ethnic, religious, and social issues that divide people in at least the bottom 80–85 percent of the social structure further limit any collective efforts to alter their common fate and put still more obstacles in the way of individual mobility. Due to their prejudices, overt and unconscious, and their emphasis on white identity, many middle-American whites cannot bring themselves to make common cause with African Americans and darker-skinned immigrants in the name of greater individual opportunity and economic equality through a progressive income tax and the kind of government programs that lifted past generations out of poverty. These intertwined dilemmas of class and race lead to a nation that celebrates individualism, equal opportunity, and diversity but is, in reality, a bastion of class privilege, castelike exclusions, and fiscal and social conservatism.

Notes

1. THE IRONIES AND UNFULFILLED PROMISES OF DIVERSITY

1. For example, see Nelson W. Aldrich Jr., *Old Money: The Mythology of America's Upper Class* (New York: Knopf, 1988); Robert C. Christopher, *Crashing the Gates: The De-WASPing of America's Power Elite* (New York: Simon & Schuster, 1989); and David Brooks, *On Paradise Drive: How We Live Now (and Always Have) in the Future Tense* (New York: Simon & Schuster, 2004).

2. "The New American Establishment," *U.S. News & World Report*, February 8, 1988, 39, 45–46.

3. "The Rise of the Overclass," *Newsweek*, July 31, 1995, 32–46.

4. Edward Pessen, *Riches, Class, and Power before the Civil War* (Lexington, MA: D. C. Heath, 1973); Edward Pessen, ed., *Three Centuries of Social Mobility in America* (Lexington, MA: D. C. Heath, 1974).

5. See Richard M. Huber, *The American Idea of Success* (New York: McGraw-Hill, 1971), 44–46; Gary Scharnhorst, *Horatio Alger, Jr.* (Boston: Twayne, 1980), 24, 29, 141. For a discussion of the general pattern by which the media eulogize tycoons as "self-made," see Richard L. Zweigenhaft, "Making Rags out of Riches: Horatio Alger and the Tycoon's Obituary," *Extra!*, January/February 2004, 27–28.

6. As C. Wright Mills wrote more than half a century ago, "Horatio Alger dies hard." C. Wright Mills, *The Power Elite* (New York: Oxford University Press, 1956), 91.

7. William Miller, "American Historians and the Business Elite," in *Men in Business*, ed. William Miller (New York: Harper & Row, 1952), 328.

8. Mabel Newcomer, *The Big Business Executive: The Factors That Made Him, 1900–1950* (New York: Columbia University Press, 1955), 55, 62–63.

9. Mills, *Power Elite*, 106.

10. Mills, *Power Elite*, 127–28.

11. See Harold R. Kerbo, *Social Stratification and Inequality* (New York: McGraw-Hill, 2006), ch. 12; the series on class in the *New York Times*, "A Portrait of Class in America,"

spring 2005; and Dennis Gilbert, *The American Class Structure in an Age of Growing Inequality*, 9th ed. (Thousand Oaks, CA: Sage, 2015).

12. Emmanuel Saez and Gabriel Zucman, "Wealth Inequality in the United States since 1913: Evidence from Capitalized Income Tax Data," *Quarterly Journal of Economics* 131, no. 2 (2016): 519–78 (the quoted material is on pp. 519–20); Edward N. Wolff, "Changes in Household Wealth in the 1980s and 1990s in the U.S." (working paper 407, Levy Economics Institute, Bard College, 2004), http://www.levy.org; see table 2, p. 30, and table 6, p. 34.

13. William Ryan, *Blaming the Victim* (New York: Vintage, 1976); Richard Sennett and Jonathan Cobb, *The Hidden Injuries of Class* (New York: Random House, 1972). See also Laura Niemi and Liane Young, "When and Why We See Victims as Responsible: The Impact of Ideology on Attitudes toward Victims," *Personality and Social Psychology Bulletin* 42, no. 9 (2016): 1227–42.

14. See Noel Ignatiev, *How the Irish Became White* (New York: Routledge, 1995); Karen Brodkin, *How the Jews Became White Folks and What That Says about Race in America* (New Brunswick, NJ: Rutgers University Press, 1998).

15. This figure is based on data through 2014. See Richard L. Zweigenhaft, "Diversity among CEOs and Corporate Directors: Has the Heyday Come and Gone?," *Who Rules America?* (blog), http://www2.ucsc.edu/whorulesamerica/power/diversity_among_ceos.html, last paragraph.

16. See Stephen Steinberg, *The Ethnic Myth: Race, Ethnicity, and Class in America* (New York: Atheneum, 1981); Richard L. Zweigenhaft and G. William Domhoff, *Jews in the Protestant Establishment* (New York: Praeger, 1982).

17. Seymour Martin Lipset and Earl Raab, *Jews and the New American Scene* (Cambridge, MA: Harvard University Press, 1995), 77–79.

18. Zweigenhaft and Domhoff, *Jews in the Protestant Establishment*, 51–52.

19. See, for example, Jose A. Delreal and Julie Zauzmer, "Trump's Vigorous Defense of Anti-Semitic Image a 'Turning Point' for Many Jews," *Washington Post*, July 8, 2016, https://www.washingtonpost.com/politics/trumps-vigorous-defense-of-anti-semitic-image-a-turning-point-for-many-jews/2016/07/08/720858e2-4450-11e6-bc99-7d269f8719b1_story.html?utm_term=.d844a3bc242e; Karen Brodkin, "How Jews Became White Folks—and May Become Nonwhite under Trump," *Forward*, December 6, 2016, http://forward.com/opinion/356166/how-jews-became-white-folks-and-may-become-nonwhite-under-Trump.

20. Gordon W. Allport, *The Nature of Prejudice*, abr. ed. (New York: Anchor, 1958), 224–26, 239.

21. E. Digby Baltzell, *The Protestant Establishment: Aristocracy and Caste in America* (New York: Random House, 1964).

22. Our decision to include a chapter on Jews but not one on Catholics does not indicate that we assume Catholics are no longer underrepresented in the power elite. In their 1982 article, drawing on 1971–1972 data about 545 "top position holders in powerful political, economic, and social institutions in the United States," Richard Alba and Gwen Moore found that non-Irish Catholics were underrepresented in most or all sectors (Irish Catholics were represented at or above their population proportion in most sectors, especially in labor and politics). See Richard A. Alba and Gwen Moore, "Ethnicity in the American Elite," *American Sociological Review* 47 (1982): 373–83. Similarly, Alba has found that Italian Americans are underrepresented on the faculties of elite universities; see Richard Alba and Dalia Abdel-Hady, "Galileo's Children: Italian Americans' Difficult Entry into the Intellectual Elite," *Sociological Quarterly* 46 (2005): 3–18. In a study of the religious affiliations of the men and women listed in *Who's Who in America* from the 1930s through the 1990s, Ralph Pyle and Jerome Koch found that, as of 1992, Catholics remained underrepresented, although they have increased their representa-

tion over time, and "are likely to achieve parity shortly" (132). See Ralph E. Pyle and Jerome R. Koch, "The Religious Affiliations of American Elites, 1930s to 1990s: A Note on the Pace of Disestablishment," *Sociological Focus* 34, no. 2 (2001): 125–37. Our decision to focus on Jews, rather than Catholics, allows us to examine a group that has gone from underrepresentation in the higher circles to overrepresentation.

23. For the census figures, see Lynette Clemetson, "Hispanics Now Largest Minority," *New York Times*, January 22, 2003, http://www.nytimes.com/2003/01/22/us/hispanics-now-largest-minority-census-shows.html, and "The American Indian and Alaska Native Population: 2014," https://www.census.gov/newsroom/facts-for-features/2014/cb14-ff26.html. There were only 377,000 American Indians in 1950, before the new social movements made an Indian identity both respectable and useful. Many of those who now identify themselves as Native Americans have only one grandparent or great-grandparent who was Indian.

24. See Mary B. Davis, ed., *Native America in the Twentieth Century: An Encyclopedia* (New York: Garland, 1994). Determining who is, and who is not, has become quite a contentious issue. See, for example, Brooke Jarvis, "Who Decides Who Counts as Native American?," *New York Times*, January 18, 2017, https://www.nytimes.com/2017/01/18/magazine/who-decides-who-counts-as-native-american.html. The most visible Native American in an important position in American society for the past decade or so has been Ben Nighthorse Campbell, who was elected to the US Senate as a Democrat in 1992 and then switched to the Republican Party shortly thereafter. He was reelected in 1998 but chose not to run in 2004. Campbell's father was part Apache, part Pueblo Indian, and part Cheyenne. His mother was a Portuguese immigrant. Following his father's advice, as a young man, Campbell did not acknowledge his Native American heritage. He did not decide to investigate his Indian background until the mid-1960s, when he was in his thirties. In 1980, at the age of forty-seven, he became a member of the Northern Cheyenne tribe and adopted the middle name "Nighthorse" (*Current Biography* [1994]: 86–90).

25. See John D. Skrentney, *The Minority Rights Revolution* (Cambridge, MA: Harvard University Press, 2002), for a detailed discussion of how these two factors combined to force a diversification of employment and education for African Americans that was soon expanded to include women and other previously excluded groups with much less contention.

2. JEWS IN THE POWER ELITE

1. Albert Lee, *Henry Ford and the Jews* (New York: Stein and Day, 1980), 3, 46.

2. Not all Jewish midshipmen at the Naval Academy in the early 1920s were "sent to Coventry," but various forms of hazing were widespread, and no one escaped it completely. Two members of the class of 1923 who may have been Jewish (one was named Seltzer and the other Wetherstine, but neither had listed himself as Jewish on arrival) attempted suicide as a result of the vicious hazing they experienced. This led to a congressional investigation. Norman Polmar and Thomas B. Allen, *Rickover: Controversy and Genius* (New York: Simon and Schuster, 1982, 51–52, 55–57).

3. See, for example, E. Digby Baltzell, *The Protestant Establishment: Aristocracy and Caste in America* (New York: Random House, 1964), ch. 10.

4. Baltzell, *Protestant Establishment*, 248.

5. Richard L. Zweigenhaft and G. William Domhoff, *Jews in the Protestant Establishment* (New York: Praeger, 1982), 47–60.

6. Zweigenhaft and Domhoff, *Jews in the Protestant Establishment*, 31–33.

7. Zweigenhaft and Domhoff, *Jews in the Protestant Establishment*, 59–60.

8. Stephen D. Isaacs, *Jews and American Politics* (Garden City, NY: Doubleday, 1974).

9. Baltzell, *Protestant Establishment*, 210–11; M. G. Synnott, *The Half-Opened Door: Discrimination at Harvard, Yale and Princeton, 1900–1970* (Westport, CT: Greenwood, 1979), 14–17; Dan A. Oren, *Joining the Club: A History of Jews and Yale* (New Haven, CT: Yale University Press, 1985); Susanne Klingenstein, *Jews in the American Academy, 1900–1940* (New Haven, CT: Yale University Press, 1991); and Jerome Karabel, *The Chosen: The Hidden History of Admission and Exclusion at Harvard, Yale, and Princeton* (Boston: Houghton Mifflin, 2005). The estimate on Harvard's faculty is from Seymour Martin Lipset and David Riesman, *Education and Politics at Harvard* (New York: McGraw-Hill, 1975), 307. The estimate on Yale's law school faculty is from Robert A. Burt, *Two Jewish Justices: Outcasts in the Promised Land* (Berkeley: University of California Press, 1988), 1. The estimate on the percentage of Jewish students at Harvard, Yale, Princeton, and Columbia and the information about the Ivy League presidents are from Edward S. Shapiro, "The Friendly University: Jews in Academia since World War II," *Judaism* 46, no. 3 (1997): 365–74.

10. Seymour Martin Lipset and Earl Raab, *Jews and the New American Scene* (Cambridge, MA: Harvard University Press, 1995), 27.

11. Jane Mayer, "Trump's Boswell Speaks," *New Yorker*, July 25, 2016, 22. It is not clear that Trump had read the book—when asked about it, he was unsure whether it was a collection of Hitler's speeches titled *My New Order* or his more well-known *Mein Kampf.*

12. In January 2017, Obama joined Woodmont Country Club in suburban Maryland, an exclusive and predominantly Jewish club with an $80,000 initiation fee, but not without controversy. Some members vociferously protested granting him a membership because of their unhappiness with his policies toward Israel. See Mark Landler, "Despite Country Club Members' Rift, Obama Gets an Invitation," *New York Times*, January 24, 2017, A16.

13. Richard L. Zweigenhaft and G. William Domhoff, *The New CEOs: Women, African American, Latino, and Asian American Leaders of* Fortune *500 Companies* (Lanham, MD: Rowman & Littlefield, 2014), table 5.5, 89–91.

14. G. William Domhoff, *The Power Elite and the State: How Policy Is Made in America* (Hawthorne, NY: Aldine de Gruyter, 1990), 246–47. See also H. E. Alexander, "The Role of the Volunteer Political Fundraiser: A Case Study in New York in 1952" (PhD diss., Yale University, 1958); H. E. Alexander, *Financing the 1968 Election* (Lexington, MA: Heath Lexington Books, 1971); and Val Burris and James Salt, "The Politics of Capitalist Class Segments: A Test of Corporate Liberalism Theory," *Social Problems* 37, no. 3 (1990): 341–59.

15. Melville Herskovits, "Who Are the Jews?" in *Jewish-American Literature: An Anthology*, ed. Abraham Chapman (New York: New American Library, 1974), 473.

16. Ronald Steel, *Walter Lippmann and the American Century* (Boston: Little, Brown, 1980), 195. For a fascinating account of how Steel came to realize that Lippmann's Jewish background was a source of great personal anguish and should be an important component of his biography, see Ronald Steel, "Living with Walter Lippmann," in *Extraordinary Lives: The Art and Craft of American Biography*, ed. William Zinsser (Boston: Houghton Mifflin, 1986), 121–60.

17. Tisch, interview with Zweigenhaft, July 23, 1980; see also Zweigenhaft and Domhoff, *Jews in the Protestant Establishment*, 102.

18. "Dianne Feinstein," *Current Biography* (1979): 128.

19. Irving Shapiro, interviewed by Richard Zweigenhaft, Wilmington, Delaware, February 23, 1981. When Shapiro died twenty years later, the *New York Times* obituary made no mention that Shapiro was the first Jewish CEO of a major *Fortune* 500 company not founded by Jews,

or even that he was Jewish. The obituary referred to Shapiro's father as "a Lithuanian immigrant who ran a dry-cleaning business in Minneapolis." Claudia H. Deutsch, "Irving Shapiro, 85, Lawyer and Ex-Chairman of DuPont," *New York Times*, September 15, 2001, B7.

20. William Miller, "American Historians and the Business Elite," in *Men in Business*, ed. William Miller (New York: Harper & Row, 1952), 324.

21. Mabel Newcomer, *The Big Business Executive: The Factors That Made Him, 1900–1950* (New York: Columbia University Press, 1955), 46–49.

22. Richard D. Alba and Gwen Moore, "Ethnicity in the American Elite," *American Sociological Review* 47 (1982): 373–83.

23. Charles G. Burck, "A Group Profile of the *Fortune* 500 Chief Executive," *Fortune*, May 1976, 174–75.

24. Frederick D. Sturdivant and Roy D. Adler, "Executive Origins: Still a Gray Flannel World," *Harvard Business Review*, November–December 1976, 125–33.

25. See Zweigenhaft and Domhoff, *Jews in the Protestant Establishment*, 25–46.

26. Charles E. Silberman, *A Certain People: American Jews and Their Lives Today* (New York: Summit, 1985), 96–97.

27. Maggie McComas, "Atop the *Fortune* 500: A Survey of the C.E.O.," *Fortune*, April 28, 1986, 26–31. In 1956, in addition to its list of the top five hundred industrial corporations, *Fortune* began to publish a list of nonindustrial companies. By 1983, that list had become the Service 500, with companies grouped in several categories (banks, diversified financial services, life insurance, etc.). In 1995, because of the considerable blurring of lines caused by mergers and acquisitions, *Fortune* decided to combine the industrial and service companies into a single list. See Thomas A. Stewart, "A New 500 for the New Economy," *Fortune*, May 15, 1995, 166.

28. Robert A. Bennett, "No Longer a WASP Preserve," *New York Times*, June 29, 1986, F28.

29. Harold S. Himmelfarb, R. Michael Loar, and Susan H. Mott, "Sampling by Ethnic Surnames: The Case of American Jews," *Public Opinion Quarterly* 47 (1983): 247–60. They conclude that the distinctive Jewish name (DJN) technique is particularly useful for those who are interested "in explanatory rather than descriptive studies (i.e., studies which are interested in explaining patterns rather than making accurate estimates of population characteristics)" (254).The thirty-five distinctive Jewish names are Berman, Bernstein, Caplan, Cohen, Cohn, Epstein, Feldman, Friedman, Ginsberg, Gold, Goldberg, Goldman, Goldstein, Greenberg, Grossman, Horowitz, Kahn, Kaplan, Katz, Levin, Levine, Levinson, Rosen, Rosenbaum, Rosenbloom, Rosenthal, Rothman, Rubin, Samuels, Shapiro, Siegel, Silverman, Weinberg, Weiner, and Weinstein.

Ira Rosenwaike, in "Surnames among American Jews," *Names* 38 (1990): 31–38, demonstrates not only that many Jews have names that are not at all distinctively Jewish, such as "Gordon" and "Miller," but that even among those people with distinctive Jewish names, such as Cohen, a small percentage are not Jewish. His data, based on a 1982 survey of 1.2 million American men and women, conducted by the American Cancer Society, indicate that about 89 percent of those with the names on the thirty-five-name DJN list are Jewish. Even taking this into account, the estimates that we will present of the number of Jewish directors on *Fortune* 500 boards are still substantially higher than the percentage of Jews in the larger population.

30. For a more complete description of the data set, and some findings that go beyond those reported here, see Richard Zweigenhaft, "Diversity among CEOs and Corporate Directors: Has the Heyday Come and Gone?" (paper presented at the annual meeting of the American Sociological Association, August 12, 2013, New York City); a revised version of this paper can be seen on the Who Rules America? blog, http://www2.ucsc.edu/whorulesamerica/power/

diversity_among_ceos.html. See also the 2014 edition of Richard L. Zweigenhaft and G. William Domhoff, *The New CEOs: Women, African American, Latino, and Asian American Leaders of* Fortune *500 Companies* (Lanham, MD: Rowman & Littlefield, 2014; paperback edition with new introduction, xxii–xxv).

31. These percentages are based on an average board size of 16 in 1975 and 1985, 14 in 1995, and 11.2 in 2004. For the 1975, 1985, and 1995 size estimates, see Murray Weidenbaum, "The Evolving Corporate Board," *Society*, March/April 1995, 12; for the 2004 estimate, we summed the number of board members on these two hundred boards and divided by two hundred. The figure we came up with (11.2) corresponded to that reported in Mark Thomsen, "*Fortune* Names Worst Corporate Boards," *Sustainability Investment News*, May 3, 2001, at http://www.socialfunds.com/news/article.cgi?sfArticleId=569.

32. Just how much the percentage of Jews in the general population has decreased is the topic of much debate in the Jewish community. A major report released in 2002 by the National Jewish Population Survey estimated that the number of American Jews had dropped by 300,000 from 1990 to 2000, reducing the number to 5.2 million (http://www. jewishvirtuallibrary.org/u-s-national-jewish-population-survey-october-2002). Critics claimed that the number of Jews was actually considerably higher ("It's utter nonsense," said one). The disagreements are based largely on how one defined who is a Jew. See Daniel J. Wakin, "A Count of U.S. Jews Sees a Dip; Others Demur," *New York Times*, October 9, 2002, A25. For our estimate of the number of Jews in 2004 (2.2 percent), we have used the 6.2 million estimate provided in the *American Jewish Yearbook* for 2002. The National Jewish Population Survey estimate of 5.2 million would lower the percentage to 1.9. Either way, the percentage of Jews in the larger population has declined.

33. Barry Rubin, *Assimilation and Its Discontents* (New York: Crown, 1995), 64.

34. Milton Gordon, *Assimilation in American Life* (New York: Oxford University Press, 1964), 8; Lipset and Raab, *Jews and the New American Scene*, 53.

35. Ruby Jo Reeves Kennedy, "Single or Triple Melting Pot? Intermarriage Trends in New Haven, 1870–1940," *American Journal of Sociology* 49, no. 4 (1944): 331–39; Ruby Jo Reeves Kennedy, "Single or Triple Melting Pot? Intermarriage in New Haven, 1870–1950," *American Journal of Sociology* 58, no. 1 (1952): 56–59.

36. Richard Alba, *Ethnic Identity: The Transformation of White America* (New Haven, CT: Yale University Press, 1991), 14.

37. Steven M. Cohen, "The Coming Shrinkage of American Jewry: A Review of Recent Research," in *Renascence or Oblivion: Proceedings of a Conference on Jewish Population, 1978*, ed. Judith Zimmerman and Barbara Trainin (New York: Federation of Jewish Philanthropies, 1978), 1–25.

38. For an estimate of 50 percent, see Steven Steinberg, "The Melting Pot and the Color Line," in *Reinventing the Melting Pot: The New Immigrants and What It Means to Be American*, ed. Tamar Jacoby (New York: Basic, 2004), 239. Lipset and Raab cite a National Jewish Population Survey (NJPS) that found that, for the five-year period prior to 1990, the figure was 57 percent (*Jews and the New American Scene*, 45). These estimates have been controversial. When the NJPS released its "long-anticipated" study in 2003 based on data gathered in 2000 and 2001, the authors of the study explained that the previous estimates were inflated because they had included people who said they were not raised as Jews. The revised estimates were 38 percent for 1980 to 1984 and 43 percent for 1985 to 1990; the new report estimated a 43 percent rate of intermarriage from 1990 to 1995 and a 47 percent rate by 2001. According to the project manager, among the "thorniest issues" was "how to define who is a Jew." Laurie Goodstein, "Survey Finds Slight Rise in Jews Intermarrying," *New York Times*, September 11, 2003, A13.

39. Uriel Hellman, Pew Survey of U. S. Jews: Soaring Intermarriage, Assimilation Rates, Jewish Telegraphic Agency (JTA), October 1, 2013, http://www.jta.org/2013/10/01/news-opinion/united-states/pew-survey-u-s-jewish-intermarriage-rate-rises-to-58-percent.

40. Lipset and Raab, *Jews and the New American Scene*, 72–73.

41. See Zweigenhaft and Domhoff, "Identity and Class in the Corporate Elite," ch. 5 in *Jews in the Protestant Establishment*, 89–111.

42. Richard L. Zweigenhaft, *Who Gets to the Top? Executive Suite Discrimination in the Eighties* (New York: Institute of Human Relations, 1984), 14–15.

43. Zweigenhaft, *Who Gets to the Top?*, 12.

44. Zweigenhaft and Domhoff, *Jews in the Protestant Establishment*, 89–111.

45. Zweigenhaft and Domhoff, *Jews in the Protestant Establishment*, 110.

46. See Carrie Dolan, "BankAmerica's Rosenberg Will Succeed Clausen as Chief; Dividend Lifted 66%," *Wall Street Journal*, February 6, 1990, B8. This article does not mention Rosenberg's religion, nor was it mentioned in the much briefer announcement of his appointment in the *New York Times*. Rosenberg does, however, include that he is Jewish in his *Who's Who in America* biographical sketch. The information on Eisner is from *Current Biography* (1987): 154–57.

47. Penny Schwartz, "Shira Goodman, Boston Community Leader, Named CEO of Staples," *Jewish Daily Forward*, September 28, 2016, http://forward.com/news/breaking-news/351026/shira-goodman-boston-community-leader-named-ceo-of-staples.

48. This is higher than the percentage of Jews in presidential cabinets from 1897 through 1972. In her study of presidential cabinets during those years, Beth Mintz found that, of the 166 people whose religion she could identify, six were Jewish. Jews, therefore, represented 3.6 percent of the total, a figure that was slightly higher than the percentage of Jews in the larger population at that time. Two were in the cabinets of Republican presidents (Oscar S. Straus, secretary of commerce and labor, 1906–1909, and Lewis L. Strauss, secretary of commerce, 1958–1959) and four were in the cabinets of Democratic presidents (Henry Morganthau Jr., secretary of the treasury, 1934–1945; Arthur J. Goldberg, secretary of labor, 1961–1962; Abraham A. Ribicoff, secretary of health, education, and welfare, 1961–1962; and Wilbur J. Cohen, secretary of health, education, and welfare, 1968–1969). Beth Mintz, "The President's Cabinet, 1897–1972: A Contribution to the Power Structure Debate," in "New Directions in Power Structure Research," ed. G. William Domhoff, special issue, *Insurgent Sociologist* 5, no. 3 (1975): 131–48.

49. Mukasey's nomination only made it out of the judiciary committee when two Democrats, Chuck Schumer and Dianne Feinstein (both Jewish), voted with the Republicans. He had equivocated on whether waterboarding was torture, but he vowed to enforce any legislation that Congress were to pass against waterboarding. "Mukasey One Step Closer to Becoming Second Jewish AG in US History," Associated Press and Haaretz Service, November 6, 2007, http://www.haaretz.com/news/mukasey-one-step-closer-to-becoming-second-jewish-ag-in-u-s-history-1.232594.

50. For this analysis, we have included only cabinet positions, not "cabinet-level" positions such as ambassador to the United Nations, the director of the Office of Management and Budget, or secretary for veterans' affairs, even though some presidents have accorded these positions "cabinet-level" rank. For example, some presidents (such as Eisenhower and Obama) have included the ambassador to the United Nations in their cabinets, and others (such as both Bushes) have not. In order to be consistent across presidents, we have not included these positions that sometimes have "cabinet-level" rank. Jasmine C. Lee, "Trump's Cabinet So Far Is More White and Male than Any First Cabinet since Reagan's," *New York Times*, January 23, 2017, https://www.nytimes.com/interactive/2017/01/13/us/politics/trump-cabinet-women-mino

rities.html. Nor have we counted Madeleine Albright, secretary of state during Clinton's second term, as Jewish. Albright was raised as a Catholic and later became an Episcopalian. Shortly after her confirmation as secretary of state, she learned that her parents had converted to Catholicism from Judaism and that three of her grandparents had died in the Holocaust. Her history adds another dimension to the difficult question of who is Jewish. Steven Erlanger, "Albright Grateful for Her Parents' Painful Choices," *New York Times*, April 5, 1997. For Albright's reflections on this discovery, see Madeleine Albright, "Names on the Synagogue Wall," ch. 15 in *Madam Secretary: A Memoir* (New York: Hyperion, 2003), 298–316. It should be noted that, although he appointed no Jews to his cabinet until Chertoff joined the cabinet in 2005, a number of Jews played important roles in the development of George W. Bush's foreign policy, especially Paul Wolfowitz, deputy secretary of defense, and Richard Perle, a resident fellow at the American Enterprise Institute. Also Jewish (though it is a surprise to many) is Lewis ("Scooter") Libby, who resigned as Vice President Dick Cheney's chief of staff hours after he was indicted for perjury related to the leak of the name of a CIA agent married to a critic of the White House. Libby, like George Bush, a graduate of Andover, has been a member of Temple Rodef Shalom, a Reform congregation in Falls Church, Virginia, for many years, although he apparently only attends services on the High Holidays. He is also a member of the Republican Jewish Coalition. See Ron Kampeas, "Libby Jewish? Some Wonder How Neo-con's Faith Impacts Leak Scandal," *JTA: Global News Service of the Jewish People*, November 2, 2005, http://www.jta.org/2005/11/03/archive/libby-jewish-some-wonder-how-neo-cons-faith-impacts-leak-scandal.

51. "Jews in America: By the Numbers," *Washington Week*, UNC-TV, February 21, 2017, http://www.pbs.org/weta/washingtonweek/blog-post/jews-america-numbers.

52. "W. Michael Blumenthal," *Current Biography* (1977): 77.

53. W. Michael Blumenthal, *Invisible Wall: German and Jews, a Personal Exploration* (New York: Counterpoint, 1998).

54. "Harold Brown," *Current Biography* (1977): 89.

55. Like many Jewish immigrants who came to America, Goldberg's father came with skills that stood him in good stead, even though he had to do menial work. He had been the town clerk in the Ukrainian village from which he emigrated, and, as Goldberg's biographer writes, "In order to provide for their transit and his own survival, Joseph Goldberg quickly obtained work as a peddler. For an educated man, it was a less than ideal way to make a living, but the only paying job he could find." David L. Stebenne, *Arthur J. Goldberg: New Deal Liberal* (New York: Oxford University Press, 1996), 4.

56. Gloria R. Mosesson, *The Jewish War Veterans Story* (Washington, DC: Jewish War Veterans of America, 1971), 17. In a subsequent article, in response to pressure from veterans' groups, Twain retracted these statements.

57. Mosesson, *The Jewish War Veterans Story*, 19.

58. Dr. James Zimble, interviewed by Richard Zweigenhaft, Bethesda, Maryland, August 25, 1995.

59. Rabbi Arnold Resnicoff, interviewed by telephone by Richard Zweigenhaft, August 25, 1995; Laurie Goodstein, "Air Force Chaplain Tells of Academy Proselytizing," *New York Times*, May 12, 2005, A22; "Air Force Names Rabbi to Bias Post," *New York Times*, June 28, 2005, A18; and Clarence Page, "Thou Shalt Aim for Clarity," *Greensboro News & Record*, June 30, 2005, A7.

60. Marc Perelman, "Jewish General to Pilot Evangelical-Friendly Air Force," *Jewish Daily Forward*, June 12, 2008, http://forward.com/news/13574/jewish-general-to-pilot-evangelical-friendly-air-f-02014.

61. Josefin Dolsten, "Jewish General Named Air Force Chief of Staff," *Jewish Daily Forward*, April 26, 2016, http://forward.com/news/breaking-news/339459/jewish-general-named-air-force-chief-of-staff.

62. C. Wright Mills, *The Power Elite* (New York: Oxford University Press, 1956), 195.

63. *Goldman v. Weinberger*, 475 US 503 (1986).

64. Bernard M. Kauderer, interviewed by telephone by Richard Zweigenhaft, October 27, 1995.

65. Tim Weiner, "Reluctant Helmsman for a Troubled Agency: John Mark Deutch," *New York Times,* March 11, 1995, A8; Nick Kotz, "Mission Impossible," *Washingtonian*, December 1995, 134.

66. In his cover article for *Parade* magazine, titled "Is He the CIA's Last, Best Hope?" November 19, 1995, Peter Maas makes no mention of Deutch's Jewish background. Nor is there any mention of Deutch's having attended an elite prep school: Deutch and his wife, we are told, went "to the same high school" (5). In a long article in the *New York Times Magazine* titled "The CIA's Most Important Mission: Itself," December 10, 1995, Tim Weiner did include information about Deutch's Jewish background (84). Kotz's *Washingtonian* article mentions that Deutch's family was Jewish and that his father was on the board of directors of the Washington Hebrew Congregation (66). Days after Deutch stepped down as director of the CIA in December 1996, CIA technicians discovered highly classified information on five computers in his home. In August 1999, Deutch's security clearance was suspended, which was the first time in the agency's fifty-two years that a former director had been stripped of access to highly classified information. Deutch was the subject of a criminal investigation over the security lapses, but the Justice Department decided not to press charges. A searing report by the Senate Select Committee on Intelligence revealed that Deutch "had problems before becoming director with regard to the handling of classified information." Steven Lee Myers, "Former Chief of CIA Is Stripped of Right to Classified Information," *New York Times*, August 21, 1999, A1; Steven Lee Myers, "Former CIA Director Left Secrets Open to Theft, Agency Investigator Says," *New York Times*, February 23, 2000, A17.

67. See, for example, Burton Hersh, *The Old Boys: The American Elite and the Origins of the CIA* (New York: Scribner's, 1992).

68. Richard Halloran, "Navy's Chief Discusses Morality and Weapons," *New York Times*, May 6, 1983.

69. "Distribution of Active Duty Forces by Service, Rank, Sex, and Ethnic Group," 05/31/95, Washington, DC: Department of Defense.

70. Ted Merwin, "Jews Are Underrepresented in the U.S. Military and Its Leadership," *Veterans' News Now*, December 1, 2011, http://www.shoah.org.uk/2014/10/01/jewish-lobby-14-jews-are-underrepresented-in-the-u-s-military-and-its-leadership.

71. For a detailed account of anti-Semitism and the institutional acceptance of evangelical proselytizing at the Air Force Academy, see Michael L. Weinstein and Davin Seay, *With God on Our Side: One Man's War against an Evangelical Coup in America's Military* (New York: St. Martin's, 2006).

72. Merwin, "Jews Are Underrepresented.

73. They were David Levy Yulee, Florida, 1844–1860; Judah Benjamin, Louisiana, 1852–1860; Benjamin Franklin Jonas, Louisiana, 1879–1885; Joseph Simon, Oregon, 1897–1903; Isidor Rayner, Maryland, 1905–1912; and Simon Guggenheim, Colorado, 1907–1913. See Eli N. Evans, *Judah P. Benjamin: The Jewish Confederate* (New York: Free Press, 1988), xx, 32, 47–48, and 399; Isaacs, *Jews and American Politics*, 235; and L. Sandy Maisel, ed., *Jews in American Politics* (Lanham, MD: Rowman & Littlefield, 2001), 447.

74. *Congressional Quarterly*, November 7, 1992, 9; *Congressional Quarterly*, January 25, 2003, 192. This includes Michael Bennett, whose mother (a Holocaust survivor) is Jewish and whose father is not. He was raised with both religions, and says simply that he believes in God. See Ron Kampeas, "In Colorado Primary Two Jewish Democrats Square Off," *New York Jewish Week*, July 13, 2010, http://jewishweek.timesofisrael.com/in-colorado-primary-two-jewish-democrats-square-off-on-special-interests. As various writers have noted, with ten or more Jews in the Senate, there are enough for a "minyan," the requirement for public prayer services.

75. Isaacs, *Jews and American Politics,* 10.

76. Isaacs, *Jews and American Politics,* 202; Ernest Gruening, *Many Battles: The Autobiography of Ernest Gruening* (New York: Liveright, 1973).

77. Dennis J. McGrath and Dane Smith, *Professor Wellstone Goes to Washington: The Inside Story of a Grassroots U.S. Senate Campaign* (Minneapolis: University of Minnesota Press, 1995), 253.

78. McGrath and Smith, *Professor Wellstone Goes to Washington*, 253. See also Brent Staples, "Dirty Political Ads, Reconsidered," *New York Times*, November 11, 1990, section IV, 16; and "Ousted Senator Apologizes for Letter to Jews," *New York Times*, November 10, 1990, A10.

79. When he ran against Coleman for the Senate seat, Al Franken quipped, "I don't think Minnesota is ready for a Gentile in this seat." Eric Fingerhut, "Franken: "I Don't Think Minnesota Is Ready for a Gentile in This Seat," *Jewish Telegraphic Agency*, September 24, 2008, http://www.jta.org/2008/09/24/news-opinion/the-telegraph/franken-i-dont-think-minnesota-is-ready-for-a-gentile-in-this-seat.

80. Among the millionaires are Lehman, Metzenbaum, Kohl, Lautenberg, and Feinstein. See R. W. Apple Jr., "Never Mind the Log Cabin," *New York Times*, October 16, 1994, E3.

81. *Congressional Quarterly*, November 7, 1992, 9; November 12, 1994, 11; January 4, 1997, 29; January 9, 1999, 63; January 20, 2001, 181; January 25, 2003, 193; January 31, 2005, 241; see also Michael Hoffman, "More Jews in Congress: Does It Make a Difference?" *Moment*, February 1993, 32–39.

82. Louis D. Brandeis, *Other People's Money and How the Bankers Use It* (New York: Frederick A. Stokes, 1914).

83. Robert A. Burt, "On the Bench: The Jewish Justices," in *Jews in American Politics*, ed. L. Sandy Maisel (Lanham, MD: Rowman & Littlefield, 2001), 65–80. See also Robert A. Burt, *Two Jewish Justices: Outcasts in the Promised Land* (Berkeley: University of California Press, 1988), 7, and Allon Gal, *Brandeis of Boston* (Cambridge, MA: Harvard University Press, 1980), 195.

84. Burt, "On the Bench," 66.

85. Burt, "On the Bench," 66.

86. Burt, "On the Bench," 67.

87. Burt, "On the Bench," 67; Andrew L. Kaufman, *Cardozo* (Cambridge, MA: Harvard University Press, 1998), 6. As was not unusual at the time, Cardozo spent two years at Columbia Law School but did not graduate (two-thirds of his classmates also left after the second year); see Kaufman, *Cardozo*, 49. Kaufman also notes that prior to entering Columbia as an undergraduate, Cardozo and his brother were tutored by none other than Horatio Alger.

88. Michael E. Parrish, *Felix Frankfurter and His Times: The Reform Years* (New York: Free Press, 1982), 8–9, 14–15.

89. Burt, "On the Bench," 71–73; Bruce Allen Murphy, *Fortas: The Rise and Ruin of a Supreme Court Justice* (New York: William Morrow, 1988), 3–4, 6–7, 13. See also http://goldberg.law.northwestern.edu/mainpages/bio.htm.

90. See https://www.oyez.org/justices/ruth_bader_ginsburg and https://www.oyez.org/justices/stephen_g_breyer.

91. Richard Wolf, "Nearly All Supreme Court Justices Are Millionaires," *USA Today*, June 20, 2014, http://www.usatoday.com/story/news/politics/2014/06/20/supreme-court-justices-financial-disclosure/11105985.

92. Burt, "On the Bench," 67, 71, 77; Kaufman, *Cardozo*, 25, 69. See also https://www.oyez.org/justices.

93. David L. Stebenne, author of *Arthur J. Goldberg*, in phone conversation, June 6, 2005.

94. We do not know how observant Ruth Bader Ginsburg is.

95. Lisa W. Foderaro, "At 12, Kagan Tested Her Faith's Confines," *New York Times*, May 13, 2010, A25; Sarah Wheaton, "Obama Shores Up Jewish Support at D.C. Synagogue," *Politico*, May 22, 2015, http://www.politico.com/story/2015/05/obama-jewish-support-washington-synagogue-118207.

96. See Bernard J. Wolfson, "The Soul of Judaism," *Emerge*, September 1995, 42–46. See also Karen Brodkin, *How Jews Became White Folks and What That Says about Race in America* (New Brunswick, NJ: Rutgers University Press, 1998).

97. See Karen D. Arnold, "Getting to the Top: What Role Do Elite Colleges Play?" *About Campus* 7, no. 5 (November–December 2002): 4–12.

98. Stephen Steinberg, *The Ethnic Myth: Race, Ethnicity and Class* (New York: Atheneum, 1981), 93–103.

99. Alba, *Ethnic Identity*, 309.

3. WOMEN IN THE POWER ELITE

1. C. Wright Mills, *The Power Elite* (New York: Oxford University Press, 1956), 3–4.

2. Mills, *Power Elite*, 125.

3. Mills, *Power Elite*, 129.

4. Jerry A. Jacobs, "Women's Entry into Management: Trends in Earnings, Authority, and Values among Salaried Managers," *Administrative Science Quarterly* 37 (1992): 282–301.

5. Wyndham Robertson, "The Top Women in Big Business," *Fortune*, July 17, 1978, 58–63.

6. Robertson, "Top Women."

7. Graham's father was Jewish, though she did not discover this until she enrolled at Vassar. She, like her parents, was married in a Lutheran ceremony, and she did not consider herself Jewish. See Howard Bray, *The Pillars of the Post: The Making of a News Empire in Washington* (New York: Norton, 1980), 211; Carol Felsenthal, *Power, Privilege, and the Post: The Katharine Graham Story* (New York: Putnam, 1993), 68, 98, 334, 443; and Katharine Graham, *Personal History* (New York: Knopf, 1997), 52–53.

8. "Women on Corporate Boards: The Challenge of Change," *Catalyst*, 1993, 4, http://www.catalyst.org/knowledge/women-corporate-boards-challenge-change; or as below in note 12. See also Enid Nemy, "Felice N. Schwartz, 71, Dies; Working Women's Champion," *New York Times*, February 10, 1996, 52.

9. "You've Come a Long Way, Baby—but Not as Far as You Thought," *BusinessWeek*, October 1, 1984, 126.

10. Sheila Wellington, "Women on Corporate Boards: The Challenge of Change," *Directorship Newsletter*, December 1994.

11. In a 2016 study, based on 492 of the *Fortune* 500 companies, the Alliance for Board Diversity found that women held 20.2 percent of the board seats. "The Missing Pieces Report: The 2016 Board Diversity Census of Women and Minorities on *Fortune* 500 Boards," Alliance for Board Diversity, 10, http://www.catalyst.org/system/files/2016_board_diversity_census_deloitte_abd.pdf.

12. "2003 Catalyst Census of Women Board Directors: A Call to Action in a New Era of Corporate Governance," *Catalyst*, 2003, http://www.catalyst.org/system/files/2003_Catalyst_Census_Women_Board_Directors_Fortune_500.pdf; Kirstin Downey, "Survey Finds Few Female Directors," *Washington Post*, June 18, 2004, E3; "Women and Minorities on Fortune 100 Boards," Alliance for Board Diversity, May 17, 2005; and Kimberly Weisel, "Globally, Women Gain Corporate Board Seats—but Not in the US," *Fortune*, January 13, 2015, http://fortune.com/2015/01/13/catalyst-women-boards-countries-us. See also the section later in this chapter about women elected to national office, which includes some cross-cultural comparisons.

13. Richard Zweigenhaft, "The Role of Elite Education for White Men, White Women, and People of Color in the US Corporate Elite" (paper presented at the Elite Education Conference, June 29, 2015, Toronto, Ontario, at the Ontario Institute for Studies in Education [OISE]). See also http://www2.ucsc.edu/whorulesamerica/power/elite_education.html.

14. Lauren A. Rivera, *Pedigree: How Elite Students Get Elite Jobs* (Princeton, NJ: Princeton University Press, 2015), 41. See also Lauren A. Rivera and Andras Tilcsik, "Class Advantage, Commitment Penalty: The Gendered Effect of Social Class Signals in an Elite Labor Market," *American Sociological Review* 81, no. 6 (2016): 1097–1131.

15. Beth Ghiloni, "New Women of Power: An Examination of the Ruling Class Model of Domination" (PhD diss., University of California, Santa Cruz, 1986), 156.

16. Ghiloni, "New Women of Power," 157.

17. Graham Bowley, "The Academic-Industrial Complex," *New York Times*, August 1, 2010, BU1; Nanette Asimov, "UC Regents Toughen Moonlighting Rules for Top Executives," *San Francisco Chronicle*, July 21, 2016, http://www.sfgate.com/education/article/UC-regents-toughen-moonlighting-rules-for-top-8401943.php. According to Equilar, a research firm that tracks board membership and executive compensation, in 2015 the median pay for directors at large public corporations was $270,000. See Pui-Wing Tam, "Join Our Board: Companies Hotly Pursue New Wave of Women in Tech," *New York Times*, December 30, 2016, http://www.nytimes.com/2016/12/30/technology/join-our-board-companies-hotly-pursue-new-wave-of-women-in-tech.html.

18. Susan Mulcahy, "A College That Paid Bills by Selling Its Art," *New York Times*, July 27, 2016, C1.

19. Ghiloni, "New Women of Power," 163–64.

20. Ghiloni, "New Women of Power," 159–62.

21. "Women on Board: Survey Indicates Inroads into the Male-Dominated Business World," *Los Angeles Times*, April 19, 1995. Such insensitivity on the part of the men in the corporate world is not rare. At one point, as she rose through the management ranks, Carly Fiorina, former CEO of Hewlett-Packard, was told by a colleague that a business lunch had been scheduled at a strip club and that she therefore could not attend. Because the lunch was with an important client, Fiorina showed up anyway and sat through the uncomfortable lunch. Nate DeGraff, "Former CEO Offers Advice for Rough Times," *Greensboro News & Record*, May 8, 2005, B1. Fiorina's willingness to tolerate male boorishness paid off: even though she was fired from her job as CEO of Hewlett-Packard in February 2005, she left the company with a compensation package worth more than $42 million. See Eric Dash, "Fiorina Exiting Hewlett-Packard with More Than $42 Million," *New York Times*, February 12, 2005, B10.

22. Rosabeth Moss Kanter, *Men and Women of the Corporation* (New York: Basic, 1977), 49.

23. Richard L. Zweigenhaft, *Who Gets to the Top? Executive Suite Discrimination in the Eighties* (New York: Institute of Human Relations, 1984), 17.

24. *Good for Business: Making Full Use of the Nation's Human Capital* (Washington, DC: US Government Printing Office, 1995), 28.

25. Peter T. Kilborn, "A Leg Up on Ladder, but Still Far from Top," *New York Times*, June 16, 1995.

26. Margaret Hennig and Anne Jardim, *The Managerial Woman* (New York: Pocket, 1976), 45.

27. Title IX was enacted by Congress in 1972, when many women in senior management today were in high school. At that time, one in twenty-seven high school girls participated in high school sports. As of 2004, the figure was one in three. Bill Pennington, "Title IX Trickles Down to Girls of Generation Z," *New York Times*, June 29, 2004, C22.

28. Pennington, "Title IX Trickles Down"; Alia Wong, "Where Girls Are Missing Out on High School Sports," *The Atlantic*, June 26, 2015, http://www.theatlantic.com/education/archive/2015/06/girls-high-school-sports-inequality/396782.

29. Laura Dunn, "Women in Business Q&A: Stephanie Streeter, CEO and Director of Libbey, Inc.," *Huffington Post*, March 21, 2015. http://www.huffingtonpost.com/laura-dunn/women-in-business-qa-step_b_6500824.html.

30. Brad Stone, "Settlement Was Paid in Whitman Shoving Incident," *New York Times*, June 15, 2010, A13.

31. Marcia Chambers, *The Unplayable Lie: The Untold Story of Women and Discrimination in American Golf* (New York: Golf Digest/Pocket, 1995). See also Marcia Chambers, "For Women, the Country Club Is the Big Handicap," *New York Times*, May 14, 1995; and Marcia Chambers, "The High Price of Victory," *New York Times*, April 4, 2001, C19. Some golf clubs continue to deny memberships to women. The best known is Augusta National Golf Club, the home of the Masters golf tournament. When the club's policies were challenged in 2003 by the National Council of Women's Organizations, the nation's oldest and largest organization of women's groups, its chair (William "Hootie" Johnson) reacted defiantly. In order to avoid legal challenges based on the acceptance of funds from public corporations, the tournament was telecast with no television advertisements.

The club admitted its first black members in 1990. The handful of black members, including some of the CEOs discussed in chapter 4, were under intense pressure either to persuade the club to change its policies or resign their memberships. See Clifton Brown, "Augusta Answers Critics on Admitting Women," *New York Times*, July 10, 2002, C18; Richard Sandomir, "Women's Group Lobbies Seven Augusta Members," *New York Times*, September 28, 2002, B18; Bill Pennington and Dave Anderson, "Some at Augusta National Quietly Seek a Compromise," *New York Times*, September 29, 2002, Section 8, 1; and Bill Pennington with Clifton Brown, "Members of Club Who Favor Change Told to Back Off," *New York Times*, November 13, 2002, C19.

32. Karen Crouse, "Host to Masters Drops a Barrier with Its First 2 Female Members," *New York Times*, August 21, 2012, A1.

33. Denise Benoit Scott, "The Power of Connections in Corporate-Government Affairs: A Gendered Perspective" (paper presented at the annual meeting of the American Sociological Association, Los Angeles, 1994), 16; see also Denise Benoit Scott, "Women at the Intersection of Business and Government: Are They in Places of Power?" *Sociological Spectrum* 18, no. 3 (1998): 333–63.

34. Basia Hellwic, "Executive Female's Breakthrough 50," *Executive Female*, September–October 1992, 46.

35. Dawn-Marie Driscoll and Carol R. Goldberg, *Members of the Club: The Coming of Age of Executive Women* (New York: Free Press, 1993), 163. See also Janet Lever, "Sex Differences in the Games Children Play," *Social Problems* 23 (1976): 478–87; Janet Lever, "Sex Differences in the Complexity of Children's Play and Games," *American Sociological Review* 43 (1978): 471–83; and Kathryn Ann Farr, "Dominance Bonding through the Good Old Boy Sociability Group," *Sex Roles* 18 (1988): 259–77.

36. Anne B. Fisher, "When Will Women Get to the Top?" *Fortune*, September 21, 1992, 44–56 (quotation appears on p. 56).

37. Lena Williams, "Not Just a White Man's Game," *New York Times*, November 9, 1995.

38. Kathleen Hall Jamieson, *Beyond the Double Bind: Women and Leadership* (New York: Oxford University Press, 1995), 120–45. For some more recent empirical research on the dilemmas faced by "agentic" women in management positions, see Laurie A. Rudman, "Self-Promotion as a Risk Factor for Women: The Costs and Benefits of Counterstereotypical Impression Management," *Journal of Personality & Social Psychology* 74 (1998): 629–45; Laurie A. Rudman and Peter Glick, "Prescriptive Gender Stereotypes and Backlash toward Agentic Women," *Journal of Social Issues* 57 (2001): 743–62; and Laurie A. Rudman and Kimberly Fairchild, "Reactions to Counterstereotypic Behavior: The Role of Backlash in Cultural Stereotype Maintenance," *Journal of Personality and Social Psychology* 87 (2004): 157–76.

39. Jay Pritzker, interviewed by Richard Zweigenhaft, Chicago, Illinois, October 20, 1980. See also "The Hustling Pritzkers," *BusinessWeek*, May 5, 1975, 55–62; "Billionaire Philanthropist A. N. Pritzker Dies," *Washington Post*, February 9, 1986.

40. See Jodi Wilgoren and Geraldine Fabrikant, "Knives Drawn for a $15 Billion Family Pie," *New York Times*, December 11, 2002, A1; Suzanna Andrews, "Shattered Dynasty," *Vanity Fair*, May 2003, 181–85, 231–36; and Jodi Wilgoren, "$900 Million Accord Enables Breakup of Pritzker Dynasty," *New York Times*, January 7, 2005, A17. See also Anthony Ramirez, "Jay Pritzker, Who Built Chain of Hyatt Hotels, Is Dead at 76," *New York Times*, January 25, 1999, A21. Penny Pritzker was ranked #315 on the 2017 *Forbes* list of the four hundred richest Americans, with an estimated worth of $2.6 billion; there were five other Pritzkers ahead of her and two more Pritzkers behind her on the list.

41. "The Daughter Also Rises," *BusinessWeek*, July 17, 1995, 82–83; and Danny Hakim, "Fidelity Picks a President of Funds Unit: Scion of the Founder Seen as Next Chairman," *New York Times*, May 22, 2001, C1; for the Forbes list: http://www.forbes.com/profile/abigail-johnson; for *Inside Philanthropy*, see http://www.insidephilanthropy.com/wall-street-donors/abigail-johnson.html.

42. For details of this much-covered corporate soap opera, see the following: Geraldine Fabrikant, "Redstone Heir Steps Further into Viacom Territory," *New York Times*, May 10, 2004, C1; Joe Flint and Amol Sharma, "Behind Shari Redstone's Rise at Her Father's $40 Billion Media Empire," *Wall Street Journal*, June 10, 2016, http://www.wsj.com/articles/behind-shari-redstones-rise-at-her-fathers-40-billion-media-empire-1465599114; Emily Steel, "Trial Date Is Set on Sumner Redstone Competence," *New York Times*, July 29, 2016, B5; James B. Stewart, "How Dauman Lost the Battle for Viacom," *New York Times*, August 26, 2016, B6; and Emily Steele, "Villain to Doting Daughter: How Shari Redstone Turned the Tide," *New York Times*, October 5, 2016, B2.

43. Michael Mann, "A Crisis in Stratification Theory? Persons, Households/Families/Lineages, Genders, Classes, and Nations," in *Gender and Stratification*, ed. Rosemary Crompton and Michael Mann (London: Polity, 1986), 47. See also Peta Tancred-Sheriff, "Gender, Sexuality, and the Labour Process," in *The Sexuality of Organization*, ed. Jeff Hearn, Deborah L.

Sheppard, Peta Tancred-Sheriff, and Gibson Burrell (London: Sage, 1989), 45–55. Tancred-Sheriff suggests that women in corporations use "implicit sexuality" as a form of "adjunct control" that serves to "facilitate the operation of the capitalist enterprise" (53).

44. "2002 Catalyst Census of Women Corporate Officers and Top Earners of the *Fortune* 500," *Catalyst*, 2002, 8, http://www.catalyst.org/knowledge/2002-catalyst-census-women-corporate-officers-and-top-earners-fortune-500.

45. Beth W. Ghiloni, "The Velvet Ghetto: Women, Power, and the Corporation," in *Power Elites and Organizations*, ed. G. William Domhoff and Thomas R. Dye (Newbury Park, CA: Sage, 1987), 21–36.

46. See G. William Domhoff, *The Higher Circles* (New York: Random House, 1970), 35; Susan Ostrander, *Women of the Upper Class* (Philadelphia: Temple University Press, 1984); and Diana Kendall, *The Power of Good Deeds: Privileged Women and the Social Reproduction of the Upper Class* (Lanham, MD: Rowman & Littlefield, 2002).

47. Robertson, "Top Women," 59.

48. "Where Are They Now? Business Week's Leading Corporate Women of 1976," *BusinessWeek,* June 22, 1987, 76.

49. "Where Are They Now?" 76.

50. Carol Hymowitz, "Five Future No. 1's: It's a Good Bet That One of These Women Will Lead a *Fortune* 500 Firm in the 1990s," *Wall Street Journal*, March 20, 1987. Surprisingly, only two of the five on the *Wall Street Journal* list were on the list of fifty women identified by *BusinessWeek*.

51. Although Mattel announced in August that Barad would become CEO, she did not officially take charge until January 1997. See Lisa Bannon, "Mattel Names Jill Barad Chief Executive," *Wall Street Journal*, August 23, 1996; Judith H. Dobrzynski, "Women Pass Milestone in the Board Room," *New York Times*, December 12, 1996, D4.

52. Valentina Zarya, "The Percentage of Female CEOs in the *Fortune* 500 Drops to 4%," *Fortune*, June 16, 2016; Jena McGregor, "Only One Woman Was Named CEO of a Major Company in North America in 2015," *Washington Post*, April 21, 2016; see also "Historical List of Women CEOs of the Fortune Lists: 1972–2016," *Catalyst*, March 2017.

53. See "These Are the Women CEOs Leading *Fortune* 500 Companies," *Fortune Magazine*, June 7, 2017, http://fortune.com/2017/06/07/fortune-500-women-ceos. An organization called 100x25, founded by the Rockefeller Foundation, is dedicated to increasing the number of *Fortune* 500 women CEOs to 100 by 2025. See Susan Chira, "Why Women Aren't CEOs, according to Women Who Almost Were," *New York Times*, July 21, 2017. https://www.nytimes.com/2017/07/21/sunday-review/women-ceos-glass-ceiling.html.

54. For a more detailed analysis that compares the educational backgrounds of white women, white men, African American, Latino, and Asian American *Fortune* 500 CEOs, see Zweigenhaft, "The Role of Elite Education."

55. We do not have information about the parents of some of the CEOs. In a phone interview, however, Cinda Hallman made it clear that it was quite rare for women from working-class backgrounds to make it to the highest positions in the corporate world, and that doing so was difficult: "It was extremely hard. At the time I didn't know that, and I'm glad I didn't. If you don't have the privileged background, you have to compensate in other ways. If I fell down on my face I knew I was going to get back up on my feet and try again. One other thing: how you look is important. I know how to do the hair, the makeup. Most people think I come from a rich family" (Cinda Hallman, interviewed by telephone by Richard Zweigenhaft, July 26, 2004).

56. Cait Murphy, "Sara Lee Cleans Out Its Cupboards," *Fortune*, March 7, 2005, 38, and Del Jones, "Sara Lee Biggest Company (for Now) with Female CEO," *USA Today*, February

11, 2005, Money section, 4B; and Landon Thomas Jr., "Brenda Barnes, Pepsi Chief Who Spurred a Work Life Debate, Dies at 63," *New York Times*, January 20, 2017, https://www. nytimes.com/2017/01/20/business/brenda-barnes-dead.html.

57. National Association for Law Placement, Inc., "2016 Report on Diversity in U.S. Law Firms," January 2017, https://www.nalp.org/uploads/2016NALPReportonDiversityinUS LawFirms.pdf; see also Elizabeth Olson, "Women Dominate at Law School, but Not at Law Firms," *New York Times*, July 25, 2017, B4.

58. Claudia H. Deutsch, "Women Lawyers Strive for Chance to Make It Rain," *New York Times*, May 21, 1996; Peter Truell, "Success and Sharp Elbows," *New York Times*, July 2, 1996.

59. Patrick McGeehan, "Morgan Stanley Settles Bias Suit with $54 Million," *New York Times,* July 13, 2004, A1, C9. Both data from the Equal Employment Opportunity Commission and the industry's own Security Industry Association showed that white men filled the large majority of executive management positions at major Wall Street firms. For a discussion of the frat-house behavior and settlement agreements that prevent disclosure, see Susan Antilla, "Money Talks, Women Don't," *New York Times*, July 21, 2004, A23; see also Susan Antilla, *Tales from the Boom-Boom Room: Women vs. Wall Street* (Princeton, NJ: Bloomberg, 2002). The Morgan Stanley settlement is merely part of a "deluge" of class-action suits for sex discrimination that have included Mitsubishi (settled for $34 million), Home Depot (settled for $104.5 million), Merrill Lynch (settled for an undisclosed sum), American Express (settled for $42 million), and Boeing (settled for $72.5 million). See Betsy Morris, "Sex Discrimination: How Corporate America Is Betraying Women," *Fortune*, January 10, 2005, 64–74.

60. Susan Antilla, "After Boom-Boom Room, Fresh Tactics to Fight Bias," *New York Times,* April 3, 2013, F4.

61. Susanne Craig, "Lessons on Being a Success on Wall St., and Being a Casualty," *New York Times*, April 3, 2013, F2.

62. Andrew Ross Sorkin, "Women in a Man's World," *New York Times*, April 3, 2013, F1–F2.

63. Maureen Sherry, "The Brutal Truth about Being a Woman on Wall Street," *Fortune*, August 6, 2016, http://fortune.com/2016/08/06/women-wall-street-bro-talk.

64. These figures are based on those with official cabinet status (but not those with "cabinet-level" status who do not hold cabinet positions). Thus, for example, Carol Browner and Christine Todd Whitman, who served as the heads of the Environmental Protection Agency under Clinton and George W. Bush, respectively, are not included; nor are a number of other highly visible women such as Jeane Kirkpatrick, ambassador to the UN under Reagan. We did not include Condoleezza Rice when she was George W. Bush's national security adviser, but we did include her when she became secretary of state in 2005. After the position was created, we included secretary of homeland security to the list of cabinet appointments.

65. Diane Ravitch, "The Miseducation of Betsy DeVos," *In These Times*, February 2017, 17. Trump also appointed Nikki Haley as ambassador to the UN, but this is not a traditional cabinet position (see chapter 2, note 50).

66. Thomas E. Cronin, *The State of the Presidency*, 2nd ed. (Boston: Little, Brown, 1980), 275–76.

67. Faye C. Huerta and Thomas A. Lane, "Participation of Women in Centers of Power," *Social Science Journal* 18, no. 2 (1981): 71–86. In this respect, the United States has lagged behind much of the world. As Rhodri Jeffreys-Jones wrote in *Changing Differences: Women and the Shaping of American Foreign Policy, 1917–1994* (New Brunswick, NJ: Rutgers University Press, 1995), prior to Albright's appointment as secretary of state, "Since 1960 there have been twenty-two women prime ministers and presidents worldwide, but the United States

has had no women as president, vice-president, secretary of state, secretary of defense, or chair of the Senate Foreign Relations Committee. According to this measurement American women are among the missing sisters of world politics, a predicament they have shared with the female citizens of Italy, Australia, and Chile, as well as of such supposedly less democratic countries as the former Soviet Union, Iraq, and North Korea" (2–3).

68. Beth Mintz, "The President's Cabinet, 1897–1972: A Contribution to the Power Structure Debate," in "New Directions in Power Structure Research," ed. G. William Domhoff, special issue, *Insurgent Sociologist* 5, no. 3 (1975): 131–48.

69. Laura Flanders, *Bushwomen: Tales of a Cynical Species* (New York: Verso, 2004), 113–15. See also Elizabeth Becker, "Candidate Vows to Aid Beleaguered Farmers," *New York Times*, January 19, 2001, A21.

70. See, for example, Steven Greenhouse, "Senate Panel Gives Warm Reception to New Labor Nominee," *New York Times*, January 25, 2001, A18; "Elaine L. Chao," *Current Biography* (2001): 84–87; and Elizabeth Becker, "Family History Forges Labor Secretary's Convictions," *New York Times*, February 26, 2001, A10.

71. Flanders, *Bushwomen*, 150–51.

72. See "Margaret M. Heckler," *Current Biography* (1983): 182–84; "Patricia Roberts Harris," *Current Biography* (1965): 189–91; "Donna Shalala," *Current Biography* (1991): 515; and Michael Wines, "Friend Helped Labor Nominee Move Up, Then Almost Brought Her Down," *New York Times*, March 12, 1997.

73. "Juanita Kreps," *Current Biography* (1977): 259.

74. "Elaine L. Chao," *Current Biography* (2001): 84–87; "Gale A. Norton," *Current Biography* (2001): 391–93; Becker, "Candidate Vows to Aid Beleaguered Farmers," A21; and Flanders, *Bushwomen*, 113–46, 147–82, and 218–51.

75. Flanders, *Bushwomen*, 261.

76. Keith Bradsher, "Bush Picks Nominee for Commerce Post," *New York Times*, December 27, 1991.

77. "2003 Catalyst Census of Women Board Directors." The *Fortune* rankings in this paragraph in the text, as well as those in this note, are all for 2003. The other former women cabinet members and their corporate boards were Lynn Martin on Procter & Gamble (#31), Ryder Systems (#345), SBC Communications (#27), and Ryder System (#345); Barbara Franklin on Aetna (#88) and Dow Chemical (#51); Hazel O'Leary on AES (#181) and UAL (#132); Donna Shalala on Gannett (#275), Lennar (#256), and UnitedHealth Group (#63); Alexis Herman on Cummins (#296) and MGM Mirage (#397).

78. Stephanie Strom, "Fees and Trustees: Paying the Keepers of the Cash," *New York Times*, July 10, 2003, A16.

79. "Elizabeth Dole," *Current Biography* (1983): 117.

80. "Ann McLaughlin," *Current Biography* (1988): 368.

81. Christopher Marquis, "A Washington Veteran for Labor; a Tested Negotiator for Trade," *New York Times*, January 12, 2001; Becker, "Family History Forges Labor Secretary's Convictions," A10.

82. Mills, *Power Elite*, 232.

83. Mills, *Power Elite*, 186.

84. Mills, *Power Elite*, 190.

85. Jeanne Holm, *Women in the Military: An Unfinished Revolution*, rev. ed. (Novato, CA: Presidio, 1992), 203.

86. Huerta and Lane, "Participation of Women," 75.

87. Lory Manning and Vanessa R. Wight, *Women in the Military: Where They Stand*, 4th ed. (Washington, DC: Women's Research and Education Institute, 2003), 9, 11. See also *1993*

Handbook on Women Workers: Trends and Issues (Washington, DC: US Department of Labor), 22–23; Department of Defense, *Defense 94 Almanac* 5 (1994): 30. According to Holm, the end of the draft "more than any other factor during the seventies produced an expansion of women's participation in the armed forces that was of unexpected and unprecedented proportions" (*Women in the Military*, 246).

88. The George W. Bush administration classified many formerly public documents—in fact, as of July 2005 it was classifying such documents at the rate of 125 per minute (see "The Dangerous Comfort of Secrecy," *New York Times*, July 12, 2005, A22). Among those that were classified were the previously easily accessible annual reports produced by the Department of Defense showing the number of active-duty forces by service, rank, sex, and ethnic group. We thank Captain Lory Manning, the director of the Women in the Military Project at the Women's Research & Education Institute, for sharing the 2004 data with us ("Distribution of Active Duty Forces by Service, Rank, Sex, and Ethnic Group," 09/30/04, DMDC-3035EO). The March 2017 data were made available to us by the Office of the Secretary of Defense (Military Personnel Policy), and can be found in the Table of Active Duty Females by Rank/Grade and Service in the Active Duty Master Personnel File, https://www.dmdc.osd.mil/appj/dwp/dwp_reports.jsp.

89. John Mintz, "President Nominates 1st Woman to Rank of Three-Star General," *Washington Post*, March 27, 1996.

90. John Mintz, "Clinton Nominates First Black Admiral: Woman in Line to Become Vice Admiral," *Washington Post*, May 14, 1996.

91. Mark Thompson, "Female Generals: The Pentagon's First Pair of Four-Star Women," *Time*, August 13, 2012, http://nation.time.com/2012/08/13/female-generals-the-pentagons-first-pair-of-four-star-women.

92. Wilma Vaught, interviewed by Richard Zweigenhaft, Arlington, Virginia, August 2, 1995. Unfortunately, the war in Iraq provided many women in the military with combat experience. Even though the military's 1994 rules limited women's exposure to combat by barring them from frontline units, the tactics of ambush in Iraq, as one army captain put it, meant that "the front line is everywhere." As of April 2005, thirty-five women in the military had been killed (twenty-three by hostile fire), more than 250 had been wounded, and two had been prisoners of war (women represented 15 percent of all military personnel and about 10 percent of those deployed to the Iraq theater of operations). See Lory Manning, *Women in the Military: Where They Stand*, 5th ed. (Washington, DC: Women's Research and Education Institute, April 2005), 9. See also Lawrence J. Korb and Nigel Holmes, "Two Years and Counting," *New York Times*, March 20, 2005, A13; and "More Women Dying in Iraq Combat's 'Front Line,'" *Greensboro News & Record*, December 16, 2004, A10.

93. Matthew Rosenberg and Dave Phillips, "Pentagon Opens All Combat Roles to Women: 'No Exceptions,'" *New York Times*, December 4, 2015, A1.

94. In a fifty-five-page "scathing report on prisoner abuse" written by Major General Antonio Taguba, Fast was mentioned only briefly though Karpinski's leadership was extensively and severely critiqued. Some speculated that this was because a two-star general wrote the report and Fast, unlike Karpinski, was of equal rank. As one former military man explained, "If you want to investigate a major general you need a lieutenant general" to do the investigation. See Susan Taylor Martin, "Report Steers Clear of Interrogators' Boss," *St. Petersburg Times* (online), May 8, 2004, http://www.sptimes.com/2004/05/08/Worldandnation/Report_steers_clear_o.shtml. Martin, in an article titled "Military Sidesteps Scandal," *St. Petersburg Times* (online), May 28, 2004, http://www.sptimes.com/2004/05/28/Worldandnation/Military_star_sideste.shtml, claimed that Fast was "still on track to become commander of a key U.S. military base and only the second three-star female in Army history." Fast did not become a three-star,

but she did become commander of the Army Intelligence Center at Ft. Huachuca, Arizona; she retired in 2005. Richard A. Serrano and Mark Mazzetti, "General Demoted over Prison Scandal," *Los Angeles Times*, May 6, 2005, A20. In an additional weird twist, it was revealed that several years prior to her assignment to oversee the prison at Abu Ghraib, Karpinski had been arrested for shoplifting at a domestic air force base. Somehow, the military missed, or ignored, this incident when it promoted her to brigadier general. As *New York Times* columnist Bob Herbert concluded, "The same army that's scouring Iraq for insurgents and terrorists was apparently unaware of the arrest record of the woman assigned to such a sensitive position at Abu Ghraib." Bob Herbert, "Stranger Than Fiction," *New York Times*, May 9, 2005, A23.

95. Barbara Ehrenreich, "What Abu Ghraib Taught Me," *AlterNet*, May 2004, http://alternet.org/story/18740. See also Carol Burke, *Camp All-American, Hanoi Jane, and the High and Tight: Gender, Folklore, and Changing Military Culture* (Boston: Beacon, 2004); Rita James Simon, ed., *Women in the Military* (New Brunswick, NJ: Transaction, 2001); and Francine D'Amico and Laurie Weinstein, eds., *Gender Camouflage* (New York: New York University Press, 1999). The same general point can be made about women in Congress. As Michele L. Swers shows in *The Difference Women Make: The Policy Impact of Women in Congress* (Chicago: University of Chicago, 2002), although women in Congress expand the range of issues included on the congressional agenda, "simply increasing the number of women and other minorities in Congress will not automatically lead to enhanced influence on policy design" (133); nor will it necessarily change the way Congress functions.

96. Holm, *Women in the Military,* 278.

97. Laurie Weinstein and Francine D'Amico, introduction to *Gender Camouflage*, ed. Francine D'Amico and Laurie Weinstein (New York: New York University Press, 1999), 5. Their edited anthology includes many examples of women who have been mistreated in and by the military.

98. Tom Brune, "Kirsten Gillibrand Military Sexual Assault Bill Fails in Senate," *Newsday*, June 14, 2016, http://www.newsday.com/news/nation/kirsten-gillibrand-military-sexual-assault-bill-fails-in-senate-1.11915647.

99. Helene Cooper, "Reports of Sexual Assault Increase at Two Military Academies," *New York Times*, March 15, 2017, https://www.nytimes.com/2017/03/15/us/politics/sexual-assault-military-west-point-annapolis.html.

100. David Philipps, "Nude Images of Female Marines Spur Inquiry of Male-Only Group," *New York Times*, March 7, 2017, A1. In the fall of 2013, Lt. Gen. Michelle D. Johnson became the first woman to head one of the five federal military academies. As of 2017, between 25 and 30 percent of the students at the academy were female. Throughout her four years in that position, addressing issues related to sexual assault continued to be one of her biggest challenges. See Sarah Brown, "The General Who Got the Air Force Academy Talking about Sexual Assault," *Chronicle of Higher Education*, April 2, 2017.

101. Donald E. Matthews, *U.S. Senators and Their World* (New York: Vintage, 1960), 13.

102. Martin Gruberg, *Women in American Politics* (Oshkosh, WI: Academia, 1968).

103. See Diane Kincaid, "Over His Dead Body: A Positive Perspective on Widows in the United States Congress," cited in Barbara Boxer, *Strangers in the Senate: Politics and the New Revolution of Women in America* (Washington, DC: National Press, 1994), 90.

104. Jeffreys-Jones, *Changing Differences*, 128.

105. "Nancy Kassebaum," *Current Biography* (1982): 192.

106. Jamieson, *Beyond the Double Bind*, 193. Because of the number of women elected to the Senate, the House, and state legislatures in the 1992 election, the media incessantly designated 1992 as "the year of the woman."

107. Snowe and her second husband, John R. McKernan Jr., who served as governor of Maine for two terms, were referred to as "Maine's political power couple" in the *Congressional Quarterly*, November 12, 1994, 13.

108. Erin Kelly, "Next Congress Likely to Have Record Number of Women, but Gains Still Slow," *USA Today*, November 4, 2016, http://www.usatoday.com/story/news/politics/elections/2016/10/31/congress-record-number-women-house-senate/92892630.

109. Sandra Day O'Connor and H. Alan Day, *Lazy B: Growing Up on a Cattle Ranch in the American Southwest* (New York: Random House, 2002).

110. The fact that she dated Rehnquist is drawn from Lou Cannon, "When Ronnie Met Sandy," *New York Times*, July 7, 2005, A27; see also Nancy Maveety, *Justice Sandra Day O'Connor: Strategist on the Supreme Court* (Lanham, MD: Rowman & Littlefield, 1996), 12–14 (quotation appears on p. 14).

111. See Linda Greenhouse, "When Sandra Day O'Connor Broke into the Men's Club," *New York Times*, August 4, 2016, http://www.nytimes.com/2016/08/04/opinion/when-sandra-day-oconnor-broke-into-the-mens-club.html.

112. Dahlia Lithwick, "Justice LOLZ Grumpycat Notorius R. B. G.: How a Gentle Supreme Court Justice Became a Badass Gangsta Internet Meme," *Slate*, March 16, 2015, http://www.slate.com/articles/double_x/doublex/2015/03/notorious_r_b_g_history_the_origins_and_meaning_of_ruth_bader_ginsburg_s.html.

113. Jeffrey Toobin, *The Nine: Inside the Secret World of the Supreme Court* (New York: Anchor, 2007).

114. Sonya Sotomayor, *My Beloved World* (New York: Vintage, 2014).

115. Alexander G. Higgins, "Rwanda Women Knock Sweden Out of Top Spot in Parliamentary Share," Associated Press Worldstream, October 22, 2003; see also Will Laster, "United States Lag behind Europe in Including Women in Politics," Associated Press, February 28, 2003; Alan Cowell, "Oslo Journal: Brewmaster Breaks One Tradition but Upholds Another," *New York Times*, December 24, 2004, A4.

116. Will McGraw, "Gender Segregation at Work: 'Separate but Equal' or 'Inefficient and Unfair,'" Washington Center for Equitable Growth, August 18, 2016; Bernadette D. Proctor, Jessica L. Semega, and Melissa A. Kollar, "Income and Poverty in the United States: 2015," US Census, Report Number: P 60-256, September 13, 2016.

117. Jerry Jacobs, "Detours on the Road to Equality: Women, Work, and Higher Education," *Contexts* 1, no. 2 (Winter 2003): 32–41 (quotation appears on p. 33).

118. Jacobs, "Detours on the Road"; see also Louise M. Roth, "Engendering Inequality: Processes of Sex-Segregation on Wall Street," *Sociological Forum* 19, no. 2 (2004): 203–28; Louise M. Roth, "The Social Psychology of Tokenism: Status and Homophily Processes on Wall Street," *Sociological Perspectives* 47, no. 2 (2004): 189–214; and Gail M. McGuire, "Gender, Race and the Shadow Structure: A Study of Informal Networks and Inequality in a Work Organization," *Gender & Society* 16, no. 3 (June 2002): 303–22.

119. Christine L. Williams, *Still a Man's World: Men Who Do "Women's Work"* (Berkeley: University of California Press, 1995), 20–21. See also Christine L. Williams, *Gender Differences at Work: Women and Men in Nontraditional Occupations* (Berkeley: University of California Press, 1990); Christine L. Williams, ed., *Doing "Women's Work": Men in Nontraditional Occupations* (Newbury Park, CA: Sage, 1993); Joel Heikes, "When Men Are the Minority: The Case of Men in Nursing," *Sociological Quarterly* 32, no. 3 (1991): 389–401; and Janice Yoder, "Is It All in the Numbers? A Case Study of Tokenism," *Psychology of Women Quarterly* 9, no. 3 (1985): 413–18.

120. Edward Lapham, "Women at Ford: What's the Problem? The Company's Culture Drove Them Out; It Must Be Changed," *Automotive News*, December 20, 2004, 14.

121. Chira, "Why Women Aren't CEOs."

4. BLACKS IN THE POWER ELITE

1. Larry Tye, *Bobby Kennedy: The Making of a Liberal Icon* (New York: Penguin Random House, 2016), 195.

2. David Remnick, "The Political Scene: It Happened Here," *New Yorker*, November 28, 2016, 63.

3. "Negro Lawyer Joining U.S. Industries Board," *New York Times*, June 23, 1964. U.S. Industries was #465 in the *Fortune* 500 that year.

4. Leonard Sloane, "Negroes in Business: A New Era Is Signaled by Election of 2 Directors by Big Corporations," *New York Times*, June 26, 1964.

5. "John Snyder Jr., Industrialist, 56," *New York Times*, April 25, 1965.

6. "Taking USI out of the Limelight," *BusinessWeek*, January 21, 1967, 51.

7. Sloane, "Negroes in Business."

8. Sharon M. Collins, *Black Corporate Executives: The Making and Breaking of a Black Middle Class* (Philadelphia: Temple University Press, 1997), 58.

9. Collins addresses "moral commitment" in Sharon M. Collins, "Blacks on the Bubble: The Vulnerability of Black Executives in White Corporations," *Sociological Quarterly* 34, no. 3 (1993): 434.

10. "Negro Lawyer Joining U.S. Industries Board"; Sloane, "Negroes in Business"; and "Personality: Pierce Causes Insurance Stir," *New York Times*, December 13, 1964.

11. John N. Ingham and Lynne B. Feldman, "Asa T. Spaulding," in *African-American Business Leaders: A Biographical Dictionary*, ed. John N. Ingham and Lynne B. Feldman (Westport, CT: Greenwood, 1994), 395.

12. Bill Surface, "The World of the Wealthy Negro," *New York Times Magazine*, July 23, 1967, 10, 35, 38, 40.

13. "Clifton R. Wharton, Jr.: The Nation's Highest-Paid Black Executive," *Ebony*, September 1987, 32.

14. Gerald H. Rosen, "TIAA-CREF: Declining Returns," *Academe* 78, no. 1 (January–February 1992): 8.

15. As Wharton became part of the corporate elite, so, too, did his wife, Delores. The daughter of a Harlem undertaker, Delores, who once studied dance with Martha Graham, became a director on numerous *Fortune*-level boards, including Kellogg, Phillips Petroleum, and Gannett. In 1980 she founded the Fund for Corporate Initiatives, designed to help minorities and women become CEOs and corporate directors. As of the early 1990s, each year she organized a weeklong retreat for twenty or so promising young executives from *Fortune* 500 companies. Patricia O'Toole, "Another Kind of Wharton School," *Lear's*, March 1991, 26–27.

16. Marylin Bender, "Woman Lawyer Still Awaits a Bid to Board," *New York Times*, May 3, 1971.

17. Michael E. Mueller, "Patricia Roberts Harris: Former U.S. Cabinet Secretary, Ambassador, Attorney," in *Contemporary Black Biography: Profiles from the International Black Community*, ed. Barbara C. Bigelow, vol. 2 (Detroit, MI: Gale, 1992), 99.

18. "A Black for GM's Board," *Time*, January 26, 1970, 72.

19. "After the Courtesy, a Crisis of Costs," *Fortune*, June 1970, 31; William Serrin, "For Roche of G.M., Happiness Is a 10% Surcharge," *New York Times Magazine*, September 12, 1971, 36–37, 109–25 (quotation appears on p. 116).

20. Ernest Holsendolph, "A Profile of Leon Sullivan," *Black Enterprise*, May 1975, 47–51.

21. Quoted in Ralph Nader and Joel Seligman, "The Myth of Shareholder Democracy," in *The Big Business Reader: Essays on Corporate America*, ed. Mark Green and Robert Massie Jr. (New York: Pilgrim, 1980), 447–56.

22. "Roche of General Motors: Thus Far and No Further," *Forbes*, May 15, 1971, 48.

23. Herschel Johnson, "The Making of Black Car Dealers," *Black Enterprise*, May 1974, 14.

24. When Sullivan died in 2001, the *New York Times* obituary began by highlighting the work he did to fight apartheid by developing guidelines for corporate investment in South Africa. Paul Lewis, "Leon Sullivan, 78, Dies; Fought Apartheid," *New York Times*, April 26, 2001, C17.

25. Lester Carson, "Black Directors: The 72 Black Men and Women Who Sit on the Boards of Major U.S. Corporations," *Black Enterprise*, September 1973, 17–28.

26. Jonathan Kaufman, "Black Executives Say Prejudice Still Impedes Their Path to the Top," *Wall Street Journal*, July 9, 1980.

27. George Davis and Glegg Watson, *Black Life in Corporate America* (Garden City, NY: Anchor, 1982), 77.

28. John Fernandez, *Racism and Sexism in Corporate Life* (Lexington, MA: Lexington, 1981), 10.

29. Floyd A. Bond, Herbert W. Hildebrandt, and Edwin L. Miller, *The Newly Promoted Executive: A Study in Corporate Leadership, 1983–1984* (Ann Arbor: University of Michigan, Division of Research, Graduate School of Business Administration, 1984), 26.

30. Richard Zweigenhaft, "Diversity among CEOs and Corporate Directors: Has the Heyday Come and Gone?" (paper presented at the annual meeting of the American Sociological Association, New York City, August 12, 2013). See also http://www2.ucsc.edu/whorulesamerica/power/diversity_among_ceos.html.

31. Bender, "Woman Lawyer." See also Cynthia Fuchs Epstein, "Positive Effects of the Multiple Negative: Explaining the Success of Black Professional Women," *American Journal of Sociology* 78 (1973): 912–35.

32. C. Wright Mills, *The Power Elite* (New York: Oxford University Press, 1956), 289.

33. "Donna A. James—Headed Human Resources," http://biography.jrank.org/pages/2615/James-Donna-Headed-Human-Resources.html.

34. Andrew Hacker, "Who They Are," *New York Times Magazine*, November 19, 1995, 71. At that time, the other four were Berry Gordy (of Motown Records), Reginald Lewis (of Beatrice Foods), Oprah Winfrey, and Bill Cosby.

35. Richard L. Zweigenhaft and G. William Domhoff, *Blacks in the White Establishment?: A Study of Race and Class in America* (New Haven, CT: Yale University Press, 1991), 136.

36. Estimating the exact number of African American CEOs of *Fortune* 500 companies has become more challenging since some companies have moved their headquarters from the United States. The Eaton Corporation, for example, was #163 on the 2012 *Fortune* list. It then merged with an Irish company and moved its headquarters from Cleveland to Ireland. In 2016 the company appointed Craig Arnold, an African American, as its CEO. Both Donald Trump and Hillary Clinton criticized Eaton during the 2016 campaign (see Paul R. La Monica, "Company That Trump Bashed Isn't Backing Down," *CNN Money*, February 3, 2017, http://money.cnn.com/2017/02/03/investing/eaton-donald-trump-inversion-ireland/index.html). We have not included Craig Arnold, nor did we include another African American, Arnold Donald, CEO of

Carnival, which is not headquartered in the United States and thus not on the recent *Fortune* 500 lists. Some others who have listed the African American CEOs of "major US companies" have included Craig Arnold and Arnold Donald. See for example, Carol Hymowitz, "The Number of Black C-Suite Executives Has Shrunk under Obama," *Bloomberg*, June 29, 2016, https://www.bloomberg.com/amp/news/articles/2016-07-29/black-americans-in-the-c-suite-a-look-at-the-obama-era-declines. Including these two men would not change any of the conclusions we draw in this chapter.

37. Zweigenhaft, "Has the Heyday Come and Gone?"

38. See Scott A. Ginder, Janice E. Kelly-Read, and Farrah B. Mann, "Graduation Rates for Selected Cohorts, 2007–2012," Institute of Educational Sciences, National Center for Educational Statistics, February 2017, NCES 2017-084, U.S. Department of Education. See also Richard Zweigenhaft and G. William Domhoff, *The New CEOs: Women, African American, Latino, and Asian American Leaders of Fortune 500 Companies* (Lanham, MD: Rowman & Littlefield, 2014), 120–38.

39. Richard W. Stevenson, "A Homecoming at Fannie Mae," *New York Times*, May 17, 1998, Business section, 10; David Leonhardt, "The Saga of Lloyd Ward: His Remarkable Journey to Become Maytag's CEO," *BusinessWeek*, August 9, 1999, 59–61, 64–66, 68, 70; David Rynecki, "Putting the Muscle Back in the Bull," *Fortune*, April 5, 2004, 162–70. The information on Clarence Otis's parents is from an e-mail from Otis to Richard Zweigenhaft, June 13, 2005.

40. In August 2017, Kenneth Frazier challenged Donald Trump by quitting the American Manufacturing Council after Trump initially failed to criticize the Klan and neo-Nazis when their protest in Charlottesville, Virginia, led to the murder of one woman and injuries to nineteen others. This ignited a fire. First a number of other CEOs quit or announced that they too planned to quit that council (including one woman, Denise Morrison, CEO of Campbell Soup) or another Trump council, the Strategy and Policy Forum (Gini Rometty, of IBM, announced that she was quitting it). Trump subsequently disbanded both councils. Trump singled out Frazier in "caustic Twitter attacks." Glenn Thrush, "Trump Condemns Racists but Creates Fresh Uproar," *New York Times*, August 14, 2017, A1; and David Gelles, Landon Thomas Jr., Andrew Ross Sorkin, and Kate Kelly, "Rebellion by Business Leaders Spelled End of Trump Councils," *New York Times*, August 17, 2017, A1.

41. "Clifton R. Wharton, Jr.," *Current Biography* (1987): 597–99; Timothy L. O'Brien, "Successor Is Selected to Run American Express," *New York Times*, April 27, 1999, C6; Claudia H. Deutsch, "Former Xerox Officer Gets Top Avis Job: Chairman's Post Fulfills a Long Aim," *New York Times*, November 10, 1999, C8; Lisa C. Jones, "Winning the Power Game: Erroll B. Davis, Jr., Head of WPL Holdings, Inc.," *Ebony*, November 1994, online version; and Carrie Kirby, "Newsmaker Profile: John Thompson, Man with a Plan," *SFGate*, January 29, 2002, http://www.sfgate.com.

42. The quote is from Gwendolyn Parker, a graduate of Radcliffe and the New York University business school, writing about Kenneth Chenault. She wrote, "Ken had an additional skill, which people often called his smoothness. As I saw it, that smoothness came from his recognition that his ease with white people was not merely a neutral ability, but something he could turn to his advantage." See Gwendolyn M. Parker, *Trespassing: My Sojourn in the Halls of Privilege* (Boston: Houghton Mifflin, 1997), 192–93.

43. Elijah Anderson, "The Social Situation of the Black Executive: Black and White Identities in the Corporate World," in *The Cultural Territories of Race: Black and White Boundaries*, ed. Michele Lamont (Chicago: University of Chicago Press, 1999), 12. Anderson explores the difficulties the executives he studied had in negotiating relationships with other blacks in the corporation and with whites who were both "wise" and "not so wise" to the difficulties

blacks encounter in such a predominantly white setting. Among other things, they were worried "about appearing 'too black' in one set of circumstances and 'too white' in another" (15).

44. For Rand, see Caroline V. Clarke, *Take a Lesson: Today's Black Achievers on How They Made It & What They Learned along the Way* (New York: Wiley, 2001), 162. For Parsons, see David Carr, "No Use Crying over Spilled Billions," *New York Times*, June 20, 2004, 5. For Chenault, see Nelson D. Schwartz, "What's in the Cards at AMEX?" *Fortune*, January 22, 2001, 59–70, 62. There is no mention of Wharton's interest or participation in sports in the extensive biographical material we have read about him. In one article about O'Neal, he says that he sometimes finds time to "play a bad game of golf." Susan Young, "A Long Road of Learning: Merrill Lynch's Stan O'Neal," *Harvard Business School Bulletin* (online), June 2001, 2, https://www.alumni.hbs.edu/stories/Pages/story-bulletin.aspx?num= 4388. For Clarence Otis, e-mail, June 13, 2002.

45. See, for example, Harry Edwards, "Athletic Performance in Exchange for an Education—A Contract Unfulfilled," *Crisis*, May 1983, 10–14, and, more recently, Harry Edwards, "Crisis of Black Athletes on the Eve of the 21st Century," *Society* 37, no. 3 (March–April 2000): 9–13. For a critique of Edwards's position, see Earl Smith, "There Was No Golden Age of Sport for African American Athletes," *Society* 37, no. 3 (March–April 2000): 45–48.

46. Henry Louis Gates Jr., "Breaking the Silence," *New York Times*, August 1, 2004, A11.

47. Leonhardt, "Saga of Lloyd Ward."

48. Clarke, *Take a Lesson*, 162.

49. See Richard L. Zweigenhaft, "'Penetrators' and 'Internal Elites': A Comparison between African Americans on the Boards of the Ten Largest Companies on the *Fortune* 500 and Those on the Boards of the Ten Largest Companies on the *Black Enterprise* List" (paper presented at the annual meeting of the Pacific Sociological Association, Portland, Oregon, April 16, 1999). See also Udayan Gupta, "Minority Suppliers Are Getting a Boost from Big Firms," *Wall Street Journal*, November 10, 1994, B2.

50. "*Black Enterprise* Releases Exclusive Report on African American Corporate Directors," http://www.blackenterprise.com/news/report-black-corporate-directors-study-boardro oms; Ross Kerber, "Black Presence on U.S. Boards Shrinks, Hedge Funds Cited by Some," *Reuters*, December 16, 2015, http://www.reuters.com/article/us-boardroom-race-insightidUSKBN0TZ1KY20151216.

51. Lena Williams, "Not Just a White Man's Game," *New York Times*, November 9, 1995.

52. Cora Daniels, "50 Most Powerful Black Executives in America," *Fortune*, July 22, 2002, 63. The estimate of less than 5 percent is our best guess, based on interviews we conducted for *Blacks in the White Elite* with African American executives working for *Fortune*-level companies (see Richard L. Zweigenhaft and G. William Domhoff, *Blacks in the White Elite* [Lanham, MD: Rowman & Littlefield, 2003], ch. 7, note 15).

53. Zweigenhaft and Domhoff, *New CEOs*, 135.

54. Collins, "Blacks on the Bubble," 438.

55. For a detailed account of these "corporate-mediated" programs, which include the A Better Chance program and the Summer Venture in Management Program (SVMP) at the Harvard Business School, see Zweigenhaft and Domhoff, *Blacks in the White Elite*, 166–72. See also the section on these programs in ch. 8.

56. See http://caselaw.findlaw.com/us-supreme-court/539/244.html and David Von Drehle, "Court Mirrors Public Opinion," *Washington Post*, June 24, 2003, https://www. washingtonpost.com/archive/politics/2003/06/24/court-mirrors-public-opinion/3994c2f3-5d314a67-b804-421c628e1595/?utm_term=.7a845f3aa58e.

57. National Association for Law Placement, "2016 Report on Diversity in U.S. Law Firms," January 2017, https://tinyurl.com/ko3fxej, p. 5.

58. "Vernon Jordan," *Current Biography* (1993): 297.

59. "Vernon Jordan," 299. See also Jeff Gerth, "Being Intimate with Power, Vernon Jordan Can Wield It Quietly but Effectively," *New York Times*, July 14, 1996.

60. Robin Armstrong, "Robert C. Weaver: Government Administrator, Scholar," in *Contemporary Black Biography: Profiles from the International Black Community*, ed. L. Mpho Mabunda, vol. 8 (New York: Gale Research, 1995), 259.

61. Richard Bardolph, *The Negro Vanguard* (New York: Rinehart, 1959), 255.

62. Armstrong, "Robert C. Weaver," 261.

63. "William T. Coleman, Jr.," *Current Biography* (1976): 89.

64. Richard A. Oppel Jr., "Nominee Is Picked to Replace Departing HUD Secretary," *New York Times*, December 13, 2003.

65. Benjamin O. Davis Jr., *Benjamin O. Davis, Jr., American: An Autobiography* (Washington, DC: Smithsonian Institution Press, 1991), 27.

66. Davis, *Benjamin O. Davis, Jr.*, 52. See also Richard Goldstein, "Lt. Gen. Benjamin O. Davis Jr., 89, Dies; in World War II, Led First Black Pilots Unit," *New York Times*, July 7, 2002, A19.

67. Charles C. Moskos and John Sibley Butler, *All That We Can Be: Black Leadership and Racial Integration the Army Way* (New York: Basic, 1996), 31.

68. Moskos and Butler report that, in 1995, the 145,000 blacks in the army were about half of all blacks in military uniform and accounted for about 27 percent of all those on active duty in the army. The percentage of blacks in the army, they note, was "approximately twice the proportion found in the navy, air force, or marine corps" (6).

69. John Mintz, "Clinton Nominates First Black Admiral," *Washington Post*, May 14, 1996.

70. For the September 2004 data, see "Distribution of Active Duty Forces by Service, Rank, Sex and Race, 09/30/04," Department of Defense document DMDC-3035EO. For the 2011 data, see Daniel Sagalyn, "Report: U.S. Military Leadership Lacks Diversity at Top," *PBS NewsHour*, March 11, 2011, http://www.pbs.org/newshour/rundown/military-report; the March 2017 data were provided by the Office of the Secretary of Defense (Military Personnel Policy)—thanks, especially, to Myles B. Caggins III, Lieutenant Colonel, U.S. Army, OSD Public Affairs. The three African Americans with four-star rank were army general Vincent Brooks, air force general Darren McDew, and navy admiral Michelle Howard.

71. Tom Vanden Brook, "Army Tries to Boost Number of Minority Officers," *USA Today*, October 13, 2014.

72. US Military Academy News Release No. 11–12, June 28, 2012.

73. "They Didn't See the Pride: West Point Photo Puts Race and Gender in Spotlight," *Guardian*, May 14, 2016.

74. *Black Americans in Defense of Our Nation* (Washington, DC: US Government Printing Office, 1991). The recent data for the Naval Academy and the US Military Academy are from their websites; the data for the Air Force Academy were provided by the public affairs office at the school.

75. Stephen Losey, "Race and the Air Force: The Truth about How Minorities Get Promoted," *Air Force Times*, March 1, 2016, https://www.airforcetimes.com/articles/race-and-the-air-force-the-truth-about-how-minorities-get-promoted. These findings supported those of a 2014 Rand Corporation study by Nelson Lim, Luis T. Mariano, Amy G. Cox, David Schulker, and Lawrence M. Hanser titled, "Improving Demographic Diversity in the U.S. Air Force Officer Corps," http://www.rand.org/pubs/research_reports/RR495.html.

76. Mills, *Power Elite*, 215.

77. Moskos and Butler, *All That We Can Be*, 50.

78. Moskos and Butler, *All That We Can Be*, 114.

79. In 1994, when he received the Order of Jamaica, the highest honor given to non-Jamaicans, after reminding those attending that he was an American citizen, Powell added, "But let it be clear to all present that I consider myself a Jamaican, a true son of Jamaica." "Colin Powell Honored with Order of Jamaica," *New York Times*, December 2, 1994, A6.

80. David Halberstam, "There Is Something Noble to It," *Parade*, September 17, 1995, 5.

81. Halberstam, "There Is Something Noble," 5.

82. John F. Stacks, "The Powell Factor," *Time*, July 10, 1995, 25.

83. Moskos and Butler, *All That We Can Be*, 115.

84. The interview was September 8, 2005, with Barbara Walters on ABC News. See http://abcnews.go.com/2020/Politics/story?id=1105979&page=1.

85. Horace Mann Bond, "The Negro Scholar and Professional in America," in *The American Negro Reference Book*, ed. John P. Davis (Englewood Cliffs, NJ: Prentice Hall, 1966), 559. See also Franklin E. Frazier, *The Black Bourgeoisie: The Rise of the New Middle Class* (New York: Free Press, 1957); Horace Mann Bond, *Black American Scholars: A Study of Their Beginnings* (Detroit, MI: Balamp, 1972); H. Edward Ransford, "Skin Color, Life Chances, and Anti-White Attitudes," *Social Problems* 18 (1970): 164–78; Elizabeth Mullins and Paul Sites, "The Origins of Contemporary Eminent Black Americans: A Three-Generation Analysis of Social Origins," *American Sociological Review* 49 (1984): 672–85; Cedric Herring, Verna M. Keith, and Hayward D. Horton, eds., *Skin Deep: How Race and Complexion Matter in the "Color-Blind" Era* (Urbana: University of Illinois Press, 2004); and Margaret Hunter, *Race, Gender, and the Politics of Skin Tone* (New York: Routledge, 2005).

86. Glass Ceiling Commission, *Good for Business: Making Full Use of the Nation's Human Capital, a Fact-Finding Report of the Federal Glass Ceiling Commission* (Washington, DC: US Government Printing Office, 1995), 29.

87. "Patricia Robert Harris," *Current Biography* (1965): 191. Recent research demonstrates that "Afrocentric facial features," such as a wide nose or full lips, contribute to stereotyping of individuals within, as well as between, racial groups. See Irene B. Blair, Charles M. Judd, M. S. Sadler, and C. Jenkins, "The Role of Afrocentric Features in Person Perception: Judging by Features and Categories," *Journal of Personality and Social Psychology* 83 (2002): 5–25; Irene B. Blair, Charles M. Judd, and Kristine M. Chapleau, "The Influence of Afrocentric Facial Features in Criminal Sentencing," *Psychological Science* 15 (2004): 674–79. See also Elena V. Stepanova and Michael J. Strube, "The Role of Skin Color and Facial Physiognomy in Racial Categorization: Moderation by Implicit Racial Attitudes," *Journal of Experimental Social Psychology*, 48 (2012): 867–78; and Heather M. Kleider-Offutt, Alesha D. Bond, and Shanna E. A. Hegerty, "Black Stereotypical Features: When a Face Type Can Get You in Trouble," *Current Directions in Psychological Science*, 26 (2017): 28–33.

88. The Skin Color Assessment Procedure is described in Selena Bond and Thomas F. Cash, "Black Beauty: Skin Color and Body Images among African-American College Women," *Journal of Applied Social Psychology* 22, no. 1 (1992): 874–88. The two raters had a high rate of interrater agreement (the interjudge reliability, as determined by a Pearson product moment correlation, was $r = 0.87$). The ninety magazine-quality photographs used were drawn from *Current Biography*, from various articles in *Ebony*'s fiftieth-anniversary issue in November 1995, and from the October 1994 *Ebony* article on the black interlocking directors. A regression analysis looking at the effect of both power-elite status and gender on skin-color rating was highly significant ($F = 20.23$, $p < 0.0001$). Gender was a stronger predictor (beta = 0.50, $p < 0.0001$) of skin color than power-elite status (beta = 0.20, $p < 0.02$).

89. For a more detailed account of these findings, see Zweigenhaft and Domhoff, *New CEOs*, 46–49 and 165–76.

90. Richard L. Zweigenhaft, *Who Gets to the Top? Executive Suite Discrimination in the Eighties* (New York: Institute of Human Relations, 1984), 17.

91. The description of Powell is in Henry Louis Gates Jr., "Powell and the Black Elite," *New Yorker*, September 25, 1995, 66 (quotation appears on p. 70).

92. Two blacks from Mississippi, Hiram Revels and Blanche Cruce, served in the Senate during Reconstruction. They were both selected by the state's legislature, not by the voters. "Edward W. Brooke," *Current Biography* (1967): 42.

93. "Edward W. Brooke," 41.

94. Isaac Rosen, "Edward Brooke: Former U.S. Senator, Lawyer, Consultant," in *Contemporary Black Biography: Profiles from the International Black Community*, ed. L. Mpho Mabunda, vol. 8 (New York: Gale Research, 1995), 28.

95. Rosen, "Edward Brooke," 28.

96. Rosen, "Edward Brooke," 29.

97. Carol Moseley-Braun, "Between W. E. B. Du Bois and B. T. Washington," *Ebony*, November 1995, 58.

98. Isaac Rosen, "Carol Moseley Braun: Politician, Lawyer," in *Contemporary Black Biography: Profiles from the International Black Community*, ed. Barbara C. Bigelow, vol. 4 (Detroit, MI: Gale, 1993), 28.

99. David Mendell, *Obama: From Promise to Power* (New York: HarperCollins, 2007), 36.

100. Barack Obama, *Dreams from My Father: A Story of Race and Inheritance* (New York: Times Books, 1995). Very few of the students at Punahou were poor, and almost none were black. Obama notes that his first experience with affirmative action had little to do with race: he was accepted at Punahou not because he was black but, rather, because his grandfather worked for an alumnus who had clout at the school (54).

101. William Finnegan, "The Candidate: How the Son of a Kenyan Economist Became an Illinois Everyman," *New Yorker*, May 31, 2004, 34.

102. Mendell, *Obama*, 2 and 7.

103. Remnick, "The Political Scene," 61.

104. Finnegan, "Candidate," 36.

105. For these very reasons, many African American voters in Chicago were at first wary about Obama. He was defeated in 2000 when he ran for Congress against Bobby Rush, a former Black Panther (see Finnegan, "Candidate," 36), and, as Salim Muwakkil, a senior editor at *In These Times*, put it, in 2004 some black voters "initially withheld support for Obama because he was projected as such a post-race candidate" ("Shades of 1983," *In These Times*, April 26, 2004, 13).

106. Richard Fausset, "For Scott, as the Only Black Republican Senator, the Election Is Complicated," *New York Times*, October 16, 2016, A16.

107. Jason Horowitz, "New Jersey's Cory Booker: A Perfect Senator for 'This Town'?," *Washington Post*, August 26, 2013, https://www.washingtonpost.com/politics/new-jerseys-cory-booker-a-perfect-senator-for-this-town/2013/08/26/ebf3b50a-0e81-11e3-bdf6-e4fc677d94a1_story.html.

108. Gregory L. Giroux, "A Touch of Gray on Capitol Hill," *Congressional Quarterly*, January 31, 2005, 243.

109. It should be noted that the fact that 24 percent of the blacks in the House since 1990 have been women represents a higher percentage than the percentage of women in the House—about 19.3 percent in mid-2017. Moreover, Katherine Tate, in *Black Faces in the Mirror: African Americans and Their Representatives in the U. S. Congress* (Princeton, NJ: Princeton University Press, 2003), notes that "perhaps the single most striking difference between Black women members and all other members of the House" is that they are more likely to be unmarried.

Whereas almost 90 percent of the members of the House were married at the time they were elected, since 1973 only about one-third of the black women were married at the time they were elected (the other two-thirds have been widowed, separated, divorced, or single); 46.

110. David Daley, *Ratf**ked: The True Story behind the Secret Plan to Steal America's Democracy* (New York: Liveright, 2016), 36.

111. Atwater was notorious after 1990 based on an explanation he gave to a political scientist for the use of code words to win over white voters in the South: "By 1968 you can't say 'nigger'—that hurts you. Backfires. So you say stuff like forced busing, states' rights and all that stuff. You're getting so abstract now [that] you're talking about cutting taxes, and all these things you're talking about are totally economic things and a byproduct of them is [that] blacks get hurt worse than whites." See the interview with Atwater by political scientist Alexander P. Lamis in his *The Two-Party South* (New York: Oxford University Press, 1984). These remarks were first published in the 1984 edition of this book as part of an interview with an anonymous insider, but, in the 1990 edition of the book, shortly before he died of a brain tumor (in 1991), Atwater was revealed to be the person interviewed.

112. See Seth C. McKee, *Republican Ascendency in Southern U.S. House Elections* (Boulder, CO: Westview, 2010), for the complete picture, which includes several factors.

113. McKee, *Republican Ascendency*, 72.

114. Ari Berman, *Give Us the Ballot: The Modern Struggle for Voting Rights in America* (New York: Farrar, Straus & Giroux, 2015), 203.

115. Berman, *Give Us the Ballot*, 205. See also Daley, *Ratf**ked*.

116. Juan Williams, *Thurgood Marshall: American Revolutionary* (New York: Times Books, 1998), 15, 21–22, 34–35.

117. Jane Mayer and Jill Abramson, *Strange Justice: The Selling of Clarence Thomas* (Boston: Houghton Mifflin, 1994), 37–52, 348. See also Kevin Merida and Michael A. Fletcher, *Supreme Discomfort: The Divided Soul of Clarence Thomas* (New York: Doubleday, 2007).

118. Howard Ball, *A Defiant Life: Thurgood Marshall and the Persistence of Racism in America* (New York: Crown, 1998), 15; Mayer and Abramson, *Strange Justice*, 45.

119. Williams, *Thurgood Marshall*, 50, 229, 242–44.

120. Mayer and Abramson, *Strange Justice*, 54–55, 144.

121. Mayer and Abramson, *Strange Justice*, 14.

5. LATINOS IN THE POWER ELITE

1. *Statistical Abstract of the United States* (Washington, DC: US Government Printing Office, 1985), 86.

2. These figures are from the US Census Bureau. When he died, Goizueta was eulogized as representing the American dream, with little or no attention paid to his privileged background in Cuba before the revolution. See Richard Zweigenhaft, "Making Rags out of Riches: Horatio Alger and the Tycoon's Obituary," *Extra!* January–February 2004, 27–28. Corporate chieftains (and their publicists) are not alone in their tendency to focus on the obstacles they have faced rather than the advantages they have had (for example, due to economic privilege). See Shai Davidai and Thomas Gilovich, "The Headwinds/Tailwinds Asymmetry: An Availability Bias in Assessments of Barriers and Blessings." *Journal of Personality and Social Psychology* 111, no. 6 (2016): 835–51.

3. Janet Morey and Wendy Dunn, *Famous Mexican Americans* (New York: Dutton, 1989), 65–67.

4. Morey and Dunn, *Famous Mexican Americans*, 70.

5. James A. Gross, *Broken Promise: The Subversion of U.S. Labor Relations Policy, 1947–1994* (Philadelphia: Temple University Press, 1995), 250–63.

6. Ramon A. Gutierrez, "What's in a Name? The History and Politics of Hispanic and Latino Panethnicities," in *The New Latino Studies Reader: A Twenty-First-Century Perspective*, ed. Ramon A. Gutierrez and Tomas Almaguer (Oakland: University of California Press, 2016), 20–21.

7. Rodolfo de la Garza, Louis DeSipio, F. Chris Garcia, John Garcia, and Angelo Falcon, *Latino Voices: Mexican, Puerto Rican, and Cuban Perspectives on American Politics* (Boulder, CO: Westview, 1992), 13–14. See also Suzanne Oboler, *Ethnic Labels, Latino Lives* (Minneapolis: University of Minnesota Press, 1995); and Renee Stepler and Anna Brown, *Statistical Portrait of Hispanics in the United States*, Pew Research Center, April 19, 2016, http://www.pewhispanic.org/2016/04/19/statistical-portrait-of-hispanics-in-the-united-states-key-charts.

8. There is yet another term that has arrived on the scene to refer to Latinos and Latinas, one designed to acknowledge that not all people fall into the gender binary of male and female. The term is *Latinx*. According to an article in the *Huffington Post*, "It's part of a 'linguistic revolution' that aims to move beyond gender binaries and is inclusive of the intersecting identities of Latin American descendants. In addition to men and women from all racial backgrounds, Latinx also makes room for people who are trans, queer, agender, non-binary, gender non-conforming or gender fluid." Tanisha Love Ramirez and Zeba Blay, "Why People Are Using the Term 'Latinx,'" *Huffington Post*, July 5, 2016, http://www.huffingtonpost.com/entry/why-people-are-using-the-term-latinx_us_57753328e4b0cc0fa136a159. By April 2017, even staid *Fortune* magazine was using the term. An article on diversity described Hewlett-Packard as having "a leadership team that's 29% female and 14% people of color," and went on to say that "its workforce overall is 33% women, 7% black, and 14% Latinx." Claire Zillman, "This Entrepreneur Is Ranking Tech Companies on Diversity," *Fortune*, April 10, 2017, http://fortune.com/2017/04/10/tech-diversity-blendoor-stephanie-lampkin.

So, too, did the term make it into the *New York Times*, though in quotation marks, when, in June 2017, an article reported that "about 120 students attended the third annual 'Latinx' commencement" at Harvard. Anemona Hartocollis, "Colleges Celebrate Diversity with Separate Commencements," *New York Times*, June 3, 2017, p. A11.

9. See *Mainline Protestant Churches No Longer Dominate NCC Yearbook's List of Top 25 U.S. Religious Bodies* (New York: National Council of Churches, 2005), http://www.ncccusa.org/news/050330yearbook.html.

10. Carlos H. Arce, Edward Murguia, and W. Parker Frisbie, "Phenotype and Life Chances among Chicanos," *Hispanic Journal of Behavioral Sciences* 9, no. 1 (1987): 19–32; E. A. Telles and Edward Murguia, "Phenotypic Discrimination and Income Differences among Mexican Americans," *Social Science Quarterly* 71 (1990): 682–96; Aida Hurtado, "Does Similarity Breed Respect? Interviewer Evaluations of Mexican-Descent Respondents in a Bilingual Survey," *Public Opinion Quarterly* 58 (1994): 77–95.

11. For excellent accounts of the association of color and racial exclusion in Latin America, see Laura A. Lewis, "Spanish Ideology and the Practice of Inequality in the New World," in *Racism and Anti-Racism in World Perspective*, ed. Benjamin Bowser (Thousand Oaks, CA: Sage, 1995), 46–66; Vânia Penha-Lopes, "What Next? On Race and Assimilation in the United States and Brazil," *Journal of Black Studies* 26, no. 6 (1996): 809–26; Edward Murguia and Tyrone Forman, "Shades of Whiteness: The Mexican American Experience in Relation to Anglos and Blacks," in *White Out: The Continuing Significance of Race*, ed. Ashley Doane and

Eduardo Bonilla-Silva (New York: Routledge, 2003), 63–79; Samantha Prado Robledo, "Colorism: The Relationship between Latino/a Self-Perceived Skin Color and Assimilation" (MA thesis, California State University at San Marcos, 2012); Nayeli Y. Chavez-Duenas, Hector Y. Adames, and Kurt C. Organista, "Skin-Color Prejudice and Within-Group Racial Discrimination: Historical and Current Impact on Latino/a Populations," *Hispanic Journal of Behavioral Sciences*, 36, no. 1 (2014): 3–26; and Lori L. Tharps, *Same Family, Different Colors: Confronting Colorism in America's Diverse Families* (Boston: Beacon, 2016), especially ch. 2, "*Mejorando la Raza*: Latinos and Color."

12. See the Alliance for Board Diversity, 2012 and 2016 reports, "Missing Pieces: Women and Minorities on *Fortune* 500 Boards—2012 [and 2016] Alliance for Board Diversity Census." Alliance for Board Diversity, August 15 (the quoted material appears on p. 9 of the 2012 report, and p. 20 of the 2016 report).

13. Reply to letter to the editor, *Hispanic Business*, April 1995, 8.

14. Personal communication from director of community affairs, Sears, July 29, 1996. Despite this clear statement that Martinez was not of Latino heritage, in 1998, *Hispanic Business* included him on its list of five Latinos who were CEOs of *Fortune* 1000 companies. See Maria Zate, "The Big Jump," *Hispanic Business*, January–February 1998, 32. Similarly, *Hispanic Business* included David Fuente, the CEO of Office Depot, as one of the five Latino CEOs in 1998, but the Office Depot public relations officer informed us that Fuente was born and raised in Chicago and is a Sephardic Jew. In all likelihood, his ancestors were expelled from Spain or Portugal in the fifteenth century, which stretches the meaning of "Hispanic" beyond the usual boundaries. Although *Hispanic Business* continued to include him on its "boardroom elite" list, he was listed as Caucasian, but not Hispanic, on the Investor Responsibility Research Center's *Standard & Poor's* (IRRC's S&P) 1500 list.

15. "Who's News," *Wall Street Journal*, June 8, 1995.

16. Jane Mayer, "Sweet Life: First Family of Sugar Is Tough on Workers, Generous to Politicians," *Wall Street Journal*, July 29, 1991.

17. Phyllis Berman, "The Set-Aside Charade," *Forbes*, March 13, 1995, 78–80, 82, 86; Phyllis Berman, "The Fanjuls of Palm Beach," *Forbes*, May 14, 1990, 56–57, 60, 64, 68–69; and Eric Alan Barton, "Bitter Sugar," *Miami New Times* (online), August 26, 2004, http://www.browardpalmbeach.com/news/bitter-sugar-6317770.

18. Leslie Wayne, "Foreign G.O.P. Donor Raised Dole Funds," *New York Times*, October 21, 1996; Barton, "Bitter Sugar"; Timothy L. O'Brien, "The Castro Collection," *New York Times*, November 21, 2004, section 3, 1; and Alexei Barrionuevo and Elizabeth Becker, "Mighty Lobby Is Losing Some Luster," *New York Times*, June 2, 2005, C1, C4.

19. J. P. Faber, "Chairman of the Board: Armando Codina," *South Florida CEO*, January 2004, 44–51.

20. Faber, "Chairman of the Board," 44–51.

21. William Finnegan, "Castro's Shadow," *New Yorker*, October 14, 2002, 101ff.

22. David Pedreira, "Strait-out Country; Bush Pals Vie for Charters," *Tampa Tribune*, March 28, 1999, 1.

23. Dusko Doder, "Our Tropical Terrorist Tourist Trap; As Fidel and His Critics Creak toward Irrelevance, the Push for Normalized U.S.-Cuban Relations Grows Stronger," *American Prospect*, October 7, 2002, 26.

24. Susan Rasky, "A 'Born' Republican: Katherine Davalos Ortega," *New York Times*, August 21, 1984.

25. Morey and Dunn, *Famous Mexican Americans*, 100–101.

26. Morey and Dunn, *Famous Mexican Americans*, 76.

27. US Census QuickFacts, https://www.census.gov/quickfacts/fact/table/US/RHI125216.

28. Richard Alba, "Schools and the Diversity Transition," *Daedelus, the Journal of the American Academy of Arts and Sciences* 142, no. 3 (2013), 155–69.

29. Richard L. Zweigenhaft and G. William Domhoff, *The New CEOs: Women, African American, Latino, and Asian American Leaders of* Fortune *500 Companies* (Lanham, MD: Rowman & Littlefield, 2014; paperback edition with new introduction, 62–63, 165–76).

30. Emma Jacobs, "20 Questions: Enrique Salem," *Financial Times*, April 15, 2010.

31. Zweigenhaft and Domhoff, *New CEOs*, 134–37. We subsequently expanded the sample from 25 companies to 287, and found basically the same patterns.

32. As in previous chapters, we are including only cabinet positions, but not "cabinet-level officials" such as the ambassador to the United Nations, the administrator of the Environmental Protection Agency, and the administrator of the Small Business Administration.

33. "Lauro F. Cavazos, Jr.," *Current Biography* (1989): 97.

34. Maureen Dowd, "Cavazos Quits as Education Chief amid Pressure from White House," *New York Times*, September 13, 1990.

35. "Henry G. Cisneros," *Current Biography* (1987): 87–96; "Federico F. Peña," *Current Biography* (1993): 460–64.

36. David Johnston, "Concluding That Cisneros Lied, Reno Urges a Special Prosecutor," *New York Times*, March 15, 1995; Steven A. Holmes, "Housing Secretary Resigns, Citing Financial Pressures," *New York Times*, November 22, 1996; and Mireya Navarro, "Cisneros Leaving Univision to Run Housing Company," *New York Times*, August 8, 2000, C8.

37. David Streitfeld and Gretchen Morgenson, "Building Flawed American Dreams," *New York Times*, October 18, 2008, http://www.nytimes.com/2008/10/19/business/19cisneros.html.

38. Matt Kranz, "Wells Fargo Scam Latest in String of Infractions," *USA Today*, September 11, 2016, https://www.usatoday.com/story/money/markets/2016/09/11/wells-fargo-scam-latest-string-infractions/90139724/.

39. See Carlos M. Gutierrez, "The Boss: My Many Citizenship Quests," *New York Times*, August 22, 2001, C6.

40. David Johnston and Richard W. Stevenson, "Riding an Ideological Divide: Alberto R. Gonzales," *New York Times*, November 11, 2004, A28; "The Wrong Attorney General," *New York Times*, January 26, 2005, A20; Mark Danner, "Torture and Gonzales: An Exchange," *New York Review of Books*, February 10, 2005, 44–46; Jonathan Schell, "What Is Wrong with Torture," *Nation*, February 7, 2005, 8; and David Cole, "Gonzales: Wrong Choice," *Nation*, December 6, 2004, 5–6.

41. Thomas E. Cronin, *The State of the Presidency*, 2nd ed. (Boston: Little, Brown, 1980), 275–76.

42. Obama also appointed Maria Contreras-Sweet as administrator of the Small Business Administration (SBA), which he elevated to a cabinet-level position in early 2012. However, as we have noted, the SBA is not considered a cabinet position traditionally. Bill Clinton also appointed a Latina, Aida Alvarez, a Puerto Rican businesswoman, as head of the SBA and raised that position to temporary cabinet level. These appointments may reflect, in part, attempts to achieve, or achieve the appearance of, greater diversity in presidential cabinets.

43. Amy Driscoll, "A Passion of Trump's New Labor Secretary Pick: Trafficking 'Is Evil. It Is Hideous,'" *Miami Herald*, February 16, 2017, http://www.miamiherald.com/news/local/community/miami-dade/article133142059.html.

44. The March 31, 2017, data were provided by the Office of the Secretary of Defense (Military Personnel Policy).

45. Sig Christenson, "Retired General Created Legacy, Made History," *Washington Times*, April 3, 2016, http://www.washingtontimes.com/news/2016/apr/3/retired-general-created-legacy-made-history.

46. The figures for the Naval Academy and West Point are taken from their websites; the figures for the Air Force Academy were provided by the school's public affairs office. For some slightly older data on graduation rates, see "Hispanic-American Graduates of the Military Academies, 1966–1989," in *Hispanics in America's Defense* (Washington, DC: Department of Defense, US Government Printing Office, 1990), 181.

47. Sonia Sotomayor, *My Beloved World* (New York: Knopf, 2013). The quote is from p. viii.

48. William Yeomans, "How the Right Packed the Court," *Nation*, October 8, 2012, 14–17.

49. Stepler and Brown, *Statistical Portrait*.

6. ASIAN AMERICANS AND SOUTH ASIANS IN THE POWER ELITE

1. For an excellent account of efforts to create pan-Asian institutions, see Yen Le Espiritu, *Asian American Panethnicity* (Philadelphia: Temple University Press, 1992). Espiritu begins her account by noting that she is "a Vietnamese American who is married to a Filipino American" (xi). See also Dina G. Okamoto, *Redefining Race: Asian American Panethnicity and Shifting Ethnic Boundaries* (New York: Russell Sage Foundation, 2014).

2. This is true for Asian Americans in general. In "The Committee of 100's Asian Pacific American (APA) Corporate Report Card," updated in April 2004 (http://www.committee100. org/initiatives/corporate_board/2004.04.23%20Formal%20Report.pdf), the authors note that 47 percent of APAs had college degrees compared to 27 percent for all American adults. See also Jennifer Lee and Min Zhou, *The Asian American Achievement Paradox* (New York: Russell Sage Foundation, 2015).

3. "Asian Americans: A Mosaic of Faiths," Pew Research Center, July 19, 2012. The groups vary tremendously. Whereas 71 percent of the Koreans surveyed were Christians, and 6 percent were Buddhists, only 18 percent of the Indian Americans were Christian, and 51 percent were Hindu.

4. Benjamin Pimentel, "Asian Americans' Awkward Status," *San Francisco Chronicle*, August 22, 1995.

5. See, for example, Ivan Light and Edna Bonacich, *Immigrant Entrepreneurs: Koreans in Los Angeles, 1965–1982* (Berkeley: University of California Press, 1988).

6. For comprehensive reviews and analyses of the evidence concerning discrimination against Asian Americans in corporate, governmental, and academic settings, see Deborah Woo, *Glass Ceilings and Asian Americans: The New Face of Workplace Barriers* (Walnut Creek, CA: AltaMira, 2000); and Bill Ong Hing and Ronald Lee, eds., *Reframing the Immigration Debate: A Public Policy Report* (Los Angeles: LEAP Asian Pacific American Public Policy Institute and UCLA Asian American Studies Center, 1996). For an earlier summary of the situation facing Asian Americans and other minorities in the corporate world, and essays by minority executives on their experience, see Donna Thompson and Nancy DiTomaso, eds., *Ensuring Minority Success in Corporate Management* (New York: Plenum, 1988).

7. As with Latinos, we are aware that there are some people who are not on our list who should be, and perhaps some on our list who are not Asian Americans. Our various sources all used slightly different methods to identify these men and women as Asians, but in each case we found supporting evidence for the fact that those we identified were, indeed, Asian Americans. Moreover, the estimates that we made corresponded with other estimates in which we have

confidence. For example, the estimate of 1 percent that we made, based on 128 seats held by Asians on the IRRC *Standard & Poor's* 1500 list of 13,820 directors, was exactly the same as the estimate made by the Committee of 100 in their Corporate Report Card for 2004 for Asians on *Fortune* 500 boards (see note 2 above). Similarly, in a study of *Fortune* 100 directors in 2004 by the Alliance for Board Diversity (an alliance consisting of three organizations: Catalyst, the Executive Leadership Council, and Hispanic Association of Corporate Responsibility), the researchers found that twelve of the 1,195 seats, or 1.0 percent, were held by Asian Americans (alternatively, 11 of the 995 people, or 1.1 percent, were Asian Americans). See "Women and Minorities on Fortune 100 Boards," Executive Leadership Council website, May 17, 2005, http://theabd.org/Women%20and%20Minorities%20on%20F100%20Boards_2005.pdf.

8. Stefanie K. Johnson and Thomas Sy, "Why Aren't There More Asian Americans in Leadership Positions?" *Harvard Business Review*, December 19, 2016, https://hbr.org/2016/12/why-arent-there-more-asian-americans-in-leadership-positions.

9. Zweigenhaft and Domhoff, *Diversity in the Power Elite* (Lanham, MD: Rowman & Littlefield, 2006), 233–34.

10. Andrew Martin and Eric Dash, "Naming a New Chief, MasterCard Signals It Is Open to Change," *New York Times*, April 12, 2010, B4.

11. Vikas Bajaj and Andrew Martin, "Who Needs Cash (or Borders)?" *New York Times*, October 16, 2010, Business section, 1, 4.

12. Bajaj and Martin, "Who Needs Cash," 4.

13. Marc Lacey, "First Asian-American Picked for Cabinet," *New York Times*, June 30, 2000, A15.

14. Christopher Marquis, "A Washington Veteran for Labor; a Tested Negotiator for Trade," *New York Times*, January 12, 2001; "Elaine L. Chao," *Current Biography* (2001): 84–86.

15. Thom Shanker, "Retiring Army Chief of Staff Warns against Arrogance," *New York Times*, June 12, 2003, A22.

16. Michael D. Shear and Richard A. Oppel Jr., "V.A. Chief Resigns in Face of Furor on Delayed Care," *New York Times*, May 30, 2014, https://www.nytimes.com/2014/05/31/us/politics/eric-shinseki-resigns-as-veterans-affairs-head.html.

17. Frances Robles, Richard Fausset, and Michael Barbaro, "Governor Joins the Call to Take Down Rebel Flag," *New York Times*, June 23, 2015, A1.

18. "2012 Demographics: Profile of the Military Community," Department of Defense, 24–25; the March 31, 2017 data were provided by the Office of the Secretary of Defense (Military Personnel Policy).

19. Seymour M. Hersh, "Chain of Command: How the Department of Defense Mishandled the Disaster at Abu Ghraib," *New Yorker*, May 17, 2004, 37, 42, 43.

20. Dan Froomkin, "General Accuses WH of War Crimes," *Washington Post*, June 18, 2008, http://www.washingtonpost.com/wp-dyn/content/blog/2008/06/18/BL2008061801546.html.

21. The data for the Naval Academy and West Point are drawn from their websites; the data for the Air Force Academy were provided by the school's public affairs office.

22. Bert Eljera, "Army Appoints Its Second Fil-Am General," *Asian Week*, August 26, 2006.

23. "Hiram L. Fong, 97, Senator from Hawaii in 60's and 70's," *New York Times*, August 19, 2004, C13.

24. Robert D. McFadden, "Daniel Inouye, Hawaii's Quiet Voice of Conscience in Senate, Dies at 88," *New York Times*, December 17, 2012, http://www.nytimes.com/2012/12/18/us/daniel-inouye-hawaiis-quiet-voice-of-conscience-in-senate-dies-at-88.html.

25. Lawrence Downes, "In Hawaii, a Chance to Heal, Long Delayed," *New York Times*, July 12, 2005, A22.

26. Dan Boylan, "The Immigrant Congresswoman," *Midweek*, March 21, 2007, http://archives.midweek.com/content/story/midweek_coverstory/the_immigrant_congresswoman/P1.

27. John Chase, "Duckworth Reaches Pinnacle of Senate Nearly 12 Years to Day after Iraq Crash," *Chicago Tribune*, November 9, 2016, http://www.chicagotribune.com/news/local/politics/ct-tammy-duckworth-met-20161109-story.html.

7. LGBT PEOPLE IN THE POWER ELITE

1. See, for example, Erin C. Westgate, Rachel G. Riskind, and Brian A. Nosek, "Implicit Preferences for Straight People over Lesbian Women and Gay Men Weakened from 2006 to 2013," *Collabra* 1, no. 1 (2015), Art. 1, doi: http://doi.org/10.1525/collabra.18.

2. Annette Friskopp and Sharon Silverstein, *Straight Jobs, Gay Lives: Gay and Lesbian Professionals, the Harvard Business School, and the American Workplace* (New York: Scribners, 1995), 21, 24.

3. Human Rights Campaign Foundation, "Corporate Equality Index 2017: Rating Workplaces on Lesbian, Gay, Bisexual and Transgender Equality," 2, http://hrc-assets.s3-website-us-east-1.amazonaws.com//files/assets/resources/CEI-2017-FinalReport.pdf.

4. See, for example, John D'Emilio and Estelle B. Freedman, *Intimate Matters: A History of Sexuality in America* (New York: Harper & Row, 1988); Bruce Bawer, *A Place at the Table* (New York: Poseidon, 1993), 52–54; M. V. Lee Badgett, *Money, Myths and Change: The Economic Lives of Lesbians and Gay Men* (Chicago: University of Chicago Press, 2001); John Simons, "Gay Marriage: Corporate America Blazed the Trail," *Fortune*, June 14, 2004, 42–43; Nicole C. Raeburn, *Changing Corporate America from the Inside: Lesbian and Gay Workplace Rights* (Minneapolis: University of Minnesota Press, 2005); and Richard Socarides, "Corporate America's Evolution on L.G.B.T. Rights," *New Yorker*, April 27, 2015, http://www.newyorker.com/business/currency/corporate-americas-evolution-on-l-g-b-t-rights.

5. Friskopp and Silverstein, *Straight Jobs, Gay Lives*, 71.

6. Thomas A. Stewart, "Gay in Corporate America," *Fortune*, December 16, 1991, 42–56, 50; James D. Woods, *The Corporate Closet: The Professional Lives of Gay Men in America* (New York: Free Press, 1993), 236–37; Mireya A. Navarro, "Disney's Health Policy for Gay Employees Angers Religious Right in Florida," *New York Times*, November 29, 1995.

7. Daryl Herrschaft, *The State of the Workplace for Lesbian, Gay, Bisexual and Transgender Americans: 2004* (Washington, DC: Human Rights Campaign Foundation, 2005), 15; Human Rights Campaign Foundation, "Corporate Equality Index 2017," 7. A study by Alison Cook and Christy Glass, based on data gathered from 2001 to 2010, found that those corporations that either had women CEOs or more gender-diverse boards were significantly more likely than other firms to have LGBT-friendly policies. See Alison Cook and Christy Glass, "Do Women Advance Equity? The Effect of Gender Leadership Composition on LGBT-Friendly Policies in American Firms," *Human Relations* 69, no. 7 (2016): 1431–56.

8. Woods, *Corporate Closet*, 28.

9. Friskopp and Silverstein, *Straight Jobs, Gay Lives*, 18–23.

10. Friskopp and Silverstein, *Straight Jobs, Gay Lives*, 110–11.

11. Friskopp and Silverstein, *Straight Jobs, Gay Lives*, 157. In a study of 284 respondents to a survey in *Out/Look* magazine, economist Lee Badgett found that "those whose employer has a sexual orientation nondiscrimination policy are much more likely to disclose their sexual orientation." See Badgett, *Money, Myths and Change*, 67.

12. Human Rights Campaign Foundation, "The Cost of the Closet and the Rewards of Inclusion: Why the Workplace Environment for LGBT People Matters to Employers," May 2014, http://hrc-assets.s3-website-us-east-1.amazonaws.com//files/assets/resources/Cost_of_the_Closet_May2014.pdf; see also Jennifer L. Wessel, "The Importance of Allies and Allied Organizations: Sexual Orientation Disclosure and Concealment at Work," *Journal of Social Issues* 73, no. 2 (2017): 240–54, doi:10.1111/josi.12214.

13. Scott Stringer and Todd Sears, "Expanding LGBT Diversity on Corporate Boards Is Good Business," *New York Slant*, May 31, 2016, http://nyslant.com/article/opinion/expanding-lgbt-diversity-on-corporate-boards-is-good-business.html.

14. Steve Friess, "Executive Decision," *Advocate*, April 29, 1997, 24–26, 31 (quotations appear on p. 26 and p. 25, respectively).

15. Danny Hakim, "Ford Is Said to Reappoint Ex-Executive," *New York Times*, May 18, 2002, B3; Danny Hakim, "Executive Leaves Retirement to Help Ford," *New York Times*, May 21, 2002, C10; Alex Taylor III, "Ford Finds Everyone Old Is New Again," *Fortune*, June 10, 2002, 40; "The Last Prejudice: Ex-Vice Chairman of Ford Comes Out," *Newsweek*, June 3, 2002, 8; and "Ex-Ford Exec Gilmour Named President of Wayne State in Detroit," *Automotive News*, January 18, 2011.

16. This awkward outing can be seen in the following link: http://www.dailymail.co.uk/video/news/video-1102286/Apple-CEO-Tim-Cook-accidentally-outed-gay-live-air.html.

17. See James Stewart, "Apple Chief's Coming Out: 'This Will Resonate,'" *New York Times*, October 30, 2014, A1 and B18; James Stewart, "Tim Cook's Coming Out: Reporter's Notebook," *New York Times*, October 31, 2014, http://www.nytimes.com/times-insider/2014/10/31/tim-cooks-coming-out-reporters-notebook. See also Drew Harrell, "Tim Cook Comes Out on Public Stage, Pulling Secretive Apple with Him," *Washington Post*, October 30, 2014, http://www.washingtonpost.com/business/economy/tim-cook-comes-out-on-public-stage-pulling-secretive-apple-with-him/2014/10/30/128e08f4-6058-11e4-9f3a-7e28799e0549_story.html; and Ben Morris, "Why Is Tim Cook of Apple the Only Major Gay US CEO?" *BBC News Business*, November 1, 2014, http://www.bbc.com/news/business-29852461.

18. Bernard Weinraub, "David Geffen: Still Hungry," *New York Times Magazine*, May 2, 1993, 28–31, 38–43, 68, 78 (quotation appears on p. 43).

19. Lisa Gubernick and Peter Newcomb, "The Richest Man in Hollywood," *Forbes*, December 24, 1990, 94–98; Weinraub, "David Geffen," 68.

20. Geraldine Fabrikant, "The Record Man with Flawless Timing," *New York Times*, December 9, 1990.

21. Gubernick and Newcomb, "Richest Man in Hollywood," 94.

22. Weinraub, "David Geffen," 40. The Buchanan quotation appears in David Mixner, *Stranger among Friends* (New York: Bantam, 1996), 249.

23. Brendan Lemon, "Man of the Year: David Geffen," *Advocate*, December 29, 1992, 35.

24. Lemon, "Man of the Year," 38.

25. Lucas Grindley, "The Innovators," *Advocate*, August 10, 2011.

26. Matea Gold, "Peter Thiel Plans to Make History as First GOP Convention Speaker to Announce That He Is Proud to Be Gay," *Washington Post*, July 20, 2016, https://www.washingtonpost.com/news/post-politics/wp/2016/07/20/peter-thiel-plans-to-make-history-as-first-gop-convention-speaker-to-announce-that-he-is-proud-to-be-gay/?utm_term=.

c9e98ff9a3fe; David Streitfeld, "Peter Thiel to Donate $1.25 Million in Support of Donald Trump," *New York Times*, October 16, 2016, https://www.nytimes.com/2016/10/16/technology/peter-thiel-donald-j-trump.html.

27. David Streitfeld and Jacqueline Williams, "For a Top Trump Backer, Is It America First, or New Zealand?" *New York Times*, January 26, 2017, A19, https://www.nytimes.com/2017/01/25/technology/peter-thiel-new-zealand-citizenship.html.

28. "About Kathy Levinson," https://kathylevinson.wordpress.com/about.

29. Michael Kearns, "Out on the Web," *LAWeekly.com*, November 26–December 2, 1999, http://www.laweekly.com/ink/00/01/cyber-kearns.php.

30. Laura Blumenfeld, "Schlafly's Son Out of the Closet," *Washington Post*, September 19, 1992; "Gingrich's Half-Sister Now Gay Activist," *Greensboro News and Record*, March 6, 1995; David W. Dunlap, "An Analyst, a Father, Battles Homosexuality," *New York Times*, December 24, 1995; and David Kirkpatrick, "Cheney Daughter's Political Role Disappoints Some Gay Activists," *New York Times*, August 30, 2004.

31. The log cabin myth is to presidents what the Horatio Alger myth is to captains of industry. See Edward Pessen, *The Log Cabin Myth: The Social Backgrounds of the Presidents* (New Haven, CT: Yale University Press, 1984), 25.

32. As has been the case with other gay Republicans, Von Wupperfeld has encountered antagonism from liberals in the gay community. Francis X. Clines, "For Gay G.O.P. Members, a 2d Closet," *New York Times*, September 4, 1992.

33. Kathy Sawyer, "Dole Campaign Returns Gays' Donation," *Washington Post*, August 27, 1995.

34. David Kirkpatrick, "Gay Activists in the G.O.P. Withhold Endorsement," *New York Times*, September 8, 2004, A20. According to this article, as a result of Bush's support for the marriage amendment, membership doubled from six thousand to twelve thousand.

35. Sarah Wheaton, "Log Cabin Republicans Board Votes against Endorsing Trump," *Politico*, October 22, 2016; Trudy Ring, "Why the Log Cabin Republicans Didn't Endorse Donald Trump," *Advocate*, October 29, 2016, http://www.advocate.com/election/2016/10/29/why-log-cabin-republicans-didnt-endorse-donald-trump.

36. For differing views on Gorsuch's likely rulings on LGBT issues, see Sheryl Gay Stolberg, "Court Nominee Is Not Easy to Pigeonhole on Gay Rights, Friends Say," *New York Times*, February 12, 2017, A16; and Mark Joseph Stern, "Neil Gorsuch's Disturbing Record on LGBTQ Rights," *Slate*, February 1, 2017, http://www.slate.com/blogs/outward/2017/02/01/neil_gorsuch_s_disturbing_record_on_lgbtq_rights.html.

37. Tim Bergling, "Closeted in the Capital: They're Powerful, Republican, and Gay," *Advocate*, May 11, 2004, 45.

38. Jonathan Mahler and Matt Flegenheimer, "What Donald Trump Learned from Joseph McCarthy's Right-Hand Man," *New York Times*, June 20, 2016, https://www.nytimes.com/2016/06/21/us/politics/donald-trump-roy-cohn.html.

39. Frank Rich, "Just How Gay Is the Right?" *New York Times*, May 15, 2005, section 4, 14; Sarah Wildman, "A Roy Cohn for Our Time?" *Advocate*, May 24, 2005, 32. Roy Cohn was a mentor to Donald Trump. As explained in the *New York Times*: "Mr. Cohn ushered him across the river and into Manhattan, introducing him to the social and political elite while ferociously defending him against a growing list of enemies. Decades later, Mr. Cohn's influence on Mr. Trump is unmistakable." See Mahler and Flegenheimer, "What Donald Trump Learned."

40. Kerry Lauerman, "LGBT's Worst Foe: The Closet Monster," *Salon*, http://www.salon.com/2012/06/23/lgbts_worst_foe_the_closet_monster/slide_show/3.

41. Alex Isenstadt and Katie Glueck, "Sheldon Adelson and Top GOP Donors Retreat to the Sidelines," *Politico*, April 9, 2016, http://www.politico.com/story/2016/04/sheldon-adelson-

gop-donors-sidelines-221765. Finkelstein died in August 2017. See Sam Roberts, "Arthur Fin-kelstein, Guru of Conservative Politics and Strategy, Dies at 72," *New York Times*, August 21, 2017, A23.

42. Patrick D. Healy, "Gay Republicans Soldier On, One Skirmish at a Time," *New York Times*, April 17, 2005, Week in Review section, 3.

43. The information in this and the next two paragraphs is drawn from Daniel Golden's profile of Mixner, "Mixner's Moment," *Boston Globe* (online), June 6, 1993, magazine section, 14, and from Mixner, *Stranger among Friends*.

44. Bawer, *A Place at the Table*, 52.

45. Golden, "Mixner's Moment," 4; Mixner, *Stranger among Friends*, 250.

46. Golden, "Mixner's Moment"; Mixner, *Stranger among Friends*, chs. 16–18; and Todd Purdom, "Clinton Would Sign Bill Barring Recognition to Gay Marriages," *New York Times*, May 23, 1996.

47. Chris Bull, "Baby Bills: A Crop of Candidates from the Clinton Administration Could Add New Life to Gay Political Causes," *Advocate*, October 29, 2002, 22.

48. David Mixner, "As a Sanders Supporter I'm Now Endorsing Hillary Clinton for Presi-dent," *Towleroad*, June 8, 2016, http://www.towleroad.com/2016/06/david-mixner-hillary-clinton.

49. Henry Louis Gates Jr., "Powell and the Black Elite," *New Yorker*, September 25, 1995, 63–80 (quotation appears on p. 74); Clarence Page, "Don't Ask, Don't Tell, Don't Leave," *Greensboro News & Record*, April 29, 2004, A11.

50. Quoted in Bawer, *A Place at the Table*, 149.

51. Mixner, *Stranger among Friends*, 350. See also Philip Shenon, "New Study Faults Pentagon's Gay Policy," *New York Times*, February 26, 1997.

52. Page, "Don't Ask, Don't Tell, Don't Leave," A11; John Files, "Number of Gays Dis-charged from Services Drops Again," *New York Times*, February 11, 2005, A21; Bryan Bender, "'Don't Ask' Policy Leaves Gap in Military," *Greensboro News & Record*, February 25, 2005, A1; and Gary L. Lehring, *Officially Gay: The Political Construction of Sexuality by the U.S. Military* (Philadelphia: Temple University Press, 2003), 3.

53. John Files, "Gay Ex-Officers Say 'Don't Ask' Doesn't Work," *New York Times*, De-cember 10, 2003, A14.

54. John Files, "Rules on Gays Exact a Cost in Recruiting, A Study Finds," *New York Times*, February 24, 2005, A16.

55. Associated Press, "Push On to Let Openly Gay Soldiers Serve," *Greensboro News & Record*, June 15, 2005, A3.

56. "An Openly Gay Man Runs the Army," *New York Times*, May 22, 2016, SR8. In this editorial, the *New York Times* notes that "it is embarrassing now, even shocking, to revisit the arguments and laments of those who sought to keep the military gay-free."

57. Dan Lamothe, "LGBT Advocates Launch Effort to Block Trump's 'Appalling' Army Secretary Nominee," *Chicago Tribune*, April 11, 2017, http://www.chicagotribune.com/news/nationworld/ct-lgbt-block-army-secretary-20170411-story.html. After his successful nomina-tions of Jeff Sessions and Tom Price to his cabinet, and his unsuccessful nomination of Mark Green, all of which were vehemently opposed by LGBT supporters, in July 2017, Trump nominated Richard Grenell, an openly gay man, as ambassador to Germany. If appointed, he would be the first openly gay man in the Trump administration. See Maggie Haberman, "Trump Picks Former Diplomatic Aide as Envoy to Germany," *New York Times*, July 20, 2017, A13. Less than one week later, Trump announced that he was rescinding Obama's policy on transgender people in the military, and that they would no longer be allowed to serve. See Julie Hirschfeld Davis and Helene Cooper, "Trump Says Transgender People Will Not Be Allowed

in the Military," New York Times, July 26, 2017, https://www.nytimes.com/2017/07/26/us/politics/trump-transgender-military.html.

58. Chuck Williams, "First Openly Gay General to Take Command of Army Reserve Unit at Fort Benning," *Ledger-Enquirer*, October 30, 3025.

59. Rowan Scarborough, "Army Gen. Randy Taylor Introduces His Husband at Pentagon Gay Pride Event," *Washington Times*, June 9, 2015.

60. See, for example, "Barney Frank's Story," *Newsweek*, September 25, 1989, 14–18; David W. Dunlap, "A Republican Congressman Discloses He Is a Homosexual," *New York Times*, August 3, 1996; Charles Kaiser, "When Outing Works," *Advocate*, October 12, 2004, 112; and Barney Frank, *Frank: A Life in Politics from the Great Society to Same-Sex Marriage* (New York: Farrar, Straus & Giroux, 2015).

61. Linda Rapp, "Tammy Baldwin," *glbtq.com*, February 16, 2005, http://www.glbtqarchive.com/ssh/baldwin_t_S.pdf; see Tammy Baldwin's government website at https://www.baldwin.senate.gov/; the information about Baldwin's grandfather was provided by Baldwin's press secretary.

62. Woods, *Corporate Closet*, 14.

8. THE IRONIES OF DIVERSITY

1. See, for example, Dennis Gilbert, *The American Class Structure in an Age of Growing Inequality*, 9th ed. (Los Angeles: Sage, 2015).

2. On the continuing importance of class voting in the United States, contrary to recent claims based on weak methods, see Jeff Manza and Clem Brooks, *Social Cleavages and Political Change: Voter Alignments and U.S. Party Coalitions* (New York: Oxford University Press, 1999). On class voting by Latinos, see Barry Kosmin and Ariela Keysar, "Party Political Preferences of U.S. Hispanics: The Varying Impact of Religion, Social Class and Demographic Factors," *Ethnic and Racial Studies* 18, no. 2 (1995): 336–47. In surveys of the CEOs of the largest Hispanic-owned businesses in 1989 and 1996, *Hispanic Business* found that 78 percent of them voted Republican in 1988 and that 67 percent said they were Republicans in 1996. See "CEOs and the Entrepreneurial 80s," *Hispanic Business*, April 1989, 30; "HB 500 CEOs Opt for Dole," *Hispanic Business*, June 1996, 34. On class voting by Chinese Americans, see Wendy Tam, "Asians—a Monolithic Voting Bloc?" *Political Behavior* 17, no. 2 (1995): 223–49.

3. Richard L. Zweigenhaft and G. William Domhoff, *Blacks in the White Elite* (Lanham, MD: Rowman & Littlefield, 2003), 158–60.

4. Glass Ceiling Commission, *Good for Business: Making Full Use of the Nation's Human Capital, a Fact-Finding Report of the Federal Glass Ceiling Commission* (Washington, DC: US Government Printing Office, 1995), 95. See, for example, Lori L. Tharps, *Same Family, Different Colors: Confronting Colorism in America's Diverse Families* (Boston: Beacon, 2016). In a study of black and white students at Amherst College, Elizabeth Aries uses the term "shadism" instead of "colorism." See Elizabeth Aries, *Speaking of Race and Class: The Student Experience at an Elite College* (Philadelphia: Temple University Press, 2013), 91.

5. Julia Alvarez, "A White Woman of Color," in *Half and Half: Writers on Growing Up Biracial and Bicultural*, ed. Claudine Chiawei O'Hearn (New York: Pantheon, 1998), 139–49. Alvarez's novels include *How the Garcia Girls Lost Their Accents* (New York: Plume, 1992) and *In the Time of the Butterflies* (New York: Plume, 1994).

6. See, for example, Nihah Masih, "India's Lethal Race Problem," *New York Times*, April 18, 2017, https://www.nytimes.com/2017/04/17/opinion/indias-lethal-race-problem.html.

7. Michael Mann, *The Dark Side of Democracy: Explaining Ethnic Cleansing* (New York: Cambridge University Press, 2005), 76.

8. Karl Eschbach, "The Enduring and Vanishing American Indian: American Indian Population Growth and Intermarriage in 1990," *Ethnic and Racial Studies* 18, no. 1 (1995): 89–108; Wendy Wang, "Interracial Marriage: Who Is 'Marrying Out'?" Pew Research Center, June 12, 2015, http://www.pewresearch.org/fact-tank/2015/06/12/interracial-marriage-who-is-marrying-out.

9. Glenn Loury, *The Anatomy of Racial Inequality* (Cambridge, MA: Harvard University Press, 2002), 69; Elena V. Stepanova and Michael J. Strube, "The Role of Skin Color and Facial Physiognomy in Racial Categorization: Moderation by Implicit Racial Attitudes," *Journal of Experimental Social Psychology* 48, no. 4 (2012): 867–78; Heather M. Kleider-Offutt, Alesha D. Bond, and Shanna E. A. Hegerty, "Black Stereotypical Features: When a Face Type Can Get You in Trouble," *Current Directions in Psychological Science* 26, no. 1 (2017): 28–33.

10. Michael Schwartz, *Radical Protest and Social Structure: The Southern Farmers' Alliance and Cotton Tenancy, 1880–1890* (New York: Academic Press, 1976).

11. Kevin Fox Gotham, *Race, Real Estate, and Uneven Development* (Albany: State University of New York Press, 2002); Michael K. Brown, Martin Carnoy, Elliott Currie, Troy Duster, David B. Oppenheimer, Marjorie M. Shultz, and David Wellman, *Whitewashing Race: The Myth of a Color-Blind Society* (Berkeley: University of California Press, 2003).

12. Thomas M. Shapiro, *The Hidden Cost of Being African American: How Wealth Perpetuates Inequality* (New York: Oxford University Press, 2004); for a more current analysis, see Thomas M. Shapiro, *Toxic Inequality—How America's Wealth Gap Destroys Mobility, Deepens the Racial Divide, and Threatens Our Future* (New York: Basic, 2017). See also Robert B. Williams, *The Privileges of Wealth: Rising Inequality and the Growing Racial Divide* (New York: Routledge, 2017).

13. Paul F. Campos, "White Economic Privilege Is Alive and Well," *New York Times*, July 30, 2017, Sunday Review, 3.

14. Shapiro, *Toxic Inequality*, 18.

15. Devah Pager and Bruce Western, "Discrimination in Low-Wage Labor Markets: Results from an Experimental Audit Study in New York City" (paper presented at the annual meeting of the American Sociological Association, Philadelphia, PA, 2005); Deirdre A. Royster, *Race and the Invisible Hand: How White Networks Exclude Black Men from Blue-Collar Jobs* (Berkeley: University of California Press, 2003).

16. Lawrence Bobo and Ryan Smith, "From Jim Crow to Laissez-Faire Racism: The Transformation of Racial Attitudes," in *Beyond Pluralism: The Conception of Groups and Group Identities in America*, ed. Wendy Katkin, Ned Landsman, and Andrea Tyree (Urbana: University of Illinois Press, 1998), 182–220; Eduardo Bonilla-Silva, *Racism without Racists: Color-Blind Racism and the Persistence of Racial Inequality in the United States*, 5th ed. (Lanham, MD: Rowman & Littlefield, 2017).

17. James M. Jones, *Prejudice and Racism*, 2nd ed. (New York: McGraw-Hill, 1997); John F. Dovidio, "On the Nature of Contemporary Prejudice: The Third Wave," *Journal of Social Issues* 57, no. 4 (2001): 829–49; and John F. Dovidio, Samuel L. Gaertner, and Adam R. Pearson, "Racism among the Well-Intentioned: Bias without Awareness," in *The Social Psychology of Good and Evil*, 2nd ed., ed. Arthur G. Miller (New York: Guilford, 2016), 95–118.

18. Mary Waters and Marisa Gerstein Pineau, eds., *The Integration of Immigrants into American Society* (Washington, DC: National Academies Press, 2015), http://www.nap.edu/21746.

19. Edward Murguia and Tyrone Foreman, "Shades of Whiteness: The Mexican-American Experience in Relation to Anglos and Blacks," in *White Out: The Continuing Significance of Race*, ed. Ashley Doane and Eduardo Bonilla-Silva (New York: Routledge, 2003), 63–79.

20. Lawrence Bobo and Devon Johnson, "Racial Attitudes in a Prismatic Metropolis: Mapping Identity, Stereotypes, Competition, and Views on Affirmative Action," in *Prismatic Metropolis*, ed. Lawrence Bobo, Melvin L. Oliver, James H. Johnson Jr., and Abel Valenzuela (New York: Russell Sage Foundation, 2000), 81–166.

21. Douglas S. Massey and Nancy A. Denton, *American Apartheid: Segregation and the Making of the Underclass* (Cambridge, MA: Harvard University Press, 1993), 61.

22. Camille Zubrinsky Charles, "Neighborhood Racial-Composition Preferences: Evidence from a Multiethnic Metropolis," *Social Problems* 47, no. 3 (2000): 379–407.

23. Massey and Denton, *American Apartheid*, 67, 223.

24. William Clark and Sarah Blue, "Race, Class, and Segregation Patterns in U.S. Immigrant Gateway Cities," *Urban Affairs Review* 39 (2004): 667–88; John Iceland, Cicely Sharpe, and Erika Steinmetz, "Class Differences in African American Residential Patterns in US Metropolitan Areas: 1990–2000," *Social Science Research* 34 (2005): 252–66.

25. Douglas S. Massey, "Residential Segregation Is the Linchpin of Racial Stratification," *City & Community* 15, no. 1 (2016): 4–7. doi: 10.1111/cico.12145.

26. Richard Rothstein, *The Color of Law: A Forgotten History of How Our Government Segregated America* (New York: Liveright, 2017).

27. Mary Pattillo-McCoy, *Black Picket Fences: Privilege and Peril among the Black Middle Class* (Chicago: University of Chicago Press, 1999). See also Bart Landry, *The New Black Middle Class* (Berkeley: University of California Press, 1987).

28. Karyn R. Lacy, *Blue Chip Black: Race, Class, and Status in the New Black Middle Class* (Berkeley: University of California Press, 2007), 71–72.

29. Patrick Sharkey, "Review of *Blue-Chip Black: Race, Class, and Status in the New Black Middle Class* by Karyn R. Lacy," *Contemporary Sociology* 37, no. 4 (2008), 324–26.

30. Jerry A. Jacobs and Teresa Labov, "Asian Brides, Anglo Grooms: Asian Exceptionalism in Intermarriage," Department of Sociology, University of Pennsylvania, October 1995; Jerry A. Jacobs and Teresa Labov, "Sex Differences in Intermarriage: Exchange Theory Reconsidered," Department of Sociology, University of Pennsylvania, September 1995.

31. Gretchen Livingston and Anna Brown, "Intermarriage in the U.S. 50 Years after Loving v. Virginia," Pew Research Center, May 18, 2017.

32. Sheryll Cashin, *Loving: Interracial Intimacy in America and the Threat to White Supremacy* (Boston: Beacon, 2017), 130.

33. Cashin, *Loving*, 133.

34. See also Wang, "Interracial Marriage."

35. William Frey, *Diversity Explosion: How New Racial Demographics Are Remaking America* (Washington, DC: Brookings Institution Press, 2015), 18.

36. Mary C. Waters, "Explaining the Comfort Factor: West Indian Immigrants Confront American Race Relations," in *The Cultural Territories of Race: Black and White Boundaries*, ed. Michelle Lamont (Chicago: University of Chicago Press, 1999), 63–96; Mary C. Waters, *Black Identities: West Indian Immigrant Dreams and American Realities* (Cambridge, MA: Harvard University Press, 1999).

37. Philip Kasinitz, *Caribbean New York: Black Immigrants and the Politics of Race* (Ithaca, NY: Cornell University Press, 1992), 76, 220–21.

38. For information on the children of foreign-born blacks at twenty-eight highly selective colleges and universities, see Douglas S. Massey, Camille Z. Charles, Garvey F. Lundy, and Mary J. Fischer, *The Source of the River: The Social Origins of Freshmen at America's Selective Colleges and Universities* (Princeton, NJ: Princeton University Press, 2003), 40. At a forum during a 2004 reunion of black Harvard alumni, law professor Lani Guinier and Henry Louis Gates Jr., the chair of the African and African American Studies Department, reported that at least a majority, and perhaps as many as two-thirds, of the then current undergraduates at Harvard were either West Indian and African immigrants, their children, or the children of biracial couples. See Sara Rimer and Karen W. Arenson, "Top Colleges Take More Blacks, but Which Ones?" *New York Times*, June 24, 2004, A1. Douglas S. Massey, Margarita Mooney, and Kimberly C. Torres, "Black Immigrants and Black Natives Attending Selective Colleges and Universities in the United States," *American Journal of Education* 113 (February 2007): 243–71.

39. Waters, "Explaining the Comfort Factor."

40. Waters, "Explaining the Comfort Factor," 82.

41. Eduardo Bonilla-Silva, "'New Racism,' Color-Blind Racism, and the Future of White-ness in America," in *White Out: The Continuing Significance of Race*, ed. Ashley Doane and Eduardo Bonilla-Silva (New York: Routledge, 2003), 271–84; Herbert Gans, "The Possibility of a New Racial Hierarchy in the Twenty-First Century United States," in *The Cultural Territories of Race: Black and White Boundaries*, ed. Michelle Lamont (Chicago: University of Chicago Press, 1999), 371–90.

42. Thomas F. Pettigrew, "Integration and Pluralism," in *Modern Racism: Profiles in Controversy*, ed. Phyllis A. Katz and Dalmas A. Taylor (New York: Plenum, 1988), 19–30, 24–26. For detailed evidence on the difficulties black Americans, including members of the middle class, still face, see Lois Benjamin, *The Black Elite* (Chicago: Nelson Hall, 1991), and Joe R. Feagin and Melvin P. Sikes, *Living with Racism* (Boston: Beacon, 1994).

43. See Sharon Collins, *Black Corporate Executives: The Making and Breaking of a Black Middle Class* (Philadelphia: Temple University Press, 1997). For a systematic empirical demonstration of the importance of such government policies using time series data, see Martin Carnoy, *Faded Dreams: The Politics and Economics of Race in America* (New York: Cambridge University Press, 1994).

44. "Defense of the Negro Race—Charges Answered. Speech of Hon. George H. White, of North Carolina, in the House of Representatives," January 29, 1901. Washington, DC: US Government Printing Office, 1901, http://docsouth.unc.edu/nc/whitegh/menu.html.

45. In focusing on these eleven states, it should not be overlooked that there were seventeen states and territories that practiced slavery on the eve of the Civil War, and that all of them had legalized school segregation until the 1954 *Brown v. Board of Education* Supreme Court decision unanimously ruled that it was unconstitutional, which reignited massive Southern resistance. Those other states, some of which have been changed in varying degrees by the growth of the Washington metropolitan area, are Delaware, Kentucky, Maryland, Missouri, Oklahoma, and West Virginia (West Virginia gradually gained its independence from Virginia between 1861 and 1863 but did not abolish slavery).

46. Bernard Grofman and Chandler Davidson, "The Effect of Municipal Election Structure on Black Representation," in *Quiet Revolution in the South: The Impact of the Voting Rights Act, 1965–1990*, ed. Chandler Davidson and Bernard Grofman (Princeton, NJ: Princeton University Press, 1994), 320, 449n83.

47. Lisa Handley and Bernard Grofman, "The Impact of the Voting Rights Act on Minority Representation: Black Office Holders in Southern State Legislatures," in *Quiet Revolution in*

the South: The Impact of the Voting Rights Act, 1965–1990, ed. Chandler Davidson and Bernard Grofman (Princeton, NJ: Princeton University Press, 1994), 336.

48. Handley and Grofman, "Impact of the Voting Rights Act," 337–38.

49. Chandler Davidson and Bernard Grofman, "The Voting Rights Act and the Second Reconstruction," in *Quiet Revolution in the South: The Impact of the Voting Rights Act, 1965–1990*, ed. Chandler Davidson and Bernard Grofman (Princeton, NJ: Princeton University Press, 1994), 383.

50. Ari Berman, *Give Us the Ballot: The Modern Struggle for Voting Rights in America* (New York: Farrar, Straus & Giroux, 2015), 187.

51. Tim Alberta, "Will Hurd Is the Future of the GOP—If He Can Hold on to the Toughest Seat in Texas," *Politico*, May 5, 2017, http://www.politico.com/magazine/story/2017/05/05/congressman-will-hurd-texas-republican-profile-215102.

52. Seth C. McKee, *Republican Ascendency in Southern U.S. House Elections* (Boulder, CO: Westview, 2010), 95–99. As noted in chapter 4, these potentially Republican districts are redrawn in such a way that white Democratic incumbents have as few of their former voters left in the district as possible, which makes it likely that the new voters will draw on their recently developed Republican identities rather than incumbency in making their voting choices.

53. Steve Bickerstaff, *Lines in the Sand: Congressional Redistricting in Texas and the Downfall of Tom DeLay* (Austin: University of Texas Press, 2007), 270.

54. Berman, *Give Us the Ballot*, 189.

55. Zweigenhaft and Domhoff, *Blacks in the White Elite*. See Richard Zweigenhaft and G. William Domhoff, *The New CEOs: Women, African American, Latino, and Asian American Leaders of Fortune 500 Companies* (Lanham, MD: Rowman & Littlefield, 2014), table A3.1 for a highly detailed accounting of how corporate, family, and community foundations finance the corporate pipeline that supports the educations of low-income students of color from middle school through college.

56. Brian T. Downes, "A Critical Re-examination of the Social and Political Characteristics of Riot Cities," *Social Science Quarterly* 51 (1970): 349–60.

57. John D. Skrentny, *The Ironies of Affirmative Action: Politics, Culture, and Justice in America* (Chicago: University of Chicago Press, 1996), ch. 4 and 7.

58. Skrentny, *Ironies of Affirmative Action*, 78–91; G. William Domhoff, *The Myth of Liberal Ascendancy: Corporate Dominance from the Great Depression to the Great Recession* (New York: Routledge, 2013), 158–59.

59. Domhoff, *Myth of Liberal Ascendancy*, 212–13.

60. John D. Skrentny, *The Minority Rights Revolution* (Cambridge, MA: Harvard University Press, 2002).

61. Erin Kelly and Frank Dobbin, "How Affirmative Action Became Diversity Management: Employer Responses to Antidiscrimination Law, 1961–1996," in *Color Lines: Affirmative Action, Immigration, and Civil Rights Options for America*, ed. John D. Skrentny (Chicago: University of Chicago Press, 2001), 87–117. For a more complete discussion of the shift from "affirmative action" to "diversity," see Zweigenhaft and Domhoff, *New CEOs*, 106–16.

62. Skrentny, *Minority Rights Revolution*, ch. 10.

63. Stephen C. Wright, "Restricted Intergroup Boundaries: Tokenism, Ambiguity, and the Tolerance of Injustice," in *The Psychology of Legitimacy: Emerging Perspectives on Ideology, Justice, and Intergroup Relations*, ed. John Jost and Brenda Major (New York: Cambridge University Press, 2001), 223–54; Stephen C. Wright, "Strategic Collective Action: Social Psychology and Social Change," in *Blackwell Handbook of Social Psychology: Intergroup Processes*, vol. 4, ed. Rupert Brown and Samuel Gaertner (Malden, MA: Blackwell, 2001), 409–30.

64. John Jost and Brenda Major, *The Psychology of Legitimacy: Emerging Perspectives on Ideology, Justice, and Intergroup Relations* (New York: Cambridge University Press, 2001).

65. Sara Rimer, "Fall of a Shirtmaking Legend Shakes Its Maine Hometown," *New York Times*, May 15, 1996. See also Floyd Norris, "Market Place," *New York Times*, June 7, 1996; and Stephanie Strom, "Double Trouble at Linda Wachner's Twin Companies," *New York Times*, August 4, 1996. Strom's article reveals that Hathaway Shirts "got a reprieve" when an investor group stepped in to save it.

66. Claudia Luther and Steven Churm, "GOP Official Says He OK'd Observers at Polls," *Los Angeles Times*, November 12, 1988; Jeffrey Perlman, "Firm Will Pay $60,000 in Suit over Guards at Polls," *Los Angeles Times*, May 31, 1989.

67. See Zweigenhaft and Domhoff, *New CEOs*, 96–101.

68. See, for example, Lisa E. Cohen, Joseph P. Broschak, and Heather A. Haveman, "And Then There Were More? The Effect of Organizational Sex Composition on the Hiring and Promotion of Managers," *American Sociological Review* 63, no. 5 (1998): 711–27.

69. Alison Cook and Christy Glass, "The Power of One or Power in Numbers? Analyzing the Effect of Minority Leaders on Diversity Policy and Practice," *Work & Occupations* 42, no. 2 (2014): 183–215, doi:10.1177/0730888414557292.

70. Cook and Glass, "Power of One," 207. See also Cheryl R. Kaiser, Brenda Major, Ines Jurcevic, Tessa L. Dover, Laura M. Brady, and Jenessa R. Shapiro, "Presumed Fair: Ironic Effects of Organizational Diversity Structures," *Journal of Personality and Social Psychology* 104, no. 3 (2012): 501–19, doi:10.1037/a0030838.

71. Frank Dobbin, Kim Soohan, and Alexandra Kalev, "You Can't Always Get What You Need: Organizational Determinants of Diversity Programs," *American Sociological Review* 76, no. 3 (2011): 387–88, 392.

72. Frank Dobbin and Alexandra Kalev, "The Origins and Effects of Corporate Diversity Programs," in *The Oxford Handbook of Diversity and Work*, ed. Quinetta Roberson (New York: Oxford University Press, 2013), 253–81. The quoted passage above is on p. 273.

73. Nancy DiTomaso, *The American Non-Dilemma: Racial Inequality without Racism* (New York: Russell Sage Foundation, 2013), xx.

74. DiTomaso, *American Non-Dilemma*, xxi.

75. DiTomaso, *American Non-Dilemma*, 4, table 1.

76. William Ryan, *Blaming the Victim* (New York: Vintage, 1976).

77. DiTomaso, *American Non-Dilemma*, 4.

78. Seval Gündemir and Adam D. Galinsky, "Multicolored Blindfolds: How Organizational Multiculturalism Can Conceal Racial Discrimination and Delegitimize Racial Discrimination Claims," *Social Psychological and Personality Science* (2017), advance online publication, doi:10.1177/1948550617726830.

79. Natasha K. Warikoo, *The Diversity Bargain* (Chicago: University of Chicago Press, 2016); W. Carson Byrd, *Poison in the Ivy: Race Relations and the Reproduction of Inequality on Elite College Campuses* (New Brunswick, NJ: Rutgers University Press, 2017).

80. J. Bricker, L. Dettling, A. Henriques, J. Hsu, L. Jacobs, K. Moore, et al. (2017), "Changes in U.S. Family Finances from 2013 to 2016: Evidence from the Survey of Consumer Finances," *Federal Reserve Bulletin* 103, no. 3: 1–41; see, especially, p. 10, box 3; Edward N. Wolff, "Changes in Household Wealth in the 1980s and 1990s in the U.S." (working paper 407, Levy Economics Institute, Bard College, 2004), http://www.levy.org; Edward N. Wolff, *Household Wealth Trends in the United States, 1962–2013: What Happened Over the Great Recession?* (Cambridge, MA: National Bureau of Economic Research, 2014); Edward N. Wolff, *A Century of Wealth in America* (Cambridge, MA: Harvard University Press, 2017).

Index

About the Authors

Richard L. Zweigenhaft is Charles A. Dana Professor of Psychology at Guilford College. He is the author or coauthor of numerous articles, chapters, and books. Most recently, he was the coeditor (with Eugene Borgida) of *Collaboration in Psychological Science: Behind the Scenes*.

G. William Domhoff is Distinguished Professor Emeritus and Research Professor of Sociology at the University of California, Santa Cruz. He is the author of many books, including *Who Rules America?*, *The Triumph of the Corporate Rich*, and *Studying The Power Elite: Fifty Years of Who Rules America?*

Over the past three decades, the authors have written a series of books together, including *Jews in the Protestant Establishment*, *Blacks in the White Elite: Will the Progress Continue?*, and *The New CEOs: Women, African American, Latino, and Asian American Leaders of Fortune 500 Companies*.